P9-CRS-507

© THE BAKER & TAYLOR CO.

Discovering Man in Psychology: A Humanistic Approach

Discovering Man in Psychology: A Humanistic Approach

Frank T. Severin

Saint Louis University

McGraw-Hill Book Company

New York   St. Louis   San Francisco   Düsseldorf   Johannesburg
Kuala Lumpur   London   Mexico   Montreal   New Delhi   Panama
Rio de Janeiro   Singapore   Sydney   Toronto

Library of Congress Cataloging in Publication Data

Severin, Frank T   ed.
    Discovering man in psychology.

    First published in 1965 under title: Humanis-
tic viewpoints in psychology; a book of readings.
    Bibliography: p.
    1.   Humanistic psychology—addresses, essays, lec-
tures.   I. Title. [DNLM: 1. Psychology—Collected
works. BF 21 S498d 1973]
BF204.S48 1973   150'.19'2   72-7335
ISBN 0-07-056341-1
ISBN 0-07-056340-3 (pbk.)

Discovering Man in Psychology:
A Humanistic Approach

1 2 3 4 5 6 7 8 9 0 DODO 7 9 8 7 6 5 4 3

This book was set in Press Roman by Creative Book Services, division of McGregor &
Werner, Inc. The editors were Walter Maytham, John Hendry, and Helen Greenberg; the
designer was Art Ritter; and the production supervisor was Sally Ellyson.
The printer and binder was R. R. Donnelley & Sons Company.

Contents

List of Contributors

Gordon W. Allport, formerly Professor of Psychology, Harvard University.

J. Bernard Berelson, President, Population Council, New York, N.Y.

Charlotte Buhler, Clinical Psychologist in private practice and Assistant Clinical Professor of Psychiatry, School of Medicine, University of Southern California.

Ernst Cassirer, formerly Professor of Philosophy, Columbia and Yale Universities.

James C. Coleman, Professor of Psychology, University of California at Los Angeles.

Herman Feifel, Chief Psychologist, VA Outpatient Clinic, Los Angeles; Clinical Professor of Psychiatry (Psychology) University of Southern California Medical School.

Viktor Frankl, Professor of Neurology and Psychiatry, University of Vienna Medical School; Professor of Logotherapy, U.S. International University; former President, Austrian Medical Society for Psychotherapy.

Erich Fromm, Professor, National University of Mexico and Adjunct Professor, New York University.

Frieda Fromm-Reichmann, formerly Supervisor of Psychotherapy, Chestnut Hill Sanitarium, Rockville, Maryland.

John W. Gardner, Chairman of Common Cause; former U.S. Secretary of Health, Education, and Welfare.

J. Barnard Gilmore, Professor of Psychology, University of Toronto.

Amedeo Giorgi, Professor of Psychology, Duquesne University.

John Hipple, Counselor, University of Idaho.

Jerome Kagan, Professor of Developmental Psychology, Harvard University.

Herbert C. Kelman, Richard Clarke Cabot Professor of Social Ethics, Harvard University; Board of Directors, American Psychological Association; Board of Directors, Institute of Society Ethics, and the Life Sciences.

Kenneth Keniston, Professor of Psychology (Psychiatry); Director of the Behavioral Sciences Study Center, Yale Medical School.

Peter Koestenbaum, Professor of Philosophy, San Jose State College.

Roy Lachman, Professor of Psychology, University of Kansas.

Edwin A. Locke, Associate Professor of Business Administration and Psychology, University of Maryland.

Noel Mailloux, Professor and Chairman, Department of Psychology, University of Montreal; Technical Director, Centre d' Orientation; President, Centre de Recherches en Relations Humaines.

Abraham H. Maslow, formerly Professor of Psychology, Brandeis University; former Resident Fellow, W. P. Laughlin Foundation.

Rollo May, Practicing Psychoanalyst and Author.

Clarke E. Moustakas, The Merrill-Palmer Institute, Detroit, Michigan.

Herbert J. Muller, Distinguished Professor of English, Indiana University.

Carl R. Rogers, Resident Fellow, Center for Studies of the Person, La Jolla, California, 1125 Torrey Pines Road, La Jolla, California 92037

William A. Sadler, Jr., Professor of Sociology, Bloomfield College.

Juilus Seeman, Professor of Psychology, George Peabody College.

Erwin M. Segal, Associate Professor of Psychology, State University of New York at Buffalo.

Lawrence D. Simkins, Professor and Director of Clinical Training, University of Missouri at Kansas City.

Donald Snygg, formerly Professor of Psychology and Chairman of the Department, State University of New York at Oswego.

Pitirim A. Sorokin, formerly Professor of Sociology, Harvard University.

Gary A. Steiner, formerly Professor of Psychology, School of Business, University of Chicago.

Gordon H. Turner, Professor of Psychology, The University of Western Ontario.

J. H. van den Berg, Professor of Psychological Phenomenology, University of Leiden, Holland.

Rolf von Eckartsberg, Associate Professor of Social Psychology, Duquesne University.

C. Gilbert Wrenn, Associate, Edward Glaser & Associates; Visiting Professor, Arizona State University; Professor, Macalester College.

Preface

When I edited *Humanistic Viewpoints in Psychology* in 1965 as the first attempt to sketch the meaning of humanistic or third force psychology, terms which had recently come into use, there were no guidelines to follow. Using selections from the most articulate spokesmen for this point of view, I formulated an idiosyncratic notion of what humanistic psychology is about. Perhaps this was inevitable since humanistic psychology is, in effect, all of psychology viewed through a wide-angle lens, as will be explained in the Introduction. An interpretation such as the present one, which grows out of an experimental background, will stress different concerns and interests than would that of a clinician or a psychologist in some other area.

The task of preparing this book was greatly facilitated by the increased volume of humanistic literature during the past few years. The attitudes of psychologists have also changed perceptibly, judging from many of the articles appearing in the *American Psychologist* and other journals. As a result, some of the earlier criticism of our profession by humanistic psychologists now needs to be qualified.

As the change of title indicates, *Discovering Man in Psychology* is more than just a revision of *Humanistic Viewpoints in Psychology*. While my basic aim—to present a broad picture of contemporary humanistic psychological thought—has not changed, I have tried to achieve it in a rather different way. *Humanistic Viewpoints in Psychology* was organized in the more or less conventional "reader" format. *Discovering Man in Psychology* is also largely composed of materials by others. But now the editorial commentary is much more extensive, and it is integrated with the selections in such a way as to provide much more continuity of thought than is usually found in a book of readings. Each chapter ends with a number of discussion topics and a list of suggested readings. The range of subject matter is sufficiently broad to serve as a supplement for a variety of courses or as the framework for a course in humanistic psychology.

Humanistic psychology is especially interesting to the student because it includes topics of deep concern to him as an individual which are usually bypassed because of the difficulty of treating them scientifically. This does not indicate a lack of concern about rigorous investigation on the part of humanistic psychologists, but rather a willingness to begin, if necessary, with naturalistic observation and then progress by steps to more meticulous methods of study. Some of the most interesting human problems are the most resistant to systematic research, but this is no reason to ignore them or to disclaim them as part of the subject matter of psychology.

Part One samples some of these areas. Many others could have been added, such as humor, courage, trust, spontaneity, and happiness. Part Two deals with the image of man. Depending upon one's presuppositions about science in general and psychology in particular, conflicting concepts of the human individual will emerge. Earlier theories which considered scientific methods totally objective and began with the dogma that all human functioning can be reduced to quasi-mechanical conditioned responses arrived at a different picture of man than the one presented here.

Part Three examines some values that are inherent in every science, especially social science. Although few psychologists today deny the presence of value judgments in their work, there is still a tendency to overlook them.

Part Four discusses some newer insights into the theory of science which are familiar to physicists and philosophers but which psychologists are only now beginning to assimilate. From a logical point of view this topic should be treated first, since the theory of science which the reader adopts will determine whether or not many of the issues raised in this book can be satisfactorily resolved. It was placed last in the belief that exposure to the thinking of humanistic psychologists would better prepare him to grasp the deeper implications of his choice. When this text is used for classroom instruction, the teacher may wish to begin with Part Four.

It is a pleasure to acknowledge a deep debt of gratitude to Robert J. Sardello for reading the entire manuscript and for many helpful suggestions, to Richard Blackwell for reading Part Four of the manuscript, and to Bernice Morris for typing the final copy. My thanks are also due to Doris Winter, Mary Schrappen, and Judith McGee for clerical assistance.

Frank T. Severin

Introduction

If a public opinion poll were to ask the question "What is the most interesting topic on earth?", most people would probably answer, "My own self." No one else, even those nearest to us, can share in the same intimate way this center of centers where all life and mental activity take place. Every waking hour is filled with one's own personal thoughts and with emotions that only he can experience firsthand. They may, of course, be communicated to others or inferred from external behavior, but nonetheless they are uniquely one's own. Every interaction with the outside world occurs in a frame of reference involving how one thinks and feels about himself. Nothing at all, not even the most disinterested altruism, can ever escape from the ego as one terminal of a relationship.

Since psychology is primarily concerned with the human individual that in the concrete is myself, it is not surprising that it should appeal to almost everyone. Writers sometimes traffic in this interest by using the term in the title of semitechnical publications. Most of us have seen articles on the psychology of golf, the psychology of fishing, or even the psychology of choosing an automobile. Many students register for an introductory course in psychology because they are eager to know more about themselves and people in general. The issues they are most concerned about are not always clearly formulated, but questions such as the following are frequently asked: "How can I improve my personality?", "Why is it that I seem unable to change some of the things I dislike about myself?", "What practical solutions does psychology have for the pressing social problems of our day?"

Some of the original charm begins to disappear when the student buys a textbook and casually pages through it before the first class. Instead of ready-made prescriptions for his hangups and a set of directions for ending social tensions or bringing ghetto dwellers into the mainstream of American life, he finds himself confronted with highly technical discussions which seem strangely irrelevant to any human purpose. A great deal is made of animal conditioning, statistics, research methodology, and engineeringlike studies which seem to contribute very little to understanding human beings. In part this mild disenchantment may be traced to a misapprehension of the student about the nature of science, but it is also the fault of psychology itself.

On behalf of psychology it should be noted that every academic discipline is organized around certain basic principles which serve as a conceptual framework for all that follows. Such a blueprint for the scientific study of man should specify different levels of functioning. Most basic of all is what goes on in the nervous system and the biological organism in general. The other levels of behavior can be divided and subdivided into a multitude of processes such as perception, emotion, remembering, thinking, and choosing. A student who wishes to understand human behavior in depth cannot confine his study to just those topics which are immediately rewarding anymore than an architect can devote all his attention to designing the main floor of a building without concern for the foundation and upper stories. Similarly, if a psychologist wishes to know exactly what "consciousness-expanding" drugs do to the brain, he must first learn many elementary facts about physiology and neuroanatomy. Laying the groundwork for understandings to be gained later on can be a grueling task, especially when the connection with the things one is most anxious to know is not immediately evident. The situation is similar to that of scientists blazing new trails in research. If they were not genuinely enthusiastic about their work, it would be drudgery. The occasional peak experiences that are triggered by brilliant new insights or exciting discoveries are usually separated by broad plains of lonely effort.

Likewise, developing the skills necessary for success in any field may prove to be as tedious as acquiring the technical background. The few hours of glory that astronauts spend on the moon are preceded by years of training so painfully routine that few persons could endure it. A new recruit in the NASA program might not be able to see the relevance of much of it to flying a spaceship, just as most beginning psychology students wonder why they should bother with statistics or the physiological mechanisms underlying behavior.

Even after taking this into consideration there is cause for mixed feelings about psychology. On the one hand certain things do impress the student as he works his way through an introductory textbook to gain an overview of the field. First and foremost is the enormous amount of research being carried on by psychologists and their passion for reliable and valid measurement. Their articles are documented with references to scores of journals devoted entirely to the publication of original studies. The student frequently catches a glimpse of teamwork, ingenuity, and technical know-how which would challenge NASA's flawless performance at Cape Kennedy.

Nonetheless as he reads further, he may be haunted by the uneasy feeling that something important is being omitted. Granted that abstract theories and generalizations are a prime necessity in science, how are these related to one's experience of himself and his growth as a person? What does psychology tell us that is authentic in dealing with friends, parents, and people in general? There is not likely to be found in the entire chapter on motivation a single suggestion that man has the freedom to make some choices just because he wants to. The typical assumption is that, like other animals, the human individual is propelled this way and that in all his actions by nonrational drives and acquired conditioned responses without any say on his part.

Seldom if ever is an allusion made to the personal **experience** of love, joy, fear, or anger in the discussion of emotions. What is emphasized are the underlying physiological processes, the bodily expression of emotion, the brain centers associated with affective behavior, and so on. Any young lovers who have just become engaged to marry know firsthand that the thrill they feel cannot be described in terms of a racing heart, sweaty palms, and an altered GSR. Nor does a flurry of sympathetic nervous activity adequately explain why a neurotic person often avoids self-actualizing experiences in situations that arouse anxiety.

Too frequently what goes on in a person's head, when not bypassed altogether in psychology, is merely tolerated instead of being welcomed with open arms into the discussion as the most characteristic of all human activities. The problem is not one of overemphasis on "pure" research to the exclusion of everyday applications, nor do psychologists feel that their science must be dull in order to be rigorous. The explanation is to be found in the choice of an inappropriate model for the study of mankind. Sigmund Koch (1961) observes that "psychology has been more concerned with being a science than with courageous and self-determining confrontation of its historically constituted subject matter. Its history has been largely a matter of emulating the methods, forms, symbols of the established science, especially physics "

The current trend began with John B. Watson (1914, p. 27), the founder of behaviorism, who insisted that psychology is a purely objective, experimental branch of natural science that needs introspection as little as physics and chemistry. What he failed to appreciate was that the natural sciences were originally developed to study inanimate nature. Consciousness could be safely ignored because insensate objects neither think nor feel. The problem is quite different when we come to man. Werner Heisenberg (1958, p. 106), a Nobel prize winner in physics who was greatly concerned with the theoretical basis of science, remarks, "if we . . . include psychology in the discussion, then there can scarcely be any doubt but that the concepts of physics, chemistry, and evolution together will not be sufficient to describe the facts . . . for an understanding of psychic phenomena we would start from the fact that the human mind enters as object and subject into the scientific process of psychology." To ignore or minimize the mental life of human beings in order to rely exclusively upon scientific methods devised for a different kind of subject matter seems rather incongruous for anyone who professes to have something significant to say about people. Certain **isolated human processes** can be investigated in this manner, but such research should not be confused with the study of **man**. Traditionally science has been largely analytical. It shows us how to take things apart, not how to put them together. If we wish to understand an integral person in a living context, we must also develop techniques of integration to see how he functions when each ongoing process influences every other one.

In summary, students who look forward to an introductory course in psychology with a great deal of enthusiasm may find that their hopes are not all fulfilled. Many have not had sufficient exposure to any science to realize that psychology is a highly systematic discipline that requires the acquisition of many facts and skills in order to become intensely rewarding. But the science of psychology as presently constituted has its limitations too, as we have already suggested. Among these limitations is the prevalent conception of man that denies him freedom of choice and uniqueness among animal species. Another limitation is the almost exclusive dependence upon the methods of natural science which are incapable of dealing adequately with inner experience. As a result many psychologists have all but renounced interest in consciousness, even though human existence would have little meaning without it. Seldom or never do they mention what it is like to feel anxiety or to think. Such questions are taboo for anyone who relies wholly on methods originally developed by physicists for the study of nature. Instead he attempts to account for all conscious experience in terms of conditioned responses or other behavioral processes that are basically physiological. This emphasis on stimuli and passive responding rather than spontaneous striving and choosing creates another vacuum. Not enough attention has been devoted to translating abstract theory into practical, everyday living. Much is said about the nature of wholesome personality traits and their measurement, but very little about how to acquire them. While it is true that education for competence in any content area is quite distinct from education for personal growth, Maslow (1970a) felt that both could be achieved and that psychologists should take the lead in discovering the necessary techniques.

Dissatisfaction with the truncated image of man discussed above has been rapidly intensifying. The past decade has seen the origin of a "third force"* composed of behavioral scientists with similar convictions who are working alone or in organized groups for the restoration of the whole person to psychology. They do not speak with a single voice, they do not constitute a separate school of thought, nor do they specialize in any specific content area. All that unites them is the common goal of humanizing psychology. Many basic philosophies are represented ranging from those of certain neo-Freudians, gestalt psychology, and existentialism, through phenomenology, personalism, and the more recent self-theories. Depending upon the point of view that is emphasized, some "third force" approaches to the study of man have been designated by such adjectives as humanistic, existential, perceptual, transactional, and proactive. The majority of behavioral scientists involved in this broad movement work in applied fields such as psychotherapy where the limitations of a psychology modeled on physics first become apparent. Many others are engaged in the study of personality, cognitive psychology, developmental psychology, psycholinguistics, and social psychology.

In spite of so much diversity there is substantial agreement on a number of points (Bugental, 1966).

1 Memory, learning, perception, and other psychological functions studied in isolation from the whole individual are less than human and do not add up to a complete person. Emphasis on the concept of **self** serves to remind the psychologist that somehow he must take into account everything that goes on in the living flesh-and-blood human being if his abstractions are to correspond to reality.

2 Within certain limits that will be discussed in Chapter 5, man is self-directing. Instead of "being lived" by drives, past conditioning, or other forces that he cannot control, he can in many circumstances freely choose to do one thing rather than another.

3 Consciousness or awareness is the most basic psychological process and is intimately involved in the design of experiments as well as in the gathering and processing of data. As a result, the so-called sub-

*Koch (1961) refers to psychology as a third force because it lies in the area of intersection between science and the humanities. More recently the expression has been used to designate the collective effort of many psychologists to supplement behaviorism and psychoanalysis, the two leading influences on American psychology, by filling in the blind spots and rectifying their distortions.

jective and objective methodologies are not as sharply differentiated as they are traditionally assumed to be.

4 Too frequently in the past, problems for research have been selected, not because of their importance to mankind, but because they would allow the investigator to make use of natural science methods. Third-force psychologists protest against this squandering of needed resources when so many pressing human problems await a solution. Despite thousands of controlled studies of reinforcement schedules, we still know very little about human motivation. Most of that comes, not from the laboratory, but from clinical interviews with emotionally disturbed persons. Still less is known about the problems of ego-identity; life goals; the prevention of crime, wars, and violence; effective methods of bridging the generation gap; the optimal conditions for personality growth; or self-fulfillment. No science, least of all psychology, can afford the luxury of working in isolated splendor from the agonies of a world overwhelmed with tensions and uncertainties. If psychology does not address itself to the legitimate needs of people, some nonscientific or pseudoscientific movement will. Fundamental human wants will not be denied; psychology must either concern itself with real-life problems or run the risk of losing its image as a relevant science.

5 Behavioristic theories of science are based to a large extent upon nineteenth-century assumptions which are no longer considered valid. These are discussed in Chapter 13. By incorporating the new insights of physicists and philosophers, psychologists should be able to devise methodologies more in keeping with their unique subject matter.

6 Humanistic psychology is unashamedly concerned with per-personal and professional responsibility, life goals, commitment, self-actualization, creativity, spontaneity, and the subtle values implied in psychological investigation. Any science that imagines itself to be value-free is long outdated. The refusal to call value judgments what they actually are does not eliminate them from pure and applied research.

7 The aim of psychology is usually defined as the prediction and control of behavior. Rather than speak a language of manipulation, behavioral scientists should think in terms of helping people understand themselves in order to be free from unwanted outside influences. Jourard (1968, p. 5) challenges the psychologists to examine carefully any commitment he makes to a sponsor who engages his services. He should ask himself, is this research to be undertaken as a psychologist-for-persons in order to enlarge individual freedom, or rather to help someone gain covert power and advantage over others?

Judging from the number of books and articles in professional journals that endorse some or all the above principles, the humanistic movement is rapidly gaining momentum. It came into existence, not to negate what is already being done, but to broaden the horizons of psychology, revamp its image of man and bring its efforts to bear on important human problems which are now being ignored. In 1971 the American Psychological Association established a new division for the study of humanistic psychology.

ADDITIONAL READINGS

Ansbacher, H. L. Alfred Adler and humanistic psychology. **Journal of Humanistic Psychology,** 1971, **11**, 53-63. Alfred Adler should be considered a charter member of the humanistic movement.

Bonner, H. **On being mindful of man: Essays toward a proactive psychology.** New York: Houghton Mifflin, 1965. "Dr. Bonner presents a proactive psychology built on the assumption that every man, however much like other men he might be, is yet unique."

Bugental, J. F. T. (Ed.) **Challenges of humanistic psychology.** New York: McGraw-Hill, 1967. The articles in this collection were written by leading figures in the humanistic movement.

Buhler, C. Basic theoretical concepts of humanistic psychology. **American Psychologist,** 1971, **26**, 378-386. This article was the presidential address at the first International Invitational Conference on Humanistic Psychology.

Chein, I. The image of man. **Journal of Social Issues,** 1962, **13**, 1-35. Theories about the human person should not be inconsistent with what we know about people by living with them.

Dubos, Rene. **So human an animal.** New York: Charles Scribner's Sons, 1968. Dubos shows how a humanized science can help us develop a society worthy of mankind.

Giorgi, A. Phenomenology and experimental psychology I. **Review of Existential Psychology and Psychiatry,** 1965, **5**, 228-238. A phenomenological approach to experimental psychology can compensate for many of its limitations.

Goble, F. **The third force: The psychology of Abraham Maslow.** New York: Grossman, 1970. Goble explains Maslow's theories in a lucid and condensed form.

Jourard, S. A. **Disclosing man to himself.** New York: Van Nostrand, 1968. The author describes a person-centered approach to psychological research.

Maddi, S. R. Humanistic psychology: Allport and Murray. In J. M. Wepman and R. W. Heine, **Concepts of personality.** Chicago: Aldine, 1963. Maddi discusses the theories of two psychologists who kept alive an interest in the whole person during an era of atomistic analysis.

Maslow, A. H. **Toward a psychology of being.** (Rev. ed.) New York: Van Nostrand, 1968. Maslow proposes a psychology of growth and self-actualization.

Matson, F. W. **The broken image.** New York: George Braziller, 1964. Matson traces the history of ideas to show how contemporary man became alienated from himself.

Rogers, C. R. Toward a science of the person. In T. W. Wann (Ed.) **Behaviorism and phenomenology: Contrasting bases for modern psychology.** Chicago: University of Chicago Press, 1964. In this article Rogers continues his search for a truly human science.

Sanford, N. Will psychologists study human problems? **American Psychologist,** 1965, **20,** 192-202. "We have produced a whole generation of research scientists who have never had occasion to look closely at any one person."

Sutich, A. J., and Vich, M. A. (Eds.) **Readings in humanistic psychology.** New York: The Free Press, 1969. This is a selection of articles from the **Journal of Humanistic Psychology.**

Part One

Underdeveloped Areas
In Psychology

We believe that every psychologist should take
as his motto Terence's famous utterance:
nihil humanum a me alienum puto ("Nothing human
is alien to me"). The exploration of every possibility
should be the psychologist's overall goal.
HUBERT BONNER

Chapter 1

Love and Altruism

*Love alone is capable of uniting living
beings in such a way as to complete and
fulfill them, for it alone takes them and
joins them by what is deepest in themselves.*

Pierre Teilhard de Chardin

LOVE

In literature and song we are told that love makes the world go round,
and from our own experience we can readily believe it. What other motive is stronger than either selfishness or hate? In the interests of love
almost everyone cheerfully sacrifices many things he would like to do
in order to accommodate the wishes of a dear one. The partners of any
successful marriage derive a feeling of fulfillment from spending themselves to bring happiness to other members of the family.

Love that is worthy of the name is outer-directed, reaching out
to and resting in some other person whose welfare becomes of paramount importance. Only secondarily is thought given to what benefits
one might derive for himself. Pathological love, in spite of the appear-

ance of authenticity, is just the opposite. Instead of the other being loved for what he is in himself, consciously or unconsciously he is covertly used to gratify one's own needs. It is a manipulative kind of affection. To borrow a term from psychoanalysis, the beloved is perceived as a love object instead of a person. For this reason some writers distinguish two kinds of love. Lewis speaks of gift and need love, Maslow of B and D love, Fromm of mature love and symbiotic union, May of eros and sex without tenderness or psychological union. Whether the deficiency be attributed to faulty family relationships during childhood (Freud, Horney, Sullivan, and many others), a commercially oriented culture in which people package and market themselves together with their products (Fromm), or the pressures of technological society that result in a banalization of tender affection and sex (May), some individuals seem incapable of either giving or receiving genuine love. What they understand by the term is, to a greater or lesser degree, the exploitation of another person for selfish reasons. Fromm (1956) astutely observes that love is not something we chance to fall into but an art that must be resolutely cultivated. The permanent state of **being** in love, in contrast with **falling** in love, requires a certain level of maturity and the development of such personality characteristics as humility, courage, faith, and discipline.

In the selection that follows, James Coleman gives an excellent overview of what psychologists have said about love.

From Psychology and Effective Behavior

Love as a Problem Emotion

Despite its central importance in human affairs, love, as a psychological phenomenon, has received very little scientific study. In fact, many psychology books do not even have the term *love* in the index, and where the term is used, it is ordinarily in connection with sex and marriage rather than in terms of its more general place in human relationships. Yet it would probably be agreed that an ability to give and receive love is one of the most important of all emotional competencies, for all the evidence points to the necessity of loving and being loved for normal human development and functioning.

Why human beings have such a great need and desire for love has been the subject of considerable speculation. Fromm (1956) believes that love develops from man's awareness of his separateness and his need to overcome the anxiety this separateness brings by achieving union with someone or something. But he stresses the point that the only healthy union is one in which the integrity of the individual is not threatened. We can achieve a feeling of union through dependence on another individual or through conformity to the group, but in so doing, we surrender our own individuality; likewise, we can achieve union through dominating others, but here the others suffer. Only through love, Fromm feels, can the needed sense of union be achieved without loss of individuality and integrity on either side. May (1968) has also emphasized the theme of aloneness as a basis for our need for love in his statement that:

> Every person, as a separate individual, experiences aloneness. And so we strive actively to overcome our aloneness by some form of love (p. 23).

Whatever its origin, the search for love is an extremely powerful force in human existence.

The meaning and forms of love

Many people have tried to define love. Prescott (1957) has described valid love in terms of the following components:

1 *Love involves* more or less *empathy* with the loved one. A person who loves actually enters into the feelings of and shares intimately the experiences of the loved one and the effects of these experiences upon the loved one.

2 One who loves is deeply *concerned for the welfare*, happiness, and development *of the beloved.* This concern is so deep as to become one of the major organizing values in the personality or self-structure of the loving person. . . .

3 One who loves finds *pleasure in making his resources available* to the loved one, to be used by the other to enhance his welfare, happiness, and development. Strength, time, money, thought, indeed all resources are proffered happily to the loved one for his use. A loving person is not merely concerned about the beloved's welfare and development, he does something about it.

4 Of course the loving person seeks a maximum of participation in the activities that contribute to the welfare, happiness, and development of the beloved. But he also *accepts fully the uniqueness and individuality of the beloved and . . . accords [him] full freedom to experience, to act, and to become what he desires to become.* A loving person has a nonpossessive respect for the selfhood of the loved one (p. 358).

There are also, of course, somewhat unique components in the love we feel for a parent, a child, a friend, and a mate. Fromm (1956) delineates five somewhat different love relationships, as described below.

1 *Brotherly love.* Perhaps the most basic kind of love is that for all of humanity. Fromm describes it as "the sense of responsibility, care, respect, knowledge of any other human being, the wish to further his life" (p. 47). Unlike the love of man and woman or mother and child, brotherly love is in no way exclusive. It is the orientation to all human relationships which finds expression in the Biblical injunction to "love thy neighbor as theyself."

2 *Motherly (parental) love.* Here Fromm emphasizes the parent's unconditional affirmation of his child's life and needs. Parental love involves care and responsibility for the child's well-being and growth, together with a willing acceptance of the fact that the child's life is his own. The parent assumes responsibility for a life entrusted to his care and finds his happiness in seeing that life fulfilled. True motherly love is nonpossessive.

3 *Erotic love.* Fromm describes erotic love as "the craving for a complete fusion, for union with one other person. It is by its very nature exclusive and not universal. . ." (pp. 52-53). Typically, of course, erotic love finds it culmination in the framework of marriage.

4 *Self-love.* Since love implies concern, respect, and responsibility, self-love is considered a necessity if the individual is to be capable of loving others. Self-deprecation and self-rejection interfere with all healthy love relationships.

5 *Love of God.* In discussing religious love, Fromm (p. 83) again emphasizes man's "need to overcome separateness and to achieve union"—in this case, union with ultimate reality. This point is elaborated further in Chapter 16 in connection with the quest for values.

UNHEALTHY LOVE RELATIONSHIPS

Distinguishing between healthy and unhealthy love is not always easy. Assuming outsiders are not being hurt by a relationship, the only yardstick we have for evaluating its healthiness is the extent to which it contributes to the happiness, well-being, and personal growth of both participants. By this criterion, the following types of love relationship would appear to be unhealthy:

1 *Conditional love*—in which the individual gives love only if the other conforms to his needs and dictates while he remains insensitive to the needs of the other.

2 *Possessive love*—in which the person views the loved object as a possession and treats him in a proprietary and exploitative way rather than as an autonomous, self-actualizing person.

3 *Overly romanticized love*—with expectations of constant excitement and continuous signs of adoration from the loved one.

4 *False or deceitful love*—in which one partner professes deep and enduring love but uses the relationship to deliberately exploit the other.

5 *Two-against-the-world love*—in which the partners view themselves as two person standing against a hostile world, indicating a defensive and self-centered orientation.

6 *Insecure and devaluating love*—in which one partner feels insecure and anxious and often jealous and in which his self-concept is devaluated rather than built up.

7 *Mutually destructive love*—in which the partners undermine and tear each other down and in which the relationship appears to be characterized more by hate than by love.

CONFLICTING ASSUMPTIONS ABOUT ROMANTIC LOVE

On the basis of intuition, personal experience, and uncontrolled observation, it has been claimed:

1 That romantic love inevitably leads to disillusionment and is the principal cause of our high divorce rate—and also that romantic love mitigates the stresses of monogamous marriage, preventing its disintegration as a social institution.

2 That romantic love is blind and irrational—and also that romantic love involves a sharpening of perception so that the other person is seen realistically but loved for himself anyway.

3 That adequate sexual relationships stem from and can be found only in the context of romantic love—and also that adequate sexual relationships often pave the way for the later development of love.

4 That finding the right person is the most important ingredient in romantic love—and also that one's capacity to give and receive love is the most important determinant.

5 That each successive love relationship is a unique and distinctive experience—and also that one loves as he has loved before so that there is a continuity in his love relationships and he will keep making the same mistakes.

6 That true romantic love leads to harmony and bliss—and also that "the path of true love never does run smooth," that the intensity of feeling in romantic love will inevitably lead to conflict and anxiety.

7 That it is possible in romantic love to lower one's defenses and let one's faults be freely seen by the partner—and also that one must be lovable to be loved and hence must always keep his best foot forward in appearance and behavior.

8 That romantic love can be felt for only one love object at a time—and also that the individual may be romantically in love with more than one person simultaneously.

Thus love may take several different forms and may have several different meanings. Central to all the forms of love, however, appears to be an attitude of care, concern, and responsibility for the loved one, and a desire to promote his growth, well-being, and concerns. Nor does an individual usually show only one form of love; more commonly, the ability for any of the particular forms of love is part of a broader orientation involving the valuing of other human beings and an eagerness to form warm bonds with other people. As Fromm has put it (1956):

> If a person loves only one other person and is indifferent to the rest of his fellow men, his love is not love but symbiotic attachment, or an enlarged egotism (p. 46).

In the remainder of this section, we shall be concerned primarily with healthy love relationships in marriage.

Romantic love vs. infatuation

Although economic factors rather than love have often been emphasized in marriage, romantic love has played an important role in most cultures (Kurland, 1953). In our contemporary society, we are constantly exposed to portrayals of idealized romantic love in movies, television, plays, novels, and popular songs. As in the case of other forms of love, however, we know very little about romantic love in real life: speculation about it by various alleged authorities casts little light on the subject.

Some of the many conflicting assumptions which have been held about romantic love are summarized [on page 17]. Interestingly, virtually the only scientific evidence we have regarding any of these assumptions concerns the last two pairs. In his study of self-actualizing people Maslow (1970b) found that these individuals were able to drop their defenses in their love relationships and be wholly themselves without fear or pretense:

> One of the deepest satisfactions coming from the healthy love relationship reported by my subjects is that such a relationship permits the greatest spontaneity, the greatest naturalness, the greatest dropping of defenses and protection against threat. In such a relationship it is not necessary to be guarded, to conceal, to try to impress, to feel tense, to watch one's words or actions, to suppress or repress. My people report that they can be themselves without feeling that there are demands or expectations upon them; they can feel psychologically (as well as physically) naked and still feel loved and wanted and secure (pp. 181-202).

Whether this finding would hold for less self-actualizing people in less healthy love relationships is a moot point.

In an early study of 500 American college girls, Ellis (1948) reported that 58 percent admitted simultaneous infatuations and 25 percent reported being in love simultaneously with two or more men. The findings of Packard (1968) with respect to the sexual patterns of college men and women suggest that the earlier findings of Ellis may be valid for today's generation as well.

Romantic love is characterized by strong feelings of attraction toward and affection for the loved person, a desire to be with him (or her), a concern for his well-being, a willingness to make more of oneself for him, and a desire to contribute to his happiness and personal growth. Usually it also includes a desire for affection from and sexual intimacy with the loved person. Such love may endure and deepen over the years or it may wither away. In some instances there appears to be a shift from romantic love to disillusionment and hurt and sometimes even to hostility and hate.

Despite all these points of similarity any given experience of romantic love is a unique, highly personal experience that may be difficult to describe to others. In fact, writers and poets have described the experience of romantic love in quite diverse ways. It seems unlikely that a person who has never experienced romantic love can understand or imagine the quality of the experience involved.

Often the question is raised as to the distinction between romantic love and infatuation. Lacking a clear understanding of either, we can make only a general distinction. Infatuation is usually considered to be an intense romantic relationship of short duration which is a purely emotional reaction and does not take into account the "fit" of the personalities or any other rational considerations. Often infatuation involves a high degree of wishful thinking in which the lover projects a halo over the head of the loved one and sees only what he wants to see instead of what is there. Once his perceptions become more realistic, the romantic aura may suddenly be lost.

Unfortunately, as Kephart (1967) has pointed out, one usually thinks of his current romantic experience as love rather than infatuation; infatuation is usually recognized as such—at least by the person involved—only after it is over.

Although infatuation may not last, it is a powerful force while it holds sway. It provides both rose-colored spectacles and a sense of urgency to its victims, and when it leads to a hasty marriage, the individual may find himself married to someone he scarcely knows, whose weak points come to him as quite a shock.

Many other irrational elements may also make it difficult for a person to tell if he is really in love. For example, even a relatively mature individual may convince himself that he wants to get married because he is in love when actually what he wants is to have someone take care of him, or to ensure his sexual satisfaction, or to protect himself from loneliness. Often, too, the individual has been indoctrinated with the romantic notion that there is only one person in the world who is right for him; in his eagerness to believe he has found that person, it is easy for him to convince himself that he is in love.

Genuine erotic love grows out of shared experiences of many kinds. The climate of a happy marriage is not necessarily one of complete harmony at all times; but it is one in which the bonds of love are deepened by shared problems as well as by happiness, and one in which both partners can continue to grow as individuals. The latter point is particularly important, for a love which feeds on dependency is apt to destroy itself. Erotic love, like brotherly and parental love, nurtures the growth of the loved one as an individual.

The ability to love

Most investigators believe that people vary greatly in their ability to love and to maintain a durable loving interaction with another person. An individual's ability to love, like other emotional competencies, appears to depend upon a number of factors, including his early experiences with his parents, the extent to which he trusts others, his degree of personal maturity and self-acceptance, and his freedom from exaggerated self-defense.

As we have seen, the ability to give and receive love apparently begins in a healthy infant-mother relationship and then expands as we build satisfying relationships with other family members, friends, and eventually a mate and children of our own. Fromm (1956) has distinguished two components which he considers of crucial importance in such early experiences: (1) the early experience of being loved unconditionally by the mother, and (2) the later experience of having to meet certain standards to ensure love. The first experience is considered a passive one in which the infant is loved simply because he exists; while the second experience, usually largely mediated by the father, shows the child that he can work for love and achieve it—that it is potentially within his control. Later these two trends are integrated into a feeling that one is basically lovable and worthy of love but also that he can behave in ways which will increase or destroy the love that other people will feel for him.

Lacking either part of this experience, the child is handicapped later on. If he has a weak and uninterested father and an indulgent mother, for example, he is not likely to be able to love since his orientation is a receptive one in which he expects others to love him regardless of his own behavior. Or, if the mother is cold and unresponsive and the father authoritarian, the child may later lack the ability for either giving or receiving unconditional love— always suspecting that there are strings attached to being loved.

Whether or not we agree with Fromm's formulation, it is of interest as a model for trying to understand the way in which early family patterns may influence our later approaches to love relationships. It seems a safe generalization that a minimally favorable emotional climate in childhood is usually necessary if the individual is to be able to give and receive love in later years. Yet love is a powerful force, and long-held patterns of self-doubt, cynicism, and of defensiveness may be dissipated by the experience of genuinely loving and being loved by another human being.

ALTRUISM

Teilhard de Chardin (1965, pp. 264-265) was among the scholars who consider love to be more than just a strongly motivating sentiment. He thought of it as a natural dynamism deeply rooted in the cosmic forces of evolution. Certain propensities present even in inanimate matter make possible the ultimate appearance and elaboration of consciousness in animals. The extent to which any species is capable of love covaries with the quality of awareness it possesses. In mammals love manifests itself in sexual passion, parental behavior, and social solidarity. Man, at the growing tip of the tree of life, experiences love of a kind that is immeasurably superior to animal affection. Still it is far from perfect. Not only is it frequently counterfeit, but the average individual does not extend his love to everyone. If we accept Teilhard's supposition that mankind as a species is still in early infancy and that **universal** brotherly love is a future end product of evolution, it should not be surprising to find that it is a rare phenomenon. But given millions of years for our species to attain full psychological and social adulthood, we might expect that the love people now feel for a few relatives and friends will then reach out to embrace all men.

One way to estimate the amount of brotherly love present in our society is to study altruistic behavior, that is, the extent to which one person will unselfishly help another who is in need. Although for practical purposes most people know the meaning of altruism, an accurate definition for purposes of research is not easy to formulate. Some psychologists place great emphasis on the **fact** of helping behavior regardless of the benefactor's intention which may be fundamentally selfish. Others consider the helper's motivation to be an essential component. Only if his actions are inspired without regard for any favorable outcome to himself can a good deed be labeled altruistic. Still other psychologists contend that since motivation is complex and since a feeling of gratification and heightened self-esteem usually accompanies unselfish helping behavior, neither point of view should be overstressed. Macaulay and Berkowitz (see Further Readings) define altruism as "behavior carried out to benefit another without anticipation of rewards from external sources."

Regardless of how altruism is defined, it remains a tremendous force for human cohesion at every level of interaction from the personal to the international. Pitirim A. Sorokin believed that without a substantial increase in unselfish brotherly love, political catastrophies and new world wars are unavoidable. The opinions and findings which he presents in the selection that follows are consistent with Teilhard's position that love has its origin in the evolutionary process and serves an important biological and psychological function.

From The Powers of Creative Unselfish Love

Moral Transformation Is Paramount Task of Our Time

The central reason for the establishment of the Harvard Research Center in Creative Altruism and of the Center's progeny—this Research Society—has been the idea that the *moral transformation of man and the man-made universe is the most important item on today's agenda of history*. Without moral transformation in altruistic directions, neither new world wars and other catastrophes can be prevented nor a new—better and nobler—social order be built in the human universe. Without a notable increase of what we call creative unselfish love in man and in the human universe, all fashionable prescriptions for prevention of wars and for building of a new order cannot achieve their purpose.

For instance, one such fashionable prescription is a political reconstruction of all nations along the lines of American democracy. Despite the popularity of this belief, it is questionable. Tomorrow, hypothetically, you could have all nations reconstructed politically along the lines of the American brand of democracy; and yet such a reconstruction would neither prevent nor decrease the chances of new world wars or of bloody internal revolutions. Why? Because study of all the wars and important internal disturbances from 600 B.C. to the present time reveals that democracies are not less belligerent, no less militant, and no more orderly than autocracies.[1] This conclusion is unpleasant. Nevertheless, it is true.

Another favorite prescription against wars and bloody strife is more education and more schooling. Again, hypothetically, tomorrow you could have all men and women at the age of sixteen and over miraculously

From Pitirim A. Sorokin. "The powers of creative unselfish love," pp. 3-11. In Abraham H. Maslow (Ed.), *New knowledge in human values.* Copyright © 1959 by Research Society for Creative Altruism. Reprinted by permission of Harper & Row, Publishers, Inc.

[1] See the detailed data in P. Sorokin, *Social and Cultural Dynamics*, American Book Company, 1937, vol. 3, Chaps. 9-14; in abridged edition of this work, see *ibid.*, Porter Sargent, 1957, Chaps. 32-35.

transformed into Ph.D.'s and super-Ph.D.'s. And yet, such a miraculous increase of education would not decrease the chances of either civil or international wars. Why? Because the prevailing forms of education and the growth of science and technology do not curb or even decrease wars and bloody revolutions. From the tenth century up to the present time, the number of schools, beginning with kindergartens and ending with universities, the percentage of literacy, the number of scientific discoveries and technological inventions, have been continuously increasing, especially during the last two centuries. Despite this enormous educational, scientific, and technological progress the curve of wars (measured either by frequency of wars or by the size of armies or by the amount of casualties per million population) has not gone down during these centuries. If anything, with great fluctuations, it has gone up. The same is true of revolutions and revolts.[2] We are living in the most scientific, most technological, and most schooled century; and the same century happens to be the bloodiest of all the preceding recorded twenty-five centuries.

The same is true of other popular prescriptions against world wars and internal disturbances—such panaceas as the establishment of a universal capitalistic or communistic or socialistic economic organization. Even the so-called religious factor has failed to alter the pattern—if, by religion, we mean just a set of beliefs, dogmas, and rituals. Among the proofs for this statement we mention here our study of seventy-three converts of popular American and English evangelists. We wanted to know if the conversion of these seventy-three persons had changed their minds and, particularly, their overt behavior in altruistic directions, by making it nearer to the sublime precepts of the Sermon on the Mount? The result was not cheerful. Out of these seventy-three persons, only one has shown a tangible change of his personality and overt behavior. About one-half of the converts changed somewhat their speech reactions: instead of profanities they more frequently began to pronounce the name of "Our Lord Jesus Christ" and so on, but their outward behavior did not change at all; and the remaining half of the converts did not change even their speech reactions.

Evidence of this sort, I believe, makes it clear why prevention of future catastrophes is hardly possible without some fundamental change of man's motivations in the direction of altruism. Still less possible becomes the building of a more harmonious and more creative social and cultural order.

The gigantic potential power of love

There is a second reason for the paramount importance of the moral transformation of man. Recent studies have shown that what we tentatively

[2] See the figures in P. Sorokin, *Reconstruction of Humanity*, Beacon Press, 1948, Chap. 3.

call "unselfish creative love" is not only one of the highest values of the Trinity of value, Truth, Goodness, Beauty, but it is also one of the three most sublime forms of energy, having gigantic potential power for the modification of man and man's universe. The last few decades have been marked in many disciplines—biology, sociology, psychology, anthropology, and others—by an emergence and growth of a *remarkable convergence toward one central point. All these disciplines have been increasingly emphasizing the all-important role of this mysterious power of love.* In recent decades rapidly growing scientific evidence tends to confirm the age-old discovery: God is Love and Love is God. Whereas the biology of the nineteenth century emphasized the role of the struggle for existence, the biology of our time more and more emphasizes—whether in evolution of species or in survival of separate species, or in maintenance of health, vitality, and longevity—the factor of mutual aid, cooperation, or friendship, all these terms being but different words designating diverse aspects of the same creative unselfish love.

Today's biology tells us that this factor has been playing at least as important a role as the factor of struggle for existence; and as time goes on the emphasis upon the power and role of love increases progressively. Among other things, contemporary biologists show clearly that, for survival and multiplication of unicellular or multicellular organisms, cooperation between parental and progeny organisms is absolutely necessary, especially in such species as homo sapiens, in which the newborn baby is helpless and, in order to survive, needs several years of help and love (Montagu, 1950, Sorokin, 1950b).

The biological, the psychological, the anthropological, and the sociological disciplines are bringing an ever-increasing body of evidence that demonstrates the vitalizing and ennobling power of unselfish love. A few examples well illustrate this point. For instance, studies of suicide show that so-called egotistic suicide (the act of anomie) is caused mainly by loneliness and psychosocial isolation of an individual, especially when it is caused by a sudden disruption of his social ties. *The best antidote against suicide is therefore a transcendence of this isolation by unselfish creative love for other human beings* (Durkheim, 1954). A number of studies, including those done by the Harvard Research Center, have shown that *love is a factor which seems to increase the duration of life.*

We have taken something like 4,500 Christian saints about whom more or less reliable data could be collected. They lived in various periods beginning with the first century of our era and ending with the present time. Among other things, we investigated the duration of their lives. More than 98 percent of these saints lived before the nineteenth century. As we approach our time, "the production of saints" rapidly decreases. Now, the average life expectation in the centuries from the first to the eighteenth was much lower than it is in the United States at the present time. Many of these saints intentionally tortured their bodies and deprived them of satisfaction of their elementary needs. About 37 percent of these saints died prematurely by martyrdom. In spite of all these adverse conditions, a rough average of life-duration of these saints happened to be at least as long as that of the contemporary American. What is the cause of this? Since most of the saints have been extraordinary apostles of unselfish love, this factor of love has possibly been the most important cause of their longevity (Sorokin, 1950a).

A number of psychological, psychiatric, sociological, and educational researches have proved that a *minimum of this love is absolutely necessary for survival of newborn babies and for their healthy growth.* Among several studies of this kind, Dr. René A. Spitz's investigation can be mentioned. He reported and filmed the death of thirty-four foundlings in a foundling house. In the foundling home these babies had all the necessities and care except motherly love. After three months of separation from their parents the babies lost appetite, could not sleep, and became shrunken, whimpering, and trembling. After an additional two months they began to look like idiots. Twenty-seven foundlings died in their first year of life, seven in the second. Twenty-one lived longer but were so altered that thereafter they could be classified as idiots.

The curative and integrating power of love shows itself in many other forms. The grace of love—in both forms of loving and being loved—is the most important condition for babies to grow into morally and mentally sound human beings. Many sociological studies show that the *bulk of juvenile delinquents are recruited from the children who in their early life did not have the necessary minimum of love. Deficiency of "the vitamin of love" is also responsible for many mental disorders.* On the other hand, in our age of psychoneuroses and juvenile delinquency, the Mennonite, the Hutterite, some Quaker, and even the Chinese communities in the United States yield either none or the lowest quota of delinquents, mentally sick persons, and drug addicts. The main reason for this is that these communities not only preach love but realize it in their daily life; they are united into a sort of a real brotherhood.

The curative power of love is also increasingly emphasized by the recent studies in psychiatry. The investigations of K. E. Appel, F. E. Fiedler, C. Rogers, V. E. Frankl, H. J. Eysenck, G. W. Allport, R. Assagioli, E. Straus, and other psychiatrists and psychologists show that the *main curative agent in the treatment of mental disorders* is not so much the specific technique used by various schools of psychiatry as the establishment of the rapport of *empathy, sympathy, kindness, and mutual trust between the patient and the therapist and the placing of the patient in a "social climate" free from inner and interhuman conflicts.*

The studies of the Harvard Research Center in Creative Altruism and of other scholars disclose other manifestations of the power of love. Despite our meager knowledge of the mysterious and sublime energy of love, its revitalizing, curative, ameliorative, and creative functions are already demonstrated by numerous converging studies of love. For instance, our experimental transformation of formerly inimical relationships between the members of each of five pairs of Harvard and Radcliffe students into amicable ones (within the period of three months, by the method of "good deeds" rendered by one of the partners of each pair to the other partner) demonstrates well the *power of love in mitigation of interhuman hatred and in elimination of interhuman strife.*

Likewise our experimental and clinical investigations of the friendly and inimical approaches and responses among the students of Harvard and Radcliffe and among the patients of the Boston Psychopathic Hospital clearly confirm the truth of the old motto that *"love begets love and hate begets hate."* Roughly from 65 to 80 percent of the responses of the friendly (or the aggressive) approaches were respectively friendly (or inimical). Similarly, our detailed study of how and why each of some five hundred Harvard and Radcliffe students happened to feel and regard a certain individual as his or her "best friend" and another individual as "the worst enemy" disclosed the fact that *in all cases of "the best friend" the friendship was started by some friendly action of the person who, continuing to be friendly, eventually became "the best friend," and in all cases of "the worst enemy" the animosity was started by an aggressive action of the person who gradually became "the worst enemy."*

I wish these experimentally tested truths could be deeply implanted into the minds and hearts of contemporary American and Soviet politicians. They seem to be trying to achieve a lasting peace by following the old method of mutual hate and vituperation, by mutual aggressive and harmful actions, and by cold and hot wars. They seem to believe in the policy of "hate begets love, and love begets hate" and "cold and hot wars beget peace." No wonder their policies have not brought peace, despite hundreds of billions of dollars spent, hundreds of thousands of lives sacrificed, and an untold amount of energy, time, health, security, and happiness of millions wasted in these absurd policies.

The constructive efficacy of love clearly manifests itself also in the life history of various societies and in the national and international life of mankind. *Creative love increases not only the longevity of individuals but also of societies and organizations.* Social organizations built by hate, conquest, and coercion, such as the empires of Alexander the Great, Caesar, Genghis-Khan, Tamerlane, Napoleon, or Hitler, have, as a rule, a short life—years, decades, or rarely, a few centuries. Often they crumble before the death of their builders. The average duration of various social organizations in which unselfish love plays an unimportant part is also comparatively modest. Thus, the average longevity of small economic establishments such as drug-grocery-hardware stores in the United States is only about four years; of big business firms (listed on English, Swiss, American stock exchanges), only about 27 years. Even the longevity of most of the states rarely goes beyond one or two hundred years. *The longest existing organizations are the great ethico-religous organizations—Taoism, Confucianism, Hinduism, Buddhism, Jainism, Christianity, Mohammedanism, and the like.* They have already lived more than one or two or even three millennia. And these organizations are motivated by, and dedicated to, the altruistic education of millions in unselfish love.[3]

The case of Emperor Asoka gives an example of *the power of love in taming war and other bloody forms of interhuman strife.* Horrified by the disastrous results of his victorious wars, Asoka, in the second half of his life, under the influence of Buddhism radically replaced his policies of war by the policies of peace, friendship, and constructive reforms; building highways, orphanages, schools, museums, temples, planting trees, digging wells; eliminating injustice, alleviating misery, and in all possible ways helping his own population as well as that of neighboring states. By this friendly policy Asoka secured peace for a period of some seventy-two years. Considering that, on the average, war occurred once in every two years in the history of Greece, Rome, and nine other main European countries in the period beginning with 600 B.C. and ending with the present time; and that a seventy-two-year-long period of peace occurred only twice in the Graeco-Roman and the Western worlds during some twenty-five centuries of their history, Asoka's realization of lasting peace is most instructive: It suggests that the policy of friendship and mutual aid can secure a lasting peace more successfully than that of hate, destructive rivalry, and war.

Finally, the gigantic power of love has manifested itself also in *the greatest and longest influence exerted by the highest apostles of love upon human beings and human history.* If we ask ourselves what sort of individuals have been most influential in human history, the answer is such individuals as Lao-Tze, Confucius, Moses, Gautama Buddha, Mahavira, Jesus, St. Paul, St. Francis of Assisi, Mahatma Gandhi and other founders of great religions, discoverers of eternal moral principles, and living incarnations of sublime, unselfish love. In contrast to the short-lived and mainly destructive influence of autocratic monarchs, military conquerers, revolutionary dictators, potentates of wealth, and other historical persons, these great apostles of spirituality and love have most tangibly affected the lives, minds, and bodies of untold millions, of many generations, during millennia of human history;

---

[3] Cf. the typical longevity of various social organizations in P. Sorokin, *Society, Culture, and Personality,* Harper, 1947, Chap. 34.

and they are tangibly influencing us at the present time. They had neither army and arms nor physical force nor wealth nor any of the worldly means of influencing the historical destinies of nations. Nor, to obtain their power, did they appeal to hate, envy, greed, and other lusts of human beings. Even their physical organism was not of the strongest kind. And yet, together with a handful of their followers, they morally transformed millions of men and women, reshaped cultures and social institutions, and conditioned the course of history. They did all this by the mere power of their sublime, pure, and overabundant love, by their unselfish spirituality and supreme wisdom.

Summing up the outlined powers of unselfish love, we can say that unselfish creative love can stop aggressive interindividual and intergroup strife and can transform inimical relationships between persons and groups into amicable ones; that love begets love, and hate begets hate (in about 70 to 85 percent of the cases studies); that love can tangibly influence international relationships and pacify international conflicts. In addition, unselfish and wise love is a life-giving force, necessary for physical, mental, and moral health; altruistic persons live longer than egotistic individuals; children deprived of love tend to become morally, socially, and mentally defective; love is a powerful antidote against criminal, morbid, and suicidal tendencies; love is the loftiest educational force for enlightenment and moral ennoblement of mankind; love performs important cognitive and aesthetic functions; love is the heart and soul of freedom and of all moral and religious values; a minimum of love is necessary for a durable, creative, and harmonious society and its progress; finally, in this catastrophic moment of human history an increased "production, accumulation, and circulation of love-energy" in the whole human universe is a necessary condition for the prevention of new wars and for the alleviation of enormously increased interindividual and intergroup strife.[4]

Fyodor Dostoievski wrote prophetic words: "Seeing the sins of men, one sometimes wonders whether one should react to them by force or by humble love. Always decide to fight them by humble love. If it is carried through, the whole world can be conquered. Humble love is the most effective force, the most terrific, the most powerful, unequaled by any other force in the world."

STUDIES OF LOVE AND ALTRUISM

In recent years a considerable number of studies of altruism have been published. Krebs (1970), in an exhaustive review of the literature, cites

[4] See for the evidential data, detailed analysis, and the literature in P. Sorokin, *The Ways and Power of Love,* Beacon Press, 1954; P. Sorokin (Ed.). *Symposium: Forms and Techniques of Altruistic and Spiritual Growth,* Beacon Press, 1954; P. Sorokin, *Studies of Harvard Research Center in Creative Altruism,* Beacon Press, 1956.

137 references. Sarason and Smith (1971) give a briefer account of progress in this area in the **Annual Review of Psychology.** Some of the variables investigated in relation to altruism were affective states, the
modeling behavior of others, interpersonal attractiveness, age, sex, or-
dinal position in the family, social class, and nationality. Few clear-cut
generalizations can be made at this time. Sarason and Smith criticize
current research for neglecting the role of such personality variables as
the need for social approval.

Research studies of love are few in number. Yet in spite of the
highly subjective nature of love, it is possible to measure expressed feelings of affection. Such information can be useful in testing theories and
in determining the qualities of love in compatable mates. Probably the
first instrument of this kind to be developed is the **Scale of Feelings and
Behavior of Love** (Swensen, 1961; Swensen & Gilner, 1964). The 125
items represent 6 factors: verbal expression of affection, self-disclosure,
toleration of the less pleasant aspects of the loved one, nonmaterial evidence of love, unexpressed feelings, and material evidence of love.
Hattis (1965) reported a pilot investigation using a questionnaire which
included numerical ratings of (1) the love feelings of twelve unmarried
couples, (2) their estimates of their partners' love feelings, and (3) the
hypothetical love feelings in an ideal marriage. Using these data he was
able to analyze (1) how these feelings were reciprocated and how accurately each partner estimated the other's sentiments, (2) differences
among actual, estimated, and hypothetical ideal love feelings, (3) inter-
correlations of different components of love feelings experienced simultaneously, and (4) the consistency of various theories of love with these
results.

What future historians will find difficult to explain is how psychologists could so long ignore love in order to concentrate upon hunger, thirst, and similar physiological drives as the basic explanation of
human behavior. One need only analyze his own experience and the
actions of most people he knows to recognize the importance of love as
an instigator to action. Love, as the term is used here, cannot be reduced to a mere drive state. It is a thinking-feeling-choosing complex of
activities that involves the person as a totality.

SUMMARY

Writers distinguish between genuine and pathological love. The former
is primarily concerned with the welfare of another person, the latter
with exploiting him or her for selfish reasons. In spite of the importance
of this subject little systematic research has been undertaken. Coleman

superbly summarizes what the better-known psychologists have written about it and adds some penetrating insights of his own. Some theorists see love as a natural dynamism deeply rooted in the forces of evolution and predict that as the human race reaches psychological maturity, love will reach beyond a small circle of relatives and friends to include all mankind. Sorokin reports on his investigation of the vitalizing and ennobling power of unselfish love. The more recent research on love and altruism is briefly reviewed.

DISCUSSION TOPICS

1 List the characteristics of wholesome love and its counterfeits.

2 How can a person be reasonably certain that what he experiences is genuine love rather than mere infatuation?

3 Why is it sometimes said that a person who unconsciously hates himself cannot relate normally to others?

4 What explanations have been proposed for the inability of some persons to give or receive love?

5 What does Rollo May mean when he refers to a new puritanism with regard to sexual love? (See Additional Readings.)

6 Describe the love relationships of the self-actualizing persons in Maslow's study. (See Additional Readings.)

7 Do you agree with Sorokin's insistence upon altruism as an essential antidote for many of society's ills?

8 What are the implications of love having its roots in biological and evolutionary processes?

ADDITIONAL READINGS

Ansbacher, H. L. Love and violence in the view of Adler. **Humanitas** (Journal of the Institute of Man, Duquesne University) 1966, **2**, 109-127. "... man is not by nature self-centered and in conflict with his men and society ... but has a natural potentiality for harmonious and cooperative social living which must be encouraged."

Bonner, H. **On being mindful of man.** Boston: Houghton Mifflin, 1965, Chap. 8. Love and sensibility are examined within the framework of a proactive psychology.

Gratton, C. Selected bibliography (love and violence). **Humanitas**, 1966, **2**, 215-221. One hundred and ninety titles are listed.

Hazo, R. G. **The idea of love.** New York: Praeger, 1967. Members of the Institute for Philosophical Research collaborated in this critical analysis of the writings of Western thinkers about love.

Lewis, C. S. **The four loves.** New York: Harcourt, Brace, 1960. A highly articulate author treats of the love of God and of fellow man.

Luijpen, W. A. **Existential phenomenology** (2d ed.) Pittsburgh: Duquesne University Press, 1969, pp. 311-326. This book on philosophy devotes a section to the phenomenology of love.

Macaulay, J., & Berkowitz, L. **Altruism and helping behavior.** New York: Academic Press, 1970. "This book is an outgrowth of a conference held at the University of Wisconsin in June 1968 dealing with research on helping and altruism."

Maslow, A. H. **Motivation and personality** (2d ed.) New York: Harper & Row, 1970, Chap. 8. The characteristics of love as experienced by psychologically healthy people are described.

May, R. **Love and will.** New York: Norton, 1969. Our dehumanized world fails to understand the true meaning of love and will. May shows how we can rediscover these values.

Menninger, K. **Love against hate.** New York: Harcourt, Brace, 1942. A noted psychiatrist writes in the psychoanalytic tradition about the struggle between conflicting human instincts.

St. Paul. First Letter to the Corinthians, Chap. 13. Paul speaks of love of God and mankind in behavioral terms.

Sorokin, P. A. **Forms and techniques of altruistic and spiritual growth.** Boston: Beacon Press, 1954. "In their totality the studies of this Symposium give an account of several basic techniques for moral and spiritual education of man, together with their philosophical background, their actual effectiveness, their scientific value, and their importance for our time."

Winthrop, H. Self-sacrifice as autonomy, ego-transcendence and social interest. **Journal of Humanistic Psychology,** 1962, **2,** 31-37. "What impresses me in the case-histories of great, self-sacrificing personalities, is that they create their own directions and organize their own values, even where these are at variance with the world's."

Chapter 2

Play

To stop playing is not to grow up; it is to cease living authentically.

William A. Sadler, Jr.

Nothing is more characteristic of early life than the impulse to play; the phenomenon is universal. No one has to teach a baby to play. So long as a baby is healthy, comfortable, and feeling secure, play is as spontaneous and irrepressible as curiosity about the big, strange world outside. Huizinga (1950) notes the ceremonial way in which animals invite each other to make-believe games in which they adhere to the rules not to bite, or not bite very hard. They may pretend to be very angry and to attack with mock ferociousness as they romp about, taking no account of the lavish expenditure of energy. Obviously play is enjoyable judging from the whole demeanor of lambs gamboling in the fields, puppies chasing each other, or an infant babbling the same sounds over and over.

Fortunately, play enjoyment is no monopoly of the very young. The desire to amuse oneself remains throughout life. Some theorists even see a play element in war, diplomacy, business transactions, and social and religious rituals. It has been said that man's greatest ingenuity appears in the invention of his games. The dedicated way in which they are played also says something about his persistence. Track and swimming records are routinely surpassed in national and international competition, even though long ago many people believed that the upper physiological limits had almost been reached. But even the youngster who participates in these sports just for fun is likely to practice incessantly and compete with a determination that psychologists cannot overlook. Such a powerful impulse in both animals and man calls for an explanation. To have survived even in the human race seems to indicate that play serves some fundamental evolutionary role, whether that be biological, psychological, or social, or a combination of all three.

What complicates the problem is that play itself is not usually instrumental; that is, it serves no obviously useful purpose outside itself. It is as though the play activity were its own end without being directed toward securing anything else. The fun element also is puzzling. Why is it fun for some people to run a mile or to climb the sheer face of a mountain, and for everyone to participate in his own favorite recreation regardless of what it is? Kerr (1962), in his **Decline of Pleasure**, describes the modern tragedy of approaching amusement with a work mentality, as if it were a practical problem to be solved. Enraptured delight is not the concomitant of organized joy but of a passive yielding of one's self to an apt experience.

THEORIES OF PLAY

What seems strange is that play should have remained a mystery for so long. Every small boy knows what it means to play, but so far not a single adult has been able to propose either a definition or an explanation of the phenomenon that is generally accepted. In the selection that follows, J. Barnard Gilmore succinctly summarizes the theories that have been advanced over the years.

From Play: A Special Behavior

Certainly everyone knows what play is not, even if everyone can't agree on just what play is. Play seems to represent that definitionally impossible "wastebasket" category of behavior, the unmotivated act. Consider these

From "Play: A special behavior" by J. Barnard Gilmore. In Current research in motivation, edited by Ralph Norman Haber. Copyright © 1966 by Holt, Rinehart and Winston, Inc. Reprinted by permission of Holt, Rinehart and Winston, Inc.

traditional definitions of play (they are actually miniature theories of play) as drawn from Mitchell and Mason (1934):

> Spencer: Activity performed for the immediate gratification derived, without regard for ulterior benefits; Lazarus: Play is activity which is in itself free, aimless, amusing or diverting; Seashore: Free self expression for the pleasure of expression; Dewey: Activities not consciously performed for the sake of any result beyond themselves; Stern: Play is voluntary, self-sufficient activity; Patrick: Those human activities which are free and spontaneous and which are pursued for their own sake alone, interest in them is self-sustaining, and they are not continued under any internal or external compulsion; Allin: Play refers to those activities which are accompanied by a state of comparative pleasure, exhilaration, power, and the feeling of self-initiative; Curti: Highly motivated activity which, as free from conflicts is usually though not always, pleasurable (pp. 86-87).

It is clear that the person who wishes to understand play behavior has set himself a difficult task if he uses either his intuitive sense of the term or the above comments as a beginning point of reference, since the definition of play will determine both the theorizing about and the research done with play. To be scientifically workable, any definition must be precise; but "play" is an abstract and global sort of behavior, one that eludes precision. In the past, play has been a thing to be inferred, not the sort of behavior that elicits clear agreement with respect to its presence or absence.

It will be the purpose of this paper to explore the possible causes and effects of play in children, as suggested both by theorists of play and by research on play behavior. Play will be defined arbitrarily by the following behavioral example: a young child takes a piece of cloth and, as if the cloth were human, makes it "go to sleep." While behaviors as divergent as the dancinglike movements of apes and the sober assembly of model airplanes by adolescents have been considered to be play, we will knowingly restrict ourselves to this narrow (and not necessarily "pure") case. Perhaps in thinking about this one small play episode, concepts and distinctions will emerge that could lead to a clearer and more extensive definition of play.

Theories dealing with the causes and the effects of play fall into two general categories. First are those theories concerned only with the antecedents of play and with the inferred purposes of play; these theories regard the specific content of play behaviors as irrelevant. These theories will be termed *classical theories* of play since they spring from the psychological *zeitgeist* prior to World War I. A second general category of play theories, more recent in origin, views the specific form that play takes as being crucial for specifying the causes and effects of play. The play theories of Piaget and of psychoanalysis represent this type of theory.

The Classical Theories of Play

One of the oldest theoretical statements concerning the significance of play is attributed both to Schiller (1873) and to Spencer (1873), although it appears likely that its germ was to be found in educational literature long before their time. Briefly stated, this theory holds that play is the result of a surplus of energy, a surplus that exists because the young are freed from the business of self-preservation through the actions of their parents. The energy surplus finds its release in the aimless exuberant activities that we term play. This theory is usually referred to as the *surplus energy theory* of play. It postulates, first, a quantity of energy available to the organism and, second, a tendency to expend this energy, even though it is not necessary for the maintenance of a life balance, through goalless activity (play). In the terms of the surplus energy theory, then, the play behavior represented by the young child's making a cloth toy "go to sleep" would be seen as essentially unpredictable and meaningless behavior, pushed into being by the automatic production of unneeded energies. The going-to-sleep-play could just as well have been any other sort of playlike behavior with no consequences for the surplus energy theory of play. The surplus energy theory of play is an appealing one, and it has been put forward in a variety of forms, most notably by Tolman (1932), Tinklepaugh (1942), and Alexander (1958).

A second classical theory of play sees this activity not as the product of a surplus of energy, but rather as the product of a deficit of energy. Play is here seen as a method by which spent energy can be replenished. This theory, the *relaxation theory* of play is associated primarily with Lazarus (1883) and with Patrick (1916). Essentially, play is seen by these men as a mode of dissipating the inhibition built up from fatigue due to tasks that are relatively new to the organism. Thus, play is found most often in childhood. Play not only replenishes energy for the as-yet-unfamiliar cognitive activities of the child, but, because it also reflects "deep-rooted race habits" (by which is meant phylogenically acquired behaviors that are *not* therefore new to the organism), play is the one activity that shows very little buildup of inhibition over time. This theory of play would view the "making-the-toy-sleep" episode as a simple restful activity reflecting perhaps an inherited ability to show simple symbolization, an activity caused by the fact that the child was psychically too fatigued to do anything else.

A great many of the general theorists who have considered the meaning of play have seen it as a form of instinctive behavior. The number of theorists who have seen play in this light approaches two dozen, as cited by Britt and Janus (1941) and by Beach (1945). Perhaps the most eloquent of these theorists is Karl Groos (1898, 1908a) whose theory has come to be known as the *preexercise theory* of play. Play for Groos is seen as the product of emerging instincts, something that fixes these instincts and exercises them in preparation for their maturation time. The episode of play we have taken for our working definition would be explained by the preexercise theory as possibly the first stirrings of a parental instinct.

At about the time Karl Groos' preexercise theory was becoming known, G. Stanley Hall (1906) put forward his *recapitulation theory,* which saw play not as an activity that developed future instinctual skills, but rather one that served to rid the organism of primitive and unnecessary instinctual skills carried over by heredity. Hall was the first to conceive of stages of play; he postulated that each child passes through a series of play stages corresponding to, and recapitulating, the cultural stages in the development of races. Wundt (1913) was another well-known proponent of the recapitulation theory of play. The recapitulation theory would seem to place the episode of "making-the-cloth-toy-sleep" in the category of a vestigal primitive behavior, perhaps magicoreligious in original intent.

Another theorylike approach to play came from the work of Appleton (1910). She studied play in primitive cultures and in children, and she concluded that play is a response to a generalized drive for growth in the organism; it is not instinctual preexercise as conceived by Groos. Appleton saw as the basis for play a hunger in the organism for growth to a stage at which the instinct can operate. Thus, play serves to facilitate the mastery of skills necessary to the function of adult instincts. The child plays because he wants this mastery and he "knows" that play is the method by which he may achieve it. There are other theories of play, mostly in the educational literature, which are akin to this one in their stress of a self-actualizing basis for play, but they will not be traced here. Theories of play such as Appleton's we will term *growth theories.*

Similar to the growth theories are the ego-expanding theories of play put forward first by K. Lange (1901), and later by Claparède (1911, 1934). "Ego" here means the reality-meeting and reality-mapping aspects of cognitive life. Thus, Lange sees play as being nature's way of completing the ego and Claparède sees play as an expressive exercising of the ego and the rest of the personality, an exercising that strengthens developing cognitive skills and aids the emergence of additional cognitive skills.

These, then, are the purely classical theories of play. They are classical insofar as all of them view the specific content of play behaviors as being more or less incidental to the causes of play generally. Surprisingly, there are essentially no research data relevant to these theories of play, so that if one wishes to evaluate their worth he must rely on observations and personal impressions (see Hurlock, 1934). This is not to imply that the classical theories of play are untestable. On the contrary. A direct consequence of the surplus energy theory of play, for instance, is that children should play more when rested than when they are fatigued. Speaking generally, this seems to be the case, yet the limits of this "truth" need empirical testing. A direct consequence of the relaxation theory of play would be that any person should do better on a new task following a period of play than after having done some different new task. Perhaps there is more reason to question this hypothesis than was the case with the hypothesis drawn from the surplus energy theory of play.

The preexercise theory of play is only as impressive as the concept of human instincts. If one grants the existence of a parental instinct, then it should be possible to design an experiment that denies the opportunity for parent-role play and evaluates the influence of this restriction on later parental behavior. The recapitulation theory predicts that children's play should mirror the development of cultures, so that we should never see a child play at a "higher" function before he first plays at a "lower" one. Of those we have called classical theories of play, only the growth theories and the ego-expanding theories of play admit of no ready, testable derivatives. From the standpoint of the person who wishes to understand the causes and the effects of play, the classical theories have only two major drawbacks. First, they do not undertake to explain the wide individual differences found in human play behavior, and second, they have produced no important research data to support their various positions.

The newer theories of play differ from the classical play theories primarily in that they invoke explanations of play behavior based on dynamic factors of individual personality, and they are geared to explaining individual shifts in play behavior. These newer theories of play will be called the *infantile dynamics theories* of play, after Piaget. The most elaborated of the infantile dynamics theories are those of Piaget and psychoanalysis; but two early theories belonging in this category are those of Lewin (1933) and Buytendijk (1934).

For Lewin, play occurs because the cognitive life-space of the child is still unstructured, resulting in a failure to discriminate between the real and the unreal. It is easy then, for the child to pass into the region of playful unreality where things are changeable and arbitrary. Lewin does not elucidate this thesis further, except to state that in childhood a force or tendency arises to leave the region of reality, especially when this region is dominated by an "overstrong pressure."

Like Lewin, Buytendijk holds that a child plays because he is a child, because his cognitive "dynamics" do not allow any other way of behaving. The four main characteristics of the child's dynamics that determine this fact for Buytendijk are: a lack of motor and mental coherence or coordination, an inability to delay or detour, a need to achieve sympathetic understanding (what he has called a "pathic" attitude) as opposed to objective knowledge, and an ambivalence toward all objects, especially strange ones. Thus, play is an expression of the child's uncoordinated approach to the environment; it allows a pathic understanding of the environment and achieves immediate ends. But play is also ambivalent and reflects only a temporarily prepotent approach tendency to objects. Play for Buytendijk is rhythmic, reflecting the relaxation phase of a tension-relaxation cycle. Finally, Buytendijk's infantile dynamics theory asserts that children (as well as animals) "play" only with images, which constitute the actual expression of the child's pathic understanding. Within the framework of the infantile dynamics theory, play is the child's way of thinking. In these last theories of play the explanation of our definitional example of play would be that it represents a straightforward working outcome of the "forces" identified in the theories. Thus, the play of "making-the-cloth-sleep" is the symbolic way children come to comprehend the act of going to sleep, when they try to think about such a thing. Piaget's theory would offer a generally similar explanation for such play behavior.

The Cathartic and Psychoanalytic Theories of Play

The cathartic theory of play has roots that extend as far back as the writings of Aristotle (see Mitchell & Mason, 1934). Briefly, the cathartic theory sees play as reflecting the child's attempt to master situations that at first were too much for him. Carr (1902) was among the earliest to put forward this theory of play. Groos (1908b) extended his preexercise theory of play somewhat to include a cathartic aspect. Reaney (1916), Robinson (1920), and Curti (1930), all have elaborated variations on the cathartic theory of play.

The psychoanalytic theory of play is a special case of the more general cathartic theory. The psychoanalytic play theory was first introduced by Freud (1908, 1920, 1926) incidental to considerations of phantasy and repetition behaviors. Freud thought of play as being closely related to phantasy behavior, in fact he defined play as phantasy woven around real objects (toys), as contrasted with pure phantasy, which is daydreaming. Play, for Freud, shares many of the unconscious determinants that shape dream life, and in this respect Freud's theory of play is similar to that of Piaget.

Freud distinguished two classes of wishes, either of which he considered to be a necessary source of play. First, there are the wishes a child has to be big, grownup, or in the shoes of someone more fortunate. Thus, in accordance with an inherited tendency to seek immediate pleasure, even if this pleasure must be in part hallucinated, the child fantasies some situation he would like to see exist. Second, the child can be driven into play by his wishes to take the active role in all painful encounters that have been passively suffered. Play arising from this source does so in accordance with an inherited tendency to repeat, over and over, any experience that has been too much for the child. Thus, Erikson has observed:

[Individual child play] often proves to be the infantile way of thinking over difficult experiences and of *restoring a sense of mastery*, comparable to the way in which we repeat, in ruminations and in endless talk, in daydreams and in dreams during sleep, experiences which have been too much for us (1959, p. 85).

In the psychoanalytic theory of play "a sense of mastery" is the most typically cited *effect* of play. It is important to note, however, that this mastery feeling is necessarily restricted to play that serves to reverse a previous painful experience. Play that is purely wish fulfillment will have as its effect the feeling of "pleasure" that is presumed to be inherent in all reductions of psychic tension according to psychoanalytic theory. Play that springs from wishes can have the effect not only of a circumvention of reality, but, as Waelder (1933) has pointed out, play can also circumvent the action of the superego. In play one can presumably achieve the physically or the morally impossible.

More recently there have been some important refinements of, and additions to, the more general psychoanalytic theory of play described so far. Anna Freud (1936) has pointed out that one effect of imitative play, in those cases where the imitated object is feared, is a lessening and binding of the fear either of the object or of what the object may represent for the child. Thus, play may serve not only to lower anxiety around a given context through promotion of active coping devices, but it may serve a *defensive* purpose as well by denying any grounds for anxiety. The exact formula under which imitative play may accomplish any defensive ends has not been suggested. One could speculate, however, that it does so under the magic formula: "Since the object and I are so alike, it will fear me just as I fear it; it will also love me just as I love me, and it will not surprise me by anything it may do, for I would be likely to do similar things myself."

Erikson (1937, 1940, 1950, 1951, 1959) is well known for his recent contributions to a psychoanalytic theory of play. While agreeing with Freud regarding the major sources of play, Erikson has emphasized the coping effects of play. He has said: "I propose the theory that the child's play is the infantile form of the human ability to deal with experience by creating model situations and to master reality by experiment and planning" (1950, p. 195). Perhaps more important has been Erikson's contribution of the concept of play disruption. Not only does anxiety lead to play of a relevant nature, suggests Erikson, but play can get out of hand, as it were, thus mobilizing the very anxiety with which it is trying to deal. The result is an abrupt stop in play behavior. Says Erikson: "The human animal not only plays most and longest, it also remains ready to become deadly serious in the most irrational contexts" (1940, p. 562). In addition to Erikson, a number of psychoanalytic theorists have put forward their own elaborations of the theory of play introduced by Freud. Among the most notable are Klein (1929), Peller (1954), and Alexander (1958).

With this background on the cathartic theories of play, consider how they would account for the making-the-rag-go-to-sleep play of our working example: There is a certain degree of psychic pain caused the young child when he is told to go to sleep, for the child wishes both to comply and to remain awake. Further, the child does not want to feel he must submit to adult demands. Thus, the sleep play of our example occurs as a cathartic, wish-impelled response to this lingering psychic pain. It is regrettable that the precise manner in which psychic conflict produces play behavior is not spelled out in any of the cathartic theories. While the implication that play occurs as a response instrumental to the reduction of psychic pain is always strong, the cathartic theories of play have never quite made the full distinction that pain reduction as an *effect* of play does not demonstrate that pain is necessarily a *cause* of play behavior.

Gilmore also explains Piaget's rather complex theory of play, which is based on two opposing aspects of mental functioning. If we postulate that new information is received and used in terms of what is already known, the immature child must necessarily distort reality somewhat in order to make it fit in with what he already knows. At the same time he cannot avoid noticing new features of the things and events he encounters and modifying his mental schema and behavior to deal with them more effectively. These two processes known as **assimilation** and **accommodation** exist side by side, although one may predominate over the other. "Play for Piaget is all behavior in which the aspect of adjustment to fit reality (that is, the aspect of mental accommodation to things as they really are) is deemphasized. Play occurs insofar as behavior is purely one of 'taking in,' of bending reality to fit one's existing forms of thought." In other words, in play the child imposes his own mental scheme of things onto the external world, distorting some thoughts and objects in the process and ignoring certain logical aspects of things somewhat as in dreaming. For this reason there is a close relationship between play and dreams.

According to Piaget all behavior, not just play, involves the interaction of assimilation and accommodation. Consequently play is not an all-or-none activity but is represented to some degree in everything that the child does. Even adults often amuse themselves by doodling and similar playful diversion. The grownup plays less than children because his wealth of experience enables him to respond to things more nearly as they are in the external world rather than on the basis of how he has pictured them in the past.

In searching for evidence to construct a theory of free fantasy, Klinger (1969) calls attention to the close relationship between imaginative behavior and play. He notes, as did Peller and Piaget before him, that formal games differ significantly from other types of play activity. The definition he constructed for his purpose excludes games with rules and socially prescribed rituals when these occur in contexts where such behavior is sanctioned and enforced. Included in play would be a make-believe race but not an athletic contest; a girl pretending to cook for her husband but not a wife actually doing it.

More than one author has called attention to play elements not only in art, literature, and social ritual, but even in morality. This will seem less strange if we remember that modern drama had its roots in the morality and miracle plays of the Middle Ages, which were presented on festive occasions with a great deal of good humor, spontaneity, and pageantry. They were meant to be fun as well as instructive. Piaget finds that children's early notions of morality are gained through an understanding of the rules of games which carry with them the notion of "ought." These are applied much more rigidly and absolutely by small children than by older ones who begin to discover that rules can be changed by common consent.

In an opposite vein, Menniger (1942) mentions Harry Emerson Fosdick's discovery of rules enforced in an American school of 1784, which read as follows: "We prohibit play in the strongest terms. . . . The students shall rise at five o'clock in the morning, summer and winter. . . . The students shall be indulged in nothing which the world calls **play.** Let this rule be observed with strictest nicety; for those who play when they are young will play when they are old." Although such regulations have long since fallen into disuse, a trace of their spirit remains in our culture. Many persons are unable to give themselves wholeheartedly to play without feeling guilty of wasting time that should be devoted to something more practical.

In discussing the characteristics of play, William A. Sadler, Jr., makes a number of interesting observations.

From Creative Existence

For play to unfold there must be an attitude of trust; as I have tried to show elsewhere, the ground of play is love (Sadler, 1966, pp. 237-245). In his study of children playing Erikson (1963, pp. 216-222) discovered that often they enter into play with a precarious sense of their own space-time. Play enables them to construct model situations whereby they can master reality through planning and experimentation, thus warding off anxiety threats. However, it would be a mistake to think of play emerging as a result of or in response to anxiety. To get children to play with him Erikson found that he had to put them at ease, to get them to trust him. As a therapist he was naturally most concerned to detect the therapeutic value of play in ridding a person of the crippling effects of anxiety. However, there is no reason to see play or any other creative activity necessarily occurring against the dark background of anxiety. The latter widespread notion is a hangover from spurious Romantic mythology. Play is therapeutic, not simply because it provides a means for dealing with problems in a novel way, but because it is an essentially human, creative unfolding of one's personal world and a way of discovering one's identity. Play does more than help one see his problem more clearly and to rise above it; more significantly, it enables him to perceive more distinctly his total situation within which a particular problem is located. In play we recover a larger personal perspective. Creative reorientation through play helps us to be more realistically aware of our world, more objective about ourselves and better prepared to receive new information and insight. Instead of concentrating upon the human response to anxiety, I think it will prove to be much more enlightening and beneficial if we focus instead upon creative behaviour emerging from love and trust, such as play.

Most likely you have been looking for a definition of play, hoping to pin down in your own mind just exactly what we have been discussing. However, it is impossible to formulate an adequate definition of play, just as it is impossible to provide one for art or love or life itself. Existential phenomenology has tried to point out that freedom in any form cannot be fitted into a formula. Nevertheless it is possible to delineate structural features of basic existential phenomena. I think a few are now in the clear, which in turn help us to realize what play means to human beings. One characteristic feature of play's perception is its openness. In many other perceptual modes the framework of interpretation is set. In taking a drink of water when thirsty, the meaning of the action is predetermined. In play, however, there is a release from set patterns of behavior and interpretation; thereby one's world opens up for the possible emergence of new forms of activity, relationship, and learning. A basic meaning of play is constituted by the intentional structure of openness. Play is the primary way a human being continues to open his world to fresh insight and creative development.

A second feature of play is that it modifies our habitual and pragmatic mode of perception. This modification constitutes a creative alteration of experience, of our personal being in the world. By throwing oneself into play one also breaks loose from the prison of a corrupted consciousness; he gains distance from repressive forces which threaten to obscure his vision and thus sets a new direction in his way through the world. Play is a creative mode of being, not so much in what it produces but in the way it "sees." Play is not the pinnacle of creativity nor the substance of art; but it is a foundation of creative human perception and as such is basic to the growth of creativity in art and in life. The focal attention of play opens man to new possibilities of free personal existence and inaugurates a creative transformation of his world.

Play and the Creation of Community

Before concluding this address I want to call attention to a further important dimension of play, namely, its creative power with respect to interpersonal relationships and community. Thus far we have considered play only in terms of an individual's experience and behavior. Certainly play has tremendous significance for the development of an individual's personality; yet we should fail to account for much of its meaning if we neglected its capacity to create strong ties between persons.

In an extremely illuminating study Professor David Bakan has reminded us of the *duality* of human existence. Our humanity cannot be fully understood in terms of individuality alone; there is also the essential dimension of reciprocal personal coinherence, what phenomenologists often call *intersubjectivity,* or what Baken labels *communion.* His argument is that the individualistic, or what he calls the *agentic,* mode of existence has become so overdeveloped in our society that we are finding it extremely difficult to appreciate and establish communion. Our agentically biased existence operates with a mode of perception which is highly analytical, one which is specially geared towards the manipulation of and mastery over one's environment. However, when man stands alone as an autonomous agent he is visited by demons of lust for power, a profound sense of alienation, a deficiency of personal understanding, repression, morbid sexuality, and an intolerable fear of death, which may be related to our society's high rate of terminal cancer. Bakan (1966) cogently argues that we in the West are at a turning point in our history. The agency feature has been predominant in our planning of life strategies; yet now we have the opportunity of turning aside from an exaggerated concentration upon "making a living" to the imaginative nurturing of children and learning to live with each other sympathetically and creatively. His moral is that agency should be mitigated with communion.

If we accept his thesis, we still must discover the most appropriate ways to develop communion. Merely to repeat the platitude that we must love each other is not sufficient; one simply cannot turn love on. To find a way beyond a strictly agentic mode will require no less than an alteration of an agentic mode of perception. What we have discovered about the capacity of play to open up one's personal world has relevance to the communal world as well. Very briefly I want to propose that play can also be remarkably creative with respect to our being with others. Through play we may learn to overcome the isolation of agency and to establish a world marked by communion.

A friend of mine was extremely eager to bring together a group of fellow clergymen from different traditions so that a friendly and cooperative association could be formed among them. Numerous attempts to achieve his goal were fruitless. Believing as he does that more things are wrought for God on a golf course than this world dreams of, he decided to plan an experiment. He invited a number of prestigious clergy, who would barely speak to each other, to play golf with him. However, he altered the rules of the game somewhat. Each man was given only one club. During the course of play they had to trade these clubs back and forth. For the first few holes the game was stiff, the conversation paltry, and the relationships customarily cool. By the end of nine holes all the men were calling each other by first names, even nicknames, joking, sharing experiences and stories, and feeling very much part of a community. From that time on the clergy association has been a success and a benefit to both church and society. This group of stiff strangers became relaxed and developed into a community of warm friendship. Through this rather ingenious form of play men well advanced in years and position discovered again the creative experience of playing with others and thereby overcoming alienation and achieving communion.

Let us go back for a minute to the snowman. An adult does not ordinarily engage in this kind of behavior all by himself. It is more usual for him to do it with his children. Together parent and children transform their lawn into a playground. In so doing they step outside the ordinary boundaries of authority and concern. Rules of etiquette, practical objectives, and a pragmatic sense of time and space are set aside. "Shall we make our snowman with a fat body and a small head, or with a long body and a fat head? Shall we put a broom under his arm? But, which lump is the arm? That's a nice nose you've made, Lisa. But why did you place it on his back?" In the event of playing together parents and children discover a way of closing the generation gap. As they become partners in play they create together something new and wonderful. The most important product is not the snowman, which parents may easily forget when they try to add on esthetic touches to impress the neighbors with their latent artistic talents. The most important meaning of this play is the recreation of a common world, which probably was originally meant by the now misused term "recreation." No matter what the chronological age difference, play partners have an opportunity to create a common history in which all partners move within the same space and time. In the act of playing together there is a reciprocal exchange of insight and interpretation. "Hey, Dad, I think our snowman looks like Santa Claus." "No, silly; there aren't any whiskers." Who cares really what it looks like?

What matters is that the players stand together in a common ecstasy where they find the freedom to create communion that will outlast a thousand snowmen.

To appreciate play's creative role in the formation of communion many more examples need to be considered and carefully elucidated. Play has an important, perhaps decisive part in the development of basic human institutions which depend upon communion, such as sex and family life, friendship, education, athletics, the arts, and even religion. The phenomenology of play points to a relatively unchartered area of human existence. Through a deeper understanding of being in the world as play we may uncover new possibilities of developing the turning point in our history towards greater creativity and communion. The scope of play's meaning is much wider than we had supposed. Play includes the exercise of man's physical nature; but even more important, it is essential to the development of the highest potentialities of distinctively human nature. The late Dutch theologian Gerardus van der Leeuw (1963) has provocatively suggested that play is even the doorway through which man must pass to find communion with God:

> The game points beyond itself: downward, to the simple, ordinary, rhythm of life; upward, to the highest form of existence. . . . Play is the prerequisite for those forms of existence which strive toward a communion with the other, and finally for a meeting with God.

In our highly individualistic, work-oriented world, in which leisure is often mistreated as an opportunity for regression to impulsive behavior, it is necessary for men and women to learn how to play if they are going to discover and actualize the richest meanings of being human. In the construction of civilization individuals had to learn how to be both workers and fighters. It seems, however, that fighting and working have come to represent our highest values. Yet as the military-industrial complex gains ascendency in our culture, the future of civilization begins to look bleak. The modes of war and work are set to control the old world; the intentional structure of play opens towards the creation of a new and fundamentally personal world. In our society in which individuals experience fantastic difficulty in forming deeply meaningful interpersonal relations, play offers us an important mode of existence not merely for the development of a healthy, creative personality but also a communion. For the good of our health, our culture, our human spirit, and the future of man it is necessary for adults to rediscover the art of playing. To paraphrase a wise old saying, unless we become as children in play, we shall never attain the destiny that is rightfully ours as human beings (St. Matthew 18:3).

SUMMARY

The conclusions one draws from reading what thoughtful men have
written about play is that, far from being merely a harmless diversion
or at worst a shameful waste of time, play serves a number of important
purposes. The fact that young animals of virtually every species engage
in play strengthens this impression. Depending upon a theorist's point
of departure, biological, psychological, or social functions of play can
be described. It can be seen, for example, as an opportunity for the
child to practice responses which will be necessary or useful in later life.
The ability to give oneself wholeheartedly to play is not only a characteristic of wholesome personality but also contributes to a healthy state
of mind. There are play elements in art, literature, social ritual, and
religion. Learning the rules of games may even contribute to a child's
earliest understanding of personal moral standards. In a social context
play breaks down many of the barriers that keep others at a distance.
As a possible antidote for loneliness, hostility, and interpersonal tensions, play deserves to be seriously studied by psychologists.

DISCUSSION TOPICS

1 Which theory or combination of theories of play do you favor?

2 How do games with rules and athletic contests differ from other
forms of play? Should they be included in the same concept?

3 How is play related to fantasy?

4 What significant human purposes does play serve in childhood? In
adult life?

5 Has today's world achieved the proper balance between work and
play?

6 Does the existentialist emphasis on the tragic aspects of life have any
negative influence on people's ability to have fun?

7 Is there any relationship between creative ability, play activity, and
artistic sensitivity?

8 Discuss play as a technique for breaking down interpersonal barriers.

ADDITIONAL READINGS

Britt, S. H., & Janus, S. Q. Toward a psychology of human play. **Journal of
Social Psychology,** 1941, **13**, 351-384. Studies of play preference are
reviewed.

Giddens, A. Notes on the concept of play and leisure. **Sociological Review,**
1964, **12,** 73-89. A sociologist looks at play. Numerous references.

Greenwald, H. Play and self-development. In H. Otto and J. Mann (Ed.), **Ways** of growth. New York: Grossman, 1968. A therapist explains how a playful attitude can sometimes help patients achieve insight into their problems.

Huizinga, Johan. **Homo Ludens.** Boston: Beacon Press, 1950. The subtitle of this work is "A study of the play-element in culture."

Humanitas (Journal of the Institute of Man), 1969, **5**(1). This issue is a symposium on personality and play.

1 Herbert Fingarette analyzes adult play within the framework of psychoanalysis and philosophy.

2 Hilde Hein treats play as an aesthetic concept.

3 F. A. Isambert observes that "our present day public festivities are but a pale reflection of the authentic public celebrations of archaic people."

4 Edward Norbeck, using Japan as an example, shows that sports are adopted in a manner that is congruent with the culture.

5 William A. Sadler, Jr., "attempts to show that play is a basic form of creativity and . . . can operate in the formation of one's personal world and in the development of love and community."

6 Vanina Sechi explains that art is not just an accident of life. While playful in nature, it can still be serious and even transform human interests.

7 Carolyn Gratton review selected works on personality and play and presents a bibliography of 181 titles.

Hurlock, E. B. Experimental investigations of childhood play. **Psychological Bulletin,** 1934, **31,** 47-66. The earlier studies of play are reviewed.

Klinger, E. Development of imaginative behavior: Implications of play for a theory of fantasy. **Psychological Bulletin,** 1969, **72,** 277-298. In search of a theory of fantasy, Klinger critically evaluates the research on play and notes major gaps.

Levin, H., & Wardell, E. The research uses of doll play. **Psychological Bulletin,** 1962, **59,** 27-56. A good summary of the literature is given.

Menninger, K. **Love against hate.** New York: Harcourt, Brace & World, 1942, Chap. 7. "I have tried to show why both work and play are necessary, not only from the economic standpoint, not only from the social standpoint, but even more urgently from the psychological standpoint."

Millar, S. **The psychology of play.** Baltimore: Penguin, 1968. This scholarly book addressed to the general reader reviews theories of play and the main lines of research.

Neale, R. E. (1969) **In praise of play.** New York: Harper & Row. Play is distinguished from work "by those elements of peace, freedom, delight, and illusion that occur in the modes of story and games."

Sadler, W. A. Play: A basic human structure involving love and freedom.

Review of Existential Psychology and Psychiatry, 1966, **6**, 237-245. Play is considered to be a form of freedom grounded in love.

Slobin, D. I. The fruits of the first season: A discussion of the role of play in childhood. **Journal of Humanistic Psychology,** 1964, **4**, 59-79. The question, "Why are children playing this game?" turns out, on closer inspection, to be seven questions which the author attempts to answer. Forty-seven references are given.

Whitman, R. M. Psychoanalytic speculation about play: Tennis—the duel. **Psychoanalytic Review,** 1969, **56**, 197-214. Tennis illustrates how play develops and the strong aggression-guilt factor that is present.

Chapter 3

Loneliness and Death: Twin Specters of Human Existence

Loneliness is as much a reality of life as night and rain and thunder, and it can be lived creatively, as any other experience.

Clark Moustakas

Life is not comprehended truly or lived fully unless the idea of death is grappled with honestly.

Herman Feifel

One of the most dreaded human experiences is being isolated physically and psychologically from other people. The stark terror of a little child who becomes separated from its parents in a crowd or lost in the woods on an outing bears mute testimony to the presence of a fundamental need that does not disappear in adulthood. All our lives we are dependent upon satisfying relationships with others, not only to achieve peace of mind and happiness, but even to maintain the feeling of self-worth. In the absence of any expression of positive regard from other human beings, a person soon begins to experience debilitating self-doubts—an observation that has contributed to the success of the so-called brainwashing techniques developed by certain totalitarian regimes.

Primitive peoples found the need for human companionship a sufficient sanction for maintaining intact over many centuries a complex web of customs and magical taboos. There was only one "right" way to do things: the way they had always been done. Anyone who thought that he had a better idea was subjected to ridicule or even ostracism. The longing for empathy and understanding has not diminished in our own day. Any individual who comes to believe that no one at all cares what happens to him is likely to harbor thoughts of suicide.

Existential writers have emphasized the tragic aspect of human existence, particularly one's ultimate aloneness, the contingency and possible failure of all his plans, with death inevitably marking the end of of a short life-span. The more vividly a person comes to recognize himself as a unique individual apart from everyone else, the more keenly he experiences loneliness. The existential anxiety arising out of this human condition is a universal heritage from which there is no escape other than courageous confrontation. Paradoxically it is this "courage to be" that brings out the best in human nature, as Clark Moustakas explains.

From Loneliness

The basic message . . . is that loneliness is a condition of human life, an experience of being human which enables the individual to sustain, extend, and deepen his humanity. Man is ultimately and forever lonely whether his loneliness is the exquisite pain of the individual living in isolation or illness, the sense of absence caused by a loved one's death, or the piercing joy experienced in triumphant creation. I believe it is necessary for every person to recognize his loneliness, to become intensely aware that, ultimately, in every fibre of his being, man is alone—terribly, utterly alone. Efforts to overcome or escape the existential experience of loneliness can result only in self-alienation. When man is removed from a fundamental truth of life, when he successfully evades and denies the terrible loneliness of individual existence, he shuts himself off from one significant avenue of his own self-growth.

I first began to discover the roots of my own loneliness during a family crisis when neither man nor reason could assuage the searing pain in my heart. This crisis was the instrument through which I plunged deeply into an intensive and timeless experience of the self. The sudden recognition and depth of my own loneliness was a revelation which changed the nature of my life. I could never again see the evening sun fading into oblivion without feeling lonely. I could never again pass a troubled person or see pain, misery, suffering, poverty around me without being deeply and sharply touched. This recognition of my own basic loneliness, this penetrating awareness of my own isolated existence, opened within me a flood of painful feeling and left me in a barren and eroded state. At the same time I saw life and nature in more vibrant forms than I had ever experienced before. Each aspect of my life took on a color, a distinctness and vividness, entirely new for me. Something extremely powerful took root in me and I came to know myself in a more honest and fuller sense than I ever thought possible. I learned that I could thrive in lonely silence. This recognition and meaningful awareness of myself as an utterly lonely person opened the way to deeper human bonds and associations and to a fuller valuing of all aspects of life and nature. I realized that man's inevitable and infinite loneliness is not solely an awful condition of human existence but that it is also the instrument through which man experiences new compassion and new beauty. It is this terror in loneliness which evokes new senses and makes possible the experiencing of deep companionship and radiant beauty.

My awareness of loneliness did not come as an idea but from the involvement of my whole being in loneliness. What I have written [here] is an experience of my own existence as a solitary individual, as well as the existence of others, and of the meaning which loneliness has for human growth. One can come to a recognition of loneliness as a condition of human life only through a deep and penetrating voyage of one's own solitary nature. I hope the experiences presented . . . will provide a primary source, an impetus to self-discovery, and to feeling-knowledge. I know that no person can remain unchanged once he opens himself to loneliness and surrenders himself to the terror and beauty of a totally isolated existence.

It is a great gift to be suddenly awakened, to perceive the world from vast, expansive inner openings and new pathways, to see light where there had been darkness, to find beauty in broken bits of stone, to see color where all had been dingy and gray, to hear a human voice and absorb a smile as a precious treasure, to see into the heart of life and to recognize the brevity of life and the necessity of making each moment count, to realize the ecstasy of human companionship—and when someone else sees this vital strand of lonely being not as an insight but with all the feeling of an informed heart, then how sweet is the confirmation. When someone cares enough to see into the deepest roots of one's nature, though it is heart-rending to be known in this naked sense, it brings the deepest measure of unique and thrilling sensations.

Loneliness for me started with a family crisis but my voyage took me into literature and music and art, into history and science. For many, many months I opened myself to the loneliness which surrounded me in my everyday living, to the lonely experiences of my colleagues, friends, and neighbors, to books and articles. I have concluded that loneliness is within life itself, and that all creations in some way spring from solitude, meditation, and isolation.

This work is not an exhaustive or comprehensive study, but is a pointed selection of lonely experiences and lonely persons, along with commentary on some of the conditions which penetrate human life and precipitate man's aloneness.

This book grows out of my own search to come to an understanding, awareness, and respect for myself as a solitary, isolated, lonely individual and the gripping, painful, exhilarating, and beautiful experience of being utterly alone and separated from others. In a sense, the book is an inquiry or search, perhaps a personal disclosure into the meaning and essence of loneliness itself, the loneliness of my life and the loneliness of others, which has shaken and stirred me profoundly and opened new channels of awareness and beauty in the world.

PATHOLOGICAL LONELINESS

Psychologists and psychiatrists who write about loneliness generally distinguish between existential loneliness, aloneness occasioned by the absence of loved ones, and pathological loneliness. In the case of aloneness the individual's feelings of love are directed outward toward other people rather than inward onto himself (Zilboorg, 1938). But even here a germ of narcissism betrays itself in the loss of interest in other things for a time and emotional withdrawal into one's own private world. This is not a permanent state of affairs, since the person gradually cures himself as in the case of someone mourning the death of a close relative.

Pathological loneliness is of a different type. Regardless of how successful the individual may be, how well his name is known to admiring fans seeking his autograph, or the number of people who would like to be his friend, he is continually haunted by an inner sense of isolation that nothing can break through. It causes him to be peevish and sometimes even to explode with thinly veiled hostility. Frieda Fromm-Reichmann explores the antecedents of this condition.

From Loneliness

Before entering into a discussion of the psychiatric aspects of what I call real loneliness, I will briefly mention the types of loneliness which are not the subject [here]. The writings of modern sociologists and social psychologists are widely concerned with culturally determined loneliness, the "cut-offness and solitariness of civilized men"—the "shut-upness," in Kierkegaard's (1944; Fromm, 1941) phrase which they described as characteristic of this culture. While this is a very distressing and painful experience, it is by definition the common fate of many people of this culture. Unverbalized as it may remain, it is nevertheless potentially a communicable experience, one which can be shared. Hence it does not carry the deep threat of the uncommunicable, private emotional experience of severe loneliness, with which this paper will be concerned.

I am not here concerned with the sense of solitude which some people have, when, all by themselves, they experience the infinity of nature as presented by the mountains, the desert, or the ocean—the experience which has been described with the expression, "oceanic feelings" (Freud, 1939, p. 8). These oceanic feelings may well be an expression of a creative loneliness, if one defines creativity, with Paul Tillich (1952, p. 46), in the wider sense of the term, as "living spontaneously, in action and reaction, with the contents of one's cultural life."

I am also not concerned [here] with the seclusion which yields creative artistic or scientific products. In contrast to the disintegrative loneliness of the mental patient, these are states of constructive loneliness, and they are often temporary and self-induced, and may be voluntarily and alternately sought out and rejected. Nearly all works of creative originality are conceived in such states of constructive aloneness; and, in fact, only the creative person who is not afraid of this constructive aloneness will have free command over his creativity. Some of these people, schizoid, artistic personalities in Karl Menninger's (1930, p. 79) nomenclature, submit to the world, as a product of their detachment from normal life, "fragments of their own world—bits of dreams and visions and songs—that we—out here don't hear except as they translate them." It should be added that an original, creative person may not only be lonely for the time of his involvement in creative processes, but subsequently because of them, since the appearance of new creations of genuine originality often antedates the ability of the creator's contemporaries to understand or to accept them.

I am not talking here about the temporary aloneness of, for instance, a

From Frieda Fromm-Reichmann. Loneliness. **Psychiatry,** 1959, **22,** 1-15. Reprinted by special permission of the William Alanson White Psychiatric Foundation, Inc., copyright holder.

person who has to stay in bed with a cold or on a pleasant Sunday afternoon while the rest of the family are enjoying the outdoors. He may complain about loneliness and feel sorry for himself, for to the "other-directed" types of the culture, "loneliness is such an omnipotent and painful threat ... that they have little conception of the positive values of solitude, and even at times are very frightened at the prospect of being alone" (May, 1953, p. 26; Reisman, 1950). But however much this man with a cold may complain about loneliness, he is, needless to say, not lonely in the sense I am talking about; he is just temporarily alone.

While the loneliness of the person who suffers the sense of loss and of being alone following the death of someone close to him is on another level, it too does not concern me here. Freud (1935, p. 36-37; 1934 pp. 152-170, especially p. 160) and Abraham (1937, Ch. 6.) have described the dynamics by which the mourner counteracts this aloneness by incorporation and identification; this can often be descriptively verified by the way in which the mourner comes to develop a likeness in looks, personality, and activities to the lost beloved one. By such incorporation and identification the human mind has the power of fighting the aloneness after the loss of a beloved person. Somewhat similar is the sense of lonesomeness which lovers may suffer after a broken-off love affair. Daydreams, fantasies, and the love songs of others—or sometimes original compositions—help the unhappy lover to overcome his temporary solitude: "Out of my great worry I emerge with my little songs," as the German poet Adelbert von Chamisso put it.

The kind of loneliness I am discussing is nonconstructive, if not disintegrative, and it shows in, or leads ultimately to, the development of psychotic states. It renders people who suffer it emotionally paralyzed and helpless. In Sullivan's (1953, p. 290) words, it is "the exceedingly unpleasant and driving experience connected with an inadequate discharge of the need for human intimacy, for interpersonal intimacy." The longing for interpersonal intimacy stays with every human being from infancy throughout life; and there is no human being who is not threatened by its loss.

I have implied, in what I have just said, that the human being is born with the need for contact and tenderness. I should now like to review briefly how this need is fulfilled in the various phases of childhood development—if things go right—in order to provide a basis for asking and answering the question, What has gone wrong in the history of the lonely ones? That is, what has gone wrong in the history of those people who suffer from their failure to obtain satisfaction of the universal human need for intimacy?

The infant thrives in a relationship of intimate and tender closeness with the person who tends him and mothers him. In childhood, the healthy youngster's longing for intimacy is, according to Sullivan, fulfilled by his participation in activities with adults, in the juvenile era by finding compeers and acceptance, and in preadolescence by finding a "chum." In adolescence and in the years of growth and development which should follow it, man feels the need for friendship and intimacy jointly with or independently of his sexual drive (Sullivan, 1953, pp. 261-262).

A number of writers have investigated what may happen, at various stages of development, if the need for intimacy goes unsatisfied. For example, René Spitz (Spitz & Wolf, 1946, pp. 313-342) demonstrated the fatal influence of lack of love and of loneliness on infants, in what he called their "anaclytic depression." An interesting sidelight on this is provided by experiments in isolation with very young animals, in which the effect of isolation can be an almost completely irreversible lack of development of whole systems, such as those necessary for the use of vision in accomplishing tasks put to the animal.[1] Sullivan (1953) and Suttie (1952) have noted the unfortunate effects on future development if a person's early need for tenderness remains unsatisfied, and Anna Freud (1954), in her lecture at the 1953 International Psychoanalytic meetings in London, described sensations of essential loneliness in children under the heading of "Losing and Being Lost."[2]

Both Sullivan and Suttie have particularly called attention to the fact that the lonely child may resort to substitute satisfactions in fantasy, which he cannot share with others. Thus his primary sense of isolation may subsequently be reinforced if, despite the pressures of socialization and acculturation, he does not sufficiently learn to discriminate between realistic phenomena and the products of his own lively fantasy. In order to escape being laughed at or being punished for replacing reports of real events by fictitious narratives, he may further withdraw, and may continue, in his social isolation, to hold on to the uncorrected substitutive preoccupation. An impressive example of the results of such a faulty development has been presented by Robert Linder (1955, pp. 221-293) in his treatment history of Kirk Allen, the hero of the "true psychoanalytic tale," "The Jet-Propelled Couch."

Incidentally, I think that the substitutive enjoyment which the neglected child may find for himself in his fantasy life makes him especially lonely in the present age of overemphasis on the conceptual differentiation between subjective and objective reality. One of the outcomes of this scientific attitude is that all too frequently even healthy children are trained to give up prematurely the subjective inner reality of their normal fantasy life and, instead, to accept the objective reality of the outward world.

[1] John C. Lilly has referred to these experiments in "Mental Effects of Reduction of Ordinary Levels of Physical Stimuli on Intact, Healthy Persons," *Psychiatric Research Reports*, No. 5; American Psychiatric Association, June, 1956.

[2] An interesting description by a layman of the impact of loneliness in childhood is given by Lucy Sprague Mitchell, in her *Two Lives: The Story of Wesley Clair Mitchell and Myself* (New York, Simon and Schuster, 1953). In this book she vividly contrasts her own childhood loneliness with the affection, approval and security her husband had as a child.

The process by which the child withdraws into social isolation into his substitutive fantasies may occur if the mothering one weans him from her caressing tenderness before he is ready to try for the satisfactions of the modified needs for intimacy characteristic of his ensuing developmental phase. As Suttie (1954, pp. 87-88) has put it, separation from the direct tenderness and nurtural love relationship with the mother may outrun the child's ability for making substitutions. This is a rather serious threat to an infant and child in a world where a taboo exists on tenderness among adults. When such a premature weaning from mothering tenderness occurs, the roots for permanent aloneness and isolation, for "love-shyness," as Suttie has called it, for fear of intimacy and tenderness, are planted in the child's mind; and the defensive counterreactions against this eventuality may lead to psychopathological developments.

Zilboorg (1938), on the other hand, has warned against psychological dangers which may arise from other types of failure in handling children—failures in adequate guidance in reality testing. If the omnipotent baby learns the joy of being admired and loved but learns nothing about the outside world, he may develop a conviction of his greatness and all-importance which will lead to a narcissistic orientation to life—a conviction that life is nothing but being loved and admired. This narcissistic-megalomanic attitude will not be acceptable to the environment which will respond with hostility and isolation of the narcissistic person. The deeply seated triad of narcissism, megalomania, and hostility will be established, which is, according to Zilboorg (1938), at the root of the affliction of loneliness.

The concepts of Sullivan, Suttie, and Zilboorg are all based on the insight that the person who is isolated and lonely in his present environment has anachronistically held on to early narcissistic need fulfillments or fantasied substitutive satisfactions. According to Sullivan and Suttie, it may be the fulfillment of his early needs which has been critical; or, according to Zilboorg, the failure may have been in meeting his needs later on for adequate guidance in reality testing.

Karl Menninger (1930) has described the milder states of loneliness which result from these failures in handling infants and children in his "isolation types of personality"—that is, lonely and schizoid personalities. The more severe developments of loneliness appear in the unconstructive, desolate phases of isolation and real loneliness which are beyond the state of feeling sorry for oneself—the state of mind in which the fact that there were people in one's past life is more or less forgotten, and the possibility that there may be interpersonal relationships in one's future life is out of the realm of expectation or imagination. This loneliness, in its quintessential form is of such a nature that it is incommunicable by one who suffers it. Unlike other noncommunicable emotional experiences, it cannot even be shared empathically, perhaps because the other person's empathic abilities are obstructed by the anxiety-arousing quality of the mere emanations of this profound loneliness.[3]

I wonder whether this explains the fact that this real loneliness defied description, even by the pen of a master of conceptualization such as Sullivan. As a matter of fact, the extremely uncanny experience of real loneliness has much in common with some other quite serious mental states, such as panic. People cannot endure such states for any length of time without becoming psychotic—although the sequence of events is often reversed, and the loneliness or panic is concomitant with or the outcome of a psychotic disturbance. Subject to further dynamic investigation, I offer the suggestion that the experiences in adults usually described as a loss of reality or as a sense of world catastrophe can also be understood as expressions of profound loneliness.

On the other hand, while some psychiatrists seem to think of severe psychotic loneliness as part of, or as identical with, other emotional phenomena, such as psychotic withdrawal, depression, and anxiety, I do not agree with this viewpoint, in general. I shall elaborate on the interrelationship between loneliness and anxiety later. So far as psychotic withdrawal is concerned, it constitutes only seemingly a factual isolation from others; the relationship of the withdrawn person to his interpersonal environment, and even his interest in it, is by no means extinguished in the way that is true of the lonely person. So far as depressed patients are concerned, every psychiatrist knows that they complain about loneliness; but let me suggest that the preoccupation with their relationships with others, and the pleas for fulfillment of their interpersonal dependency-needs—which even withdrawn depressives show—are proof that their loneliness is not of the same order as the state of real detachment I am trying to depict.

The characteristic feature of loneliness, on which I shall elaborate later, is this: It can arouse anxiety and fear of contamination which may induce people—among them the psychiatrists who deal with it in their patients—to refer to it euphemistically as "depression." One can understand the emotional motivation for this definition, but that does not make it conceptually correct.

People who are in the grip of severe degrees of loneliness cannot talk about it; and people who have at some time in the past had such an experience can seldom do so either, for it is so frightening and uncanny in character that they try to dissociate the memory of what it was like, and even

---

[3] Some attention has been given to this interference of anxiety with the freedom of utilizing intuitive abilities by a seminar in which I participated, dealing specifically with intuitive processes in the psychiatrist who works with schizophrenics. See "The 'Intuitive Process' and its Relations to Work with Schizophrenics," introduced by Frieda Fromm-Reichman and reported by Alberta Szalita-Pemow, *J. Amer. Psychoanal. Assn.* (1955) 3.7-18.

the fear of it. This frightened secretiveness and lack of communcation about loneliness seems to increase its threat for the lonely ones, even in retrospect; it produces the sad conviction that nobody else has experienced or ever will sense what they are experiencing or have experienced.

Even mild borderline states of loneliness do not seem to be easy to talk about. Most people who are alone try to keep the mere fact of their aloneness a secret from others, and even try to keep its conscious realization hidden from themselves. I think that this may be in part determined by the fact that loneliness is a most unpopular phenomenon in this group-conscious culture. Perhaps only children have the independence and courage to identify their own loneliness as such—or perhaps they do it simply out of lack of imagination or an inability to conceal it. One youngster asked another, in the comic strip "Peanuts," "Do you know what you're going to be when you grow up?" "Lonesome," was the unequivocal reply of the other.

Incidentally, one element in the isolation of some lonely psychotics may be the fact that, perhaps because of their interpersonal detachment, some of them are more keen, sensitive, and fearless observers of the people in their environment than the average nonlonely, mentally healthy person is. They may observe and feel free to express themselves about many painful truths which go unobserved or are suppressed by their healthy and gregarious fellowmen. But unlike the court jester, who was granted a fool's paradise where he could voice his unwelcome truths with impunity, the lonely person may be displeasing if not frightening to his hearers, who may erect a psychological wall of ostracism and isolation about him as a means of protecting themselves. Cervantes (1951, pp. 760-796), in his story, "Man of Glass," has depicted a psychotic man who observes his fellowmen keenly and offers them uncensored truths about themselves. As long as they look upon him as sufficiently isolated by his "craziness," they are able to laugh off the narcissistic hurts to which he exposes them.

I would now like to digress for a moment from the subject of real, psychotogenic loneliness to consider for a moment the fact that while all adults seem to be afraid of real loneliness, they vary a great deal in their tolerance of aloneness. I have, for example, seen some people who felt deeply frightened at facing the infinity of the desert, with its connotations of loneliness, and others who felt singularly peaceful, serene, and pregnant with creative ideas. Why are some people able to meet aloneness with fearless enjoyment, while others are made anxious even by temporary aloneness—or even by silence, which may or may not connote potential aloneness? The fear of these latter people is such that they make every possible effort to avoid it—playing bridge, by looking for hours at television, by listening to the radio, by going compulsively to dances, parties, the movies. As Kierkegaard (1944, p. 107) has put it, ". . . one does everything possible by way of diversions and the Janizary music of loud-voiced enterprises to keep lonely thoughts away. . . ."

Perhaps the explanation for the fear of aloneness lies in the fact that, in this culture, people can come to a valid self-orientation, or even awareness of themselves, only in terms of their actual overt relationships with others. "Every human being gets much of his sense of his own reality out of what others say to him and think about him," as Rollo May (1953, p. 32) puts it. While alone and isolated from others, people feel threatened by the potential loss of their boundaries, of the ability to discriminate between the subjective self and the objective world around them. But valid as this general explanation for the fear of loneliness may be, it leaves unanswered the question of why this fear is not ubiquitous.

Generally speaking, I believe that the answer lies in the degree of a person's dependence on others for his self-orientation, and that this depends in turn on the particular vicissitudes of the developmental history. Here, you may recall, I am talking about aloneness, and not what I term real loneliness; and whether the same holds true for loneliness, I do not know. Only an intensive scrutiny of the developmental history of the really lonely ones might give the answer; and the nature of real loneliness is such that one cannot communicate with people who are in the grip of it. Once they emerge from it, they do not wish—or they are unable—to talk about their loneliness or about any topic which is psychologically connected with it, as I suggested earlier.

Descriptively speaking, however, one can understand why people are terrified of the "naked horror"—in Binswanger's term—of real loneliness. Anyone who has encountered persons who were under the influence of real loneliness understands why people are more frightened of being lonely than of being hungry, or being deprived of sleep, or of having their sexual needs unfulfilled—the three other basic needs which Sullivan assigns to the same group as the avoidance of loneliness. As Sullivan (1953, p. 262) points out, people will even resort to anxiety-arousing experiences in an effort to escape from loneliness, even though anxiety itself is an emotional experience against which people fight, as a rule, with every defense at their disposal. Needless to say, however, the person who is able to do this is not fully in the grip of true, severe loneliness, with its specific character of paralyzing hopelessness and unutterable futility. This "naked horror" is beyond anxiety and tension; defense and remedy seem out of reach. Only as its all-engulfing intensity decreases can a person utilize anxiety-provoking defenses against it. One of my patients, after she emerged from the depths of loneliness, tried unconsciously to prevent its recurrence by pushing herself, as it were, into a pseudo-manic state of talkativeness, which was colored by all signs of anxiety.

Another drastic defensive maneuver which should be mentioned is compulsive eating. As Hilde Bruch's (1957) research on obesity has shown, the attempt to counteract loneliness by overeating serves at the same time as a means of getting even with the significant people in the environment, whom the threatened person holds responsible for his loneliness. The patient I have just mentioned, who resorted to pseudo-manic talkativeness as a defense against loneliness, told me that her happiest childhood memory was of sitting in the darkened living room of her home, secretly eating stolen sweets. In her first therapeutic interview, she said to me, "You will take away my gut pains (from overeating), my trance states (her delusional states of retreat), and my food; and where will I be then?" That is, if she gave up her defenses against her loneliness, where would she be then?

Sullivan, it should be added, thought that loneliness—beyond his description of it in terms of the driving force to satisfy the universal human need for intimacy—is such an intense and incommunicable experience that psychiatrists must resign themselves to describing it in terms of people's defenses against it. Freud's (1935, pp. 36 37) thinking about it seems to point in the same direction, in his reference to loneliness and defenses against it in *Civilization and Its Discontents.*

DEATH

Nowhere is the sense of aloneness more vividly portrayed than in dying. At a time when the skill of physicians and the desire of others to be of assistance are to no avail, the dying person is thrown completely on his own resources. Much has been written about the dread of leaving everything behind and the efforts people make to escape facing this reality. It is not so much the thought of death that is frightening as the imaginary anticipation of dying and the mystery surrounding it. There is no way of knowing what it will be like. We can speculate that, other things being equal, one's personal philosophy and the meaning that life has for him will be powerful determinants. For the individual who believes with Camus that life is altogether without meaning and that death is the climax of an absurd existence, the experience must be frustrating indeed. One who, like Frankl, is able to perceive significance even in dying should be in a better position to encounter it with calm courage. The earnest Christian who is convinced that "the meaning of life is consummated in its termination" will see death in still a different light.

Death signifies more to the individual than the mere cessation of physical existence. As a profound symbol it enters into the lower levels of consciousness where it may interact with painful experiences of the distant past that have been repressed. "When we fear death intensely and unremittingly, we fear instead, often, some of the unconscious irrational symbolic equivalences of death. A steadily increasing body of clinical evidence shows us how manifold these may be" (Wahl, 1965).

Another aspect of the dread of dying not frequently mentioned is the forced evaluation of how well one has used his abilities and the opportunities that came his way. At a time when the individual's life is all but history, he must ask himself, "How well did I do?" and accept the record as he made it. In this moment of truth he is likely to see himself in a more objective and detached manner than was previously possible.

In the following selection, Herman Feifel describes the attempts of various investigators to account for the fear of death, particularly in normal people.

From The Meaning of Death

A discerning passage from the Talmud states that "for all creatures, death has been prepared from the beginning." To be alive is to face the possibility of death, of nonbeing. As far as we can determine, man is the only animal who knows consciously that he has to die. Death is something that we all must sooner or later, come to grips with. Life insurance, Memorial Day, the belief in immortality—all attest to our interest and concern. Historical and ethnological information (Caprio, 1946) reveals that reflection concerning death extends back to the earliest known civilization and exists among practically all peoples. Some investigators (Caprio, 1950; Zilboorg, 1943) hold that fear of death is a universal reaction and that no one is free from it. Freud (1922), for instance, postulates the presence of an unconscious wish in people which he connects with certain tendencies to self-destruction. We have only to think of sports like bobsledding and bullfighting, the behavior of the confirmed alcoholic or addict, the tubercular patient leaving the hospital against medical advice, etc. Melanie Klein (1948) believes fear of death to be at the root of all persecutory ideas and so indirectly of all anxiety. Paul Tillich (1952), the theologian, whose influence has made itself felt in American psychiatry, bases his theory of anxiety on the ontological statement that man is finite, or subject to nonbeing. Others (Heidegger, 1927) feel that time has meaning for us only because we realize we have to die. Stekel (1949) went so far as to express the hypothesis that every fear we have is ultimately a fear of death.

Death themes and fantasies are prominent in psychopathology. Ideas of death are recurrent in some neurotic patients (Bromberg & Schilder, 1936; Teicher, 1953) and in hallucinations of many psychotic patients (Boisen, 1954). There are the stupor of the catatonic patient, sometimes likened to a death state and the delusions of immortality in certain schizophrenics. It may well be that the schizophrenic denial of reality functions, in some way, as a magical holding back, if not undoing, of the possibility of death. If living leads inevitably to death, then death can be fended off by not living. Also, a number of psychoanalysts (Fenichel, 1945; Schilder, 1939; Silberman, 1940) are of the opinion that one of the main reasons that shock measures produce positive effects in many patients is that these treatments provide them with a kind of death-and-rebirth fantasy experience.

In broader perspective—the meaning of death is no side issue but the central core not only of the Babylonian epic of Gilgamesh but of some of our most important present philosophicoreligious systems, e.g., existentialism, and its striking preoccupation with dread and death; Christianity, where the meaning of life is brought to full expression in its termination. This orientation has enormous practical consequences in all spheres of life, economic and political, as well as moral and religious.

Death is one of the essential realities of life. Despite this, camouflage and unhealthy avoidance of its inexorableness permeate a good deal of our thinking and action in Western culture. Even the words for death and dying are bypassed in much of everyday language by means of euphemisms. It is not the disquieting, "I die," but rather the anonymous, "one passes on," "one ends his days." *The Christian Science Monitor*, one of our outstanding newspapers, did not permit the word to be mentioned in its pages until recently. American movies, for the most part, shy away from tragedy and death and give us "happy endings." Forest Lawn, a cemetery in Los Angeles, proudly claims to minister "not to the dead, but to the living." And one of our industries has as its major interest the creation of greater "lifelike" qualities in the dead. Geoffrey Gorer (1955), the English anthropologist, has commented that death has become, in a certain sense, as unmentionable to us as sex was to the Victorians. He points out that in the nineteenth century most Protestant countries would seem to have subscribed to Pauline beliefs concerning the sinfulness of the body and the certainty of an afterlife. With the weakening of these concepts in the twentieth century, there appears to be a concomitant decrease in the ability of people to contemplate or discuss natural death and physical decomposition.

The underemphasis on the place of the future in psychological thinking is surprising because, in many moments, man responds much more to what is coming than to what has been. Indeed, what a person seeks to become may, at times, well decide what he attends to in his past. The past is an image that changes with our image of ourselves. It has been said that we may learn looking backward—we live looking forward. A person's thinking and behavior may be influenced more than we recognize by his views, hopes, and fears concerning the nature and meaning of death.

Feifel's observation that our burial customs are part of a general tendency to camouflage death seems all too true. The obsession to create lifelike qualities in the deceased person using wax and cosmetics, displaying him in a fluffy upholstered casket to give the impression of normal sleep, burying him in a sealed vault guaranteed to keep out moisture for a century or more, all seem to be ways of shutting out an unpleasant reality. Nonetheless death is a fact that must be faced, accepted, and lived with. To attempt to escape the inescapable will, in the long run, create more anxiety than it disguises.

Because most people are not comfortable with the thought of dying, they are ill at ease in dealing with terminal patients and often fail to supply the moral support needed by someone standing on the brink of the unknown. Physicians and professional hospital personnel are no exception. In testing the hypothesis that physicians are more uneasy in such situations than the general population, Feifel (1963) found a group of forty doctors to be more afraid of death than one control group of patients and one of nonprofessionals. Perhaps the desire to achieve some control over it may be what it is that initially attracts certain young people into the field of medicine. Another factor may be the sense of helplessness and failure experienced by the physician who cannot prolong the life of someone who depends upon him. Nurses, too, have been found to avoid contact with terminal patients as much as is consistent with good physical care, especially if the individual is not aware of the seriousness of his condition or refuses to accept its significance.

Feifel (1963) experienced extraordinary difficulty in gaining access to terminal patients in his investigation of attitudes toward death, even though a pilot study had indicated that the great majority of them welcomed an opportunity to express their feelings about death. Many remarked that as a result of doing so they were better able to understand and control their emotions. Studies have shown that while most physicians do not favor telling seriously ill patients their true condition, most patients feel that they have the right to know. Glaser and Strauss (1965, p. 6) point out that the issue is a moral one involving professional ethics, and social and personal values. Is it proper to keep a dying person ignorant of his precarious situation when he might wish to settle his affairs, make peace with his conscience, and control his style of dying? Someone must decide if and when to give the patient this information. Nurses cannot do so without the permission of the attending physician. Even if this is given, their training, at least in the past, has not prepared them for the psychological aspects of dealing with terminal patients.

In the selection that follows, Van den Berg addresses himself to some of these issues.

From The Psychology of the Sickbed

It can only be expected that modern man will be a difficult patient because the sickbed dictates to him the task for which he is least prepared: the confrontation with the vulnerability of his body and the transience of his life. Neither will he be a very helpful sickbed-visitor. For a healthy person is neither able nor prepared to speak of illness and death because, out of an ill-conceived sense of self-preservation, he has abolished every thought of these from his own existence.

Silence About Death

Compelled by his sickbed to take notice of these things, a patient may try to discuss them; for only a discussion can bring greater clarity to his thoughts. But he finds that no one can help him; often not even his doctor. The latter, like every healthy person, frequently prefers a false optimism to the seriousness which his human task—and certainly his medical task—imposes upon him, a seriousness which could really relieve this patient's heart, and his own. But he also arms himself with the medical sophism that to realize the seriousness of an illness and to consider death is always, and at any time, something that aggravates the illness and accelerates death. In connection with this, we would like to make the following remarks.

The first and principal demand medical action must meet is not to do any harm (*nil nocere*). This demand is not solely or even primarily directed toward the actual condition of the patient, but aims at his whole life. When a doctor is asked for advice whether or not a marriage should be considered and he knows that the hereditary taints of both partners make it medically certain that the children will be seriously affected, he is justified in advising against marriage, even if he knows that with this advice he is harming the present situation of the man and the woman. But he considers their lives as a whole, and because he wants to prevent these lives as a whole from being damaged, he pronounces his negative advice. Similarly, a neurosurgeon will refuse to remove the tortures of a compulsive neurosis if he has reason to believe that a lobotomy would damage the complete personality to such an extent that the gain does not balance the loss. The doctor who is convinced that his patient's sickbed will be his deathbed and who forbids himself and others to speak of these things, even if the patient emphatically asks for it, acts as if death were only significant at the time of its occurrence, as if death were a symptom of a disease rather than of life itself. But death is even a norm of life. Thus, the physician's silence is not right.

From J. H. van den Berg. **The psychology of the sickbed,** pp. 50-58. Copyright © 1966 by the Duquesne University Press. Reprinted by permission.

Death, Symptom of Life

Eugene Minkowski, in his *Le Temps Vécu* (1933), compares life to a long march of which the last milestone represents death. This last milestone, he says, is decisive for the whole march. Our walking is a continuous communication with the end. We walk in one way when this end is far away, another when it is near; one way when it is clear in our minds and another when it threatens to disappear. However emphatically we may ban death from our lives, we actually never cease to communicate with it; it determines our way of life. The forty-year-old person is so often inclined to give an entirely new form to his existence because he realizes that he has passed the halfway mark; the new presentation of death invites him to reset his sails before it is too late. Immanuel Kant lived with such iron discipline and with such a never abating sense of duty largely because death was never out of his mind. We may expect that the life of a person who convulsively closes his eyes to the reality of a personal end, is viewed differently from the life of a person for whom the *memento mori* is no longer frightening but constitutes the real issue of his life.

Death is a quality of life, *the* quality of life, the index of value of human existence. As a march is completed by the last milestone, so is life completed by death. To deny a person the right to contemplate approaching death actually means denying him the right to see his life as a whole, to live it as a complete life. If the end is reached in complete ignorance, a march has no sense, however many pleasant relaxations the way may have provided. If the goal, which caused such exertion, is entered blindfolded, a pilgrimage loses all sense, however many marvelous views the traveller may have enjoyed on the way. If we withhold the unmistakable seriousness of his sickbed from him, if we do not allow him to speak of death on his deathbed, we debase the life of the human being who is about to meet his end.

Truth at the Sickbed

It should not be concluded from all this that every patient indiscriminately has to be told the truth about his sickbed. There are patients who never in any way ask for such information. There are patients who ask with such an evident fear that it can be assumed that they lack every preparation for the harsh reality of their condition. There are deathbeds on which it is impossible to make up for the neglect of a lifetime. So also there are deathbeds where the discussion has been going on for a long time and where it is held with such seriousness that our own seriousness would mean a disturbance of the peace in which the discussion occurs. In all these cases it is better not to say anything. But if a patient shows how much these questions are torturing him, if it is apparent that he wants to know in order to survey his life with this knowledge, in order to examine, to order and to rectify his life, if he desires this knowledge to give meaningful wholeness to his life, then it is certainly wrong, both morally and medically, to lie to him by urging a false expectation of health upon him, however much he may be asking for that as well.

It is doubtful whether such patients will die sooner if they are told the truth and if they are allowed to discuss it. But even if life would be shortened by a few hours, or days or perhaps even weeks, does not the benefit of a really human end balance this loss of time? Is it really so important to lengthen the time in a sickbed if it consists of nothing but a continued self-deception from which even the patient himself yearns to be delivered? What is more important: the length or the content of a life? Is not the overemphasized medical interest in a longer and longer average lifespan an incorrect overaccentuation of one of the many medical tasks? The very pleasing statistics prove much in favor of the effectiveness of medical management, but in some respects they do not prove anything. The duty of a doctor is to save the life of his patients, to aid health in its struggle against disease. But human life is misunderstood if there is only an interest in the number of years and if medical care only includes the condition of the body.

For most general practitioners these are superfluous words. However, for hospital doctors and specialists, it seems that this is not always so. For they do not know their patients very well; they know little, if anything, of the patient's healthy life. They see him for only a short time, and the short duration of the contact has to be completely used, as a rule, for the care of the physical disease. Their reserve in discussions with patients is understandable though not always excusable. The hospital chaplain can do much good here. This does not mean that the clergyman is a colleague of the undertaker; the chaplain's duties still concern, like those of the doctor, the living person; the specific part of his task, however, is that he sees life in perspectives in which death can naturally be considered.

Wolfle (1970) points out how our well-intentioned efforts to be helpful may increase rather than decrease the anxiety of dying patients. Most terminal patients have lost the opportunity their grandfathers had of dying at home in familiar surroundings, lovingly attended by family and friends. With the progress of medical science more and more people die of a lingering illness. Not infrequently life is prolonged after all hope for recovery has been abandoned and the person is no longer conscious—all of which makes death more stressful and expensive for the family. It has even been found that the death rate among close relatives of the deceased is twice as high if the patient passed away in a hospital or nursing home than in his own home.

Wolfle goes on to raise a number of ethical questions. When and how long should physicians use heroic means to extend life for a few days or weeks? Is a heart transplant worth $20,000 or more, seeing that patients do not survive very long and maintenance costs are high? Would a billion dollars spent for 50,000 heart transplants secure greater human returns if used in another way? Who should have access to limited facilities of this kind?

Until the mid-1950s psychologists devoted very little attention to the problem of dying. In 1957 Alexander, Colley, and Alderstein were able to summarize the empirical research in two sentences: "Normal people show little conscious concern about death. Children, old people, and those in psychopathological or socially marginal states express somewhat more conscious interest in the problem." Since that time the number of systematic investigations of death and dying has continued to increase. The 150 entries in **Psychological Abstracts** of 1970 represents a 250 per cent gain over the previous year. Favorite topics for research are attitudes toward death, fear of death, death anxiety, suicide, adjustment and defenses of dying patients. Quantitative scales have been developed for the first three items mentioned.

Research in this area has been neglected for so many years that the stage has not yet been reached where broad theories can be tested.

DISCUSSION TOPICS

1 Explain the difference between existential loneliness, the feeling of aloneness, and pathological loneliness.

2 Do self-actualizing persons experience loneliness from time to time?

3 What special problems contribute to the feeling of loneliness in adolescence? In old age?

4 How can the dread of loneliness and death be reduced?

5 Compare the theories of the fear of death proposed by such writers as Freud, Tillich, and Klein.

6 Discuss modern taboos associated with death and dying.

7 What explanation can you give for the finding that fewer people die just before their birthdays and other events that are important to them?

8 Should a terminal patient be informed of his true condition? If so, when?

9 How can a consideration and acceptance of death as a reality enhance one's living?

ADDITIONAL READINGS

Buhler, C. Loneliness in maturity. Journal of Humanistic Psychology, 1969, **9**, 167-181. This insightful article deals with loneliness in adulthood, especially in old age.

Choron, J. **Death and Western thought.** New York: Collier, 1963. Choron surveys the great philosophers' thoughts on death.

Farebow, N L. (Ed.) **Taboo topics.** New York: Atherton, 1963. Death is among the taboos.

Fulton, R. (Ed.) **Death and identity.** New York: Wiley, 1965. The twenty-eight essays in this collection sample a wide variety of opinions.

Gorer, G. The pornography of death. In S. Spender, I. Kristol, & M. J. Lasky. **Encounter: An anthology from the first ten years of Encounter magazine.** New York: Basic Books, 1963. The content of prudery has shifted in the twentieth century. In place of sex it is death as a natural process that has become unmentionable

Jung, C. G. The soul and death. In H. Feifel (Ed.), **The meaning of death.** New York: McGraw-Hill, 1959. One of the three pioneers of modern psychiatry speaks of death from his broad experience as a clinician.

Kubler-Ross, E. **On death and dying.** New York: Macmillan, 1969. This book grew out of an interdisciplinary seminar in a hospital setting.

Lepp, I. **Death and its mysteries.** New York: Macmillan, 1968. A Christian psychologist looks at death. "Today I believe in personal immortality as a result of meditating on universal evolution."

Lifton, R. J. **Death in life: Survivors of Hiroshima.** New York: Random House, 1967. This is an account of the death imprint on those who barely survived the bombing.

Moustakas, C. The sense of self. **Journal of Humanistic Psychology**, 1961, **1**, 20-34. The author shows how aloneness can be exhilarating.

Pearson, L. (Ed.) **Death and dying: Current issues in the treatment of the dying person.** Cleveland: Case Western Reserve University Press, 1969. The patient's experience of dying and his interaction with the medical staff and the family are discussed in this collection of five essays. A 104-page selected bibliography on most aspects of death is included.

Reisman, D. **The lonely crowd.** New Haven, Conn.: Yale University Press, 1950. The middle-class, urban, outer-directed American is unable to feel close either to himself or to other people.

Rogers, C. R. The loneliness of contemporary man. **Review of Existential Psychology and Psychiatry,** 1961, **1**, 94-101. A case study is used to illustrate the development of loneliness to tragic proportions.

Chapter 4

Encounter Groups

*Our way of seeing a person is different
from our way of seeing a thing. A thing
we perceive, a person we meet. To meet
means not only to come upon, to come
within the perception of, but also to
come into the presence of, or association
with, a person. To meet means not only
to confront but also to agree, to join, to
concur.*

Abraham J. Heschel

Few developments in the social sciences have attracted as much attention on the part of the general public as group dynamics. The discovery
that spontaneous, authentic interaction between several persons can
serve as an instrument for promoting self-insight and personal growth
has resulted in an ever-increasing demand for this special kind of experience. Requests for trained group leaders come from a variety of
sources. Many large corporations and other agencies are interested in
sensitivity training for executives and a better understanding of the
conditions that promote harmonious working relationships. Mental

hospitals consider group psychotherapy a standard procedure. School systems are experimenting with the application of group techniques to education. Growing numbers of students, housewives, and people in diverse occupations participate in T-groups in all their variations. Obviously this experience must satisfy some deeply felt inner need such as the hunger for relatedness. For whatever reason a person might wish to assign—the dehumanizing effects of a highly technical society, the failure to establish satisfactory love relationships in infancy, overindulgence of children resulting in their expectation that the adult world will take up where their ever loving parents left off—for whatever reason, people are lonely. The selection by Frieda Fromm-Reichmann in Chapter 3 describes the acute pain of loneliness and the measures that human beings will often take to escape it.

In the special environment of a properly conducted encounter group a new microculture develops. Mere convention and meaningless formalities give way to sincere, honest discussion including the disclosure of feeling. Each individual allows himself to be known and, in turn, attempts to understand every other participant, not in terms of preconceived ideas or psychological abstractions, but from the inside—the way the person himself thinks and feels. Frequently people who had forgotten how to experience deep emotion suddenly come to life again. As the group process runs its course, participants who were strangers feel themselves drawn into a kind of relatedness that is reserved for special friends. The personal gain is not exclusively in the sphere of emotion. As each person gains courage to drop his defenses, he begins to see himself as he appears to other people. Simultaneously he discovers that being his own authentic self gains rather than loses the respect of others. Perhaps he feared that if people knew him as he really is they would reject him out of hand. To his surprise he finds that he can both be himself and be loved. It is this enhancement of the self-image that seems to be chiefly responsible for the personality growth that occurs.

Carl Rogers gives a fuller account of what goes on in the typical encounter group.

The Process of the Basic Encounter Group

I would like to share with you some of my thinking and puzzlement regarding a potent new cultural development—the intensive group experience. It has, in my judgment, significant implications for our society. It has come very suddenly over our cultural horizon, since in anything like its present form it is less than two decades old.

I should like briefly to describe the many different forms and different labels under which the intensive group experience has become a part of our modern life. It has involved different kinds of individuals, and it has spawned various theories to account for its effects.

As to labels, the intensive group experience has at times been called the *T-group* or *lab group*, "T" standing for training laboratory in group dynamics. It has been termed *sensitivity training* in human relationships. The experience has sometimes been called a *basic encounter group* or a *workshop*—a workshop in human relationships, in leadership, in counseling, in education, in research, in psychotherapy. In dealing with one particular type of person—the drug addict—it has been called a *synanon*.

The intensive group experience has functioned in various settings. It has operated in industries, in universities, in church groups, and in resort settings which provide a retreat from everyday life. It has functioned in various educational institutions and in penitentiaries.

An astonishing range of individuals have been involved in these intensive group experiences. There have been groups for presidents of large corporations. There have been groups for delinquent and predelinquent adolescents. There have been groups composed of college students and faculty members, of counselors and psychotherapists, of school dropouts, of married couples, of confirmed drug addicts, of criminals serving sentences, of nurses preparing for hospital service, and of educators, principals, and teachers.

The geographical spread attained by this rapidly expanding movement has reached in this country from Bethel, Maine (starting point of the National Training Laboratory movement), to Idyllwild, California. To my personal knowledge, such groups also exist in France, England, Holland, Japan, and Australia.

In their outward pattern these group experiences also show a great deal of diversity. There are T-groups and workshops which have extended over three to four weeks, meeting six to eight hours each day. There are some that have lasted only 2½ days, crowding twenty or more hours of group sessions into this time. A recent innovation is the "marathon" weekend, which begins on Friday afternoon and ends on Sunday evening, with only a few hours out for sleep and snacks.

As to the conceptual underpinnings of this whole movement, one may almost select the theoretical flavor he prefers. Lewinian and client-centered theories have been most prominent, but gestalt therapy and various brands of psychoanalysis have all played contributing parts. The experience within the group may focus on specific training in human relations skills. It may be closely similar to group therapy, with much exploration of past experience and the dynamics of personal development. It may focus on creative expression through painting or expressive movement. It may be focused primarily upon a basic encounter and relationship between individuals.

Simply to describe the diversity which exists in this field raises very properly the question of why these various developments should be considered to belong together. Are there any threads of commonality which pervade all these widely divergent activities? To me it seems that they do belong together and can all be classed as focusing on the intensive group experience. They all have certain similar external characteristics. The group in almost every case is small (from eight to eighteen members), is relatively unstructured, and chooses its own goals and personal directions. The group experience usually, though not always, includes some cognitive input, some content material which is presented to the group. In almost all instances the leader's responsibility is primarily the facilitation of the expression of both feelings and thoughts on the part of the group members. Both in the leader and in the group members there is some focus on the process and the dynamics of the immediate personal interaction. These are, I think, some of the identifying characteristics which are rather easily recognized.

There are also certain practical hypotheses which tend to be held in common by all these groups. My own summary of these would be as follows: In an intensive group, with much freedom and little structure, the individual will gradually feel safe enough to drop some of his defenses and facades; he will relate more directly on a feeling basis (come into a basic encounter) with other members of the group; he will come to understand himself and his relationship to others more accurately; he will change in his personal attitudes and behavior; and he will subsequently relate more effectively to others in his everyday life situation. There are other hypotheses related more to the group than to the individual. One is that in this situation of minimal structure, the group will move from confusions, fractionation, and discontinuity to a climate of greater trust and coherence. These are some of the characteristics and hypotheses which, in my judgment, bind together this enormous cluster of activities which I wish to talk about as constituting the intensive group experience.

As for myself, I have been gradually moving into this field for the last twenty years. In experimenting with what I call *student-centered teaching,* involving the free expression of personal feelings, I came to recognize not only the cognitive learnings but also some of the personal changes which occurred. In brief intensive training courses for counselors for the Veterans Administration in 1946, during the postwar period, I and my staff focused more directly on providing an intensive group experience because of its impact in producing significant learning. In 1950, I served as leader of an intensive, full-time, one-week workshop, a postdoctoral training seminar in psychotherapy for the American Psychological Association. The impact of those six days was so great that for more than a dozen years afterward, I kept hearing from members of the group about the meaning it had had for them. Since that time I have been involved in more than forty ventures of what I would like to term—using the label most congenial to me—*basic encounter groups.* Most of these have involved for many of the members experiences of great intensity and considerable personal change. With two individuals, however, in these many groups, the experience contributed, I believe, to a psychotic break. A few other individuals have found the experience more unhelpful than helpful. So I have come to have a profound respect for the constructive potency of such group experiences and also a real concern over the fact that sometimes and in some ways this experience may do damage to individuals.

The Group Process

It is a matter of great interest to me to try to understand what appear to be common elements in the group process as I have come dimly to sense these. I am using this opportunity to think about this problem, not because I feel I have any final theory to give, but because I would like to formulate, as clearly as I am able, the elements which I can perceive at the present time. In doing so I am drawing upon my own experience, upon the experiences of others with whom I have worked, upon the written material in this field, upon the written reactions of many individuals who have participated in such groups, and to some extent upon the recordings of such group sessions, which we are only beginning to tap and analyze. I am sure that (though I have tried to draw on the experience of others) any formulation I make at the present time is unduly influenced by my own experience in groups and thus is lacking in the generality I wish it might have,

As I consider the terribly complex interactions which arise during twenty, forty, sixty, or more hours of intensive sessions, I believe that I see some threads which weave in and out of the pattern. Some of these trends or tendencies are likely to appear early and some later in the group sessions, but there is no clear-cut sequence in which one ends and another begins. The interaction is best thought of, I believe, as a varied tapestry, differing from group to group, yet with certain kinds of trends evident in most of these intensive encounters and with certain patterns tending to precede and others to follow. Here are some of the process patterns which I see developing, briefly described in simple terms, illustrated from tape recordings and personal reports, and presented in roughly sequential order. I am not aiming at a high-level theory of group process but rather at a naturalistic observation out of which, I hope, true theory can be built.[1]

Milling around

As the leader or facilitator makes clear at the outset that this is a group with unusual freedom, that it is not one for which he will take directional responsibility, there tends to develop a period of initial confusion, awkward silence, polite surface interaction, "cocktail-party talk," frustration, and great lack of continuity. The individuals come face-to-face with the fact that "there is no structure here except what we provide. We do not know our purposes; we do not even know one another, and we are committed to remain together over a considerable period of time." In this situation, confusion and frustration are natural. Particularly striking to the observer is the lack of continuity between personal expressions. Individual A will present some proposal or concern, clearly looking for a response from the group. Individual B has obviously been waiting for his turn and starts off on some completely different tangent as though he had never heard A. One member makes a simple suggestion such as, "I think we should introduce ourselves," and this may lead to several hours of highly involved discussion in which the underlying issues appear to be, "Who is the leader?" "Who is responsible for us?" "Who is a member of the group?" "What is the purpose of the group?"

Resistance to personal expression or exploration

During the milling period, some individuals are likely to reveal some rather personal attitudes. This tends to foster a very ambivalent reaction among other members of the group. One member, writing of his experience, says:

> There is a self which I present to the world and another one which I know more intimately. With others I try to appear able, knowing, unruffled, problem-free. To substantiate this image I will act in a way which at the time or later seems false or artifical or "not the real me." Or I will keep to myself thoughts which if expressed would reveal an imperfect me.
>
> My inner self, by contrast with the image I present to the world, is characterized by many doubts. The worth I attach to this inner self is

---

[1] Jack and Lorraine Gibb have long been working on an analysis of trust development as the essential theory of group process. Others who have contributed significantly to the theory of group process are Chris Argyris, Kenneth Benne, Warren Bennis, Dorwin Cartwright, Matthew Miles, and Robert Blake. Samples of the thinking of all these and others may be found in three recent books: Bradford, Gibb, & Benne (1964); Bennis, Benne, & Chin (1961); and Bennis, Schein, Berlew, & Steele (1964). Thus, there are many promising leads for theory construction involving a considerable degree of abstraction. This chapter has a more elementary aim—a naturalistic descriptive account of the process.

subject to much fluctuation and is very dependent on how others are reacting to me. At times this private self can feel worthless.

It is the public self which members tend to reveal to one another, and only gradually, fearfully, and ambivalently do they take steps to reveal something of their inner world.

Early in one intensive workshop, the members were asked to write anonymously a statement of some feeling or feelings which they had which they were not willing to tell in the group. One man wrote:

I don't relate easily to people. I have an almost impenetrable facade. Nothing gets in to hurt me, but nothing gets out. I have repressed so many emotions that I am close to emotional sterility. This situation doesn't make me happy, but I don't know what to do about it.

This individual is clearly living inside a private dungeon, but he does not even dare, except in this disguised fashion, to send out a call for help.

In a recent workshop when one man started to express the concern he felt about an impasse he was experiencing with his wife, another member stopped him, saying essentially

Are you sure you want to go on with this, or are you being seduced by the group into going further than you want to go? How do you know the group can be trusted? How will you feel about it when you go home and tell your wife what you have revealed, or when you decide to keep it from her? It just isn't safe to go further.

It seemed quite clear that in his warning, this second member was also expressing his own fear of revealing *him*self and *his* lack of trust in the group.

Description of past feelings

In spite of ambivalence about the trustworthiness of the group and the risk of exposing oneself, expression of feelings does begin to assume a larger proportion of the discussion. The executive tells how frustrated he feels by certain situations in his industry, or the housewife relates problems she has experienced with her children. A tape-recorded exchange involving a Roman Catholic nun occurs early in a one-week workshop, when the discussion has turned to a rather intellectualized consideration of anger:

Bill: What happens when you get mad, Sister, or don't you?
Sister: Yes, I do—yes I do. And I find when I get mad, I, I almost get, well, the kind of person that antagonizes me is the person who seems so unfeeling toward people—now I take our dean as a person in point

because she is a very aggressive woman and has certain ideas about what
the various rules in a college should be: and this woman can just send
me into high "G"; in an angry mood. *I mean this.* But then, I find,
I. . . .
Facil.:[2] But what, what do you do?
Sister: I find that when I'm in a situation like this, that I strike out in a
very sharp, uh, *tone,* or else I just refuse to respond—"All right, this
happens to be her way"—I don't think I've ever gone into a tantrum.
Joe: You just withdraw—no use to fight it.
Facil.: You say you use a sharp tone. To *her,* or to other people you're
dealing with?
Sister: Oh, no. To *her.*

This is a typical example of a *description* of feelings which are obviously current in her in a sense but which she is placing in the past and which she
describes as being outside the group in time and place. It is an example of
feelings existing "there and then."

Expression of negative feelings

Curiously enough, the first expression of genuinely significant "here-and-
now" feeling is apt to come out in negative attitudes toward other group
members or toward the group leader. In one group in which members
introduced themselves at some length, one woman refused, saying that she
preferred to be known for what she was in the group and not in terms of her
status outside. Very shortly after this, one of the men in the group attacked
her vigorously and angrily for this stand, accusing her of failing to cooperate,
of keeping herself aloof from the group, and so forth. It was the first *personal
current feeling* which had been brought into the open in the group.

Frequently the leader is attacked for his failure to give proper guidance
to the group. One vivid example of this comes from a recorded account of an
early session with a group of delinquents, where one member shouts at the
leader (Gordon, 1955, p. 214):

You will be licked if you don't control us right at the start. You have to
keep order here because you are older than us. That's what a teacher is
supposed to do. If he doesn't do it we will cause a lot of trouble and
won't get anything done. [Then, referring to two boys in the group
who were scuffling, he continues.] Throw 'em out, throw 'em out!
You've just got to make us behave!

An adult expresses his disgust at the people who talk too much, but
points his irritation at the leader (Gordon, 1955, p. 210):

[2] The term "facilitator" will be used throughout . . .although sometimes he is
referred to as "leader" or "trainer."

It is just that I don't understand why someone doesn't shut them up. I would have taken Gerald and shoved him out the window. I'm an authoritarian. I would have told him he was talking too much and he had to leave the room. I think the group discussion ought to be led by a person who simply will not recognize these people after they have interrupted about eight times.

Why are negatively toned expressions the first current feelings to be expressed? Some speculative answers might be the following: This is one of the best ways to test the freedom and trustworthiness of the group. "Is it really a place where I can be and express myself positively and negatively? Is this really a safe place, or will I be punished?" Another quite different reason is that deeply positive feelings are much more difficult and dangerous to express than negative ones. "If I say, 'I love you,' I am vulnerable and open to the most awful rejection. If I say, 'I hate you,' I am at best liable to attack, against which I can defend." Whatever the reasons, such negatively toned feelings tend to be the first here-and-now material to appear.

Expression and exploration of personally meaningful material

It may seem puzzling that following such negative experiences as the initial confusion, the resistance to personal expression, the focus on outside events, and the voicing of critical or angry feelings, the event most likely to occur next is for an individual to reveal himself to the group in a significant way. The reason for this no doubt is that the individual member has come to realize that this is in part *his group.* He can help to make of it what he wishes. He has also experienced the fact that negative feelings have been expressed and have usually been accepted or assimilated without any catastrophic results. He realizes there is freedom here, albeit a risky freedom. A climate of trust (Gibb, 1964, Ch. 10) is beginning to develop. So he begins to take the chance and the gamble of letting the group know some deeper facet of himself. One man tells of the trap in which he finds himself, feeling that communication between himself and his wife is hopeless. A priest tells of the anger which he has bottled up because of unreasonable treatment by one of his superiors. What should he have done? What might he do now? A scientist at the head of a large research department finds the courage to speak of his painful isolation, to tell the group that he has never had a single friend in his life. By the time he finishes telling of his situation, he is letting loose some of the tears of sorrow for himself which I am sure he has held in for many years. A psychiatrist tells of the guilt he feels because of the suicide of one of his patients. A woman of forty tells of her absolute inability to free herself from the grip of her controlling mother. A process which one workshop member has called a "journey to the center of self," often a very painful process, has begun.

Such exploration is not always an easy process, nor is the whole group always receptive to such self-revelation. In a group of institutionalized adolescents, all of whom had been in difficulty of one sort or another, one boy revealed an important fact about himself and immediately received both acceptance and sharp nonacceptance from members of the group:

> *George:* This is the thing. I've got too many problems at home-uhm, I think some of you know why I'm here, what I was charged with.
> *Mary:* I don't.
> *Facil.:* Do you want to tell us?
> *George:* Well, uh, it's sort of embarrassing.
> *Carol:* Come on, it won't be so bad.
> *George:* Well, I raped my sister. That's the only problem I have at home, and I've overcome that, I think. (*Rather long pause.*)
> *Freda:* Oooh, that's *weird*!
> *Mary:* People have problems, Freda, I mean ya know. . . .
> *Freda:* Yeah, I know, but *yeOUW*!!!
> *Facil.* (*to Freda*): You know about these problems, but they still are weird to you.
> *George:* You see what I mean; it's embarrassing to talk about it.
> *Mary:* Yeah, but it's O.K.
> *George:* It *hurts* to talk about it, but I know I've got to so I won't be guilt-ridden for the rest of my life.

Clearly Freda is completely shutting him out psychologically, while Mary in particular is showing a deep acceptance.

The expression of immediate interpersonal feelings in the group

Entering into the process sometimes earlier, sometimes later, is the explicit bringing into the open of the feelings experienced in the immediate moment by one member about another. These are sometimes positive and sometimes negative. Examples would be: "I feel threatened by your silence." "You remind me of my mother, with whom I had a tough time." "I took an instant dislike to you the first moment I saw you." "To me you're like a breath of fresh air in the group." "I like your warmth and your smile." "I dislike you more every time you speak up." Each of these attitudes can be, and usually is, explored in the increasing climate of trust.

The development of a healing capacity in the group

One of the most fascinating aspects of any intensive group experience is the manner in which a number of the group members show a natural and spontaneous capacity for dealing in a helpful, facilitative, and therapeutic fashion with the pain and suffering of others. As one rather extreme example of this, I think of a man in charge of maintenance in a large plant who was one of the low-status members of an industrial executive group. As he informed us, he had not been "contaminated by education." In the initial phases the group tended to look down on him. As members delved more deeply into themselves and began to express their own attitudes more fully, this man came forth as, without doubt, the most sensitive member of the group. He knew intuitively how to be understanding and acceptant. He was alert to things which had not yet been expressed but which were just below the surface. When the rest of us were paying attention to a member who was speaking, he would frequently spot another individual who was suffering silently and in need of help. He had a deeply perceptive and facilitating attitude. This kind of ability shows up so commonly in groups that it has led me to feel that the ability to be healing or therapeutic is far more common in human life than we might suppose. Often it needs only the permission granted by a freely flowing group experience to become evident.

In a characteristic instance, the leader and several group members were trying to be of help to Joe, who was telling of the almost complete lack of communication between himself and his wife. In varied ways members endeavored to give help. John kept putting before Joe the feelings Joe's wife was almost certainly experiencing. The facilitator kept challenging Joe's facade of "carefulness." Marie tried to help him discover what he was feeling at the moment. Fred showed him the choice he had of alternative behaviors. All this was clearly done in a spirit of caring, as is even more evident in the recording itself. No miracles were achieved, but toward the end Joe did come to the realization that the only thing that might help would be to express his real feelings to his wife.

Self-acceptance and the beginning of change

Many people feel that self-acceptance must stand in the way of change. Actually, in these group experiences, as in psychotherapy, it is the *beginning* of change. Some examples of the kind of attitudes expressed would be these: "I *am* a dominating person who likes to control others. I do want to mold these individuals into the proper shape." Another person says, "I really have a hurt and overburdened little boy inside of me who feels very sorry for himself. I *am* that little boy, in addition to being a competent and responsible manager."

I think of one governmental executive in a group in which I participated, a man with high responsibility and excellent technical training as an engineer. At the first meeting of the group he impressed me, and I think others, as being cold, aloof, somewhat bitter, resentful, and cynical. When he spoke of how he ran his office it appeared that he administered it "by the book," without any warmth or human feeling entering in. In one of the early sessions, when he spoke of his wife, a group member asked him, "Do you love your wife?" He paused for a long time, and the questioner said, "OK, that's answer enough." The executive said, "No. Wait a minute. The reason I didn't respond was that I was wondering if I ever loved anyone. I don't think I *ever* really *loved* anyone." It seemed quite dramatically clear to those of us in the group that he had come to accept himself as an unloving person.

A few days later he listened with great intensity as one member of the group expressed profound personal feelings of isolation, loneliness, and pain, revealing the extent to which he had been living behind a mask, a facade. The next morning the engineer said, "Last night I thought and thought about what Bill told us. I even wept quite a bit by myself. I can't remember how long it has been since I have cried, and I really *felt* something. I think perhaps what I felt was love."

It is not surprising that before the week was over, he had thought through new ways of handling his growing son, on whom he had been placing extremely rigorous demands. He had also begun genuinely to appreciate the love which his wife had extended to him and which he now felt he could in some measure reciprocate.

In another group one man kept a diary of his reactions. Here is his account of an experience in which he came really to accept his almost abject desire for love, a self-acceptance which marked the beginning of a very significant experience of change. He says (Hall, 1965):

> During the break between the third and fourth sessions, I felt very droopy and tired. I had it in mind to take a nap, but instead I was almost compulsively going around to people starting a conversation. I had a begging kind of feeling, like a very cowed little puppy hoping that he'll be patted but half afraid he'll be kicked. Finally, back in my room I lay down and began to know that I was sad. Several times I found myself wishing my roommate would come in and talk to me. Or, whenever someone walked by the door, I would come to attention inside, the way a dog pricks up his ears; and I would feel an immediate wish for that person to come in and talk to me. I realized my raw wish to receive kindness.

Another recorded excerpt, from an adolescent group, shows a combination of self-acceptance and self-exploration. Art had been talking about his "shell," and here he is beginning to work with the problem of accepting himself, and also the facade he ordinarily exhibits:

> *Art:* I'm so darn used to living with the shell; it doesn't even bother me. I don't even know the real me. I think I've uh, well, I've pushed the

shell more away here. When I'm out of my shell—only twice—once just a few minutes ago—I'm really me, I guess. But then I just sort of pull in the [latch] cord after me when I'm in my shell, and that's almost all the time. And I leave the [false] front standing outside when I'm back in the shell.

Facil.: And nobody's back in there with you?

Art (crying): Nobody else is in there with me, just me. I just pull everything into the shell and roll the shell up and shove it in my pocket. I take the shell, and the real me, and put it in my pocket where it's safe. I guess that's really the way I do it—I go into my shell and turn off the real world. And here: that's what I want to do here in this group, ya know, come out of my shell and actually throw it away.

Louis: You're making progress already. At least you can talk about it.

Facil.: Yeah. The thing that's going to be hardest is to stay out of the shell.

Art (still crying): Well, yeah, if I can keep talking about it, I can come out and stay out, but I'm gonna have to, ya know, protect me. It hurts; it's actually hurting to talk about it.

Still another person reporting shortly after his workshop experience said, "I came away from the workshop feeling much more deeply that 'It is all right to be me with all my strengths and weaknesses.' My wife has told me that I appear to be more authentic, more real, more genuine."

This feeling of greater realness and authenticity is a very common experience. It would appear that the individual is learning to accept and to *be* himself, and this is laying the foundation for change. He is closer to his own feelings, and hence they are no longer so rigidly organized and are more open to change.

The cracking of facades

As the sessions continue, so many things tend to occur together that it is difficult to know which to describe first. It should again be stressed that these different threads and stages interweave and overlap. One of these threads is the increasing impatience with defenses. As time goes on, the group finds it unbearable that any member should live behind a mask or a front. The polite words, the intellectual understanding of one another and of relationships, the smooth coin of tact and cover-up—amply satisfactory for interactions outside—are just not good enough. The expression of self by some members of the group has made it very clear that a deeper and more basic encounter is *possible,* and the group appears to strive, intuitively and unconsciously, toward this goal. Gently at times, almost savagely at others, the group *demands* that the individual be himself, that his current feelings not be hidden, that he remove the mask of ordinary social intercourse. In one group there was a highly intelligent and quite academic man who had been rather perceptive in his understanding of others but who had not revealed himself at all. The attitude of the group was finally expressed sharply by one member when he said, "Come out from behind that lectern, Doc. Stop giving us speeches. Take off your dark glasses. We want to know *you*."

In Synanon, the fascinating group so successfully involved in making persons out of drug addicts, this ripping away of facades is often very drastic. An excerpt from one of the "synanons," or group sessions, makes this clear (Casriel, 1963, p. 81):

> *Joe (speaking to Gina):* I wonder when you're going to stop sounding so good in synanons. Every synanon that I'm in with you, someone asks you a question, and you've got a beautiful book written. All made out about what went down and how you were wrong and how you realized you were wrong and all that kind of bullshit. When are you going to stop doing that? How do you feel about Art?
> *Gina:* I have nothing against Art.
> *Will:* You're a nut. Art hasn't got any damn sense. He's been in there, yelling at you and Moe, and you've got everything so cool.
> *Gina:* No, I feel he's very insecure in a lot of ways but that has nothing to do with me. . . .
> *Joe:* You act like you're so goddamn understanding.
> *Gina:* I was *told* to act as if I understand.
> *Joe:* Well, you're in a synanon now. You're not supposed to be acting like you're such a goddamn healthy person. Are you so well?
> *Gina:* No.
> *Joe:* Well why the hell don't you quit acting as if you were.

If I am indicating that the group at times is quite violent in tearing down a facade or a defense, this would be accurate. On the other hand, it can also be sensitive and gentle. The man who was accused of hiding behind a lectern was deeply hurt by this attack, and over the lunch hour looked very troubled, as though he might break into tears at any moment. When the group reconvened, the members sensed this and treated him very gently, enabling him to tell us his own tragic personal story, which accounted for his aloofness and his intellectual and academic approach to life.

The individual receives feedback

In the process of this freely expressive interaction, the individual rapidly acquires a great deal of data as to how he appears to others. The "hail-fellow-well-met" discovers that others resent his exaggerated friendliness. The executive who weighs his words carefully and speaks with heavy precision may find that others regard him as stuffy. A woman who shows a somewhat excessive desire to be of help to others is told in no uncertain terms that some group members do not want her for a mother. All this can be decidedly upsetting, but as long as these various bits of information are fed back in the context of caring which is developing in the group, they seem highly constructive.

Feedback can at times be very warm and positive, as the following recorded excerpt indicates:

> *Leo (very softly and gently):* I've been struck with this ever since she talked about her waking in the night, that she has a very delicate sensitivity. *(Turning to Mary and speaking almost caressingly.)* And somehow I perceive—even looking at you or in your eyes—a very—almost like a gentle touch and from this gentle touch you can tell many—things—you sense in—this manner.
> *Fred:* Leo, when you said that, that she has this kind of delicate sensitivity, I just felt, *Lord yes!* Look at her eyes.
> *Leo:* M-hm.

A much more extended instance of negative and positive feedback, triggering a significant new experience of self-understanding and encounter with the group, is taken from the diary of the young man mentioned before. He had been telling the group that he had no feeling for them, and felt they had no feeling for him (Hall, 1965):

> Then, a girl lost patience with me and said she didn't feel she could give any more. She said I looked like a bottomless well, and she wondered how many times I had to be told that I *was* cared for. By this time I was feeling panicky, and I was saying to myself, "My God, can it be true that I can't be satisfied and that I'm somehow compelled to pester people for attention until I drive them away!"
> At this point while I was really worried, a nun in the group spoke up. She said that I had not alienated her with some negative things I had said to her. She said she liked me, and she couldn't understand why I couldn't see that. She said she felt concerned for me and wanted to help me. With that, something began to really dawn on me, and I voiced it somewhat like the following. "You mean you are all sitting there, feeling for me what I say I want you to feel, and that somewhere down inside me I'm stopping it from touching me?" I relaxed appreciably and began really to wonder why I had shut their caring out so much. I couldn't find the answer, and one woman said: "It looks like you are trying to stay continuously as deep in your feelings as you were this afternoon. It would make sense to me for you to draw back and assimilate it. Maybe if you don't push so hard, you can rest awhile and then move back into your feelings more naturally."
> Her making the last suggestion really took effect. I saw the sense in it, and almost immediately I settled back very relaxed with something of a feeling of a bright, warm day dawning inside me. In addition to taking the pressure off of myself, however, I was for the first time really warmed by the friendly feelings which I felt they had for me. It is

difficult to say why I felt liked only just then, but, as opposed to the earlier sessions, I really *believed* they cared for me. I never have fully understood why I stood their affection off for so long, but at that point I almost abruptly began to trust that they did care. The measure of the effectiveness of this change lies in what I said next. I said, "Well, that really takes care of me. I'm really ready to listen to someone else now." I *meant* that, too.

Confrontation

There are times when the term "feedback" is far too mild to describe the interactions which take place, when it is better said that one individual *confronts* another, directly "leveling" with him. Such confrontations can be positive, but frequently they are decidedly negative, as the following example will make abundantly clear. In one of the last sessions of a group, Alice had made some quite vulgar and contemptuous remarks to John, who was entering religious work. The next morning, Norma, who had been a very quiet person in the group, took the floor:

> *Norma (loud sigh):* Well, I don't have *any* respect for you, Alice. *None!* *(Pause.)* There's about a hundred things going through my mind I want to say to you, and by God I hope I get through 'em all! First of all, if you wanted us to respect you, then why couldn't you respect *John's* feelings last night? Why have you been on him today? Hmm? Last night—couldn't you—couldn't you accept—*couldn't you* comprehend in any way at all that—that *he felt* his unworthiness in the service of God? Couldn't you accept this, or did you have to dig into it today to find something *else there?* And his respect for womanhood—he *loves* women—yes, he does, because he's a real person, but you—you're not a real woman—to me—and thank God, you're not my mother! ! ! ! I want to come over and beat the hell out of you! ! ! I want to slap you across the mouth so hard and—oh, and you're so, you're many years above me—and I respect age, and I respect people who are older than me, *but I don't respect you, Alice. At all!* And I was so *hurt* and *confused* because you were making someone else feel *hurt* and confused. . . .

It may relieve the reader to know that these two women came to accept each other, not completely, but much more understandingly, before the end of the session. But this *was* a confrontation!

The helping relationship outside the group sessions

No account of the group process would, in my experience, be adequate if it did not make mention of the many ways in which group members are of assistance to one another. Not infrequently, one member of a group will spend hours listening and talking to another member who is undergoing a painful new perception of himself. Sometimes it is merely the offering of help which is therapeutic. I think of one man who was going through a very depressed period after having told us of the many tragedies in his life. He seemed quite clearly, from his remarks, to be contemplating suicide. I jotted down my room number (we were staying at a hotel) and told him to put it in his pocket and to call me anytime of day or night if he felt that it would help. He never called, but six months after the workshop was over he wrote to me telling me how much that act had meant to him and that he still had the slip of paper to remind him of it.

Let me give an example of the healing effect of the attitudes of group members both outside and inside the group meetings. This is taken from a letter written by a workshop member to the group one month after the group sessions. He speaks of the difficulties and depressing circumstances he has encountered during that month and adds:

> I have come to the conclusion that my experiences with you have profoundly affected me. I am truly grateful. This is different than personal therapy. None of you *had* to care about me. None of you had to seek me out and let me know of things you thought would help me. None of you had to let me know I was of help to you. Yet you did, and as a result it has far more meaning than anything I have so far experienced. When I feel the need to hold back and not live spontaneously, for whatever reasons, I remember that twelve persons, just like those before me now, said to let go and be congruent, to be myself, and, of all unbelievable things, they even loved me more for it. This has given me the *courage* to come out of myself many times since then. Often it seems my very doing of this helps the others to experience similar freedom.

The basic encounter

Running through some of the trends I have just been describing is the fact that individuals come into much closer and more direct contact with one another than is customary in ordinary life. This appears to be one of the most central, intense, and change-producing aspects of such a group experience. To illustrate what I mean, I would like to draw an example from a recent workshop group. A man tells, through his tears, of the very tragic loss of his child, a grief which he is experiencing *fully*, for the first time, not holding back his feelings in any way. Another says to him, also with tears in his eyes, "I've never felt so close to another human being. I've never before felt a real physical hurt in me from the pain of another. I feel *completely* with you." This is a basic encounter.

Such I-Thou relationships (to use Buber's term) occur with some frequency in these group sessions and nearly always bring a moistness to the eyes of the participants.

One member, trying to sort out his experiences immediately after a workshop, speaks of the "commitment to relationship" which often developed on the part of two individuals, not necessarily individuals who had liked each other initially. He goes on to say:

> The incredible fact experienced over and over by members of the group was that when a negative feeling was fully expressed to another, the relationship grew and the negative feeling was replaced by a deep acceptance for the other. . . . Thus real change seemed to occur when feelings were experienced and expressed in the context of the relationship. "I can't *stand* the way you talk!" turned into a real understanding and affection for you the *way* you talk.

This statement seems to capture some of the more complex meanings of the term "basic encounter."

The expression of positive feelings and closeness

As indicated in the last section, an inevitable part of the group process seems to be that when feelings are expressed and can be accepted in a relationship, a great deal of closeness and positive feelings result. Thus as the sessions proceed, there is an increasing feeling of warmth and group spirit and trust built, not out of positive attitudes only, but out of a realness which includes both positive and negative feeling. One member tried to capture this in writing very shortly after the workshop by saying that if he were trying to sum it up, ". . . it would have to do with what I call confirmation—a kind of confirmation of myself, of the uniqueness and universal qualities of men, a confirmation that when we can be human together something positive can emerge."

A particularly poignant expression of these positive attitudes was shown in the group where Norma confronted Alice with her bitterly angry feelings. Joan, the facilitator, was deeply upset and began to weep. The positive and healing attitudes of the group, for their own *leader,* are an unusual example of the closeness and personal quality of the relationships.

> *Joan (crying):* I somehow feel that it's so *damned* easy for me to—to put myself *inside* of another person and I just guess I can feel that—for John and Alice and for you, Norma.
> *Alice:* And it's *you* that's hurt.
> *Joan:* Maybe I am taking some of that hurt. I guess I am. *(Crying.)*
> *Alice:* That's a wonderful gift. I wish I had it.
> *Joan:* You have a lot of it.

Peter: In a way you bear the—I guess in a special way, because you're the—facilitator, ah, you've probably borne, ah, an extra heavy burden for all of us—and the burden that you, perhaps, you bear the heaviest is—we ask you—we ask one another; we grope to try to accept one another as we are, and—for each of us in various ways I guess we reach things and we say, *please* accept me. . . .

Some may be very critical of a "leader" so involved and so sensitive that she weeps at the tensions in the group which she has taken into herself. For me, it is simply another evidence that when people are real with each other, they have an astonishing ability to heal a person with a real and understanding love, whether that person is "participant" or "leader."

Behavior changes in the group

It would seem from observation that many changes in behavior occur in the group itself. Gestures change. The tone of voice changes, becoming sometimes stronger, sometimes softer, usually more spontaneous, less artificial, more feelingful. Individuals show an astonishing amount of thoughtfulness and helpfulness toward one another.

Our major concern, however, is with the behavior changes which occur following the group experience. It is this which constitutes the most significant question and on which we need much more study and research. One person gives a catalog of the changes which he sees in himself which may seem too "pat" but which is echoed in many other statements:

I am more open, spontaneous. I express myself more freely. I am more sympathetic, empathic, and tolerant. I am more confident. I am more religious in my own way. My relations with my family, friends, and coworkers are more honest, and I express my likes and dislikes and true feelings more openly. I admit ignorance more readily. I am more cheerful. I want to help others more.

Another says:

Since the workshop there has been a new relationship with my parents. It has been trying and hard. However, I have found a greater freedom in talking with them, especially my father. Steps have been made toward being closer to my mother than I have ever been in the last five years.

Another says:

It helped clarify my feelings about my work, gave me more enthusiasm for it, and made me more honest and cheerful with my coworkers and also more open when I was hostile. It made my relationship with my wife more open, deeper. We felt freer to talk about anything, and we felt confident that anything we talked about we could work through.

Sometimes the changes which are described are very subtle. "The primary change is the more positive view of my ability to allow myself to *hear*, and to become involved with someone else's 'silent scream.' "

At the risk of making the outcomes sound too good, I will add one more statement written shortly after a workshop by a mother. She says:

The immediate impact on my children was of interest to both me and my husband. I feel that having been so accepted and loved by a group of strangers was so supportive that when I returned home my love for the people closest to me was much more spontaneous. Also, the practice I had in accepting and loving others during the workshop was evident in my relationships with my close friends.

Disadvantages and risks

Thus far one might think that every aspect of the group process was positive. As far as the evidence at hand indicates, it appears that it nearly always is a positive process for a majority of the participants. There are, nevertheless, failures which result. Let me try to describe briefly some of the negative aspects of the group process as they sometimes occur.

The most obvious deficiency of the intensive group experience is that frequently the behavior changes, if any, which occur, are not lasting. This is often recognized by the participants. One says, "I wish I had the ability to hold permanently the 'openness' I left the conference with." Another says, "I experienced a lot of acceptance, warmth, and love at the workshop. I find it hard to carry the ability to share this in the same way with people outside the workshop. I find it easier to slip back into my old unemotional role than to do the work necessary to open relationships."

Sometimes group members experience this phenomenon of "relapse" quite philosophically:

The group experience is not a way of life but a reference point. My images of our group, even though I am unsure of some of their meanings, give me a comforting and useful perspective on my normal routine. They are like a mountain which I have climbed and enjoyed and to which I hope occasionally to return.

Some data on outcomes

What is the extent of this "slippage?" In the past year, I have administered follow-up questionnaires to 481 individuals who have been in groups I have organized or conducted. The information has been obtained from two to twelve months following the group experience, but the greatest number were followed up after a three- to six-month period.[3] Of these individuals, two (i.e., less than one-half of 1 percent) felt it had changed their behavior in ways they did not like. Fourteen percent felt that experience had made no perceptible change in their behavior. Another fourteen percent felt that it had changed their behavior but that this change had disappeared or left only a small residual positive effect. Fifty-seven percent felt it had made a continuing positive difference in their behavior, a few feeling that it had made some negative changes along with the positive.

A second potential risk involved in the intensive group experience and one which is often mentioned in public discussion is the risk that the individual may become deeply involved in revealing himself and then be left with problems which are not worked through. There have been a number of reports of people who have felt, following an intensive group experience, that they must go to a therapist to work through the feelings which were opened up in the intensive experience of the workshop and which were left unresolved. It is obvious that, without knowing more about each individual situation, it is difficult to say whether this was a negative outcome or a partially or entirely positive one. There are also very occasional accounts, and I can testify to two in my own experience, where an individual has had a psychotic episode during or immediately following an intensive group experience. On the other side of the picture is the fact that individuals have also lived through what were clearly psychotic episodes, and lived through them very constructively, in the context of a basic encounter group. My own tentative clinical judgment would be that the more positively the group process has been proceeding, the less likely it is that any individual would be psychologically damaged through membership in the group. It is obvious, however, that this is a serious issue and that much more needs to be known.

Some of the tension which exists in workshop members as a result of this potential for damage was very well described by one member when he said, "I feel the workshop had some very precious moments for me when I felt very close indeed to particular persons. It had some frightening moments when its potency was very evident and I realized a particular person might be deeply hurt or greatly helped but I could not predict which."

Out of the 481 participants followed up by questionnaires, two felt that the overall impact of their intensive group experience was "mostly damaging." Six more said that it had been "more unhelpful than helpful." Twenty-one, or 4 percent, stated that it had been "mostly frustrating, annoying, or confusing." Three and one-half percent said that it had been neutral in its impact. Nineteen percent checked that it had been "more

---

[3] The 481 respondents constituted 82 percent of those to whom the questionnaire had been sent.

helpful than unhelpful," indicating some degree of ambivalence. But 30 percent saw it as "constructive in its results," and 45 percent checked it as a "deeply meaningful, positive experience."[4] Thus for three-fourths of the group, it was *very* helpful. These figures should help to set the problem in perspective. It is obviously a very serious matter if an intensive group experience is psychologically damaging to *anyone*. It seems clear, however, that such damage occurs only rarely, if we are to judge by the reaction of the participants.

Other hazards of the group experience

There is another risk or deficiency in the basic encounter group. Until very recent years it has been unusual for a workshop to include both husband and wife. This can be a real problem if significant change has taken place in one spouse during or as a result of the workshop experience. One individual felt this risk clearly after attending a workshop. He said, "I think there is a great danger to a marriage when one spouse attends a group. It is too hard for the other spouse to compete with the group individually and collectively." One of the frequent aftereffects of the intensive group experience is that it brings out into the open for discussion marital tensions which have been kept under cover.

Another risk which has sometimes been a cause of real concern in mixed intensive workshops is that very positive, warm, and loving feelings can develop between members of the encounter group, as has been evident from some of the preceding examples. Inevitably some of these feelings have a sexual component, and this can be a matter of great concern to the participants and a profound threat to their spouses if these feelings are not worked through satisfactorily in the workshop. Also the close and loving feelings which develop may become a source of threat and marital difficulty when a wife, for example, has not been present, but projects many fears about the loss of her spouse—whether well founded or not—onto the workshop experience.

A man who had been in a mixed group of men and women executives wrote to me a year later and mentioned the strain in his marriage which resulted from his association with Marge, a member of his basic encounter group:

> There was a problem about Marge. There had occurred a very warm feeling on my part for Marge, and great compassion, for I felt she was *very* lonely. I believe the warmth was sincerely reciprocal. At any rate she wrote me a long affectionate letter, which I let my wife read. I was

---

[4] These figures add up to more than 100 percent since quite a number of the respondents checked more than one answer.

proud that Marge could feel that way about *me* [Because he had felt very worthless]. But my wife was alarmed, because she read a love affair into the words—at least a *potential* threat. I stopped writing to Marge, because I felt rather clandestine after that.

My wife has since participated in an "encounter group" herself, and she now understands. I have resumed writing to Marge.

Obviously, not all such episodes would have such a harmonious ending.

It is of interest in this connection that there has been increasing experimentation in recent years with "couples workshops" and with workshops for industrial executives and their spouses.

Still another negative potential growing out of these groups has become evident in recent years. Some individuals who have participated in previous encounter groups may exert a stultifying influence on new workshops which they attend. They sometimes exhibit what I think of as the "old pro" phenomenon. They feel they have learned the "rules of the game," and they subtly or openly try to impose these rules on newcomers. Thus, instead of promoting true expressiveness and spontaneity, they endeavor to substitute new rules for old—to make members feel guilty if they are not expressing feelings, are reluctant to voice criticism or hostility, are talking about situations outside the group relationship, or are fearful of revealing themselves. These old pros seem to be attempting to substitute a new tyranny in interpersonal relationships in the place of older, conventional restrictions. To me this is a perversion of the true group process. We need to ask ourselves how this travesty on spontaneity comes about.

Implications

I have tried to describe both the positive and the negative aspects of this burgeoning new cultural development. I would like now to touch on its implications for our society.

In the first place, it is a highly potent experience and hence clearly deserving of scientific study. As a phenomenon it has been both praised and criticized, but few people who have participated would doubt that *something* significant happens in these groups. People do not react in a neutral fashion toward the intensive group experience. They regard it as either strikingly worthwhile or deeply questionable. All would agree, however, that it is *potent.* This fact makes it of particular interest to the behavioral sciences since science is usually advanced by studying potent and dynamic phenomena. This is one of the reasons why I personally am devoting more and more of my time to this whole enterprise. I feel that we can learn much about the ways in which constructive personality change comes about as we study this group process more deeply.

In a different dimension, the intensive group experience appears to be one cultural attempt to meet the isolation of contemporary life. The person who has experienced an I-Thou relationship, who has entered into the basic encounter, is no longer an isolated individual. One workshop member stated this in a deeply expressive way:

> Workshops seem to be at least a partial answer to the loneliness of modern man and his search for new meanings for his life. In short, workshops seem very quickly to allow the individual to become that person he wants to be. The first few steps are taken there, in uncertainty, in fear, and in anxiety. We may or may not continue the journey. It is a gutsy way to live. You trade many, many loose ends for one big knot in the middle of your stomach. It sure as hell isn't easy, but it is a *life* at least—not a hollow imitation of life. It has fear as well as hope, sorrow as well as joy, but I daily offer it to more people in the hope that they will join me. . . . Out from a no-man's land of *fog* into the more violent atmosphere of extremes of thunder, hail, rain, and sunshine. It is worth the trip.

Another implication which is partially expressed in the foregoing statement is that it is an avenue to fulfillment. In a day when more income, a larger car, and a better washing machine seem scarcely to be satisfying the deepest needs of man, individuals are turning to the psychological world, groping for a greater degree of authenticity and fulfillment. One workshop member expressed this extremely vividly:

> [It] has revealed a completely new dimension of life and has opened an infinite number of possibilities for me in my relationship to myself and to everyone dear to me. I feel truly alive and so grateful and joyful and hopeful and healthy and giddy and sparkly. I feel as though my eyes and ears and heart and guts have been opened to see and hear and love and feel more deeply, more widely, more intensely—this glorious, mixed-up, fabulous existence of ours. My whole body and each of its systems seems freer and healthier. I want to feel hot and cold, tired and rested, soft and hard, energetic and lazy. With persons everywhere, but especially my family, I have found a new freedom to explore and communicate. I know the change in me automatically brings a change in them. A whole new exciting relationship has started for me with my husband and with each of my children—a freedom to speak and to hear them speak.

Though one may wish to discount the enthusiasm of this statement, it describes an enrichment of life for which many are seeking.

Rehumanizing human relationships

This whole development seems to have special significance in a culture which appears to be bent upon dehumanizing the individual and dehumanizing our human relationships. Here is an important force in the opposite direction, working toward making relationships more meaningful and more personal, in the family, in education, in government, in administrative agencies, in industry.

An intensive group experience has an even more general philosophical implication. It is one expression of the existential point of view which is making itself so pervasively evident in art and literature and modern life. The implicit goal of the group process seems to be to live life fully in the here and now of the relationship. The parallel with an existential point of view is clear cut. I believe this has been amply evident in the illustrative material.

There is one final issue which is raised by this whole phenomenon: What is our view of the optimal person? What is the goal of personality development? Different ages and different cultures have given different answers to this question. It seems evident from our review of the group process that in a climate of freedom, group members move toward becoming more spontaneous, flexible, closely related to their feelings, open to their experience, and closer and more expressively intimate in their interpersonal relationships. If we value this type of person and this type of behavior, then clearly the group process is a valuable process. If, on the other hand, we place a value on the individual who is effective in suppressing his feelings, who operates from a firm set of principles, who does not trust his own reactions and experience but relies on authority, and who remains aloof in his interpersonal relationships, then we would regard the group process, as I have tried to describe it, as a dangerous force. Clearly there is room for a difference of opinion on this value question, and not everyone in our culture would give the same answer.

Conclusion

I have tried to give a naturalistic, observational picture of one of the most significant modern social inventions, the so-called intensive group experience, or basic encounter group. I have tried to indicate some of the common elements of the process which occur in the climate of freedom that is present in such a group. I have pointed out some of the risks and short-comings of the group experience. I have tried to indicate some of the reasons why it deserves serious consideration, not only from a personal point of view, but also from a scientific and philosophical point of view. I also hope I have made it clear that this is an area in which an enormous amount of deeply perceptive study and research is needed.

As in the case of many other new developments in psychology, the encounter movement is still a controversial issue and not all psychologists are convinced of its value. Numbered among its sternest critics is Sigmund Koch (1969, 1970), who disavows the image of man that he considers implicit in the basic assumptions of this technique. ". . . All these methods," he writes, "are based on **one** fundamental assumption: that total psychic transparency—total self-exposure—has therapeutic and growth-releasing potential. More generally they presuppose an ultimate theory of man as socius; man as an undifferentiated and diffused region in a social space inhabited concurrently by all other men thus diffused. . . . This entire, far-flung 'human potential' movement is a threat to human dignity. It challenges any conception of the person that would make life worth living, in a degree far in excess of behaviorism."

Most psychologists do not take such a dim view of the movement, although they do call attention to a number of unresolved issues such as those discussed below.

In one sense the very success of the small group movement has become something of a problem. Social scientists might wish for more time to refine this instrument before placing it in the hands of less competent practitioners. The science of group dynamics is not a finished product but is still in the experimental stage. There is no generally accepted theory to explain the growth that takes place in encounter. A psychologist may take his choice of gestalt theory, self-insight, sensory awareness, the feeling of relatedness, the opening up or oneself to any and all inner experience, or any other conceptualization he may favor. The kind of sessions he conducts will obviously bear some relation to what he thinks is going on.

Rigorous evaluation of the outcome is another item of unfinished business. How many people are helped? How much are they helped and for how long a time? What is the extent of the psychological harm suffered occasionally by participants? What procedures should be instituted to screen out persons who might be injured by intense group interaction? If similar questions must be answered to the satisfaction of public health officials before powerful new wonder drugs are placed on the market, they would seem to be relevant here. Yet at a time when adequate guidelines and ethical norms are only beginning to be hammered out by leaders in the field, workshops and growth centers are springing up everywhere. The promotional literature sent out in such profusion does not always provide information on how competently they are conducted.

Lakin (1969) points up a number of ethical issues in sensitivity training that have not received sufficient attention. An increasing number of psychologically unstable persons seeking a solution for their problems are being attracted to encounter groups. Such individuals are not easy to identify even when some screening is attempted. If admitted as participants, their contractual relationship with the trainer would seem to resemble that of patients undergoing psychotherapy rather than "normal" persons intent on actualizing their potentialities. More serious, perhaps, is the absence of training standards for group facilitators. Frequently persons whose only qualification is that they have participated in one or two group experiences undertake sensitivity training. They do not seem to be aware that a trainer cannot easily absolve himself from all responsibility for the outcome of dramatic, emotionally charged confrontations on the plea that he is merely one of the participants in a democratic type of interaction. In spite of every disavowal of the use of authority he cannot, because of his role, avoid exerting a significant influence upon the group. If he has sufficient expertise in group dynamics, he can make the participants aware of how this influence is operating and, when occasion warrants, use it to minimize harmful pressures exerted on certain individuals.

In spite of his criticism, Lakin is not unsympathetic to sensitivity training. On the contrary he considers it to be not only a compelling psychological experience but a promising vehicle for learning as well. This does not blind him to the fact that the encounter group movement is still suffering from the growing pains of a vigorous adolescence.

SUMMARY

Many persons are finding that encounter groups which are expertly conducted serve to promote self-insight and personal growth. Carl Rogers explains the basic process of these intensive group experiences. The theory underlying group dynamics as well as the ethical standards to be applied by the leaders are still undergoing development.

DISCUSSION TOPICS

1 Describe the various phases through which a typical encounter group passes.

2 What are the immediate goals and more remote goals of group dynamics?

3 Why are so many people with diverse interests anxious to participate in encounter groups?

4 Is there danger of covert pressures being exerted upon individuals in a group to conform to the majority opinion?

5 Examine the charge that encounter groups can seriously harm some participants.

6 What type of guidelines should be established for the training of facilitators?

7 If you were setting up an encounter group, what ethical issues would you take into account?

8 Suggest how T-groups might be used effectively for (a) improving communications between college administrators, faculty, and students, (b) promoting the feeling of solidarity among neighbors and a willingness to cooperate in residential block programs.

9 Discuss the issues Maslow (see Additional Readings) raises with regard to the application of sensitivity techniques to scientific and professional training.

ADDITIONAL READINGS

Bach, G. R. The marathon group: Intensive practice of intimate interaction. **The Discoverer,** 1967, **4**(5), 1-6. Ten commandments or ground rules for participants in marathon therapy are suggested.

Bennis, W. G. Goals and meta-goals in laboratory training. In W. G. Bennis et al., **Interpersonal dynamics: Essays and readings in human interaction** (Rev. ed.). Homewood, Ill.: Dorsey Press, 1968, pp. 680-687. This paper describes the proximate and the more ultimate goals of the activities associated with the National Training Laboratories.

Bennis, W. G., Benne, K. D., and Chin, R. **The planning of change: Readings in the applied behavioral sciences.** New York: Holt, Rinehart, 1966. Chapter 6 contains a number of pertinent readings on group dynamics.

Blanchard, W. H. Ecstasy without agony is baloney. **Psychology Today,** 1970, **3**(8), 8-10, 64. The discussion centers around some psychological and ethical problems of workshops for awareness and human growth.

Bradford, L. P., Gibb, J. R., & Benne, K. D. (Eds.) **T-group theory and laboratory method.** New York: Wiley, 1964. "While this book attempts to describe the general development of laboratory training, its emphasis if upon the T (training) group."

Bugental, J. F. T. (Ed.) **Challenges of humanistic psychology.** New York: McGraw-Hill, 1967. Part Five is devoted to growthful encounter.

Burton, A. (Ed.) **Encounter.** San Francisco: Jossey-Bass, 1969. Among the thirteen contributors to this book are Rogers, Gibb, Burton, Thomas, Ellis, and Shapiro.

The Counseling Psychologist, 1970, **2**(2). All articles in this issue deal with encounter groups.

Egan, G. **Group process for interpersonal growth.** Belmont, Calif.: Brooks/ Cole, 1970. In attempting to identify the general principles underlying the growth properties of encounter groups, Egan summarizes and integrates a great deal of related material.

Golembiewski, R. T. (Ed.) **Sensitivity training and the laboratory approach.** Itasca, Ill.: Peacock, 1970. This is a book of readings about the theory and applications of the T-group method.

Jourard, S. M. Growing awareness and awareness of growth. In H. Otto & J. Mann (Eds.) **Ways of growth.** New York: Grossman, 1968. "I am going to speak here of growth from an 'inside' point of view, of growth of experience and the changed experience that is growth."

Lifton, W. M. **Working with groups: Group process and individual growth.** New York: Wiley, 1961. ". . . This book is intended both to provide some immediate help for the beginner and help the potential group workers to recognize their need for formal professional training."

Mann, J. **Encounter: A weekend with intimate strangers.** New York: Grossman, 1970. This book reports the interaction between thirteen members of an encounter group during a period of 40 hours.

Maslow, A. H. Humanistic education vs. professional education: Further comments. **New Directions in Teaching** (Dept. of Education, Bowling Green State University), 1970, **2**(2), 3-10. "During recent months I have come to feel even more strongly the need and the usefulness of a distinction between instrinsic and extrinsic education, education for personal growth as over against professional and skilled and content education; i.e., education for competence."

Moustakas, C. **The authentic teacher: Sensitivity and awareness in the classroom.** Cambridge: Doyle, 1966. Moustakas devotes a chapter to creating the authentic relationship.

Shepard, M., & Lee, M. **Marathon 16.** New York: Putnam, 1970. This interesting account of an encounter group is directed to a lay audience.

Strassburger, R. Ethical guidelines for encounter groups. **APA Monitor,** 1971, **27**(2), 32. Quite reasonable standards are proposed for the conduct of encounter groups. The complete article from which these were excerpted can be obtained from the author at the APA Central Office.

van Kamm, A. Encounter and its distortion in contemporary society. **Humanitas,** 1967, **2,** 271-284. The author analyzes the nature of human encounter and its distortion in today's world.

Part Two

An Image
of Man

*There is no issue about which so many
contradictory statements have been made,
no issue so important, no issue so obscure.
Psychology, biology, sociology have sought to explore
the nature of man. And yet man remains an enigma.*

ABRAHAM J. HESCHEL

Chapter 5

Man's Nature

Do you want to know where to find a free man, a man who acts as if he were free and thinks of himself as free (and how much freer could he be that that?). Go to him who is earnestly trying to persuade you that all men are robots. He will not claim that his ardor was designed into him and has no necessary connection with the validity of what he is saying.

Edwin G. Boring

Several centuries before the present era a psalmist asked, "What is man?" We are still searching for the answer to this urgent question, for even today there is no agreement about the matter. This fact would occasion little surprise had the psalmist been inquiring about something we are not familiar with, such as the planet Uranus but he was referring to ourselves. In effect he was saying to each of us, "What are you like?"

And after experiencing the selves that we are every waking moment
from birth, we still respond with a wide variety of conflicting answers.
For example, philosophers during the so-called Age of Reason exaggerated the extent to which our lives are ruled by logical thinking. Even as
late as the Victorian period (May, 1969, Ch. 7) sheer will power was
believed to account for virtually all human behavior. Freud reacted to
this immoderate view by elaborating a notion of man that is just as
extreme but in the opposite direction. For him conscious motives are
not important: it is the unconscious ones that ultimately determine
what a person does. Where formerly man was pictured as "captain of
his soul" actively directing his life, he now appeared as a driven creature
devoid of any real influence over his own actions. In fact, Freud spoke
of him as "being lived by the unconscious."

　　　Another limiting aspect of psychoanalytic theory is its failure to
adequately account for the unity of the human individual. Instead of
stressing harmony and integration Freud looked upon conflict between
id, ego, and superego as an essential component of personality. Watson
and the behaviorists in general also rejected reasoned choice in favor of
a model of behavior based on conditioned responses. To humanistic
psychologists this construct seems unable to account for the autonomy,
spontaneity, and creativity we experience both in ourselves and other
people. This matter will be discussed in greater detail later in the chapter.

　　　Some inconsistencies between the models of man proposed by
scholars in different disciplines are due to the vantage points from
which human nature is viewed. Each scholar is intent upon one particular aspect of the human design which lends itself to the study methods
he uses. Cartoonists sometimes capitalize on similar differences in outlook by drawing caricatures of how the same person appears to his employer, his banker, his dentist, his daughter, and his minister. One
would scarcely expect fields as diverse as philosophy, theology, and
behavioral science to give identical answers to our question. They do
not even ask it the same way. Psychologists, for example, instead of
inquiring, What is man? are more likely to investigate how man differs
from everything else in the universe: primates, lower animals, and even
computers (Adler, 1967, p. 12). Thus transformed into a hypothesis no
response can be given without making a host of comparisons and taking
into account all the relevant scientific information that is available. At
one time or another in the past each of the above-mentioned disciplines
shaped the dominant world view, and in doing so, modified the image
of man. Bernard Berelson and Gary A. Steiner describe the outcome.

From Human Behavior

If all we knew about man came from the behavioral sciences, what would he appear to be? How does this image compare with other images developed in the Western world over the ages?

What have been some of the key terms? The philosophical image of man in the ancient world centered on virtue and reason: man apprehending virtue through the use of reason and following its demands. The Christian image added sin and love. The political image of the Renaissance introduced power and will, and the economic image of the eighteenth and nineteenth centuries rationalized man's interest in property, things, money. The psycho-analytic image of the early twentieth century, currently so fashionable, dealt with ego and instinct, with the unconscious and the libido. The behavioral science image may be the latest contribution of this great stream of thought about human nature; it certainly is not the last.

How, in a similar way, might we characterize the man of the behavioral sciences? As we have seen, he is a creature far removed from his animal origins even in such instinctual matters as sexual or maternal behavior; a creature of enormous plasticity, able to live in a wide range of physical environments and an even wider range of cultural or social ones; a creature who simplifies reality in order to cope with it effectively; a creature subject to a variety of complex "forces" from the outside and the inside, such that almost nothing is caused by any other single thing; a creature who is subject to the probabilities of influence; to whom everything he is familiar with seems natural, and most other things unnatural; a creature who can adapt to a variety of experiences if given time and social support.

He is extremely good at adaptive behavior—at doing or learning to do things that increase his chances of survival or satisfaction. He is also, it must be stressed, extremely good at adapting his attitudes and expectations and perceptions to what external reality demands of him.

When he cannot achieve "realistic" satisfaction, he tends to modify what he sees to be the case, what he thinks he wants, what he thinks others want. For example, again as we have seen, he tends to remember what fits his needs and expectations; he not only works for what he wants but wants what he has to work for; he sees and hears not simply what is there but what he prefers to see and hear; he seeks out congenial groups in order to be comfortable about his actions and his opinions; he is skilled in engaging in private fantasies and "defense mechanisms" in order to lighten the human load; he tends to believe that the people around him agree with him more fully than in fact they do. Animals adjust to their environment more or less on its terms; man maneuvers his world to suit himself, within far broader limits.

The point is that nearly all of these findings, all except a few that deal with near-physiological aspects of behavior, put the individual in direct touch with other people—not only for facts and beliefs about the actual nature of the world, but also for what he has learned to want, to value, to consider right and good, to worship. Again, as examples, support from the small group around one is often more important than the larger issues involved; in political affairs one votes with one's friends as well as for the candidate; from religion to etiquette, what one's peers agree is right is typically seen as indeed right; even a person's perception of himself rests on how he is regarded by others.

So behavioral science man is social man—social product, social producer, and social seeker—to a greater degree than philosophical man or religious man or political man or economic man or psychoanalytic man, or the man of common observation and common sense, for that matter. The prime motivating agents stressed in the traditional images of man have been reason or faith or self-interest or impulse. The behavioral science image stresses the social definition of all of these. In these pages, the individual appears less "on his own," less as a creature of the natural environment, more as a creature making others and made by others.

The reader should not conclude from what has been said that at least social scientists are in agreement about the nature of human beings. Nothing could be farther from the truth. There is no more compatibility among their theories than among those of other scholars. Gordon W. Allport shows why this is true by describing several approaches to the study of man together with the basic assumptions from which conflicting theories flow.

From Pattern and Growth in Personality

Today people are asking more urgently than ever before, *What sort of creature is man?* Has he the potential for continued evolution and growth so that he may yet master the calamitous problems that face him—ideological schism, overpopulation, atomic disaster, and widespread disrespect of nation for nation and race for race?

Although the question is often addressed to philosophers and theologians, to historians and poets, the inquirer turns with special hope to the biological, psychological, and social sciences. For in an age of science he wants to hear what these relevant studies have to say.

So far as psychology is concerned, there is less agreement than we could wish for. Like other scientists and like philosophers, psychologists offer different sorts of answers—often only bare hints of answers, half-hidden in a network of unexpressed assumptions. Our task is to make some of the leading psychological answers explicit.

Positivist Formulations

We use the term *positivist* to stand for the traditional main stream of psychological science as it has existed in Western lands since the time of Locke and Comte. It is the empirical, experimental, chiefly associationist, and increasingly quantitative tradition known to all.

Perhaps the simplest way to characterize the positivist view of man is to say that he is regarded as a *reactive* being. What he does is determined by outer forces or by inner drives. Like traditional natural science, positive psychology sees movement as caused and determined by pressures. Man is like inanimate objects (including machines) and like elementary organisms.

The positivist view of man is seldom explicitly stated. Psychologists are too busy studying this reaction or that, in men or rats, to draw final implications from their work. They merely assume, in line with their procedures, that the human person is a purely reactive being. As pointed out [elsewhere], even a cursory view of the psychologist's vocabulary shows that terms such as *reflex, reaction, response, retention* are far more common— perhaps a hundred times more common—than terms with *pro* prefixes, such as *proactive, programing, propriate, proceeding, promise*. Terms commencing with *re* connote againstness, passivity, being pushed or maneuvered. Terms with *pro* suggest futurity, intention, forward thrust. Psychology for the most part looks at man not in terms of *proaction* but of *reaction*.[1]

The only real difficulty with the positivist formulation is that it does not know (or rarely knows) that it is a prisoner of a specific philosophical outlook, also of a specific period of culture, and of a narrow definition of "science." Positivism seldom defends its deterministic, quasi-mechanical view of the human person; it merely takes it for granted. Its metaphysics is unexamined, and, as the philosopher Whitehead once said, "No science can be more secure than the unconscious metaphysics which it tacitly presupposes."

It is certainly unfair to blame the positivist outlook in psychological and social science for the present plight of mankind, although many critics do so. Positivism is more a reflection than a cause of the fragmentation of personality in the modern world. The worst that can be said is that by

---

[1] See also G. W. Allport, The open system in personality theory. In *Personality and social encounter: selected essays* (Boston: Beacon, 1960), Ch. 3.

keeping itself "method-centered" rather than "problem-centered" positivism has brought forth an array of "itty bitty" facts at the expense of a coherent view of the human person as a whole (Maslow, 1970b, Ch. 2). In fairness, however, we should thank positivism for the wholesome safeguards it places on undisciplined speculation, and for many useful, if disconnected findings.

Psychoanalytic Formulations

Much has been written concerning the psychoanalytic image of man. Indeed, the image is so well known that only the briefest comment is needed here to supplement our discussion [elsewhere].

In some respects the picture is like that of positivism. Man is a quasi-mechanical reactor, goaded by three tyrannical forces: the environment, the id, and the superego. Man adjusts as well as he can within this triangle of forces. His vaunted rationality is of little account. Since he is full of defenses and prone to rationalize, his search for final truth is doomed to failure. If perchance he claims to find truth in religion, this discovery is dubbed an illusion and charged up to his neurosis.

There is a deep pessimism in orthodox psychanalytic doctrine (Freudian style). Man is so heavily dominated by unconscious id forces that he never fully escapes the ferocity and passion in his nature. Sublimation is the best we can hope for. There is no genuine transformation of motives.

Grim as the picture is, no theory of modern man can safely overlook its elements of truth. How can we hope to see man whole unless we include the dark side of his nature? Many present-day psychoanalysts, however, feel that the image overweights the role of unconscious and libidinal forces in personality. Neo-Freudian "ego-psychology" has broadened the perspective, and would agree in many respects with the school of thought we shall next consider.

Personalistic Formulations

There are several versions of personalistic thought.[2] They all agree that the individual person as a patterned entity must serve as the center of gravity for

[2] The most detailed system is found in the writings of the German psychologist William Stern. See *General psychology from the personalistic standpoint* (Transl. by H. D. Spoerl; New York: Macmillan, 1938); also G. W. Allport, The personalistic psychology of William Stern, *Charact. & Pers.*, 1937, 5, 231-246. The American philosophical school of personalism is exemplified in E. S. Brightman, *Introduction to philosophy* (New York: Holt, Rinehart and Winston, 1925); also in P. A. Bertocci, Psychological self, ego, and personality, *Psychol. Rev.*, 1945, 52, 91-99. For a critical discussion see G. W. Allport, The psychological nature of personality. In *Personality and social encounter*, Chap. 2. A Thomistic version of personalism is M. B. Arnold and J. A. Gasson (Eds.), *The human person* (New York: Ronald, 1954). An eclectic textbook approach is that of G. Murphy, *Introduction to psychology* (New York: Harper, 1951).

psychology. The intention of personalism is to rewrite the science of mental life entirely around this focus.

Why should such thoroughgoing reconstruction be demanded by the personalists? The reasons they advance are too numerous to be given in full. A brief hint of some of the arguments must suffice.

> Without the coordinating concept of *person* (or some equivalent, such as *self* or *ego*), it is impossible to account for the interaction of psychological processes. Memory affects perception, desire influences meaning, meaning determines action, and action shapes memory; and so on indefinitely. This constant interpenetration takes place within some *boundary,* and the boundary is the person. The flow occurs for some purpose, and the purpose can be stated only in terms of service to the person.
>
> The organization of thought or behavior can have no significance unless viewed as taking place within a definite framework. Psychological states do not organize themselves or lead independent existences. Their arrangement merely constitutes part of a larger arrangement—the personal life.
>
> Such concepts as *function, adaptation, use* have no significance without reference to the person. If an adjustment takes place it must be an adjustment *of* something, *to* something, *for* something. Again, the person is central.
>
> All the evidence—introspective and otherwise—that forces psychology to take account of the *self* is here relevant. The very elusiveness of the self—James says that to grasp it fully in consciousness is like trying to step on one's own shadow—proves that it is the ground of all experience. Although seldom salient itself, it provides the platform for all other experience.
>
> We cannot talk about strata of personality . . . or of propriate, as distinguished from peripheral, states without implying that a superior totality includes both.
>
> A creative person is presupposed in the creeds he creates. Even a scientist of the positivist persuasion intentionally limits his interest, designs his experiments, interprets the results. No sense could be made of this sequence without the assumption that the scientist himself is a prior creative unity. . . .

To sum up, the personalistic point of view is based partly on philosophical argument and partly on appeal to immediate experience (phenomenology). It is in essence a rebellion against positivist science that tends to regard the individual as a bothersome incident. Different lines of personalism would answer somewhat differently the question, What sort of a creature is man? But they all agree that the final answer will disclose a creative unity, a purposive, growing individual—and not a dismembered reactor as pictured by positivism. The secret of man will not be found in a reductive analysis of his *being*, but only by tracing coherently the course of his *becoming*.

Existentialist Formulations

Existentialism, like personalism, has no single answer to our question concerning the nature of the human person. Indeed, in this movement we can find answers that in some respects are diametrically opposed to one another. One existentialist tells us that "man is a useless passion"; another, that "man is a being who exists in relation to God." Existentialism is theistic and atheistic, despairing and hopeful, empirical and mystical—all depending on the devotee.

Yet certain features are common. One is the conviction that positive science alone cannot discover the nature of man as a being-in-the-world. Each special science is too narrow. None is synoptic. And the methods of positive science tend to rule out the most appropriate tool for research· phenomenology. It is not enough to know how man reacts: we must know how he feels, how he sees his world, what time and space are to *him* (not to the physicist), why he lives, what he fears, for what he would willingly die. Such questions of *existence* must be put to man directly, and not to an outside observer.

Common also is a passion not to be fooled about man's nature. If the Victorian image of man was perhaps too pretty, the Freudian image may be too grim. But grim or pretty, *all* knowledge about man must be faced. The findings of biology, psychology, anthropology are important, but so, too, are the findings of history, art, philosophy. We seek to know man in his entirety. Life demands that we know the worst and make the best of it.

It is probably true to say that all forms of existentialism hope to establish a new kind of psychology—a psychology of mankind. The pivot of such a psychology will lie in the perennial themes and crises of human life. Mere stimulus-response sequences, drives, habits, repetitions tend to miss the catastrophic coloring of life. Psychology should be more urgently human than it is. . . .

To sum up, there is a tendency among existentialist writers to seek for one basic intentional theme in human life. A fairly wide range of proposals is the result—and yet the varied proposals seem for the most part to be complementary and concordant, not in actual opposition. Man is inherently restless and anxious, desiring both security and freedom. He strives to counter his condition of alienation by seeking a meaning for existence which will cover the tragic trio of suffering, guilt, death. By making commitments he finds that life can become worth living. Along the way he enhances his own value experiences. If necessary he will sacrifice his life in order that some primary value can continue to be served. He is capable of taking responsibility, of answering by his deeds the questions life puts to him. In this way he rises above his own organic and spiritual urgencies, and achieves true self-transcendence. Although different writers place emphasis on different parts of this formula, the picture is consistent.

While Allport's general classifications are skillfully constructed, some personality theories contain elements from more than one category. Rogers' (1959) and Maslow's (1970a) will serve as examples. In contrast to the image of man as a reactive being, both authors think of the person as a unique individual who strives actively toward achieving self-fulfillment, including a strong positive regard for himself. Both authors also state their constructs as hypotheses which can be tested by appropriate research methods.

Rogers in particular believes that behavior depends upon how the person perceives himself and the things around him. An individual whose past experience causes him to view the world as a threatening place to live will act quite differently than one who sees people as friendly and lovable. The attitude of the former will change, if and only if, he begins to perceive his life-situation in a different way. Meanwhile in response to real or imagined threats, he may restrict his perceptions in an attempt to screen out everything that runs contrary to his feeling of self-worth. By remaining oblivious to sensations and feelings that produce anxiety, he can take the edge off the discomfort they cause. But doing so exacts an exorbitant price; he becomes less effective as a person. His distorted perceptions do not accurately mirror his inner experience nor does the self-image he clings to so desperately correspond to actuality. Such a percarious state of affairs can be maintained only by relying heavily upon defensive tactics which set his motives at cross purposes with each other. Eventually the incongruence between the self and his experience may reach the point where personality disorganization sets in.

To reverse this destructive trend, he must remove the distorting lenses from his perceptions so that he views self and the outside world less defensively. In the process he will probably discover that situations that formerly frightened him are not as threatening as he imagined. No longer is it necessary to surrender his personhood and smother his real feelings in order to keep defenses working effectively; he can relax and open himself freely to all experiences regardless of what they are. As the feeling of control over his own life increases, his positive regard for himself and others is enhanced. His style of living becomes more socialized, more mature, more creative. In short he is on his way to becoming a fully functioning person.

LIVING OR BEING LIVED: THE PROBLEM OF HUMAN AUTONOMY

The Danish Prince Hamlet was more modern than he knew when he proposed the question, "To be or not to be," without being able to opt for either alternative. Almost from the beginning, psychology has been in a similar quandary about whether Hamlet or anyone else is really capable of making a choice on his own initiative. Is it possible that in spite of the overwhelming perception of freedom a human being is merely the pawn of previous conditioning, inner conflicts, or environmental influences? After trying repeatedly to solve this riddle, William James (1894, 1897, 1904) concluded that, although every psychologist must sooner or later face the problem of freedom, it cannot be resolved on strictly psychological grounds. His own decision was to accept the phenomenon of freedom as a reality.

Hard Determinism

Immergluck (1964) adopts an opposite attitude, which is typical of the position of "hard" determinists as opposed to that of "soft" determinists. The latter, while admitting that human behavior is caused, includes among the causes the "self-determining" powers of the individual (Coleman, 1969, p. 23). Immergluck notes that although the majority of psychologists accept determinism as a valid working hypothesis, a growing number are becoming concerned about the paradox it occasions. In spite of commitment to a deterministic model that presupposes a causal relationship between behavior and its antecedents, the nagging doubt remains that somehow man must be free. As a result many psychologists are beginning to waiver. He is distressed at the thought that the "hard-won battle" for determinism may soon be relinquished. "I firmly believe," he continues, "that it would serve conceptual clarity if we regarded determinism and free will as representing two basically different and divergent views in modern psychology which cannot simply be dealt with through the fiat notion that 'both are somehow right' within their own limited frameworks, or that they really complement one another in jointly reflecting the total realities of psychological life." Accordingly he insists upon hard determinism, not only as a methodological principle, but also as the basic philosophy of psychology. This implies that regardless of how much freedom a person experiences in making a decision, his choice is in reality coerced by forces over which he has no control—he is subject to laws of behavior as rigid and invariant as those governing the behavior of chemical as they enter into combination.

Among other considerations that Immergluck advances to support this supposition are the following: (1) The constant search for
causes of such conditions as schizophrenia, feeblemindedness, and anxiety presupposes determination by their antecedents. (2) Lawful determinants are being found for creative behavior and there is every reason
to believe that they will also be discovered for even the most complex
psychological processes. (3) Our inability to predict behavior in a concrete situation does not rule out the existence of precise laws. No one
can forecast the exact time it will take a leaf to fall or the path it will
take, because there is no way of knowing all the vectors of force influencing its descent. (4) Man's behavior differs from an insect's not only
because he is presented with more alternatives, but also because he is
subjected to more internal and external stimuli. (5) Man is free neither
in a totalitarian nor in a democratic society. In one he is determined by
external factors, in the other by internal ones. (6) There are two levels
of analysis: **experiential**, such as the self-perception of freedom in
choosing, and **experimental** or scientific investigation. The former,
Immergluck contends, is direct, unanalyzed, and global while the latter
is detailed and precise in a way that is not possible under the circumstances of daily life. He believes that unless we probe beyond the phenomenological level of the feeling of freedom, we are likely to err,
because no sensory knowledge is free from distortion.

A Different Point of View

Other psychologists have not been slow to point out flaws in Immergluck's arguments. Within a year after his article appeared, six letters
were published in **American Psychologist** taking issue with him. This
would be sufficient proof, if any were needed, that the problem of
freedom was not laid to rest with William James. Begelman (1966)
points out that Immergluck's appeal to science to settle the argument
is invalid since the scientific method itself is based upon the **presupposition** of a deterministic world. To use it as a means of confirming a
lack of freedom in human beings would be equivalent to assuming the
very thing to be proved. Moreover, no one has yet specified the conditions under which deterministic claims could be falsified empirically.
Edwin A. Locke (1964) points to another fallacy in the deterministic
position.

Determinism

Immergluck's (1964) defense of psychological determinism contains an epistemological contradiction that refutes the validity of the very point he attempts to make. This contradiction, which is inherent in any form of psychological determinism, has been made previously by Branden (1963) and will be summarized here.

Determinism asserts that everything man does, thinks, or believes is determined by forces beyond his control. If a man believes something, he had to believe it. If he does something, he had to do it. If this is true, it follows that no knowledge or understanding of objective reality is possible to man. ". . . if the actions and content of his [man's] mind are determined by factors that may or may not have anything to do with reason, logic, and reality—then he can never know if his conclusions are true or false [pp. 17, 19]." If no knowledge is possible, then by what right and by what standard can the determinist claim any validity for his conclusions? If everything we say is determined, then all the determinist can say is that he was helpless to say otherwise. He cannot assert at the same time that what he says is true, except by claiming that he alone is an exception to a principle that he claims applies to all men.

To deny the possibility that man can have knowledge, however, is a self-contradiction. To conclude, as a determinist must, that we can know nothing assumes that: (a) there is something to know, and (b) that we have the means of determining whether we know it or not (i.e., whether our conclusions are valid). Yet it is precisely this possibility that determinism denies; thus the determinist argument refutes itself. "Determinism is a theory whose claim to truth is incompatible with its own content [p. 20]." Far from being necessary for the existence of science, psychological determinism would make all science impossible.

The point that Locke makes is a convincing one. In setting up any experiment a scientist must guide his thinking and activities in keeping with the logical and technical requirements of the situation. Not only must he select an appropriate experimental design, and make decisions about the variables to be controlled, the type of instruments to be used, and the kinds of data to be collected, but, in addition, he must ponder the meaning of his experimental observations in order to deduce their logical implications. Obviously it is not enough for a scientist merely to know what should be done without being at liberty to carry out his plans in every detail. His choices must be both free and reasonable,

Edwin A. Locke. Determinism. **American Psychologist,** 1964, **19,** 846-847. Copyright 1964 by the American Psychological Association.

since the operations of science cannot be entrusted to random, non-rational determining forces. Bertocci (1967) observes that "there are at least two critical points in being reasonable that to me seem to involve the freedom of will, that is, the freedom to execute, to the best of one's ability, one of the possible alternatives. The first point, already emphasized is that at which one insists on logically weeding out what is relevant. The reasonable man selects, from the plethora of data or memories that come flooding in, not what pleases, not what he's used to, but what will help solve the problem at hand. At this point he must struggle to affirm the hypothesis, however unpalatable to him, which best fits the evidence." An experimenter who would base his decisions on anything other than the logical demands of the situation would not add significantly to the body of scientific literature except, perhaps, as a case history. However adamantly the assumption of determinism is held, the experimenter must always exempt himself from its implications.

Immergluck (1964) argues that the personal experience of freedom is nothing more than an illusion although a necessary one for human beings to function as they do. If we are to assume that such a clear and compelling awareness—involving as it does not only perception but the total integration of all ongoing conscious processes—can be illusory, then where do we stop? What is seen with the eyes is no more convincing than the experience of freedom. Why trust meter readings or measurement in general? Or, for that matter, why believe in a world of reality outside one's self? We cannot cry "illusion" only when convenient for our purposes. The logical extension of such an assumption would make the acquisition of all knowledge impossible (see Chapter 11, pp. 218-221).

Herbert Muller identifies some tangled threads in the skein of reasoning about determinism. Prominent among these is a misunderstanding of what is meant by a law of behavior. As he explains, it is not a totally coercive force as is often imagined.

From Issues of Freedom

On scientific grounds, the problem of human freedom in a lawful universe has been confused by common-sense notions of law and causation. A scientific law is a statement of certain uniform sequences, as of the regular falling of apples in accordance with the law of gravitation. It is not a universal commandment, not a description of a force that makes the apples fall, not a final explanation of why all the apples fall. The cause assigned to a sequence of events is in any case selective, never the whole or the "real" cause. If a chicken is run over by an automobile, its death may be attributed to the laws of mechanics, the nature of living organisms, the stupidity of chickens, the carelessness of the driver, the sins of American automobile designers, or the curse of an industrial society. A similar set of causes may be assigned to all human behavior, from the most mechanical to the seemingly spontaneous. "Free" activity need not mean activity that is uncaused or unaffected by the environment. If it did, freedom would be a nightmare in which nobody could understand or count on the behavior of others, everybody could enjoy only the freedom of lunatics.

The essential idea is that some human actions are not simply mechanical, wholly predetermined, absolutely predictable, but are to some extent self-determined and unpredictable. Although this "self" is always conditioned by its whole past, in a given culture, it still has live options and may say yes or no. If behavior becomes broadly more predictable when a man has character and acts on principle, his decisions are then more clearly his own; and there is still a margin for judgment, ingenuity, imagination—the brilliant decision. We may predict that a poet will keep on writing poetry becaue of an inner compulsion, but we cannot possibly predict his next happy phrase or far-fetched metaphor.

Let us consider even routine behavior, as of a man who gets up in the morning when his alarm clock goes off. The ringing of the clock is a mechanical, automatic event. It was predetermined by the designer of the clock, through creative powers of mind, and then by this man's setting the alarm. His own behavior involves both reflexes and reflection. He set it out of habit because he had to get up, go to work, make his living—because of necessities that limit his freedom, but also help him to achieve his living purposes. Even so, he might decide not to get up, instead to lie in bed a while—possibly to chuck the whole business. In either case his behavior is not causeless. Call it rational or irrational, one can find reasons for it. The point remains that once he is awake he is not behaving like an automaton. Unlike other animals, he is not merely following instincts either, but is thinking ahead, exercising some conscious judgment.

EVEN HARD DETERMINISTS MUST ASSUME
THAT THEY ARE FREE

What seems inconsistent, as Allport noted long ago, is that many of the psychologists who deny freedom are in the forefront of movements pressing for freedom of speech, civil rights, and other forms of individual liberty. Surely they must presume that either they or the persons they are attempting to persuade or both have some control over their behavior. Similarly, insight therapy of any variety presupposes the client's ability to change his style of life; otherwise the interviews would be pointless. Even Freud, who denied self-determination, found himself forced to speak in terms of freedom when explaining the goal of psychoanalytic treatment.

The mental set of a hard determinist is not too difficult to maintain as long as one speculates in the abstract about human behavior. But in real life everyone, whether he likes it or not, is forced to act on an opposite set of assumptions. He cannot avoid decisions ranging from what he wishes to make of himself to problems of occupation, marriage, and the homely details of everyday living. Few determinists think of themselves as going through a meaningless ritual in weighing the pros and cons of problem situations or of consciously indulging an illusion in attempting to make any decision at all.

Noel Mailloux calls attention to an important aspect of the problem which has not received sufficient emphasis.

From Psychic Determinism, Freedom, and Personality Development

To clear the ground from the start, we must say that the formulation of the question of the relationship between determinism and freedom has been entirely misleading. In fact, as long as the thesis of physicalism was triumphant in psychology, either under the form of behaviorism or of operationism, physical determinism was accepted as a scientific dogma. Moreover, such determinism was regarded as the alternative of free will. It is rather amazing that such a gross confusion could persist so long in the mind of many a scientist and philosopher. Here, let us remember that the real alternative of determinism, as Knight (1946, p. 262) expressed it with lapidary precision, is not free will, but indeterminism, which implies chaos, unpredictability, and a denial of cause and effect relationships in human affairs.

Noel Mailloux goes on to speak of the small child overcoming the original indeterminacy of its motivation through a rather mechanical process which is equivalent to establishing a type of psychic determinism. Behavior at this stage of development is largely habitual and characterized by extreme rigidity and "schematic" adaptation. But once the child discovers values and the possibility of controlling his own behavior, he is on the way to achieve autonomy. He must, how-

From Noel Mailloux, Psychic determinism, freedom, and personality development. Canadian Journal of Psychology, 1953, 7, 1-11. Reprinted by permission.

ever, face the anxiety accompanying indeterminacy that makes the acquisition of freedom such a painful struggle. Some unconscious elements will remain in the newly elaborated function of free choice since it represents the **completion** of a whole hierarchy of processes "which it does not suppress but integrates, which are still used even if surpassed." Mailloux continues:

It is now becoming clear enough that psychic determinism, far from being opposed to freedom, is a necessary step or condition for its acquisition. Moreover, it cannot be surpassed without being integrated, since freedom can no more be exercised without using psychic automatisms than without using biological mechanisms. It is only in the case of a neurotic condition that, on account of the lack of integration, these two levels of functioning will appear as conflicting, the lower one maintaining its autonomy. After what has been said already, it seems easier to introduce here a few other considerations about the psychological nature and the development of free activity, which have important clinical implications.

Free activity, corresponding to the most perfect activity of which man is capable, is certainly the activity in which least is left to indeterminacy and unpredictability. In other words, such behavior is fully controlled precisely because it is fully determined, because it constitutes the most adequate and accurate answer one can give to the more or less complicated set of demands imposed by reality at a given moment. It is easy to see that the more one has developed some skill and can master a situation, the more he takes account of even its minutest details. Each aspect of his activity corresponds to a definite element of reality, and finds in it its ultimate determination. The more complex the situation to which we have to adapt, the more necessary it is to surpass the gross and rigid determination achieved through mechanization or automatization. The extremely precise adaptability of the artist, of the craftsman, of the professional player, requires nothing less than the plasticity of free determination—free because it has to be complete.

But as free determination implies self-determination, what we call free activity is nothing else than self-determined activity. This means that such activity, far from losing the advantages gained through determination, namely, intentionality, structuralization, and organization, possesses the additional property of extreme flexibility, which makes it possible for it to respond in an integrated way to situations which are as varied as they are unique. Again, this point of view has been quoted by Knight, who writes: "That man is free who is conscious of being the author of the law that he obeys" (13, p. 256). This man, of course, instead of being determined by any particular motivation, is himself actively determining that particular motivation which will be the spring of his individual action. Moreover, he remains capable of changing it at any time.

Obviously self-determination implies the highest level of consciousness, that is, the only level at which deliberation and choice can occur. In fact, any free activity is one which proceeds from deliberate willing, or one in which the motivation has been rationally elaborated. It presupposes, therefore, a clear perception of the relationship existing between ends and means, and the ability to explore, invent, or create the means leading to the desired end. In brief, as science facilitates inventiveness and originality of vision, freedom facilitates creativeness and originality of action. And here we reach the root of an old misunderstanding which has been a serious obstacle to the development of psychology. Because creativeness and originality (which are the characteristics of free activity) were confused with indeterminacy, freedom came to be synonymous with unpredictability, and was discarded from the realm of science. It took the work of such men as Bergson and Scheler to rehabilitate freedom in the eyes of science. Now, however, it is more and more clearly understood that free behavior, far from being unpredictable, is the most predictable behavior, though it is not predictable in the same way as behavior which is the result of a deterministic process or of a repetition compulsion. Confronted with a difficult and problematic situation, the man who is really free is the only one who is entirely reliable, the only one whose behavior remains predictable, because he is the only one capable of making the right choice and of executing it. On the one hand, we always know that this man is going to do the only thing which ought to be done, namely, the right thing; but on the other hand, we also know that such an achievement, like any genuine discovery, escapes all our prevision.

Several points that Mailloux makes deserve further elaboration. The first is that a certain amount of psychic determinism is not only consistent with freedom but even necessary for it to be exercised just as biological mechanisms are. Herbert Muller spells out some further implications of this notion.

From Issues of Freedom

Now there is no gainsaying all that we have learned about the physical, physiological, psychological, and social determinants of human behavior. Yet there is no human necessity of gainsaying it, or reason to be simply distressed

From Herbert J. Muller. Issues of freedom, pp. 41-42. Copyright © 1969 by Herbert J. Muller. Reprinted by permission of Harper & Row, Publishers, Inc.

by it. One who believes that man is in some sense a free agent, and hopes that collectively he is still free to make his history, should be the first to welcome all such knowledge. It is valuable knowledge precisely because man can then do something about it, just as he acquired it by his own determination. Having discovered natural laws, he can bend them to his own purposes, as he has triumphantly done through science and technology. Once aware of conditioned reflexes, the drives of the unconscious, the mechanisms of heredity, the compulsions of custom, the tyranny of the past, he can hope to be no longer wholly at their mercy. Early American behaviorists gave the most curious proof of his effective freedom: insisting that his so-called mental activity was absolutely conditioned by mechanical processes—and also insisting that they could so condition a youngster as to make him whatever they had a mind to.

How man can be free in a lawful world may be a metaphysical mystery (though no less mysterious than how he could get his illusion of freedom if his behavior were completely determined). The empirical fact remains that he is able to do a great many things to suit his own purposes. The plain source of this ability is his highly developed brain; intelligence itself is a power of deliberate choice. On biological grounds his powers of mind remain mysterious because they enable him to defy the strongest and most essential of instincts, self-preservation; but again the empirical fact remains that he can determine even to kill himself. If we cannot absolutely prove man's freedom, we can at least find sound reasons for our living belief.

Mailloux's (1953) observation, that only in mentally disturbed persons does the integration between free activity and psychic automatisms break down to the extent that the latter function autonomously, has received some empirical confirmation. If, in his article, we substitue the term "psychotic condition" for "neurotic condition," his conclusion is in agreement with the findings of Baumgold, Temerlin, and Ragland (1965). These investigators asked twenty neurotic, twenty psychotic, and twenty normal subjects to respond to three sets of concepts referring to the determinants of behavior, namely, external or fate concepts, internal and personal (self) concepts, and things having no relation to the determination of behavior (control concepts). No significant differences were found between neurotic and normal subjects. Both typically described **self** as the active agent in behavior, whereas psychotics responded in terms of **fate**. "These results," they say, "are consistent with the idea that the experience of freedom to choose is related to the integrity of the personality as a whole, for they suggest that psychotics experience the most salient determinants of their behavior as external and nonpersonal; in short, as factors other than the preferences and choices of an experienced identity." Rollo May's clinical experience leads him to a similar conclusion.

From Psychology and the Human Dilemma

The data we get from our work with patients in psychotherapy seems to me clearly to support my thesis. When people come for therapy, they typically describe themselves as "driven," unable to know or to choose what they want, and they experience various degrees of dissatisfaction, unhappiness, conflict, and despair. What we find as we begin working with them is that they have blocked off large areas of awareness, are unable to feel or be aware of what their feelings mean in relation to the world. They may think they feel love when actually they only feel sex; or they think they feel sex when they actually wish to be nursed at mother's breast. They will often say in one way or another: "I don't know what I feel; I don't know who I am." In Freud's terms, they have "repressed" significant experiences and capacities of all sorts. The symptomatic results are the wide gamut of conflicts, anxiety, panic and depression.

At the beginning of therapy, thus, they present the picture of *lack* of freedom. The progress of therapy can be gauged in terms of the increase of the patient's capacity to experience the fact he is the one who *has* the world and can be aware of it and move in it. One could define mental health, from one side, as the capacity to be aware of the gap between stimulus and response, together with the capacity to use this gap constructively. Thus, mental health, in my judgment, is on the opposite side of the spectrum from "conditioning" and "control." The progress of therapy can be measured in terms of the progress of "consciousness of freedom."

LAWFUL BEHAVIOR

Another familiar argument directed against the possibility of personal autonomy is that the purpose of science is to discover uniformities in nature. If the human person were free to control some of his actions, invariable laws of behavior as we find in physics and chemistry could never be established. In other words, psychology would not be a true science. The argument stops here, but the implication is that since those who raise it are determined on **a priori** grounds to have a genuine science of behavior, come what may, man **has to be** determined by something other than his own choices. In addition to the fact that a scientist must begin with reality as he finds it rather than attempt to shape it to his wishes, the above assumption is altogether unnecessary. Although no one will ever be able to predict behavior with the accuracy of a physicist, it can be forecast with fair accuracy. In the foregoing selection Mailloux remarks that the freer a person is, the more predictable he becomes because he is less likely to be determined by non-rational processes. In a difficult choice situation he alone can be relied upon to make a logical decision. The closer he approaches the ideal of a fully integrated personality, the smaller the probability that he will be coerced by drives, needs, or defenses. One might say that he is freer to interpret situations as they really are and to act logically and consistently. Freedom in the sense of self-determination does not imply the absence of characteristic patterns of behavior. In addition to the influence of psychic mechanisms and habitual ways of acting previously referred to, the person who is not confused by unresolved conflicts tends to integrate his behavior around a set of goals and values that give direction to his striving. To sum up, free behavior is more "lawful" than behavior coerced by factors other than personal choice and reason.

UNCONSCIOUS MOTIVES AND FREEDOM

So far we have said little about the role of unconscious motivation. How can an act be free when not all the reasons for the choice are known? First of all it should be recognized that the term **unconscious** has several meanings. What it usually implies is that the person is aware of the motive but not of its origin. A neurotic patient may be all too conscious of a compulsion to wash his hands repeatedly. The unconscious element lies in his inability to know **why** he does it. Nuttin (1962) explains that in decision making the origin of the motive is not important. What is critical is its "felt-value" and the way it enters into the choice. Even natural tendencies and needs, exemplified by hunger and thirst, arise from unconscious biological states of the organism. Furthermore, the origin of most likes, whether in food, clothing, or anything else, are not usually clear to the individual. Preferences grow out of a multitude of experiences over too long a period of time to be remembered. In this respect they resemble unconscious motives which are believed to result from the repression of anxiety-producing thoughts and feelings. Although none of the above motives is known in its source, each may play the role of a junior partner in making a decision. Ordinarily unconscious motives manifest themselves as insistent urges, similar to unreasonable preferences or aversions, that may persuade the person to turn a blind eye to certain evidence or cause him to dread coming to any conclusion at all. While this will to a greater or lesser degree influence his choices, it need not rob him of all freedom. Most of us can remember being in such situations—perhaps strongly impelled to buy a car or expensive camera that we could not afford. In spite of powerful emotions urging us to say "yes" it is still possible to say "no." Neither the victim of a "con" man nor a girl who only dimly realizes that she is marrying to escape an unhappy home life has necessarily lost the ability to make an opposite choice.

There are, to be sure, instances where unconscious motives may be so compelling as to overwhelm the individual's capacity for freedom. Many neurotic and psychotic patients behave in such a way as to suggest that control over at least some of their actions has been temporarily suspended. Posthypnotic suggestions provide another example, but even here it is not clear that a subject will carry out ruthless commands if they violate deeply held ethical principles.

Perhaps it would be well to think of human motivation as occupying a continuum between the two poles of coercion and freedom. A surprising amount of behavior, although seemingly spontaneous, is not technically free. Any habitual act tends to run its course mechanically with less and less attention as time goes on. In routine everyday activities when very little is at stake we tend to follow fixed patterns which frequently parallel the path of least resistance. To the extent that we switch to automatic pilot instead of steering a deliberate course, our actions, while characteristic, may not be free. The situation is quite different when a momentous decision is to be made. Typically we then weigh the matter from every vantage point while attempting to compensate for any strong feelings that may be tugging against our better judgment.

Some of the conclusions that psychologists reach have little relevance for everyday living. The verdict that one method of rote learning is superior to another is not likely to shatter anyone's self-concept. Not so with the answer to the question, "Am I capable of deliberate choices, or is freedom an illusion?" One's attitude toward personal responsibility, ego-development, and society in general hinges on his reply. Anyone who believes that personality is not something that just happens to him, as physical growth, who believes that he can within limits become the kind of person he wishes to be, who believes in the possibility of self-actualization, also believes in freedom. Regardless of the terms used or the explanation given, if a human being is able to exert a significant influence over some of his activities by his decision to do so, he is exercising self-determination. Whether this be referred to as soft-determinism or called by any other name is of secondary importance. We would only insist that freedom not be granted by the right hand and then taken away with the left, as, for example, saying that the perceptual field is not originally determined, but once established it coerces behavior.

In this chapter we did not touch upon the principle of homeostasis, which many hard determinists consider to be a substitute for self-determination. It will be discussed in relationship to values in the next chapter.

To anticipate a topic treated in Part Four, it should be noted that all images of man are mental constructions based upon certain kinds of evidence. While each may tell something true about man, no single one gives a comprehensive explanation. Adler (1967, p. 13) is correct in insisting that the problem of man is a mixed one and that scientists must join forces with philosophers in order to unravel the truth about human nature. We might add that they must also take into account the insights of historians, theologians, artists, writers, in short those of every discipline that views man in a different way if the picture is ever to be completed.

SUMMARY

A wide variety of answers have been given to the ever-recurring question, "What is man?" Berelson and Steiner compare the composite behavioral science image of the human being with other images developed by Western thinkers. Allport describes some basic assumptions that result in conflicting models of the person. Not all personality theories fit neatly into any one of his categories. A brief sketch of Rogers' theory was given as an example.

Although the question of human freedom is a very ancient one, it is still much alive today. "Soft" determinists, while admitting that behavior is caused, allow some room for self-determination. "Hard" determinists do not. In spite of the all but overwhelming feeling of freedom, they assume that every human activity is coerced by underlying forces over which the person has no control. The opposite opinion of a number of scholars and their reasons for holding them were presented. The problem of how unconscious motives can coexist with freedom was also explored. Personal responsibility, ego-development, and self-actualization were seen to imply autonomy. Regardless of the name by which it is called or the explanation given, if an individual can, by his

own choosing, influence some of his activities, he is to that extent
capable of self-determination

The task of defining the nature of man is not the sole responsibility of psychologists. Scholars from many fields must contribute to
the effort.

DISCUSSION TOPICS

1 List the characteristics that you believe should be included in a
description of the nature of man.

2 Compare your image of man with those proposed by various
psychologists.

3 Why are the attempts to define humanness usually incomplete?

4 What biases are introduced by the way the question about human
nature is asked, for example, What is man? Who is man? How does man
compare with animals? What does it mean to be human?

5 Why bother with such a theoretical issue as the nature of man?

6 Describe Rogers' (1961) notion of the fully functioning person.

7 How does a healthy self-image develop and how is it maintained
(Hamachek, 1970)?

8 What do you understand by the terms (a) hard determinism, (b)
soft determinism, (c) self-determination?

9 What are the impliations of hard determinism for:
human society in general?
law and morality?
creativity and self-actualization?
psychotherapy?

10 What empirical evidence, if any, is there to confirm either self-
determination or its alternative?

11 Is the problem of freedom a purely scientific matter, a philosophical matter, or an interdisciplinary one?

12 How can the notions of unconscious motivation and personal
freedom be reconciled?

13 What are the main factors that limit self-determination?

14 Police departments can estimate with fair accuracy the number of
cars to be stolen within the following month. Does this fact have any bearing
on the problem of freedom?

15 List the reasons that you find most convincing for the belief you
hold with respect to hard determinism versus self-determination.

ADDITIONAL READINGS

Adler, M. J. **The idea of freedom.** Garden City, N.Y.: Doubleday, 1958. This two-volume work is the first of a series of studies by the Institute of Philosophical Research taking stock of Western thinking about topics of continuing interest.

Allport, G. W. **Becoming.** New Haven, Conn.: Yale University Press, 1955. Dissatisfied with an "empty organism" image of man, Allport looks at what it means to be human.

Bonner, H. The proactive personality. In J. F. T. Bugental (Ed.), **Challenges of humanistic psychology.** New York: McGraw-Hill, 1967. "In this paper I have tried to present as precise a description of the proactive personality as present evidence and discussion permit."

Boring, E. G. When is behavior predetermined? **Scientific Monthly,** 1957, **84,** 189-196. "To get rid of freedom would change our whole civilization. Yet we need not attempt that, for causality is only the form of a model, and freedom is also a model, and we can use our models at will without letting them dominate us."

Bugental, J. F. T. **The search for authenticity.** New York: Holt, Rinehart & Winston, 1965. The first part of this book describes the condition of being human from an existentialist point of view.

Cantril, H. A fresh look at the human design. In J. F. T. Bugental (Ed.). **Challenges of humanistic psychology.** New York: McGraw-Hill, 1967. The author discusses eleven characteristics of human beings.

Chein, I. The image of man. **Journal of Social Issues,** 1962, **18**(4), 1-35. This article describes man as he appears to a humanistic social scientist.

Coleman, J. C. **Psychology and effective behavior** (2d ed.) Glenview, Ill.: Scott, Foresman, 1969. Chapter 1 deals with the problem of man's basic nature.

Frankl, V. E. The concept of man in logotherapy. **Journal of Existentialism,** 1965, **6,** 53-58. "Insofar as logotherapy is concerned its concept of man is based on three pillars: (1) freedom of will; (2) will to meaning; (3) and meaning in life."

Heschel, A. J. **Who is man?** Stanford, Calif.: Stanford University Press, 1965. In this beautifully written book Heschel reflects on the nature of man and his transcendental strivings.

Hitt, W. D. Two models of man. **American Psychologist,** 1969, **24,** 651-658. The author contrasts the behavioristic and phenomenological models debated in a published account of the Rice University symposium sponsored by the APA Division on Philosophical Psychology.

Kelman, H. C. **A time to speak.** San Francisco: Jossey-Bass, 1968. Chapter 1 discusses the manipulation of behavior versus the enhancement of freedom in social research.

Maslow, A. H. **Toward a psychology of being** (Rev. ed.) Princeton, N.J.: Van Nostrand, 1970. Maslow proposed a psychology of self-actualization.

Matson, F. W. **The broken image.** New York: George Braziller, 1970. This brilliant overview of the history of social science shows how exclusive reliance upon methods derived from natural science has dehumanized man's image of himself.

May, R. **Psychology and the human dilemma.** Princeton, N.J.: Van Nostrand, 1967. Part IV deals with the topics of freedom and responsibility.

May, R. **Love and will.** New York: Norton, 1969. A large portion of this book is devoted to freedom and its pathology.

Nuttin, J. **Psychoanalysis and personality** (2d ed.) New York: Sheed & Ward, 1962. (Also published as a Mentor-Omega paperback.) Among other topics, Nuttin treats of the relationship between the unconscious and freedom.

Review of Existential Psychology and Psychiatry, 1961, **1**(3). The entire issue consists of articles on freedom, decision, and responsibility.

Rogers, C. R. A humanistic conception of man. In R. E. Farson (Ed.), **Science and human affairs.** Palo Alto, Calif.: Science and Behavior Books, 1965. Rogers's view of human nature reflects his long experience as a client-centered therapist.

Rosenthal, B. G. **The images of man.** New York: Basic Books, 1971. The broad aspirations and value patterns of Athenian Greece, Italian Renaissance, and the high Middle Ages are presented as guideposts for contemporary psychology in developing a new and more humanistic image of man.

Royce, J. E. **Man and his meaning.** New York: McGraw-Hill, 1969. Chapter II is concerned with a self-determination and its limitations.

Skinner, B. F. **Beyond freedom and dignity.** New York: Knopf, 1971. Skinner's behavioristic image of man contrasts sharply with the one presented in this chapter.

Symposium: Freedom and responsibility—values or not. **The Catholic Psychological Record,** 1966, **4,** 106-129. This symposium was jointly sponsored by ACPA and APA.

Temerlin, M. K. On choice and responsibility in a humanistic psychotherapy. **Journal of Humanistic Psychology,** 1963, **3,** 35-48. ". . . In a humanistic psychotherapy oriented toward the wholeness of the personality the responsibility-avoiding function of defense needs to be thoroughly analyzed, for when defenses reduce responsibility and anxiety, the person pays a high price: a reduction of selfhood."

Went, F. W. The size of man. **American Scientist,** 1968, **56,** 400-413. If man were not precisely the size that he is, culture as we know it would be impossible.

Chapter 6

Personal Values and Commitment

Above all, human wholeness means a capacity for commitment, dedication, passionate concern, and care—a capacity for wholeheartedness, and singlemindedness, for abandon without fear of self-annihilation and loss of identity.

Kenneth Keniston

Charlotte Bühler (1962) observes that everyone is constantly concerned about values. Consciously or unconsciously they are reflected in everything a person does, especially in his choice of goals and objectives. Values so permeate his whole development and personality that they can never be left out of the picture by anyone who wishes to understand human behavior.

Needless to say, such a conception of motivation stresses the image of man as an active instigator of behavior that contrasts sharply with the positivistic and psychoanalytic models described by Allport in Chapter 5. The latter theories rely upon the explanatory principle of homeostasis, or the tendency of an organism to maintain a constant internal state. In general homeostatic mechanisms operate somewhat similar to the thermostat on a furnace. Whenever the temperature varies beyond a certain predetermined range, the heat is automatically turned on or off as required to bring it back to normal.

As applied to motivation, the single homeostatic objective is to achieve a state of minimal tension. The behaviorist tradition speaks in terms of drives such as hunger or thirst. When a person feels this particular form of discomfort he is motivated to seek food or water in order to relieve it. As soon as his hunger or thirst is satisfied, the motivation ceases for the time. What about one's other choices, such as to become a lawyer or to marry a particular person? The behaviorist answer would be that through a long series of conditioned responses such acquired motives have become associated with the reduction of drives which are basically physiological. In spite of the feeling of choosing freely, the built-in tendency to relieve inner tensions ultimately determines one's decisions as inexorably as a thermostat regulates room temperature. Orthodox Freudians apply the principle of homeostasis in a slightly different way but with similar results. In place of drives they substitute inner conflicts among the id, the ego, and the superego as they interact with the environment. The controlling objective of the individual, as conceived by Freud, is to keep such conflicts at a minimum.

Kurt Goldstein was among the first psychologists to point out the shortcomings of the original homeostasis postulate as an explanation of the autonomous and spontaneous functioning of an organism. The discharge of tension may describe the process by which a constant internal state is maintained, but does it account for it? What about change, such as adaptation, growth, and reproduction? Bühler (1959) contends that in place of a single process such as homeostasis we should think in terms of a complex system of activities which can be divided into two general categories. The first group of activities, which can be referred to as need-satisfaction, is concerned with restoring inner equilibrium and energy reserves. The second group is concerned with such functions as the internal organization of the individual. In accordance with these and other biological considerations, she postulates four basic tendencies with corresponding psychological correlates which explain more satisfactorily the cognitive factors that shape one's whole life pattern (Bühler, 1959), and through the years has tested these conclusions using a variety of empirical methods (Bühler, 1965).

As she explains in private correspondence with the author:

Already in my first book (Bühler, 1933) on **The Course of Human Life as a Psychological Problem** I conceived as the ultimate goal "fulfillment." Fulfillment is reached, as I presented perhaps clearest in the coming book of M. Allen and myself, **Introduction to Humanistic Psychology,** by way of need satisfaction and accomplishment. The dynamics in their direction are the four basic tendencies, **need satisfaction, self-limiting adaptation, creative expansion,** and **upholding** the **internal order.** These operate in complementing each other, although they may at times also conflict with each other. Need satisfaction is the fulfillment specifically of psychological and ego needs, but beyond that also is belonging and fitting in, expanding creatively and upholding the inner order (through acting in an organized way as well as in harmony with the own conscience) are ultimately satisfying. Accomplishment is the constructive contribution to the creation of values the individual believes in. They are a constant concern of most individuals (Bühler, 1959). Self-realization on the one hand and dedication on the other are implied in these pursuits.

Another approach to the study of life goals that accounts for the observed facts better than mere tension reduction is known as self-realization (Jung, Horney, and Fromm) or self-actualization (Goldstein, Maslow, and Rogers). Existential psychologists propose a variation on the same theme (May, 1958). The broad scope of these theories with their positive approach to creative activity has much to recommend them. Whether or not they are completely successful will be discussed later.

Rogers' notion of self-actualization was alluded to in the brief description of his theory in Chapter 5. Maslow (1970b, 1968) uses the term with reservation because it might seem to imply selfishness rather than altruism, neglect of duty or dedication to life's task, and a denial of self-transcendence. "It refers to man's desire for self-fulfillment, namely, to the tendency for him to become actualized in what he is potentially. This tendency might be phrased as the desire to become more and more what one idiosyncratically is, to become everything that one is capable of becoming (1970b, p. 46)." In other words he thinks of it as denoting "full-humanness" within the context of a growth psychology.

Maslow's theory is rooted in biology. He emphasizes the notion of instinctoid needs which are innate in human beings and basic in the sense that they must be adequately dealt with in order to maintain psychological health and to achieve the fullest growth. According to their urgency he places them in hierarchical order. Most pressing of all

are the (1) physiological needs, such as those for air, water, food, and
shelter and (2) the safety needs that imply absence of fear, threats, or
physical danger. The needs that follow—(3) belongingness or acceptance
by some group, (4) the desire to love someone and be loved in return,
and (5) esteem or recognition of a person's worth and competence both
by himself and others—are on progressively higher levels. At the top of
the motivational pyramid lie the self-actualization needs which along
with fulfillment include the desire for knowledge as well as aesthetic
and similar values. Maslow (1968, Ch. 3) calls these metaneeds or D
(deficiency) needs which consist in a deprivation of satisfactions in the
areas of safety, belongingness, love, respect, or self-esteem.

    Although the inborn urge to actualize one's inherent potentials is
the most important factor in personality dynamics, it may, to a greater
or lesser degree, be stifled by the clamor of unfilled lower needs. Higher
needs at any level must await the satisfaction of lower ones. A man who
is starving is likely to have very few interests outside of food. A soldier
on the firing line devotes more attention to controlling fear and pre-
serving his life than to perfecting his skills in interpersonal relations.
The individual who perceives himself as unloved and unlovable is less
concerned about full humanness than in escaping the torture of loneliness.

    The degree of psychological health a person enjoys depends upon
the need level at which he typically operates. A life-style geared to the
service of lower needs can never be gratifying. By contrast anyone who
has achieved a feeling of belonging and rootedness, who finds himself
loved and respected, and who enjoys a reasonable sense of self-worth
needs only small amounts of positive feedback from others to quiet
these yearnings. The bulk of his motivation can be directed toward the
metaneeds related to self-actualization.

    To test his observations Maslow (1970b, Ch. 11) made a careful
study of forty-nine persons who exemplified self-fulfillment at its best.
Among the many characteristics that he discovered were a more objective perception of reality; the ability to accept themselves, other
people, and nature; spontaneity; problem-centeredness rather than ego-
centeredness; a positive liking for solitude and privacy; independence;
resistance to overconformity; occasional peak experiences; a deep
feeling of sympathy for all mankind; and more profound interpersonal
relations than other adults.

    In commenting on self-actualization theories in general, Bühler
(1959) notes that in spite of their vast superiority over homeostatic descriptions of motivation, a number of questions remain unanswered. What are the dynamics of this tendency toward self-

fulfillment and how is it related to the individual's biological "groundplan"? Should we seek its origin in conscious or unconscious motivation? Is the notion of "drive" (Goldstein) or "need' (Maslow) too limited to explain such an all-encompassing tendency? In order to achieve fulfillment an individual may have to deny pressing needs and, in extreme circumstances, even forfeit his life. Moreover the notion of self-realization is not confined to the present moment as is the typical drive or need but embraces the whole life as a unit: past, present, and future. How is it related to different levels of adjustment, to maturation, and to development in general? How are conflicts between the divergent tendencies of adaptation and productivity resolved? In short is self-actualization a specific process or is it a name given to a whole group of processes? The question is especially pertinent if self-realization is taken to mean the total development of the individual in an optimal way.

Bühler notes that even those who propose this theory do not seem to consider self-realization as the ultimate objective of human striving. First of all they go one step further and add the notion of fulfillment. In other words, the objective accomplishment of actualizing one's potential appears to be subservient to achieving a more basic goal: a gratifying subjective experience. Furthermore fulfillment refers primarily to the outcome of a process—its satisfactory completion or its incompletion—rather than to the process itself. Whether or not the individual experiences fulfillment or disappointment will depend upon how he evaluates both himself and the present situation. Charlotte Bühler explains how one man's success can be another man's failure.

From Theoretical Observations about Life's Basic Tendencies

This assessment or evaluation as we may now say, means that human beings do not live their lives just as a process, but as a process related to a value and subject to evaluation. In other words, human beings live their lives as self-transcendent, as related to factors outside and beyond the process of life as such.

This factor of human life's self-transcendence has been most strongly emphasized by existentialists. Rollo May (1958), in discussing it, points out the following: First of all, human existence always transcends the present moment and the present situation and brings past and future into the

From Charlotte Bühler. Theoretical observations about life's basic tendencies. American Journal of Psychotherapy, 1959, **13**, 561-581. Reprinted by permission.

immediate presence. Secondly, reason and the use of symbols allow for the human being's conscious self-relatedness. This accounts thirdly for the experience of freedom as well as of conscience. It is a freedom which, as Kurt Goldstein demonstrated, is lost in certain brain-injured cases. Equipped with this freedom, with consciousness, and conscience, man becomes what he makes of himself, as Kierkegaard pointed out.

The postulated goal of life and the goal of psychotherapy on this basis is then that man, having become aware of his existence as well as of his potentialities, would find himself enabled to make of himself what he wanted to be. This he should do according to Tillich (1952), in spite of living "in the grip of doubt and meaninglessness" which is to be accepted with "the courage of despair."

Perhaps this is what man should experience. But is it what he actually does experience?

People the world over and at all times of history have seen fulfillment of life not primarily, or certainly not exclusively, in having become what they wanted to be or what potentially they were able to be; but nearly always also in terms of what they thought they should have become. This "should" has always implied more than fulfillment of potentialities or self-realization. It implied through the history of mankind always the fulfillment of some "law."

This law is experienced by the human mind in terms of values in which he believes and the reasons for these beliefs he projects more often than not into the Universe. Frequently, he says with Einstein: "I cannot believe that God plays dice with the world." He believes in his existence as participating in some generally meaningful process. He may reason that since he is made so as to believe in meaning that this must be part of some all-inclusive meaningfulness outside of him.

If he does not believe in the meaningfulness of his existence in the Universe, man still has always set up moral codes for himself and given his life the meaning of measuring up to these values. These have always represented the consideration of other men, usually with secondary consideration being given to self-realization. Only our Western culture gives it primary concern.

Fulfillment to the healthy individual with a well-rounded personality is to have had "happiness." That is, the fulfillment of the most essential wishes; to have found sufficient self-realization in successful creative accomplishments; to have helped and not been detrimental to the welfare of others; and to have found "peace of mind" in the resultant internal order.

Viktor E. Frankl points out even more forcibly the need of every individual to discover values that will give purpose to his being and focus his energies upon the pursuit of meaningful goals. Enthusiasm and zest for living are not the concomitants of an idle or aimless existence but are by-products of using one's abilities to accomplish something of significant value. What years in a Nazi death camp and his experiences as a clinician has taught Frankl is that life without commitment is as dreary as it is purposeless.

From Address before the Third Annual Meeting of the Academy of Religion and Mental Health, 1962

Ever more frequently psychoanalysts report that they are confronted with a new type of neurosis that is mainly characterized by loss of interest and by lack of initiative. They complain that in such cases conventional psycho-analysis is not effective. Time and again, the psychiatrist is consulted by patients who doubt that life has any meaning. This condition I have called "existential vacuum" (Frankl, 1959). As to the frequency of this phenom-enon I refer to a statistical survey made among my students at the University of Vienna: only 40% of the students (German, Swiss and Austrian) who attend my lectures held in German stated that they knew from their own experience that feeling of ultimate absurdity, while not 40 but 81% of the students (American) who attend my lectures held in English professed to the same experience. From these percentages we must not draw the conclusion that the existential vacuum is predominantly an American disease, but rather that it is apparently a concomitant of industrialization.

The existential vacuum seems to issue from man's twofold loss; the loss of that instinctual security which surrounds an animal's life, and the further, more recent loss of those traditions which governed man's life in former times. At present, instincts do not tell man what he has to do, nor do traditions direct him toward what he ought to do; soon he will not even know what he wants to do and will be led by what other people want him to do, thus completely succumbing to conformism.

Is psychotherapy prepared to deal with the present need? Above all, I consider it dangerous to press man's search for a meaning into stereotype interpretations such as "nothing but defense mechanisms" or "secondary rationalizations." I think that man's quest for, and even his questioning of a meaning to his existence, i.e., his spiritual aspirations as well as his spiritual

From Address of Viktor E. Frankl, M.D., Ph.D., President of Austrian Medical Society for Psychotherapy, and Professor of Neurology and Psychiatry on the Medical Faculty of the University of Vienna, before the Third Annual Meeting of the Academy of Religion and Mental Health, 1962. Universitas, Zeitschrift fur Wissenschaft, Kunst und Literatur (Quarterly English Language Edition), 1962, **5**, 273-286. Wissenschaftliche Verlagsgesellschaft mbH., Stuttgart, W. Germany. Reprinted by permission.

frustrations should be taken at face value and should not be tranquilized or analyzed away. Therefore, I cannot share Freud's (1960) opinion as he stated it in a letter to Princess Bonaparte: "The moment a man questions the meaning and value of life he is sick." I rather think that such a man only proves that he is truly a human being. I remember how my science teacher in high school once explained that life, in the final analysis, was nothing but a process of oxidation. At this I jumped up and passionately asked: "If that is so, then what meaning does life have?" It might well be that with this question I actualized spiritual self-hood for the first time. . . .

Professor Tweedie (1961) in his book on logotherapy jokingly makes the following distinction: "In psychoanalysis the patient lies on a couch and tells the analyst things which are disagreeable to say; in logotherapy he sits in a chair and is told things which are disagreeable to hear. . . ." In logotherapy the patient is, indeed, confronted with meanings and purposes and is challenged to fulfill them. At this point the question might be raised whether the patient is not overburdened with such a confrontation. However, in the age of the existential vacuum, the danger lies much more in man's not being burdened enough. Pathology does not only result from stress but also from relief of stress which ends in emptiness. Lack of tension as it is created by the loss of meaning is as dangerous a threat in terms of mental health as is too high a tension. Tension is not something to be avoided indiscriminately. Man does not need homeostasis at any cost, but rather a sound amount of tension such as that which is aroused by the demanding quality (Aufforderungs-charakter) inherent in the meaning for human existence. Like iron filings in a magnetic field, man's life is put in order through his orientation toward meaning. Thereby a field of tension is established between what man is and what he ought to do. In this field existential dynamics, as I call it, is operating (Frankl, 1961). By this dynamics man is rather pulled than pushed; instead of being determined by meaning, he decides whether his life is to be structured by the demanding character of a meaning for his existence.

It is a tenet of logotherapy that meaning can be found in life not only through acting or through experiencing values, but also through suffering. This is why life never ceases to have and to retain a meaning to the very last moment. Even facing an ineluctable fate, e.g., an incurable disease, there is still granted to man a chance to fulfill even the deepest possible meaning. What matters is, then, the stand he takes in his predicament. Life can be made meaningful 1. by what we give to the world in terms of our creation; 2. by what we take from the world in terms of our experience; and 3. by the stand we take toward the world, that is to say, by the attitude we choose toward suffering.

Let me illustrate what I mean; an elderly general practitioner once consulted me because of his severe depression. He could not overcome the loss of his wife whom he had loved above all and who had died two years before. How could I help him? What should I tell him? Instead of telling him anything, I asked him: "Doctor, what would have happened if you had died first and your wife would have had to survive you?" "Oh," he said, "for her this would have been terrible; how she would have suffered!" Whereupon I replied: "You see, doctor, she was spared such a suffering, and you are sparing her this suffering; but now you have to pay for it by surviving and mourning her." He said nothing but shook my hand and calmly left my office. Somehow suffering ceases to be suffering when it finds a meaning— such as here the meaning of a sacrifice.

Of course, this was no therapy in the proper sense since first of all his despair was no disease, and secondly I could not change his fate, I could not revive his wife. But I at least succeeded in changing his attitude toward his unalterable fate so that from this time on he could at least see a meaning to his suffering. Logotherapy insists that man's main concern is not to seek pleasure or to avoid pain, but rather to find a meaning to his life. Thus we saw that man is ready to suffer if only he can be satisfied that his suffering has a meaning.

As logotherapy teaches, human freedom is in no way a freedom from conditions but rather the freedom to take a stand toward conditions. There-fore, choosing a stand toward suffering means exerting freedom. In doing so, man, in a sense, transcends the world and his predicament therein. Let me try to illustrate this with an experience I had during my first days at the concentration camp in Auschwitz. The odds of surviving there were no more than one in twenty. Not even the manuscript of a book which I had hidden in my coat seemed likely ever to be rescued. This manuscript was the first version of my book, The Doctor and the Soul: An Introduction to Logo-therapy, that was later, in 1955, published by Alfred A. Knopf in New York. At the concentration camp I had to surrender my clothes with the manu-script. Thus I had to overcome the loss of my spiritual child, as it were, and had to face the question whether this loss did not make my life void of meaning. An answer to this question was given to me soon: in exchange for my clothes I was given the rags of an inmate who had already been sent to the gas chamber; in a pocket I found a single page torn from a Hebrew prayer book. It contained the main Jewish prayer Shema Yisrael, i.e., the command "Love thy God with all thy heart, and with all thy soul, and with all thy might," or, as one might interpret it as well, the command to say yes to life despite whatever one has to face, be it suffering or even dying. A life, I told myself, whose meaning stands or falls on whether one can publish a manu-script ultimately would not be worth living. Thus I saw in that single page which replaced the many pages of my manuscript a symbolic call henceforth to live my thoughts instead of merely putting them on paper. . . . In contrast to those existential writers who declare that man has to stand the ultimate absurdity of being human, it is my contention that man has to stand only his incapacity to grasp the ultimate meaning on intellectual grounds. Man is only called upon to decide between the alternatives "ultimate absurdity or ultimate meaning" on existential grounds, through the mode of existence which he chooses. In the "How" of existence, I would say, lies the answer to the question for its "Why."

Thus, the ultimate meaning is no longer a matter of intellectual cognition but of existential commitment. One might as well say that a meaning can be understood but the ultimate meaning must be interpreted. An interpretation, however, involves a decision. Reality is intrinsically ambiguous since it admits of a variety of interpretations. Man, in choosing one of these interpretations, finds himself in a situation similar to the one in a projective test. To illustrate this, let me relate the following experience.

Shortly before the United States entered World War II, I was called to the American Consulate in Vienna to receive my immigration visa. My old parents expected me to leave Austria as soon as the visa was given. However, in the last moment I hesitated: the question beset me whether I should leave my parents. One knew that any day they could be taken to a concentration camp. Shouldn't I stay with them? While pondering this question I found that this was the type of dilemma which made one wish for a hint from heaven. It was then that I noticed a piece of marble lying on a table at home. When I asked my father about it he explained that he had found it on the site where the National Socialists had burned down the largest Viennese synagogue. My father had taken this marble piece home because it was a part of the tables which contained the Ten Commandments. The piece showed one engraved and gilded Hebrew letter. My father explained that this letter is the abbreviation for only one of the Commandments. Eagerly I asked, "Which one is it?" The answer was: "Honor father and mother, and you will dwell in the land." So I stayed with father and mother in the land and decided to let the American visa lapse.

That I acknowledged this piece of marble as a hint from heaven might well be the expression that already long before, in the depth of my heart, I had decided to stay. I only projected this decision into the appearance of the marble piece. Much the same way would it be self-expression if one saw nothing but $CaCO_3$ in it—although I would call this rather a projection of an existential vacuum. . . .

Man cannot avoid decisions. Reality inescapably forces man to decide. Man makes decisions in every moment, even unwittingly and against his will. Through these decisions man decides upon himself. Continually and incessantly he shapes and reshapes himself. Thomas Aquinas' *agere sequitur esse* is but half the truth: man not only behaves according to what he is, he also becomes what he is according to how he behaves. Man is not a thing among

others—things are determining each other—but man is ultimately self-determining. What he becomes—within the limits of endowment and environment—he has made himself. In the living laboratories of the concentration
camps we watched comrades behaving like swine while others behaved like
saints. Man has both these potentialities within himself. Which one he
actualizes depends on decisions, not on conditions. It is time that this
decision character of human existence be included into the definition of man.
Our generation has come to know man as he really is: the being that has
invented the gas chambers of Auschwitz—and also the being who entered
those gas chambers upright, the Lord's prayer or the Shema Yisrael on his
lips.

SUMMARY

The theory of human motivation based on homeostasis does not do
justice to man's constant concern for values. Bühler postulates an additional group of activities which describe more fully the conscious
factors involved in goal setting. Self-actualization theories, illustrated
by Maslow's, were discussed and some limitations noted. Frankl finds
that the individual who experiences enthusiasm and zest in living is the
one who has fully committed himself to a set of meaningful values.

DISCUSSION TOPICS

1 Cite the reasons for and against considering self-actualization the
primary goal of human striving.
2 Discuss the need of commitment to a definite set of values.
3 Sketch the dynamics of mental health and mental illness in Horney's
self-actualization theory. (See Additional Readings.)
4 Compare the approaches of Bühler (1962, 1967) and Frankl (see
Additional Readings) to the study of human motivation.
5 How in Mowrer's (1961) view does morality enter into the picture?
6 Comment on Erikson's (1964) theory of identity.
7 List your own life goals in hierarchical order.

ADDITIONAL READINGS

Bühler, C. & Massarik, F. (Eds.) **The course of human life.** New York:
     Springer, 1968. "A study of life goals in the humanistic perspective."
Frankl, V. E. **Psychotherapy and existentialism.** New York: Washington
     Square Press, 1967. ". . . an adequate view of man can only properly be
     formulated when it goes beyond homeostasis, beyond self-actualization
     to that sphere of human existence in which man chooses what he will

do and what he will become in the midst of an objective world of meaning and value (Ch. 3)."

Fromm, E. Values, psychology, and human existence. In A. H. Maslow (Ed.), **New knowledge in human values.** New York: Harper & Row, 1959. Since values are rooted in the conditions of human existence we can establish values that have objective validity.

Glasser, W. Reality therapy. In O. H. Mowrer (Ed.), **Morality and mental health.** Chicago: Rand McNally, 1967. "Reality therapy, therefore, is a way in which an irresponsible man can be helped toward facing his values and learning to live responsibly and hopefully happily."

Goldstein, K. Health as a value. In A. H. Maslow (Ed.), **New knowledge in human values.** New York: Harper & Row, 1959. "Value is not a characteristic which is secondarily ascribed to something from judgments based on concepts externally determined. Value is a characteristic of the true being of man. . . ."

Horney, K. **Neurosis and human growth: The struggle toward self-realization.** New York: Norton, 1950. The author identifies and describes many of the factors that obstruct self-growth.

Huber, J. **Through an Eastern window.** Boston: Houghton Mifflin, 1965 (also published as a Bantam paperback). An American psychologist describes an enduring experience of self-transcendence achieved through Zen meditation.

Kluckhohn, C., et al. **A selected bibliography on values, ethics, and aesthetics in behavioral sciences and philosophy, 1920-1958.** New York: Free Press, 1959.

Maslow, A. H. (Ed.) **New Knowledge in human values.** New York: Harper & Row, 1959. "This volume springs from the belief, first, that the ultimate disease of our time is valuelessness; second, that this state is more crucially dangerous than ever before in history; and finally, that something can be done about it by man's own rational efforts."

May, R. **Man's search for himself.** New York: Norton, 1953. ". . . on the deepest level, the question of which age we live in is irrelevant. The basic question is how the individual, in his own awareness of himself and the period he lives in, is able through his decisions to attain inner freedom and to live according to his own inner integrity."

Mowrer, O. H. (Ed.) **Morality and mental health.** Chicago: Rand McNally, 1967. This collection of essays stresses the direct relationship between wholesome personality and ethical living.

Scheibe, K. E. **Beliefs and values.** New York: Holt, 1970. Many recent psychological studies in these areas are reviewed.

Smith, M. B. **Social psychology and human values.** Chicago: Aldine, 1969. Chapter 7 deals with personal values in social-psychological research.

Is the Human Species Unique?

It is exactly when we do regard man as an animal that we know he is not an animal.

G. K. Chesterton

Popular interest in the problem of animal intelligence is currently undergoing a revival. Experiments designed to test whether subhuman species are capable of using abstract symbols in a meaningful way have placed new emphasis on the age-old question, "Do animals possess an elementary form of human intelligence?" Since the publication of Darwin's **Origin of the Species,** many scientists have tended to answer this question in the affirmative. If man has evolved from more primitive organisms, then it would seem necessary to postulate gradually attenuating versions of all his abilities in the animal forms below him on the tree of life.

Teilhard de Chardin (1965) disagrees with this conclusion. On the basis of fossil evidence he points to the existence of several so-called thresholds which produced some discontinuity in evolution. One example is the transformation of inanimate matter into primitive plants. While every living organism contains a variety of chemical elements, simple physical and chemical forces can in no way account for such highly integrated life processes as growth and reproduction. What seems to have happened is that an inner reorganization of matter occurred at such depth that the resulting species can no longer be fully explained in terms of their antecedents but only in terms of a new internal unity.

Mankind passed through such a threshold in the transition from an anthropoid form to a human being. The distinctive characteristic that sets him apart from all his vertebrate cousins is self-reflective thought—the ability to analyze his conscious experience and to use it as a source of abstract knowledge. When other writers maintain that it is the ability to use symbols that sets man apart from other animals they are, in effect, saying the same thing. The absence of self-reflective thought forces subhuman species to rely exclusively upon concrete signs which lack some of the characteristics of genuine symbols. Bertalanffy (1965) defines symbols as special kinds of signs which have the following properties: (1) They are freely created rather than im- posed from without as in the case of conditioning or the natural con- nection between fire and being burned. (2) They are representative as illustrated by language with its vocabulary and grammar. And finally (3) they are transmitted by tradition. The last criterion is helpful in distinguishing human speech from animal communication. One or the other criterion may be found in animal behavior, but not all three together.

In defining man's uniqueness Bertalanffy speaks in terms of the ability to use symbols rather than conceptual language as we do in this chapter. Among his reaons are (1) that symbolism is not confined to language but is a much broader term and (2) that ". . . language is a highly developed form of symbolism rooted in deeper and more primi- tive layers where the junction between subhuman and human behavior may possibly be found." Because of the interest aroused by recent ex- periments in teaching language to chimpanzees, which will be reviewed later, we will approach the problem from the language point of view.

Conceptual language belongs to a different level of discourse than the mere expression of emotional states or types of animal communica- tion that link certain sounds or actions with definite behavior patterns. A pet dog may bark excitedly and wag his tail as his master begins to prepare his food dish. Obviously he knows that he is about to be fed. Past associations of the sight and sound of a certain ritual preceding the taste of food and the relief of hunger pangs cause him to expect that one set of circumstances will follow the other. There is no need to assume that the dog understands the idea of food in the same way his master does. His behavior can be better described as a concrete attitude which English and English (1958) define as a tendency to react to the immediately given object or situation in terms of sensory impressions rather than abstract relationships. Because our own mental processes do not usually stop here but go on to analyze the situation in more general terms, we may mistakenly attribute a human type of knowing to animals. A good example is the conclusion that Fields (1932) drew from his studies in concept formation. He conditioned a group of rats to respond to triangular stimuli in preference to other shapes. When the response was well established, his animals reacted correctly not only to the triangular shapes used during training but also to others they had not previously seen. Fields concluded that these animals had grasped the concept of triangularity. It would be much simpler to explain their knowledge in terms of visual experiences and concrete imagery. A one-to-one relationship between a triangular object and some behavior pattern such as a right or left turn in a maze does not presuppose an understanding of what a triangle is. A knowledge that this particular sensory impression or image goes with that definite motor reaction is all that is needed. The nature of genuine universal concepts will be discussed in Chapter 13.

At the same time it must be admitted that something equivalent to abstraction takes place at the concrete level. Generalization of stimuli occurs in conditioning because an animal is able to isolate certain sensory qualities of the stimulus object. In Fields' experiment it was the three-sided shape. Similarly a cat needs never to have seen a white mouse to know that it would make a good dinner. Although the domestic mouse differs in several respects from the wild variety, there is still enough similarity for the cat to recognize it as a favorite prey.

Ernst Cassirer (1944) defines man as an **animal symbolicum.** In pointing up the similarities and dissimilarities between human language and animal communication, he dwells at length on the difference between signs and signals, on the one hand, and symbolic thought and human language, on the other.

From An Essay on Man

For the sake of a clear statement of the problem we must carefully distinguish between *signs* and *symbols*. That we find rather complex systems of signs and signals in animal behavior seems to be an ascertained fact. We may even say that some animals, especially domesticated animals, are extremely

From **An essay on man** by Ernst Cassirer, pp. 31-35. Copyright © 1944 by the Yale University Press. Reprinted by permission.

susceptible to signs.[1] A dog will react to the slightest changes in the behavior of his master; he will even distinguish the expressions of a human face or the modulations of a human voice.[2] But it is a far cry from these phenomena to an understanding of symbolic and human speech. The famous experiments of Pavlov prove only that animals can easily be trained to react not merely to direct stimuli but to all sorts of mediate or representative stimuli. A bell, for example, may become a "sign for dinner," and an animal may be trained not to touch its food when this sign is absent. But from this we learn only that the experimenter, in this case, has succeeded in changing the food-situation of the animal. He has complicated this situation by voluntarily introducing into it a new element. All the phenomena which are commonly described as conditioned reflexes are not merely very far from but even opposed to the essential character of human symbolic thought. Symbols—in the proper sense of this term—cannot be reduced to mere signals. Signals and symbols belong to two different universes of discourse: a signal is a part of the physical world of being; a symbol is a part of the human world of meaning. Signals are "operators"; symbols are "designators" (Thorndike, 1911). Signals, even when understood and used as such, have nevertheless a sort of physical or substantial being; symbols have only a functional value. . . . In the case of the higher animals it became clear that they were able to solve rather difficult problems and that these solutions were not brought about in a merely mechanical way, by trial and error. As Koehler points out, the most striking difference exists between a mere chance solution and a genuine solution, so that the one can easily be distinguished from the other. That at least some of the reactions of the higher animals are not merely a product of chance but

[1] This susceptibility has, for instance, been proved in the famous case of "clever Hans" which a few decades ago created something of a sensation among psychobiologists. Clever Hans was a horse which appeared to possess an astounding intelligence. He could even master rather complicated arithmetical problems, extract cube roots, and so on, stamping on the ground as many times as the solution of the problem required. A special committee of psychologists and other scientists was called on to investigate the case. It soon became clear that the animal reacted to certain involuntary movements of its owner. When the owner was absent or did not understand the question, the horse could not answer it.

[2] To illustrate this point I should like to mention another very revealing example. The psychobiologist, Dr. Pfungst, who had developed some new and interesting methods for the study of animal behavior, once told me that he had received a letter from a major about a curious problem. The major had a dog which accompanied him on his walks. Whenever the master got ready to go out the animal showed signs of great joy and excitement. But one day the major decided to try a little experiment. Pretending to go out, he put on his hat, took his cane, and made the customary preparations—without, however, any intention of going for a walk. To his great surprise the dog was not in the least deceived; he remained quietly in his corner. After a brief period of observation Dr. Pfungst was able to solve the mystery. In the major's room there was a desk with a drawer which contained some valuable and important documents. The major had formed the habit of rattling this drawer before leaving the house in order to make sure that it was safely locked. He did not do so the day he did not intend to go out. But for the dog this had become a signal, a necessary element of the walk situation. Without this signal the dog did not react.

guided by insight appears to be incontestable (Koehler, 1956). If by intelligence we understand either adjustment to the immediate environment or adaptive modification of environment, we must certainly ascribe to animals a comparatively highly developed intelligence. It must also be conceded that not all animal actions are governed by the presence of an immediate stimulus. The animal is capable of all sorts of detours in its reactions. It may learn not only to use implements but even to invent tools for its purposes. Hence some psychobiologists do not hesitate to speak of a creative or constructive imagination in animals (Yerkes & Yerkes, 1929). But neither this intelligence nor this imagination is of the specifically human type. In short, we may say that the animal possesses a practical imagination and intelligence whereas man alone has developed a new form: *a symbolic imagination and intelligence.*

Moreover, in the mental development of the individual mind the transition from one form to the other—from a merely practical attitude to a symbolic attitude—is evident. But here this step is the final result of a slow and continuous process. By the usual methods of psychological observation it is not easy to distinguish the individual stages of this complicated process. There is, however, another way to obtain full insight into the general character and paramount importance of this transition. Nature itself has here, so to speak, made an experiment capable of throwing unexpected light upon the point in question. We have the classical cases of Laura Bridgman[3] and Helen Keller, two blind deaf-mute children, who by means of special methods learned to speak. Although both cases are well known and have often been treated in psychological literature, I must nevertheless remind the reader of them once more because they contain perhaps the best illustration of the general problem with which we are here concerned. Mrs. Sullivan, the teacher of Helen Keller, has recorded the exact date on which the child really began to understand the meaning and function of human language. I quote her own words:

> I must write you a line this morning because something very important has happened. Helen has taken the second great step in her education. She has learned that *everything has a name, and that the manual alphabet is the key to everything she wants to know.*
>   . . . This morning, while she was washing, she wanted to know the name for "water." When she wants to know the name of anything, she points to it and pats my hand. I spelled "w-a-t-e-r" and thought no more about it until after breakfast. . . . [Later on] we went out to the pump house, and I made Helen hold her mug under the spout while I

[3] For Laura Bridgman see Maud Howe and Florence Howe Hall, *Laura Bridgman* (Boston, 1903); Mary Smith Lamson, *Life and Education of Laura Dewey Bridgman* (Boston, 1881); Wilhelm Jerusalem, *Laura Bridgman. Erziehung einer Taubstumm-Glinden* (Berlin, 1905).

pumped. As the cold water gushed forth, filling the mug, I spelled
"w-a-t-e-r" in Helen's free hand. The word coming so close upon the
sensation of cold water rushing over her hand seemed to startle her. She
dropped the mug and stood as one transfixed. A new light came into
her face. She spelled "water" several times. Then she dropped on the
ground and asked for its name and pointed to the pump and the trellis
and suddenly turning round she asked for my name. I spelled
"teacher." All the way back to the house she was highly excited, and
learned the name of every object she touched, so that in a few hours
she had added thirty new words to her vocabulary. The next morning
she got up like a radiant fairy. She has flitted from object to object,
asking the name of everything and kissing me for very gladness. . . .
Everything must have a name now. Wherever we go, she asks eagerly for
the names of things she has not learned at home. She is anxious for her
friends to spell, and eager to teach the letters to everyone she meets.
She drops the signs and pantomime she used before, as soon as she has
words to supply their place, and the acquirement of a new word affords
her the liveliest pleasure. And we notice that her face grows more
expressive each day.[4]

The decisive step leading from the use of signs and pantomime to the use
of words, that is, of symbols, could scarcely be described in a more striking
manner. What was the child's real discovery at this moment? Helen Keller had
previously learned to combine a certain thing or event with a certain sign of
the manual alphabet. A fixed association had been established between these
things and certain tactile impressions. But a series of such associations, even if
they are repeated and amplified, still does not imply an understanding of
what human speech is and means. In order to arrive at such an understanding
the child had to make a new and much more significant discovery. It had to
understand that *everything has a name*—that the symbolic function is not
restricted to particular cases but is a principle of *universal* applicability which
encompasses the whole field of human thought. In the case of Helen Keller
this discovery came as a sudden shock. She was a girl seven years of age who,
with the exception of defects in the use of certain sense organs, was in an
excellent state of health and possessed of a highly developed mind. By the
neglect of her education she had been very much retarded. Then, suddenly,
the crucial development takes place. It works like an intellectual revolution.
The child begins to see the world in a new light. It has learned the use of
words not merely as mechanical signs or signals but as an entirely new
instrument of thought. A new horizon is open up, and henceforth the child
will roam at will in this incomparably wider and freer area.

[4] See Helen Keller, *The Story of My Life* (Doubleday, Page & Co., 1902, 1903),
Supplementary Account of Helen Keller's Life and Education, pp. 315ff.

When Cassirer speaks of a fixed association between signs and objects, we need not visualize anything as unvarying as the presence of smoke where there is flame. This is evident from his review of the Koehler and Kohts experiments later in the essay. What he is referring to here is the association of sensory impressions with objects or situations that does not include an understanding of their inner meaning.

The discovery of Helen Keller that made possible her transition from the use of words as signs to their use as genuine speech symbols seems relevant in evaluating some current attempts to teach language to chimpanzees (Gardner & Gardner, 1969a, 1969b; Premack, 1970a, 1970b, 1971). The Gardners have taught their subject, Washoe, a large number of American sign language signals which she spontaneously uses, often in combination. Premack took a different approach. He mounted plastic pieces of various shapes on metal bases which will adhere to a magnetic language board. These he calls "words." Soon his chimpanzee, Sarah, learned that placing a blue plastic triangle on the magnetic board would be rewarded by a piece of apple, a red square by a banana, and so on. Next the animal was required to use two "words"—the name of the donor and the fruit, such as, "Mary apple." Eventually it was able to place in proper order on the board the cutouts representing "Mary give apple Sarah."

In order to determine whether Sarah could answer questions, Premack taught her to place a piece of plastic which he designated as "same" between two objects that were identical and one he designated "different" between two things that were unlike. When the chimpanzee used the markers appropriately Premack concluded that she was answering the question, "What is the relation between the two objects— are they the same or different?" He then introduced a question mark and varied the procedure.

There can be no doubt about the existence of a question in the trainer's mind—the critical issue is what went on in the chimpanzee's brain? Did Sarah realize that a query was being addressed to her about information she possessed, or was she merely using markers as signs in the sense discussed above? An analysis of the training procedure seems to favor the latter assumption. The basic operation consisted in one-to-one substitution. Each new "word" was introduced at a marked location as the only unknown in a series of other plastic pieces that were familiar. One-to-one substitution was adopted as the simplest procedure because it gave a clue to "(1) which words to use and how many, (2) where to put the words in the string, and (3) which operations to use— simply addition, or rearrangement and deletion as well" (Premack, 1971). Such a procedure should maximize an animal's ability to make concrete associations, and perhaps test the ceiling of its capacity to operate at this level. It does not furnish evidence of the quality of understanding that is universal in applicability and as abstract and versatile as speech symbols are known to be. Neither does the fact that the animal continues to make approximately one error in five trials favor the assumption that it grasps the inner meaning of situations. One indication of insight in problem solving is the ability to repeat a performance with few if any mistakes.

What is said here applies also to other markers which, in the experimenter's mind, stand for "name of," "and," plural number, "is," quantifiers such as "all" or "none," and the logical connective, "if-then." While it is surprising that an animal can respond correctly to as many markers as "Sarah take apple ⊃ Mary give Sarah chocolate." the symbol ⊃ may merely mean to the chimpanzee that getting an apple and chocolate go together—the sign for a concrete association between two events—not necessarily an understanding of the logical connective, "if-then."

Cassirer notes that even in sensation an ogranism is conscious of a variety of relationships. It is not, however, mere awareness of relationships that indicates the presence of abstract thinking but an understanding of them **as relationships.**

From An Essay on Man

The mere awareness of relations cannot, therefore, be regarded as a specific feature of human consciousness. We do find, however, in man a special type of relational thought which has no parallel in the animal world. In man an ability to isolate relations—to consider them in their abstract meaning—has developed. In order to grasp this meaning man is no longer dependent upon concrete sense data, upon visual, auditory, tactile, kinesthetic data. He considers these relations "in themselves" as Plato said. Geometry is the classic example of this turning point in man's intellectual life. Even in elementary geometry we are not bound to the apprehension of concrete individual figures. We are not concerned with physical things or perceptual objects, for we are studying universal spatial relations for whose expression we have an adequate symbolism. Without the preliminary step of human language such an achievement would not be possible. In all the tests which have been made of the processes of abstraction or generalization in animals, this point has become evident. Koehler succeeded in showing the ability of chimpanzees to respond to the *relation* between two or more objects instead of to a particular

From Ernest Cassirer, **An essay on man.** New Haven, Conn.: Yale University Press, 1944, pp. 38-39. Reprinted by permission.

object. Confronted by two food-containing boxes, the chimpanzee by reason of previous general training would constantly choose the larger—even though the particular object selected might in a previous experiment have been rejected as the smaller of the pair. Similar capacity to respond to the nearer object, the brighter, the bluer, rather than to a particular box was demonstrated. Koehler's results were confirmed and extended by later experiments. It could be shown that the higher animals are capable of what has been called the "isolation of perceptual factors." They have the potentiality for singling out a particular perceptual quality of the experimental situation and reacting accordingly. In this sense animals are able to abstract color from size and shape or shape from size and color. In some experiments made by Mrs. Kohts a chimpanzee was able to select from a collection of objects varying extremely in visual qualities those which had some one quality in common; it could, for instance, pick out all objects of a given color and place them in a receiving box. These examples seem to prove that the higher animals are capable of that process which Hume in his theory of knowledge terms making a *"distinction of reason."*[1] But all the experimenters engaged in these investigations have also emphasized the rarity, the rudimentariness, and the imperfection of these processes. Even after they have learned to single out a particular quality and to reach toward this, animals are liable to all sorts of curious mistakes.[2] If there are certain traces of a *distinctio rationis* in the animal world, they are, as it were, nipped in the bud. They cannot develop because they do not possess that invaluable and indeed indispensable aid of human speech, of a system of symbols.

Premack has broadened the original Koehler and Kohts experiments on size, color, and shape by training a chimpanzee to associate these isolated perceptual factors with plastic markers. He then treats them as class concepts rather than sensory elements. In terms of the foregoing discussion, what he does it to mistake signs for authentic symbols.

As in the case of animal intelligence, the term **language** can also be defined in such a way as to maximize the similarities and to obscure the difference across species. To call Sarah's plastic "word" communication a genuine conceptual language is questionable at best. In spite of the fact that she rapidly and easily mastered the operations required of her in the laboratory, none of the careful studies of anthropoids in the wild state has discovered even the beginnings of a true language system. The absence of any animal culture approximating that of the most

[1] Hume's theory of the "distinction of reason" is explained in his *Treatise of Human Nature*, Pt. 1, sec. 7 (London, Green and Grose, 1874), 1, 332 ff.
[2] Examples are given by Yerkes (1943) in *Chimpanzees*, pp. 103 ff.

primitive human beings also points in the same direction. Without a conceptual language and something significant to say, noninstinctual social institutions would be impossible.

THE UNIQUE CHARACTERISTICS OF HUMAN LANGUAGE

Richard Ohmann (1969) discusses a simple technique to illustrate in a dramatic fashion the unique characteristics of human speech. The demonstration consists in showing to twenty-five persons the picture of a bear using a telephone with a tourist waiting outside and asking each to describe the situation in one sentence. Since speech is not determined in a rigid way by any given set of circumstances, the subjects have no need of prior associations with the scene in order to describe it, and no two descriptions are likely to be identical. Using a computer to determine all the permissible combinations and permutations of vocabulary and structures typically supplied in twenty-five responses, one finds that there are approximately 19.8 billion different ways of describing this single situation, and we might add, the average individual is likely to be able to understand every one of them. "When we reflect," Ohmann comments, "that the number of seconds in a century is only 3.2 billion, it is clear that no speaker has heard, read, or spoken more than a tiny fraction of the sentences he **could** speak or understand, and that no one learns English by learning any particular sentences of English. What speakers **have** learned is a grammar. And the examples show one requirement we must make of a grammar: that it be capable of generating an infinite number of grammatical sentences." Even the illiterate or feebleminded person must be able to distinguish intuitively between sentences and nonsentences which differ only slightly in construction. The examples Ohmann gives are:

> Got he a chance?
> Does he have a chance?
> The accident was seen by thousands.
> The accident was looked by thousands.

The vast chasm between conceptual language and animal communication becomes even more apparent when we compare Premack's training of Sarah with the way a child learns to speak. Instead of being conditioned to associate a series of concrete signs in a fixed manner so that there is only one unfamiliar item at a time, the child hears a welter of words, phrases, and meaningful and unmeaningful sentences. From these he must construct a theory of language that will enable him not only to speak but, in the years ahead, to understand billions of sentences which he has never before encountered. And the child does this regardless of the language to which he is exposed. Ohmann (1969) speculates that there must be some special innate ability to account for such creative and rapid learning of language. From what has been said above we would maintain that at the basis of it all is the capacity for self-reflective consciousness which makes possible the use of symbolism.

SUMMARY

Although the theory of evolution would seem to presuppose a quantitative rather than a qualitative difference between mankind and lower animals, this is not necessarily true. Certain steplike progressions in the process of evolution have been postulated which could account for man's unique capacity for self-reflective thinking and his use of symbolism.

Conceptual language differs from animal communication in that it involves the capacity for dealing with abstract as well as concrete relationships. Bertalanffy analyzes the nature of symbols and proposes three criteria for identifying them. Cassirer distinguishes symbols from signs, using the example of Helen Keller's discovery that everything has a name.

Two current attempts to teach language to chimpanzees were cited. In our opinion these fail to establish the presence of a true conceptual language at the subhuman level. The fact that chimpanzees in the wild have not developed a true language or anything approaching a primitive human culture reinforces this conclusion. By means of a simple technique, Ohmann demonstrates the all but infinite complexity and the uniqueness of human language which a child learns in a manner that has little in common with conditioning. We concluded that, to account for these observations, man must possess a special capacity not shared by lower animals.

DISCUSSION TOPICS

1 Discuss the characteristics of human language outlined by Ohmann (1969) and by Bronowski and Bellugi. (See Additional Readings below.)

2 Compare the main features of conceptual language and animal communication.

3 Contrast the way a child learns language with Premack's training of Sarah.

4 What is implied by the terms **word, sentence,** and **meaning?** Are your answers in agreement or disagreement with Premack's operational use of these terms?

5 Explain the nature of symbols and distinguish between symbols and signs.

6 If a true concept is a symbol and a mental image a sign, how does an idea differ from an image?

7 Compare human and animal cultures.

8 Comment on how the Clever-Hans effect (see the Additional Reading by Pfungst) might apply to other attempts to teach language to animals.

ADDITIONAL READINGS

Adler, M. J. **The difference of man and the difference it makes.** New York: Holt, Rinehart & Winston, 1967. (Also available in paperback from the World Publishing Co.) In this carefully reasoned discussion of the difference between animals and man, Adler first clarifies the issues and then critically evaluates the empirical and philosophical evidence that is available.

Bellugi, U. Learning the language. **Psychology Today,** 1970, **4**(7), 32-35 & 66. In learning language a child discovers certain regularities, analyzes them at progressively deeper levels, and arrives at generalizations which he applies in speaking. These factors are more basic than imitation and reinforcement.

Bronowski, J., & Bellugi, U. Language, name, and concept. **Science,** 1970, **168,** 669-673. A chimpanzee shares in rudimentary form some of the abilities necessary for the acquisition of knowledge, but not all. When compared with a child who is learning to speak, the animal's deficiencies become apparent.

Fellenbaum, S. Psycholinguistics. In P. H. Mussen & M. R. Rosenzweig (Eds.), **Annual review of psychology,** Palo Alto, Calif.: Annual Reviews, 1971. A masterful review of the current literature in this area, including the question of animal language is found in this chapter.

Fossey, D. Making friends with mountain gorillas. **National Geographic Magazine,** 1970, **137,** 48-67. Inspired by Jane van Lawick Goodall's study of chimpanzees in their native habitat, Miss Fossey spent many months in Africa carefully observing the behavior of mountain gorillas.

Hayes, C. **The ape in our house.** New York: Harper & Row, 1951. This book records the classic study of a chimpanzee raised in the home of a husband-wife psychologist team.

Royce, J. R. (Ed.) **Psychology and the symbol**. New York: Random House, 1965. The papers in this excellent interdisciplinary symposium were originally presented at the 1962 annual meeting of the Western Psychological Association.

Spuhler, J. N. (Ed.) **The evolution of man's capacity for culture.** Detroit: Wayne State University Press, 1959. Spuhler presents a symposium consisting of six papers and a summary.

van Lawick Goodall, J. The behavior of free living chimpanzees in the Gombe Stream Reserve. **Animal Behavior Monographs,** 1968, **1**, 165-311. This is the report of a scientist who gained the confidence of wild chimpanzees in order to study them intently at close range.

White, L. A. **The science of culture.** New York: Farrar & Straus, 1949. (1958 paperback issued by Grove Press, New York). This book contains an essay entitled "The symbol: The origin and basis of human behavior."

Chapter 8

A Human Society
That Is Human

*... the knowledge of man, his nature,
and the real possibilities of its manifestations must become one of the basic
data for any social planning.*

Erich Fromm

Although every normal individual has the potentiality to make of himself what he wishes, within the limits of natural endowment, past experience, and the opportunities within reach, still he does not grow to
personhood in isolation from everyone else. Anthropologists have long
pointed out how profoundly society influences the personality development of every individual. "No man ever looks at the world with pristine
eyes," Ruth Benedict (1934) observes. "He sees it edited by a definite
set of customs and institutions and ways of thinking." The reason for
this is obvious. No one can exist in a vacuum. If only to survive, let
alone grow to the full stature of humanness, an infant in any culture
must learn a host of conventions, skills, and attitudes. Failure to do so
would cut him off from familiar interaction with the other members of
his group. In a sense he becomes a creature of his culture. Not only

does he typically share the common attitudes and behavior patterns of his society, he also tends to regard them as normative, that is, as the most characteristically human way of acting.

We should not for this reason conclude that societal pressures are always determining ones. There is more diversity in personality patterns within any given social group than between groups. Probably few people even among primitive tribes blindly follow tradition. The higher the educational standards of a society, the more critically its members evaluate traditional folkways and rely on their own judgment as a norm for action. The sheer volume of protests raised against modern society on every side, the deliberate flouting of traditional mores, and the setting up of anitcultures demonstrate quite clearly that we are less imprisoned by our culture than many social scientists in the past had imagined. Although most people may choose to follow the path of familiar customs, there is always the possibility of dissent and, in many countries, freedom to adopt a different style of life.

CULTURAL PATHOLOGY

The chief complaint against any culture is its failure to keep pace with other developments. To give an example which has its counterpart in every society, the Plains Indians, over many thousands of years, developed a culture suited to the needs of a hunting people. Some of the attitudes and practices which were essential for the survival of huntsmen now impede adaptation to changed living conditions. In spite of this incongruity they are tenaciously and affectionately preserved as a mark of tribal identity.

Among the more eloquent critics of modern society are Erich Fromm and Rollo May. Unlike Freud, who thought of man as the architect of society, Fromm considers human personality to be more a product than a producer of social processes (Bischof, 1970). Largely as a result of the industrial revolution and its aftermath, man has transformed himself into the image of a machine whose products he worships. Goods are his new god; materialism his idolatry.

The Crossroads

A specter is stalking in our midst whom only a few see with clarity. It is not the old ghost of communism or fascism. It is a new specter: a completely mechanized society, devoted to maximal material output and consumption, directed by computers; and in this social process, man himself is being transformed into a part of the total machine, well fed and entertained, yet passive, unalive, and with little feeling. With the victory of the new society, individualism and privacy will have disappeared; feelings toward others will be engineered by psychological conditioning and other devices, or drugs which also serve a new kind of introspective experience. As Zbigniew Brzezinski (1968) put it, "In the technetronic society the trend would seem to be towards the aggregation of the individual support of millions of uncoordinated citizens, easily within the reach of magnetic and attractive personalities effectively exploiting the latest communication techniques to manipulate emotions and control reason." This new form of society has been predicted in the form of fiction in Orwell's *1984* and Aldous Huxley's *Brave New World*.

Perhaps its most ominous aspect at present is that we seem to lose control over our own system. We execute the decisions which our computer calculations make for us. We as human beings have no aims except producing and consuming more and more. We will nothing, nor do we not-will anything. We are threatened with extinction by nuclear weapons and with inner deadness by the passiveness which our exclusion from responsibile decision making engenders.

How did it happen? How did man, at the very height of his victory over nature, become the prisoner of his own creation and in serious danger of destroying himself?

In search for scientific truth, man came across knowledge that he could use for the domination of nature. He had tremendous success. But in the one-sided emphasis on technique and material consumption, man lost touch with himself, with life. Having lost religious faith and the humanistic values bound up with it, he concentrated on technical and material values and lost the capacity for deep emotional experiences, for the joy and sadness that accompany them. The machine he built became so powerful that it developed its own program, which now determines man's own thinking.

At the moment, one of the gravest symptoms of our system is the fact that our economy rests upon arms production (plus maintenance of the whole defense establishment) and on the principle of maximal consumption. We have a well-functioning economic system under the condition that we are producing goods which threaten us with physical destruction, that we transform the individual into a total passive consumer and thus deaden him, and that we have created a bureaucracy which makes the individual feel impotent.

Are we confronted with a tragic, insolvable dilemma? *Must we produce sick people in order to have a healthy economy, or can we use our material resources, our inventions, our computers to serve the ends of man? Must individuals be passive and dependent in order to have strong and well-functioning organizations?*

The answers to these questions differ. Among those who recognize the revolutionary and drastic change in human life which the "megamachine" could bring about are the writers who say that the new society is unavoidable, and hence that there is no point in arguing about its merits. At the same time, they are sympathetic to the new society, although they express slight misgivings about what it might do to man as we know him. Zbigniew Brzezinski and H. Kahn are representatives of this attitude. On the other end of the spectrum is Jacques Ellul, who in his *Technological Society* describes with great force the new society which we are approaching and its destructive influence on man. He faces the specter in its dreadful lack of humanness. His conclusion is not that the new society is bound to win, although he thinks that, in terms of probabilities, it is likely to win. But he sees a possibility that the dehumanized society may not be the victor "if an increasing number of people become fully aware of the threat the technological world poses to man's personal and spiritual life, and if they determine to assert their freedom by upsetting the course of this evolution."[1] Lewis Mumford's position may be considered similar to that of Ellul. In his profound and brilliant *The Myth of the Machine* (Mumford, 1966), he describes the "megamachine," starting with its first manifestations in Egyptian and Babylonian societies. But in contrast to those who, like the previously mentioned authors, recognize the specter with either sympathy or horror are the majority of men, those at the top of the establishment and the average citizen, who do not see a specter. They have the old-fashioned belief of the nineteenth century that the machine will help lighten man's burden, that it will remain a means to an end, and they do not see the danger that if technology is permitted to follow its own logic, it will become a cancerlike growth, eventually threatening the structured system of individual and social life. The position taken in this book[2] is in principle that of Mumford and Ellul. It is perhaps different in the sense that I see a somewhat greater possibility of restoring the social system to man's control. My hopes in this respect are based on the following factors:

1 The present social system can be understood a great deal better if one connects the system "Man" with the whole system. Human nature is not an abstraction nor an infinitely malleable and hence dynamically negligible system. It has its own specific qualities, laws, and alternatives. The study of the system Man permits us to see what certain factors in the socioeconomic system do to man, how disturbances in the system Man produce imbalances in the whole social system. By introducing the human factor into the analysis of the whole system, we are better prepared to understand its dysfunctioning and to define norms which relate the healthy economic functioning of the social system to the optimal well-being of the people who participate in it. All this is valid, of course, only if there is agreement that maximal development

---

[1] French edition, 1954; American edition, 1964, Alfred Knopf, and first Vintage Books edition, 1967.
[2] As in *Escape from Freedom* and *The Sane Society*.

of the human system in terms of its own structure—that is to say, human well-being—is the overriding goal.

2 The increasing dissatisfaction with our present way of life, its passiveness and silent boredom, its lack of privacy and its depersonalization, and the longing for a joyful, meaningful existence, which answers those specific needs of man which he has developed in the last few thousand years of his history and which make him different from the animal as well as from the computer. This tendency is all the stronger because the affluent part of the population has already tasted full material satisfaction and has found out that the consumer's paradise does not deliver the happiness it promised. (The poor, of course, have not yet had any chance to find out, except by watching the lack of joy of those who "have everything a man could want.")

Ideologies and concepts have lost much of their attraction; traditional clichés like "right" and "left" or "communism" and "capitalism" have lost their meaning. People seek a new orientation, a new philosophy, one which is centered on the priorities of life—physically and spiritually—and not on the priorities of death.

There is a growing polarization occurring in the United States and in the whole world: There are those who are attracted to force, "law and order," bureaucratic methods, and eventually to nonlife, and those with a deep longing for life, for new attitudes rather than for ready-made schemes and blueprints. This new front is a movement which combines the wish for profound changes in our economic and social practice with changes in our psychic and spiritual approach to life. In its most general form, its aim is the activation of the individual, the restoration of man's control over the social system, the humanization of technology. It is a movement in the name of life, and it has such a broad and common base because the threat to life is today a threat not to one class, to one nation, but a threat to all.

TECHNOLOGY IS NOT THE BASIC PROBLEM

Rollo May (1953, 1969) also denounces modern technology for its dehumanizing effects upon people. Not only do we find ourselves adrift without a set of central, unifying values, we have even lost the awareness of self. As a result many people feel out of touch with others and are incapable of experiencing genuine love or any other deep emotion. Little wonder, then, that the common midcentury complaint is a feeling of emptiness and superficiality. The situation, fortunately, is not hopeless. By struggling courageously to assert his freedom, the individual can regain inner strength. He need not be a passive victim of the age in which he lives because mankind is a transcender of time. "The basic question is how the individual in his own awareness of himself and the period he lives in, is able through his decisions to attain inner freedom and to live according to his own inner integrity . . . no 'well-adjusted' society can perform for the individual, or relieve him from, his task of achieving self-consciousness and the capacity for making his own choices responsibly" (May, 1953, p. 273). May is convinced that come what may, no one can deprive the individual of the privilege of deciding how to meet a traumatic situation, even if this only involves accepting his fate. Frankl's (1959) experience in a Nazi death camp confirms this view.

It should be obvious, then, that technology itself is not the villain. In point of fact, there would be no possibility of meeting the survival needs of even a much smaller world without its benefits. In the absence of a highly developed technology, millions of people today would die of starvation or disease. The recent development of high-yield rice has completely changed the food picture for several Asian nations, and airlifts of medicine and provisions to communities isolated by earthquakes or flooding have saved countless lives. On another level, instantaneous communication is slowly but surely creating a sense of world community. While in past centuries most people were aware only of what happened in their own village or at most in their own country, today television and transistor radios keep a large part of the world abreast of current events. The broadening effect of such exposure on the minds and outlook of illiterate populations can only be imagined.

Carl Rogers (1955) remarks that we never need to fear science, only people. The same is true of technology. Whatever one might take this mental construct to mean, it does not refer to some dreadful reality, as a fiery dragon, ready to pounce upon innocent, unsuspecting persons. Technology, as fire, is our servant but one that can get out of hand, especially since it is something relatively new in the human experience and we have neither learned all its danger nor how to control some that we know. Like the sorcerer's apprentice, we have set our machines to work without learning the complete formula to keep them from mastering us. The solution lies not in attempting to turn the clock back to the "good old pretechnological days" when in place of punching a time clock the laborer engaged in backbreaking work from sunup to sundown six days a week, but in seeing that our machines serve human rather than inhumane purposes.

INDIVIDUAL RESPONSIBILITY FOR SOCIETY

What can the average person do to bring about needed changes in society? The answer is that he can do much, indeed, if he has the courage. Any individual who attempts to shake people out of lethargy is bound to incur the displeasure of those who prefer the comfort of familiar ways to almost any prospect of human fulfillment. Rather than bear the brunt of their attacks it is easy to absolve one's self of personal responsibility for society by asking what seems to be an obvious question. What influence could I possibly have on the monied powers and vested interest that typically shape the destiny of any nation? Events of the past decade have done much to dispel the apparent force of such an argument. If concerted effort on the part of the least economically favored citizens of our country are slowly but surely improving their lot, why cannot similar pressures change other aspects of our culture as well? All that is needed is the climate of opinion that makes this seem a desirable thing to do. When enough ordinary people, whether in the ghettos or the suburbs, want change, it will come. Each voice added to the growing crescendo will hasten the day when it does. Perhaps Kenneth Keniston can convince the reader that he should join the chorus.

The Reconstruction of Commitment

History is always made by men, even in an era like ours when men feel they are but the pawns of history. The inability to envision a future different from the present is not a historical imposition but a failure of imagination. It is individuals, not historical trends, that are possessed by a self-confirming sense of social powerlessness. The decision to continue along our present course rather than to take a new turning is still a decision made by men. One way men sometimes have of shaping the future is to be passive and acquiescent before it. Our collective and individual future, then, will inevitably be shaped by us, whether we choose inaction and passivity, regression and romanticism, or action, imagination, and resolve. Men cannot escape their historical role by merely denying its existence. The question is therefore not *whether* Americans will shape their future, but *how* they will shape it.

What is lacking today in America Is certainly not the know-how, the imagination, or the intelligence to shape a future better than our present. Nor do we lack the values that might guide the transformation of our society to a more fully human and diverse one. Rather, we lack the conviction that these values might be implemented by ordinary men and women acting in concert for their common good. The Utopian impulse, I have argued, runs deep in all human life, and especially deep in American life. What is needed is to free that impulse once again, to redirect it toward the creation of a better society. We too often attempt to patch up our threadbare values and outworn purposes; we too rarely dare imagine a society radically different from our own.

Proposals for specific reforms are bound to be inadequate by themselves. However desirable, any specific reform will remain an empty intellectual exercise in the absence of a new collective myth, ideology, or Utopian vision. Politically, no potent or lasting change will be possible except as men can be roused from their current alienations by the vision of an attainable society more inviting than that in which they now listlessly live. Behind the need for any specific reform lies the greater need to create an intellectual, ideological, and cultural atmosphere in which it is possible for men to attempt affirmation without undue fear that their Utopian visions will collapse through neglect, ridicule, or their own inherent errors. Such an ethos can only be built slowly and piecemeal, yet is it clear what some of its prerequisites must be.

For one, we need a more generous tolerance for synthetic and constructive ideas. Instead of concentrating on the possible bad motives from which they might arise (the genetic fallacy) or on the possible bad consequences which might follow from their misinterpretation (the progenitive fallacy), we must learn to assess them in terms of their present relevance and appropriateness. To accomplish this task will be a double work. Destructively, it will require subverting the methodologies of reduction that now dominate our intellectual life. Constructively, it will require replacing these with more just measures of relevance, subtlety and wisdom, learning to cherish and value the enriching complexity of motives, passions, ethical interests, and facts which will necessarily underlie and support any future vision of the good life.

Secondly, we must reappraise our current concepts and interpretations of man and society. It is characteristic of the intellectual stagnation of our era, an era so obviously different from former times, that we continue to operate with language more appropriate to past generations than to our own. Many of our critiques and interpretations of technological society, including most discussions of alienation, apply more accurately to the America of the 1880's than to the America of the 1960's. We require a radical reanalysis of the human and social present—a reevaluation which, starting from uncritical openness to the experience, joys, and dissatisfactions of men today, can gradually develop concepts and theories that can more completely comprehend today's world. American society does not lack men and women with the fine discrimination, keen intelligence, and imagination to understand the modern world; but we have yet to focus these talents on our contemporary problems.

But above and beyond a more generous atmosphere and a more adequate understanding of our time, ordinary human courage is needed. To criticize one's society openly requires a strong heart, expecially when criticism is interpreted as pathology; only a man of high mettle will propose a new interpretation of the facts now arranged in entrenched categories. And no matter how eagerly the audience awaits or how well prepared the set, only courage can take a performer to the stage. There are many kinds of courage; needed here is the courage to risk being wrong, to risk doing unintentional harm, and, above all, the courage to overcome one's own humility and sense of finite inadequacy. This is not merely a diffuse "courage to be," without protest, in a world of uncertainty, alienation, and anxiety, but the courage to be *for* something despite the perishability and transience of all human endeavors.

Commitment, I have said, is worthy only as its object is worthy. To try to "reconstruct" commitment to American society as it exists today is less than worthy, for our society is shot through with failings, failures, and flaws. It is, as the alienated truly perceive, "trashy, cheap, and commercial"; it is also, as the alienated seldom see, unjust, distorting of human growth and dignity, destructive of diversity. It has allowed itself to be dominated by the instruments of its own triumph over poverty and want, worshiping the values, virtues, and institutions of technology even when these now dominate those they should serve. Only if we can transform the technological process from a master to a servant, harnessing our scientific inventiveness and industrial productivity to the promotion of human fulfillment, will our society be worthy of commitment. And only the vision of a world beyond technology can now inspire the commitment of whole men and women.

America today possesses a vast reservoir of thwarted and displaced idealism; there are millions of men and women who sense vaguely that something is amiss in their lives, who search for something more, and yet who cannot find it. Their idealism will not be easily redirected to the creation of better lives in a better society; it will require imagination, vigor, conviction, and strong voices willing to call for many years, before we dare raise our aspirations beyond vistas of total technology to visions of fuller humanity. But for the first time in American history, and probably in the history of the world, it is conceivable that a whole nation might come to take seriously these ancient and honored visions.

In defining this new vision of life and society, we must remember the quests of the alienated. Though their goals are often confused and inarticulate, they converge on a passionate yearning for openness and immediacy of experience, on an intense desire to create, on a longing to express their perception of the world, and, above all, on a quest for values and commitments that will give their lives coherence. The Inburns of modern American life are often self-defeating; they cannot be taken as exemplars of human integration or fulfillment. But the implicit goals they unsuccessfully seek to attain *are* those of integrated and whole men—openness, creativity, and dedication. Today we need men and women with the wisdom, passion, and courage to transform their private alienations into such public aspirations. We might then begin to move toward a society where such aspirations were more fully realized than in any the world has known.

We can hope for such new commitments in the future only if men now begin to resolve their alienations by committing themselves—through the analysis, synthesis, and reform of their own lives and worlds—to the preparation of such a new society, a society in which whole men and women can play with zest and spontaneity, can work with skill and dedication, can love with passion and care—a society that enjoys diversity and supports human fulfillment.

TRANSFORMING SOCIETY

The question of whether or not psychology as a profession should become involved in social change is a highly controversial issue. In the past most scientists believed that they should engage in this type of activity only as private citizens, not as members of professional organizations. Perhaps they feared that any kind of social activism might divert their research efforts from problems of greater scientific importance to matters of passing interest which were considered relevant for a time. At present a growing number of psychologists are beginning to feel that psychology can no longer remain a detached spectator in a world torn apart by tensions at every level of social interaction but must join in the search for an effective remedy. Although in the case of professional organizations this issue is hotly debated, no one can question the need for the student of psychology to become actively concerned about the social structure of tomorrow's world in which he will live the major portion of his life.

Anyone seriously concerned about curing society's ills soon encounters a number of thorny problems. Identifying social pathologies and protesting against them is the easiest task. There is even popular support for this. Who is not an enemy of self-alienation, unhappiness, loneliness, and apathy? But where does one find workable correctives? The romantic hope that merely wiping the slate clean by total revolution would inevitably pave the way for more wholesome living does not appear realistic. Even scholars who devote much time and thought to the problem of transforming society have misgivings about their suggestions. Maslow (1970b), for example, in proposing **eupsychia**, his version of utopia, notes that it could be achieved only by well-integrated adults and children whose personalites have not yet been distorted. In the paragraphs that follow, John W. Gardner discusses some down-to-earth issues that must be taken into account in any attempt at radical transformation of society.

From The Recovery of Confidence

In undertaking the redesign of our institutions, it is necessary to ask what kind of society we want.

We are all familiar with the young radicals who reject the world as it is but can't specify the kind of world they want. The truth is that most middle-of-the-road and conservative citizens are equally unprepared to specify the kind of society we should be striving to achieve.

It is child's play to mount a devastating critique of the existing system—any existing system. It is child's play to have unquestioning faith in the existing system. The hard task is to specify appropriate directions of change.

We must face that hard task. We cannot stand still. We cannot go back. The forces of change are altering our society whether we like it or not. We are moving on to something new. If we are to have any influence on the course of events, we must have some conception of what we would like that new thing to be. Among other things, it must be a society capable of continuous renewal.

What would be the attributes of such a society?

Let us begin with the most controversial attribute. The society capable of renewal will provide for dissent, for the emergence of alternatives to official doctrine or widely accepted assumptions. It will provide for honest appraisal of the disparity between widely professed ideals and existing conditions.

It is not just the national government or the Establishment (whatever that is) that can profit from criticism. Corporations, universities, churches, professions, government agencies—all must foster a climate in which assumptions may be questioned and settled policies challenged. We are beginning to understand that there are innumerable Establishments, many of them hardly recognizable in traditional terms. In the absence of criticism, every organization ends up being managed for the benefit of the people who run it: most schools tend to be run in such a way as to serve the purposes of the teachers; the Navy tends to be run for the benefit of naval officers; the vested interests of postal employees are the predominant factor in controlling and directing the future of the post office; the policies and practices of most universities are explicable chiefly in terms of the vested interests of the professors.

Critics who are so preoccupied with the fantasy of a single all-powerful Establishment that they ignore these facts are missing one of the most significant features of the contemporary scene.

Our society rates very high in sheer volume of expressed dissent. But much of it is fruitless. We can and must construct more effective means of criticizing the institutions and processes of our society. We have plenty of generalized caterwauling about society's faults. We need more specific, on-target criticism. For a variety of reasons, it is hard to come by.

It is easy to approve of dissent in the abstract, but often difficult in real life. The most visible dissenters are too aggressive for comfort. They carry an unwelcome message. They promise inconvenience, altercations, embarrassment. And inevitably mingled among them are the fools, neurotics, and self-aggrandizers that one finds in any segment of the population.

In short, the task of remaining open to dissent isn't just a matter of listening tolerantly, congratulating oneself all the while for exemplary open-mindedness. It is apt to be an annoying experience. But it is worth the trouble. . . .

Revolution

There are some dissenters who say, "We don't need reform, we need revolution. The whole system is rotten and should be destroyed." Of course, many who say it don't really mean it. There is an awesome theatricality about today's radicalism, and the apocalyptic assertion is much in vogue. If one patiently questions people who make such statements, not attacking them but exploring their views, one uncovers a variety of conventional radical positions, most of which have been around for a generation or more and have survived peaceably (if not necessarily comfortably) within our traditional political structure.

But, of course, some who call for destruction of the system really mean it. At first, one is puzzled by their failure to understand that when a social system is destroyed, the resulting chaos is supremely antagonistic to *any* organized purposes, including the purposes of those who initiated the destruction; and by their failure to understand that periods of chaos are followed by periods of iron rule.

Those who seek to bring societies down always dream that after the blood bath *they* will be calling the tune. But after the chaos no one knows what kind of dictator would emerge. Since physical force would probably reign supreme, the rulers would presumably be those most skilled in the use of weapons—in other words, the police and the military services. So we are asked to destroy the system, suffer the resulting chaos, put ourselves in the hands of the steel-hard inheritors of chaos, go through the long rebuilding process—all with no assurance whatever of a better outcome (or even as good an outcome). The proposal dissolves under examination.

Some of today's revolutionaries, particularly younger ones, have fallen victim to an old and naïve doctrine—that man is naturally good, humane, decent, just, and honorable, but that corrupt and wicked institutions have transformed the noble savage into a civilized monster. Destroy the corrupt institutions, they say, and man's native goodness will flower. There isn't anything in history or anthropology to confirm the thesis, but it has survived down the generations.

Of course, the assertion that society's ills are incurable often masks purposes shallower than revolution. Since the assertion cannot be proven wrong, it lends itself to those whose chief interest is in the theatricalities of debate. And since it makes remedial efforts pointless, it serves those who through laziness or impatience have no intention of mastering the processes of social change.

Although left-wing revolutionaries have managed to get most of the attention lately, we are in just as much danger from extremism of the right, from all those in our society who live with their finger on the trigger of repressive action—leaders who make political capital out of fear and anger, law-enforcement officers who are seeking an excuse for harsh measures, and all the secret militiamen who lurk in the shadows of our national life. The extreme right is fully as radical in its intentions as the extreme left. Though it mouths the pieties of flag and constitution, it would—given the opportunity—fashion a society that would be utterly unrecognizable to the authors of the Bill of Rights.

CREATING THE CLIMATE FOR CHANGE

So far our discussion has been largely theoretical. We have commented on what should be done but not how to do it. In the practical order, how can a climate of thinking be developed which will demand the humanization of our technological society? A number of proposals have been made for organizations specifically devoted to this purpose. Among them are **Common Cause** (2100 M St., N.W., Washington, D.C. 20037) and the **Urban Coalition** (1819 H St., N.W., Washington, D.C.). Common Cause is a lobby set up to represent the public interest, particularly by pressing for revitalization of the machinery of government in order to make it more responsive to the people's needs. Although of recent origin, its influence in Congress is already being felt. Common Cause is governed by a policy council of forty members headed by John W. Gardner, a former Secretary of Health, Education, and Welfare. It is now looking forward to the establishment of state and local organizations to deal with problems closer to home. Among the issues that engage the attention of Common Cause are the overhaul of government at every level, peace, negotiations to limit arms and defense spending, poverty, equal opportunities for all citizens, ecology, family planning, and suitable housing. The Urban Coalition is composed of a broad spectrum of leaders and other concerned citizens who actively address themselves to the unresolved social problems of our cities.

Erich Fromm (1968, pp. 151-162) has also suggested plans for a nonpolitical organization to deal with similar problems. The first step would consist in forming a national council to be known as the "Voice of American Conscience" composed of fifty outstanding persons whose integrity and ability could not be questioned. The national council would deliberate in an atmosphere relatively free from the pressures of special interest groups and make recommendations regarding such issues as our foreign policy in Asia, aid to underdeveloped countries, the problems of cities, values, education, and culture. In general its task would be to clarify issues, suggest alternate courses of action and possible solutions, cooperate with other social bodies, and interact with responsible critics.

Corresponding councils would be set up at the local level, consisting of "clubs" of 100 to 300 members and smaller "groups" of no more than 25. Local councils would deal with the issues of ecology, city planning, slum clearance, the relocation of industries, and similar problems. Together with the national council they would represent the voice of reason and conscience addressed to the government and the citizenry as a whole. Even without direct power they could, Fromm believes, be highly influential in a society based on knowledge, training in science, and logical thinking as a technological society must be.

PRACTICAL CONSIDERATIONS

One conspicuous aspect of human behavior is that cultural change, short of the use of naked force as we have seen in some totalitarian nations, comes about slowly with a great deal of bickering between those who expect dramatic results immediately and many others who cling tenaciously to the status quo. Perhaps this is nature's safeguard against the disrupting effects of embarking too precipitously upon untried schemes. Human interaction in society is immeasurably more complex than the economy or ecology which more than once have been damaged by well-intentioned remedies. The widespread use of DDT to prevent malaria and to increase the world's supply of food did not eliminate its disastrous side effects. Intervention in so intricate a system of interrelationships often results in unforseen consequences.

Another consideration that may be overlooked by persons interested in social change is that we are envisioning something no other age has ever been able to achieve—a society of self-actualizing persons. In estimating how far we still have to go, we should not lose sight of what has actually been accomplished. For the first time in human history modern governments take responsibility, at least in principle, for financial and medical aid to the destitute, rehabilitation of the handicapped, universal education, promotion of the arts, and support of libraries, museums, parks, and other recreational facilities. As unsatisfactory as many of our city hospitals and welfare systems may be, they are still a vast improvement over anything that has existed in the past. Pretechnological society enjoyed a number of crucial advantages which are in short supply today: a set of values commonly agreed upon, extended family relationships, a feeling of belonging, and a view of the good life that was not necessarily predicated upon a host of material possessions. But this is not the whole story. Conditions of the time were such as to prevent all except a few favored individuals from ever achieving fulfillment in our meaning of the term. The stultifying effects of hard manual labor from dawn to dusk to eke out a living left the average individual with neither the leisure nor inclination to actualize his full potential. Most people were unable to read, and even if they could, books and newspapers were not generally available. In the absence of efficient means of travel or rapid communications of any kind, there was little or nothing to raise the common person's interest above the platitudes of neighborhood gossip.

HOPE FOR THE FUTURE

One hopeful sign of progress in our day is the willingness to study our culture objectively in order to assess its weaknesses. This is something new. In the past, people took for granted that their customs were normative. Westerners coming into contact with Eastern cultures for the first time looked down on them as inferior because they were different. The Orientals, for their part, considered the foreign strangers to be barbarians. Primitive peoples, in particular, are convinced that there is only one "right" way to do things—the way they have always done them. That is why change in customs was so painfully slow prior to contact with highly developed civilizations. Innovation was not only unwelcome, but even severely punished by ridicule or ostracism.

The fact that we find so much wrong with the so-called American way of life is no excuse for pessimism. What is encouraging is that the public is becoming aware of these deficiencies. This is the first step toward improvement. Secondly, there is no dearth of trained personnel to accomplish almost anything we set our mind on doing. More scientists and scholars are alive and working today than in all the past centuries taken together. For this same reason the need for social change is greater than ever before. Not only do we have the resources to greatly improve the lot of mankind, we also have the capability of destroying our species if not most life on this planet by a third world war. But the same intelligence, training, and marvels of inventiveness that have produced the atom bomb and space travel can be put to work on social problems if we prefer. If it is possible to land a man on the moon, it should be within our ability to make him feel at home on earth as a whole person. Up until now we have been more intent upon the quest for material goods and physical comfort than upon the cultivation of social and spiritual values. Perhaps the worldwide fear of total war is a salutary reminder that "not by bread alone does man live." There are deep human cravings that transcend all egocentric gratifications.

It is sometimes stated that any attempt to transform society is likely to involve a vicious circle. Each generation is the product of its own culture and must grow to adulthood before wielding the influence necessary to effect a change. By that time society has already molded most individuals to its own image. While to some extent this is true, still the gnawing dissatisfaction felt by so many people today serves as a counterbalance. Not only in this country but throughout the world, including the Iron Curtain countries, millions of individuals feel that their lives are empty and meaningless. Even though society cannot be blamed for all our existential ills, there is a general feeling that it does not provide many of the human satisfactions we have a right to expect. It would be comforting to think that we are approaching a turning point in history where the forces of social evolution are gradually building up to the point where they will become all but irresistible. Such an outlook is compatible with the predictions of Teilhard de Chardin (1965) and Julian Huxley (1965).

CULTURE AS A PRECIOUS HERITAGE

This chapter would be incomplete with a word of appreciation for the culture we rightly criticize. No living group is ever the creator of a culture, because a million years or more of human living have gone into its making and every age has contributed something to the way of life we call modern. To cite as an example only the Neolithic period, Teilhard de Chardin (1965) observes that as mankind abandoned a nomadic hunting existence in favor of permanent settlements, human ingenuity erupted in a flurry of inventiveness. Practically all the animals we use and the grains we grow were then domesticated and empirically improved. The basic skills of weaving and pottery were developed and the techniques of wine making still in use today were perfected. Through a process of trial and error in which almost every conceivable arrangement was tried, Neolithic man devised a network of customs regulating individual rights and duties, marriage agreements, moral behavior, property ownership, and so on. Among other clever inventions of the distant past that everyone takes for granted is the written alphabet. Some scholars believe it to be so brilliant a discovery as to have occurred only once in the whole history of our race. What the invention of an alphabet has contributed to the humanization of mankind is beyond all calculation. The introduction of democracy in government is another example of how we build upon the experience of past ages.

Indeed, the foundation of our present-day society reaches back to and beyond the beginnings of civilization. Much of the wisdom it enshrines has been gained by finding out in actual practice through scores of centuries what works and what does not. Nonetheless we are painfully aware not only that society is an unfinished product, but that its deficiencies lie in the most crucial area—the development of fully functioning people. How we can make a breakthrough that previous ages have been unable to achieve is a burning question. John W. Gardner cautions us against impatience.

From No Easy Victories

How can we make people understand that if they expect all good things instantly, they will destroy everything? How do we tell them that they must keep unrelenting pressure on their social institutions to accomplish beneficial change but must not, in a fit of rage, destroy those institutions? How can we caution them against exploitative leaders, leaders lustful for power or for the spotlight, leaders caught in their own vanity or emotional instability, leaders selling extremist ideologies?

Hasty, simplistic solutions that ignore the complexities of social organization can only compound the difficulties. The Herculean task that confronts us will require the best thinking and concerted action on the part of a large segment of our nation. It should be possible to persuade enough of our citizens that the goal of shaping society to fit the needs of man rather than the reverse is well worth any effort.

SUMMARY

The rapid rise of industrialization in much of the world has exaggerated the tendency for culture in general and society in particular to lag behind current developments. Fromm and May lament the dehumanizing effects of modern technology which we must learn to use in a way that it does not allow it to

From John W. Gardner. No easy victories, p. 5, Harper & Row, 1968. Reprinted by permission of Harper & Row, Publishers, Inc.

become our master. Keniston observes that men are not puppets of history even in eras when they feel helpless. There is no lack of dedicated people today, and we have the know-how to bring about cultural change. All that is needed is to focus our enthusiasm on contemporary social problems. Gardner discusses some issues that must be squarely faced in any attempt to transform society. Among the organizations actively engaged in social renewal are Common Cause and the Urban Coalition. Fromm suggested a similar organization to be known as the Voice of American Conscience.

What is envisioned—a society of self-actualizing people—has never before been achieved. One encouraging sign of progress is the willingness of many people to objectively assess the strengths and weaknesses of our institutions. Respect is due to our culture even as we criticize it. No one group ever develops a culture. It is the heritage of a million or more years of human living.

DISCUSSION TOPICS

1 Which aspects of our society invite the commitment of young persons and which tend to alienate them?

2 Describe the major manifestations of alienation from society and given some probable causes (Keniston, 1965, Chs. 4 and 7).

3 From a historical perspective, what previous cultures, if any, were more successful than ours in helping the average person achieve fulfillment?

4 What does the relationship between social class and mental health imply? (See Additional Reading by Myers and Bean.)

5 How well does the middle-class American family measure up to the ideal society in which each individual is a whole person?

6 Cite several examples of cultural lags. To what do you attribute them?

7 Compare the utopian society proposed by Skinner (see Additional Readings) with that of Fromm, Maslow, and May.

8 Make some practical suggestions for ways in which you and your classmates can exert an influence on the course of American society.

9 How can colleges and universities help you in this respect without prejudice to their primary objective?

ADDITIONAL READINGS

Bennis, W. G., & Stater, P. E. **The temporary society.** New York: Harper & Row, 1968. "We write this book with one main goal, and that is to force into view certain changes affecting vital aspects of our key institutions, organizational life, family life, interpersonal relationships, and authority."

Bidney, D. **Theoretical anthropology** (2d ed.) New York: Schocken Books, 1967, Ch. 16. Within the context of any culture, freedom and authority are complementary principles which mutually limit each other.

Counts, G. S. The impact of technological change. In W. G. Bennis, K. D. Benne, & R. Chin. **The planning of change.** New York: Holt, 1966. Technology is changing both our civilization and ourselves.

Dubos, R. **So human an animal.** New York: Scribner's, 1968. Dr. Dubos writes brilliantly about the dehumanizing trends in today's society but is hopeful that we will be able to develop a culture that does not thwart human nature.

Erikson, E. H. **Childhood and Society.** New York: Norton, 1950. The author points out how societal pressures influence a person's sense of identity.

Feinberg, G. **The Prometheus project: Mankind's search for long-range goals.** Garden City, N.Y.: Doubleday, 1969. The inspiration for this book on mankind's need for long-term goals grew out of a series of group discussions which included scientists, social scientists, and philosophers.

Frank, J. D. **Sanity and survival: Psychological aspects of war and peace.** New York: Random House, 1967, Chs. 5 & 6. The reasons why men and nations fight are analyzed.

Halleck, S. You can go to hell in style. **Psychology Today,** 1969, **3**(6), pp. 16, 70-73. This article sketches the psychiatric portrait of the person who, in the face of a changing world, opts for immediacy, relevance, and social maneuverability in preference to planning and mastery.

Honingmann, J. J. **Personality in culture.** New York: Harper & Row, 1967. An anthropologist traces the influence of culture upon personality development.

Jung, C. G. **The undiscovered self.** Boston: Little, Brown & Co., 1958. (Also published as a Mentor paperback.) A noted psychiatrist expresses his concern about the fate of the human individual in mass society.

Levine, L. S. Some psychological prerequisites for peace. In J. F. T. Bugental (Ed.), **Challenges of humanistic psychology.** New York: McGraw-Hill, 1967. Before we can stand against war we must prepare our minds for peace.

Milner, E. **The failure of success: The middle-class crisis** (2d ed.) St. Louis: Green, 1968. This is an impassioned attack upon the debilitating effects of our affluent society.

Myers, J. K. & Bean, L. L. **A decade later: A follow-up of social class and mental illness.** New York: Wiley, 1968. A long-term investigation of the influence of social class upon mental health is reported.

Skinner, B. F. **Walden II.** New York: Macmillan, 1948. In the behavioristic utopia described in this novel, everyone would be conditioned from earliest infancy to be happy after the manner determined by the persons in charge.

Toffler, A. **Future shock.** New York: Random House, 1970. As the author notes: "This is a book about what happens to people when they are overwhelmed by change. It is about the ways in which we adapt—or fail to adapt—to the future."

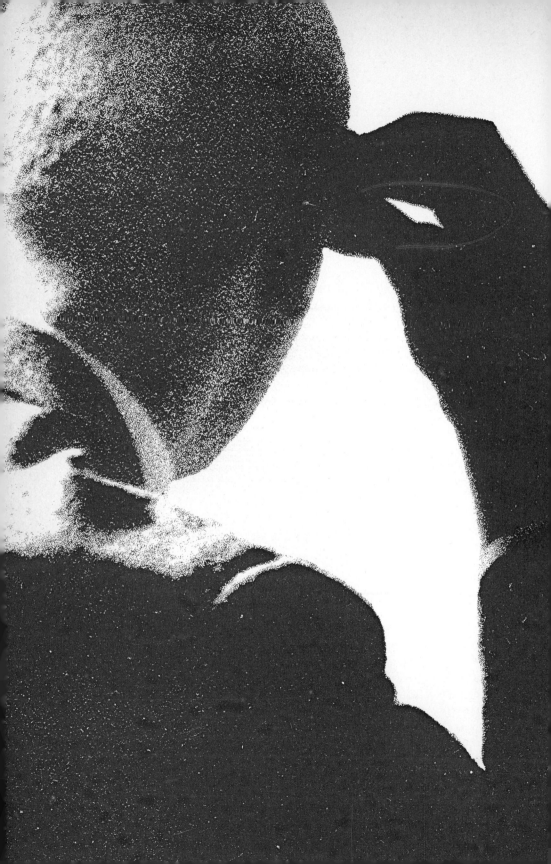

Part Three

Values in Psychology

*Of course social psychology must grapple
with human experience in society;
of course it is inextricably concerned with human values
—or so I have always thought.*

M. BREWSTER SMITH

Chapter 9

Value Judgments in the Social Sciences

We can only practice science if we value truth.

Jacob Bronowski

One human idiosyncrasy that might amuse the mythical stranger from another planet is our extraordinary ability to remain unaware of many vexing problems until they become too critical to ignore any longer. It was not yesterday that peoples of the world began polluting watercourses and strewing the earth's surface with debris. Only when the fetid wastes and nauseous gases poisoned food sources and brought tears to burning eyes did we suddenly discover that something had gone awry. Perhaps unconsciously we pursue the policy attributed to astute English diplomats of waiting until the last possible moment to make the least possible concession.

Among the urgent problems still blithely ignored is the irresponsible dissipation of natural resources that will be sorely needed by countless future generations. Whales and some edible fish are being hunted almost to extinction by sonar and other sophisticated gear.

Innumerable fertile fields are being destroyed by surface mining thin veins of coal of marginal value. With few exceptions all that the behemoth dredges leave behind is heap upon heap of worthless stones. The world's entire supply of petroleum which was millions of years in the making will probably be exhausted within a few decades.

Scientists, who in the laboratory as well as private life are human beings, sometimes suffer a similar lack of vision. The general reluctance of psychologists to deal with the problem of values is a good example. Until quite recently many even denied that their discipline has anything to do with values. Fortunately the tide is now beginning to turn in the opposite direction.

The term **value** in its most general context, according to Smith (1969, pp. 99-102), refers to the human phenomenon of caring, prizing, committing one's self, or judging as better or worse. To this might be added the scientist's passion for facts, precision, and objectivity. In studying values, attention can be focused either on the subject himself or on the object of his striving. In the former case value is identical with a disposition or attitude toward something that is prized. In the latter case it consists in some property of the goal object that attracts the individual. Some personality theorists sharpen the concept to denote general evaluative attitudes that form the backbone of one's philosophy of life.

Until quite recently the conviction that science deals only with facts, never with values, amounted almost to a dogma. "This attitude," Dukes (1955) explains, "was incorporated into psychology by Titchener, who in his zeal to make psychology scientific, imitated the classical physicists and excluded value along with meaning and utility from the new science." Herbert C. Kelman explains why he adopts a different frame of reference.

From A Time to Speak

My own approach to the value questions I have mentioned starts with the assumption that, to achieve scientific objectivity in social research, it is neither necessary nor sufficient to avoid value-laden problems, to treat the subjects of research in a completely impersonal way, to rely entirely on experimental and quantitative techniques, and to adopt simple mechanistic models. Social research, in my view, must be based on the recognition that neither the social researcher as a person, nor the process of social research can be entirely value-free; that the observations of the social scientist cannot be carried out from a wholly external vantage-point; and that the findings of social research cannot stand by themselves as scientifically validated facts about nature. A total separation of the role of scientist from the role of valuing man, of the definition of the research problem from the investigator's value preferences, of the investigator from his human subjects and subject matter, and of research findings from ideas about these findings and about the world into which they fit cannot be achieved and, what is more, the effort to achieve such separation leads to an impoverished social science. What is necessary, however, for the enhancement of scientific objectivity, is that the investigator deliberately take his values, attitudes, and expectations into account and systematically analyze their effects on the definition of the research problem, the observations obtained, and the interpretations placed on these observations. We can never eliminate the effects of values and subjective factors, but we must push against the limits to scientific objectivity that inevitably govern our efforts. In my view, the tension between the investigator's values and a recalcitrant reality world, and the constant—though never wholly successful—effort to disentangle the two, are central and constructive features of the scientific study of man.

This view of scientific objectivity has several implications for the task of the social researcher:

1 Since the role of scientist cannot be totally separated from that of human being, of citizen, and of participant in social action, I see no objection to the broadening of the social scientist's repertoire and to his enactment of a variety of roles. As I point out . . . a social scientist who engages in action research, applied research, or social engineering is making as valid a use of his scientific training as one engaged in "pure" research. It is essential, however, that the social scientist be perfectly clear, both to himself and to others, about the context in which he is operating and the role he is taking at any given time, and that he make a deliberate effort to assess the effect that his personal involvement has on his observations and conclusions.

2 Since the purposes of the research and the definition of the research problem cannot be totally separated from the investigator's value preferences, I see no reason to avoid value-laden research. There is no way of assuring objectivity by the type of problem or method we select and there is no reason, therefore, to consider any problem scientifically taboo. Those who make a sharp distinction between proper and improper research in terms of the nature of the problem and method are usually unaware of the possibility that their own research may be far from value-free. One can easily fail to notice the role of value preferences when he works within the frame of reference of the status quo, since its value assumptions are so much second nature to members of the society that they perceive them as part of objective reality. Similarly, one may miss the intrusion of value preferences when he uses experimental or quantitative methods, which give an often deceptive appearance of objectivity. Thus, the issue is not how we can keep out

intrusive values by virtue of the problems we study and the methods we use, but how we can take systematic account of the values and subjective considerations that inevitably enter into our research. . . . As long as we are actively aware of the possible effects of our values, there are many advantages to research that is avowedly based on value preferences. Because of his involvement in the problem, the investigator may be able to bring to the research a level of motivation and a depth of insight that are conducive to an especially creative effort.

3 Since the investigator cannot be totally separated from his human subjects and subject matter, I see a need for new approaches to social research that include the relationship of the investigator to the individuals and societies he is studying as a salient dimension. We have to reassess the methodological assumption that a completely impersonal relationship can be achieved in social research and explore new methodologies that call for different patterns of relationship. [Elsewhere] I discuss as one possible model a more participatory type of relationship, which attempts, not to bypass the motivations the subject brings to the research situation, but to mobilize them in support of the research enterprise. I do consider it important to maintain the separation of the investigator from his subject matter; this is, after all, one of the major differences between social science and other ways of studying man. Efforts at such separation, however, must be based on a realistic conception of the degree of "outsideness" that a social researcher is able to achieve.

4 Since research findings cannot be totally separated from ideas about these findings, I regard empirical investigations primarily as sources of new inputs into our thinking about social behavior, rather than as verifications of the laws of such behavior. The scientific study of man is, indeed, concerned with developing general propositions, but I do not feel that our experiments and observations can in any sense "establish" these propositions as proven. The gap between the observations we are able to make and the reality to which we wish to generalize is too great for that. As I point out . . . I see the basic task of the social researcher as systematic thinking about social behavior, fed and tempered by empirical evidence. Empirical research, in this view, is thus essentially an aid to thinking—albeit one that is especially and uniquely valuable and that constitues one of the central contributions of a scientific approach to the study of man.

A psychologist is even less able than the natural scientist to divorce himself from his subject matter. Try as he may, he can never stand outside the human nature he studies. C. A. Mace (1964) observes that "the educational psychologist behaves as if he knows what is good for the child. The psychotherapist behaves as if he knows what is good for the patient. The occupational therapist conducts himself as though he knows what is good for the workers. **And so in fact they do.**" It would be strange indeed if a lifetime of being human did not throw some light on what is suitable for mankind in general.

THE GOALS OF PSYCHOLOGISTS

Values always presuppose an end or goal. A small child is likely to treasure plastic tokens as long as they can be exchanged for candy in a laboratory vending machine. If the rules of the game change so that they no longer pay off, he quickly loses interest in them. Even in adult life the things one prizes profoundly influence his whole behavior pattern. For this reason knowledge of a person's value system supplies the surest key to understanding him in depth. Curious as it may seem, only a minority of personality theorists stress man's intentional striving as a significant human feature, presumably because of the traditional distrust of freedom and values. While not denying that he is a goal-oriented creature, they often prefer to bypass these central issues in favor of specific questions concerning reinforcement schedules, unconscious motivation, or other peripheral items.

Not only in theorizing but also in practice psychologists act purposively. They do things to attain certain results with a more remote goal in mind. In other words, they employ means to attain ends and their activities can be analyzed in terms of these final causes or ultimate purposes. Such an approach is labeled teleological. Because of negative attitudes historically conditioned by past debates about the nature of science, many psychologists reject the notion of teleology without bothering to examine what it implies (Rychlak, 1968, p. 236). The hard core of this resistance to the acceptance of final causes probably centers on the inability of traditional methodology to deal with the values rather than the actual presence of such aims. Most people privately acknowledge the existence of final goals in some form or other, although scientists are usually embarrassed to refer to them as such in public. More uninhibited discussions of the topic, such as the one by G. H. Turner that follows, might clarify the issues and resolve a number of misunderstandings.

From Psychology — Becoming and Unbecoming

There are taboos in psychology and one of them seems to be the consideration of ultimate aims or ends. Such delicate matters are normally shunned in
the professional literature and in conversation among psychologists, and one
does not have to go far to find reasons. The most obvious is the prevailing
philosophical climate of logical positivism or scientific empiricism, with its
futile disavowal of metaphysics. Its more deliberate devotees undoubtedly
eschew final purposes on the high grounds of personal conviction; others
seem to do so out of either indifference to, or irresolution on, these weighty
issues. Still others may know where they stand but regard it as a highly
personal matter, or may fail to speak out of respect for the taboos. Whatever
the reasons I regard this conspiracy of silence as tragic, and consequently I am
going to make the question of ends the first major concern of my talk this
evening.

Since ultimate aims or values receive such scant attention, I can hardly
be accused of laboring the obvious if I take a moment to argue that we are
lost without them in our professional as well as our private lives. How long
can an intelligent clinical psychologist function without wondering, in a
profound way, what he is trying to do? Is he there to help remove undesirable
symptoms, to reduce psychic pain, to improve efficiency, to restore a former
level of function, to contribute to growth or independence, or what? Does he
see mental health in positive terms and, if so, what is the desirable state at
which he is aiming?

The problem of the industrial psychologist is no different. Is his
function to assist in the attainment of his client's goals, to increase production and efficiency, to improve the administrative process, to share his own
perspectives with the client, to help in achieving community-oriented goals,
or what? Division XIV of the American Psychological Association brought
this problem into sharp focus for me by suggesting that graduate students in
industrial psychology be made aware of the "realities" of business and
industrial life. If I interpreted this statement aright, it meant that to be a
satisfactory consultant you must know the goals of your client and help him
attain them—a proposition that is by no means as innocent as it sounds! The
university teacher and administrator faces the same difficulties. Would he
revise the program of studies? To what end? Is the goal to impart the core
curriculum, to develop the currently fashionable skills, to turn out scientists,
or what?

Let us touch a more sensitive nerve and bring the problem closer to
home. How can we order our own lives and maintain health and stability if

From **Presidential address to the Canadian Psychological Association,** Kingston,
Ontario, June 3, 1960. G. H. Turner. Psychology—becoming and unbecoming. Canad. J.
Psychol., 1960, 14, 153-165. Reprinted with permission of the author and the University
of Toronto Press.

we have no overriding purposes or values, if we are busily treading the activity cage to nowhere? Without some hierarchy of values life must be chaotic and pointless. Without awareness of our values, how can we accept responsibility for them and avoid being slaves to whatever early cultural influences fell to our lot? If we once grant the desirability of self-awareness, of integrity and synergy of thought, feeling, and action, then professional, scientific, academic, and private problems begin to merge into one, namely: What are our ultimate objectives and how may these best be implemented in our private and professional lives?

But what do we concern ourselves with at present? To avoid becoming involved in disputes over philosophy, or, worse still, religion, we will openly admit the pursuit of only the most banal and patently penultimate or antepenultimate purposes such as increasing production, efficiency, and profit, or, even better, improving employer-employee relations, or effecting better personal adjustment, or facilitating the process of socialization, or, better still, raising standards, in the profession or training better scientists, or, best of all, adding to knowledge or advancing psychology as a science and as a profession. How perfectly respectable, how normal, but how unsatisfactory. They all leave unanswered the question, why bother? To stop short of God, Mammon, the state, the fully actualized man, or some equally final alternative, is to admit that we do not know what we are doing or that if we know, we will not say.

Going the whole distance and specifying our ultimate purpose would, of course, end in nothing but words if we were not simultaneously under the necessity of retracing our steps and establishing the hierarchies of lesser purposes that in effect constitute its definition. It is only from such a hierarchy of aims that any clear implications for behavior can emerge and by which behavior may be consistently evaluated. Thus the healthy person who is intellectually alive and growing is cognizant of his goals, ever mindful of the need to revise them and always modifying his behavior, the better to achieve them.

To expect us to reach agreement about ends is quite unreasonable, although much of our disagreement is, I am sure, semantic rather than real, but to be unwilling to be explicit about them seems indefensible. What greater barrier to effective communication could one devise? What more subtle form of misrepresentation could one practice? One can with honor admit indecision or confusion. But what can be said of those who would deny or ignore the issue?

To accept responsibility for deciding, no matter how tentatively, and for stating, no matter how provisionally, the final grounds on which we base our lives might not seem to constitute a formidable assignment since the answers are already implicit in our behavior. By our every action we commit ourselves to some purpose or other. But this is surely a taller order than I am making out. What is harder than to discover and make explicit one's assumptions? More than that, the values we assume, the ends implicit in our behavior, do not enjoy some sort of separate independent existence. On the contrary they are firmly embedded in a view of man, in some conception of the nature of the universe and of man's place in it. What is his nature, what does he need, where is he going, how can we account for him? It is how we answer these questions that determines our hierarchy of purposes.

Only our total concept of man can provide us with the master cognitive map into which all our little maps must fit if we would have a coherent view of life. But how poorly supplied we are with comprehensive models and the bits and pieces that constitute the conventional wisdoms are characterized by unrevealed assumptions, inconsistencies, grave omissions, and questionable validity. If we are so uncertain of man's nature, how can we be so sure we are doing what is best for him as consultants, counselors, clinicians, and teachers? How can we be so confident we know the best questions to ask of nature in pursuing our study of man? As we are well aware it is hard to find good answers to poor questions.

Do not think that this is none of our business, or that it concerns only the incorrigibly speculative personality theorists. Do we waive all claim to a part in policy setting? Are we content to implement the decisions of others? If this is not our business, then what is?

An objection that seems to appeal to many is that it is not of immediate concern to us as scientists, because psychologists do not at present know enough to provide a coherent picture of man. Their rejoinder is "Give us a hundred years or so and we may have something of significance to offer." The case for ignorance is easy to make out but the argument from it would be much more convincing if it were not for the fact that the self-same psychologist-scientist lives the real life of a real person at home, in the community, and among his professional colleagues, fighting for what he thinks is right and making his way in a real world, on the basis of very real assumptions about the nature of man. (Rigorous experimentalists have, by the way, been known to scorn the less certain findings of their colleagues who study children, while confidently raising their own on principles handed down with the family silver.)

I grant that our knowledge is limited and that our concept of man must be rounded out with borrowed or improvised propositions. But surely we must continually incorporate such knowledge as we have. It would be the height of irony for a psychologist to devote his life to the task of building the empirical foundations of knowledge about man while living his life on postulates that take no account of the knowledge already available in his discipline.

Let us make no mistake about it, our job is to throw light on the nature of man. As practical and realistic men, we must and do, in the interim, commit ourselves completely to those views about man we think are most worth the gamble. As psychologists, we owe it to ourselves, and to others, to say what particular assumptions we are prepared to act upon, in order to clarify our own thinking, to give more consistent direction to our action and, with respect to clients, to let them know what they are paying for.

If we do this we shall find ourselves no longer declaring knowledge to be for its own sake and no longer regarding psychology as an end in itself—a way of thinking that has crept into our textbooks and into articles discussing, for example, the importance to psychology of recruitment and proper selection, or the danger to psychology of early professionalization, and so on. This is only a manner of speaking, but perhaps it is an unfortunate one. Unintentional reification seems to develop easily into unintentional deification. While there is still so much question of psychology's effectiveness as a means, we hardly dare promote it to an end.

Man may need a lot of things but one thing he certainly needs is an adequate view of himself, one that is consistent with and grounded in his fullest knowledge of himself and of his world. This is where psychology fits in. The world does not go round in order to accommodate psychology. The study of psychology derives such significance as it has from its power to contribute to our knowledge of and perspective on man.

Some psychologists fear that concern for values will lead inevitably to problems of purpose beyond the scope of empirical investigation. Final answers to such questions as, "What is man for?" are not obtained by observing behavior in the laboratory or measuring personality traits. Raising issues about the nature of man would seem to invite endless philosophical debates. Would it not be better to ignore values altogether? First of all, we need not press the quest for values to the breaking point. "What is man for?" has many answers, some of which are implicitly assumed in the way behavioral studies are carried out and their conclusions applied to psychotherapy, counseling, human engineering, and similar areas.

Secondly, psychological laws, if there be any, are general statements that apply universally to all mankind. They are obtained as a residue after boiling away everything that differentiates one person from another. If such abstract, impersonal principles are to be useful in understanding the behavior of a unique individual, some of the original selfhood vaporized in the process of generalization must be recondensed. At the heart of each self lies a value system that serves as a road map for its journey through life. There can be no doubt that psychologists as a group as well as individuals have final purposes which chart the course of their profession. If this statement needs any proof, the **Ethical Standards of Psychologists,** now being revised by the American Psychological Association (1200 Seventeenth St., N.W., Washington, D.C. 20037), will suffice.

The disagreement about values serves as an excellent example of the way that psychology and science in general progress. Assumptions which are generally accepted at any given time tend to become outmoded and gradually change despite the reluctance of many persons to relinquish the comfort of familiar concepts. In this regard it is instructive to trace the history of some familiar construct such as gravity. Plato and other Greek philosophers of nature began by endowing space with certain geometrical characteristics which supposedly caused heavy objects to find their place below and light ones above. Countless other explanations have been proposed in modern times ranging from magnetism in general or magnetic effluvia emitted by the spinning sun, to ultramundane particles striking the surface of objects, and changes in the structure of ether produced by the presence of matter. At present the mechanistic view of gravity as a pull has been superseded by an abstract mathematical conception related to curvature of the space-time continuum. The only thing that seems certain about gravity is that our notion of it will continue to undergo development. Other mathematical ways of accounting for it have already been proposed, each involving value judgments on the part of the authors (see Chapter 11, pp. 220-221).

SUMMARY

One vestige of classical physics only now being abandoned by psychologists is the notion that science deals exclusively with facts without the intrusion of value judgments. Kelman presents an opposite view. Scientific research is neither value-free nor can it be transacted in a wholly objective manner. Consequently, an investigator must always take into account how his attitudes and values influence his conclusions.

Values presuppose goals and purposes. In spite of an almost universal refusal to speak of final purposes, the **Ethical Standards of Psychologists** gives eloquent testimony to their existence and emphasizes the need of an adequate concept of man. Psychology can deal with purpose at an intermediate level without encroaching upon the prerogatives of philosophy or becoming bogged down in useless debate.

DISCUSSION TOPICS

1 What do you understand by the term "value"? Give examples of different types of values.

2 In any type of research involving human subjects, what qualitative judgments must be made about (a) the nature of science and of man? (b) the particular kind of behavior one wishes to single out for observation? (c) the types of controls, experimental design, and statistical analysis?

3 Suppose you wish to conduct an empirical investigation of honesty in children. What implicit value judgments would be involved in addition to those mentioned above?

4 To what extent could a science that disavows values and qualitative choices deal with human problems?

5 List some obvious value judgments implied in Skinner's description of a utopian society in **Walden II.**

6 Comment on Matson's (1964, pp. 92-93) remark that the abdication of responsibility for the use or consequences of his research by a value-neutral social scientist would imply that he is "for hire."

7 Enumerate the criteria of wholesome personality. What value judgments were involved in constructing this list?

ADDITIONAL READINGS

Bertalanffy, L. von. The world of science and the world of values. In J. F. T. Bugental (Ed.), **Challenges of humanistic psychology.** New York: McGraw-Hill, 1967. We must overhaul our value system if we are to survive in this time of trouble.

Burtt, E. A. Value presuppositions in science. **Bulletin of the Atomic Scientist,** 1957, **13,** 99-106. The scientist's commitment to prediction and control must be replaced in psychology by aims more in accordance with the values of mankind.

Conant, J. B. **Modern science and modern man.** New York: Columbia University Press, 1952, pp. 65-70. Scientists, as other human beings, have biases which are reflected in the interpretation of their data.

Kelman, H. C. Value for graduate education in psychology. **American Psychologist,** 1970, **21,** 954-956. Seven value goals in the work of a psychologist are identified and explained.

Kuhn, T. S. **The structure of scientific revolution** (Rev. ed.) Chicago: University of Chicago Press, 1962. Progress in science does not consist merely in the accumulation of knowledge. It has a dialectic that changes from time to time.

Mackenzie, P. T. Fact and value. **Mind,** 1967, **76,** 228-237. Even such statements as "Jones is president of the butterfly club" involve rights and duties, and hence values.

Macklin, R. Action, causality, and teleology. **British Journal of Philosophy of Science,** 1969 **19,** 301-316. This scholarly article maintains that explanations of human action based on causality need not ignore the fact that human action is goal-directed or purposive.

Maslow, A. H. (Ed.) **New knowledge in human values.** New York: Harper & Row, 1959. Fifteen distinguished scholars answer the question, "What do we know about human values?"

Maslow, A. H. **The psychology of science: A reconnaissance.** New York: Harper & Row, 1966, Ch. 12. One goal scientists have in mind is the betterment of mankind.

Odegard, P. H. The social sciences and society. **Science,** 1964, **145**(3637), 1127. A value-free science is absurd. Social sciences by definition are concerned with man and society.

Polanyi, M. **Personal knowledge.** Chicago: University of Chicago Press, 1957. Any attempt to eliminate our human perspective from scientific investigation is doomed to failure.

Rychlak, J. F. **A philosophy of science for personality theory.** Boston: Houghton-Mifflin, 1968, pp. 237-243. Final causes are taken for granted in the personality theories of Freud, Rogers, and Skinner.

Smith, M. B. **Social psychology and human values.** Chicago: Aldine, 1969, Introduction. The attitudes of social psychologists toward the concept of value are seen in historical perspective. Also see Chapter 7 for various definitions of value.

Chapter 10

The Experimenter's Obligation to His Subjects

... every human being is a person, that is, his nature is endowed with intelligence and free will. By virtue of this, he has rights and duties of his own, flowing directly and simultaneously from his very nature, which are therefore universal, inviolable, and inalienable.

Pope John XXIII

One advantage over psychology that the physicist or chemist enjoys is that he can manipulate his subject matter with abandon. Without any qualms of conscious he can break up a rock specimen, pulverize a crystal, or smash an atom. Investigators working with animals must be more humane. In 1968 the American Psychological Association promulgated a set of principles for the care and use of animals. A copy of these principles are to be placed in every room and laboratory where animal research is carried on and any violations of the code are to be reported to the Board on Scientific Affairs.

There are circumstances in which the risk of death or permanent disability to animal subjects seems justified, such as in the research that led to the development of polio vaccine. Psychologists on occasions implant electrodes in the brains of animals to help unravel the mystery of behavior. Since brain tissue has no pain receptors, the discomfort is negligible. At other times it may be useful to rear newborn animals in the dark to learn more about the development of vision in children. Or puppies may be kept in isolation chambers for the first few months of their lives to determine whether some effects of sensory deprivation are permanent. In one series of classic experiments infant chimpanzees were raised without benefit of a mother or other simian companionship to investigate their need for monkey love.

A psychologist working with human subjects cannot allow himself such liberties. Each individual is a person of inestimable worth, endowed with certain inalienable rights that everyone must respect. Sometimes an animal may be sacrificed for the sake of science, but never a human being. The world was justly shocked by the inhuman treatment of inmates in Nazi concentration camps by a few unscrupulous investigators who used them as guinea pigs for trivial experiments. A widely publicized incident in this country involved the exposure of elderly patients to cancer to determine under what conditions they would contract the disease. These abhorrent cases are truly exceptional. Most scientists are as sensitive as other people to the needs of human beings. At the same time some psychologists have been known to infringe on the rights of their subjects through thoughtlessness rather than callousness.

Most of us know someone who becomes so engrossed in what he is doing as to lose contact with much that goes on around him. Scientists are not a breed apart. An investigator with strong introvert inclinations to live in a world of his own making may find that his single-minded pursuit of knowledge reinforces this tendency. Particularly if he is engaged in some narrow specialty that the average person cannot comprehend, communication with others is apt to become increasingly difficult. As a result he may cease to read newspapers or to take an active interest in politics and current social problems. The creative efforts of a research scientist, like those of a novelist, may intrude upon his thinking most of his waking hours and are likely to be of greater interest than most other concerns. If, in addition, he is a psychologist dedicated to the exclusive use of natural science methods originally devised to study inanimate matter his attention may focus on the goals to be accomplished rather than the people involved. In other words, he may become so intent on devising the most efficient means of collecting empirical data that he overlooks harmful side effects to the subjects. Although the risks here are less imminent and perilous than some reported in medical experimentation, the dangers do exist. In discussing the use of encounter groups in Chapter 4 attention was also called to some potential hazards of sensitivity training.

In recent years psychologists have become acutely aware of the experimenter's ethical responsibility to his human subjects. Various committees have been set up to establish ethical guidelines for discharging these obligations. The following report is an example.

Privacy and Behavioral Research

In recent years there have been growing threats to the privacy of individuals. Wiretapping, electronic eavesdropping, the use of personality tests in employment, the use of the lie detector in security or criminal investigations, and the detailed scrutiny of the private lives of people receiving public welfare funds all involve invasions of privacy. Although the social purpose is usually clear, the impact on the persons involved may be damaging. Our society has become more and more sensitive to the need to avoid such damage.

This concern has led to extensive discussion about the propriety of certain procedures in behavioral research, by the Congress, by officials in the various agencies of the Government, by university officials, by the scientific community generally, and by leaders in professional societies in the behavioral sciences. The Office of Science and Technology appointed a panel, in January 1966, to examine these issues and to propose guidelines for those who are engaged in behavioral research or associated with its support and management.

The panel has restricted its attention to issues of privacy arising in connection with programs of data collection and study which are intimately associated with behavioral research. For example, it has not reviewed a number of the programs for data collection which are sponsored by the Federal Government, such as the various censuses, health and welfare statistics, and financial information secured from business and industry. These programs may also encroach upon the privacy of individuals, either through the burden of disclosure which they impose on respondents or through their availability for unintended purposes.

It is our opinion that the principles described in this report for protection of privacy in behavioral research should apply equally to such inquiries. When response is mandatory, as in the case of information that must be furnished to the Government, there is an even greater burden on the sponsoring agency to protect the individual against disclosure unless disclosure is specifically sanctioned by statute.

The panel has not reviewed in detail the wide variety of mechanical or electronic devices which make it possible to intrude into private lives. We have become acquainted with a few of the problems in that field, however, and are dismayed to observe the disregard for human values indicated by the advocacy or actual practice of eavesdropping, the use of lie detection without clear justification, and the frequent willingness to institute surveillance procedures to handle the problems of a small proportion of our population at the risk of eroding the rights and the quality of life for the majority.

Likewise, the panel has not reviewed in detail the propriety of procedures involved in employment or social welfare activities. Enough examples have been brought to our attention, however, to make us feel that examination of procedures in these spheres is needed also.

The attitudes of various segments of our society about proper procedures for the protection of privacy and the right to self-determination have been explored by the panel. It has reviewed relevant research in the behavioral sciences and the administrative practices of universities and Government agencies. It has also consulted with the scientific community through its professional organizations.

Threats to Privacy

The right to privacy is the right of the individual to decide for himself how much he will share with others his thoughts, his feelings, and the facts of his personal life. It is a right that is essential to insure dignity and freedom of self-determination. In recent years there has been a severe erosion of this right by the widespread and often callous use of various devices for eavesdropping, lie detection, and secret observation in politics, in business, and in law enforcement. Indeed, modern electronic instruments for wiretapping and bugging have opened any human activity to the threat of illicit invasion of privacy. This unwholesome state of affairs has led to wide public concern over the methods of inquiry used by agencies of public employment, social welfare, and law enforcement.

Behavioral research, devoted as it is to the discovery of facts and principles underlying human activity of all types, comes naturally under scrutiny in any examination of possible threats to privacy. All of the social sciences, including economics, political science, anthropology, sociology, and psychology, take as a major object of study the behavior of individuals, communities, or other groups. In one context or another, investigators in all of these disciplines frequently need to seek information that is private to the men, women, and children who are the subjects of their study. In most instances this information is freely given by those who consent to cooperate in the scientific process. But the very nature of behavioral research is such that there is a risk of invasion of privacy if unusual care is not taken to secure the consent of research subjects, or if the data obtained are not given full confidentiality.

While the privacy problem in scientific research is small in comparison to that which exists in employment interviewing, social welfare screening, and law enforcement investigations, the opportunity for improper invasion is not negligible. About 35,000 behavioral scientists are engaged in research in the United States, 2,100 new Ph.Ds are graduated each year, and the total number of students enrolled for advanced degrees in the behavioral sciences exceeds 40,000 at the present time.

It is probable that relatively few of the studies undertaken by these scientists raise serious questions of propriety in relation to privacy and human dignity. From a survey of articles published in professional journals and of research grant applications submitted to Government agencies, we have concluded that most scientists who conduct research in privacy-sensitive areas are aware of the ethical implications of their experimental designs and arrange to secure the consent of subjects and to protect the confidentiality of the data obtained from them.

It cannot be denied, however, that, in a limited number of instances, behavioral scientists have not followed appropriate procedures to protect the rights of their subjects, and that in other cases recognition of the importance of privacy-invading considerations has not been as sophisticated, or the considerations as affirmatively implemented, as good practice demands. Because of this failure there has been pressure from some quarters, both within the Government and outside of it, to place arbitrary limits on the research methods which may be used. Behavioral scientists as a group do not question the importance of the right to privacy and are understandably concerned when suggestions are made that the detailed processes of science should be subjected to control by legislation or arbitrary administrative ruling. All scientists are opposed to restrictions which may curtail important research. At the same time they have an obligation to insure that all possible steps are taken to assure respect for the privacy and dignity of their subjects.

Conflicting Rights

It is clear that there exists an important conflict between two values, both of which are strongly held in American society.

The individual has an inalienable right to dignity, self-respect, and freedom to determine his own thoughts and actions within the broad limits set by the requirements of society. The essential element in privacy and self-determination is the privilege of making one's own decision as to the extent to which one will reveal thoughts, feelings, and actions. When a person consents freely and fully to share himself with others—with a scientist, an employer, or a credit investigator—there is no invasion of privacy, regardless of the quality or nature of the information revealed.

Behavioral science is representative of another value vigorously championed by most American citizens, the right to know anything that may be known or discovered about any part of the universe. Man is part of this universe, and the extent of the Federal Government's financial support of human behavioral research (on the order of $300 million in 1966) testifies to the importance placed on the study of human behavior by the American people. In the past there have been conflicts between theological beliefs and the theoretical analyses of the physical sciences. These conflicts have largely subsided, but the behavioral sciences seem to have inherited the basic conflict that arises when strongly held beliefs or moral attitudes—whether theologically, economically, or politically based—are subjected to the free ranging process of scientific inquiry. If society is to exercise its right to know, it must free its behavioral scientist as much as possible from unnecessary restraints. Behavioral scientists in turn must accept the constructive restraints that society imposes in order to establish that level of dignity, freedom, and personal fulfillment that men treasure virtually above all else in life.

The root of the conflict between the individual's right to privacy and society's right of discovery is the research process. Behavioral science seeks to assess and to measure many qualities of men's minds, feelings, and actions. In the absence of informed consent on the part of the subject, these measurements represent invasion of privacy. The scientist must therefore obtain the consent of his subject.

To obtain truly informed consent is often difficult. In the first place, the nature of the inquiry sometimes cannot be explained adequately because it involves complex variables that the nonscientist does not understand. Examples are the personality variables measured by questionnaires, and the qualities of cognitive processes measured by creativity tests. Second, the validity of an experiment is sometimes destroyed if the subject knows all the details of its conduct. Examples include drug testing, in which the effect of suggestion (placebo effect) must be avoided, and studies of persuasibility, in which the subjects remain ignorant of the influences that are being presented experimentally. Clearly, then, if behavioral research is to be effective, some modification of the traditional concept of informed consent is needed.

Such a change in no sense voids the more general proposition that the performance of human behavioral research is the product of a partnership between the scientist and his subject. Consent to participate in a study must be the norm before any subject embarks on the enterprise. Since consent must sometimes be given despite an admittedly inadequate understanding of the scientific purposes of the research procedures, the right to discontinue participation at any point must be stipulated in clear terms. In the meantime, when full information is not available to the subject and when no alternative procedures to minimize the privacy problem are available, the relationship between the subject and the scientist (and between the subject and the institution sponsoring the scientists) must be based upon trust. This places the scientist and the sponsoring institution under a fiduciary obligation to protect the privacy and dignity of the subject who entrusts himself to them. The scientist must agree to treat the subject fairly and with dignity, to cause him no inconvenience or discomfort unless the extent of the inconvenience and discomfort has been accepted by the subject in advance, to inform the subject as fully as possible of the purposes of the inquiry or experiment, and to put into effect all procedures which will assure the confidentiality of whatever information is obtained.

Occasionally, even this degree of consent cannot be obtained. Naturalistic observations of group behavior must sometimes be made unbeknownst to the subjects. In such cases, as well as in all others, the scientist has the obligation to insure full confidentiality of the research records. Only by doing so, and by making certain that published reports contain no identifying reference to a given subject, can the invasion of privacy be minimized.

Basically, then, the protection of privacy in research is assured first by securing the informed consent of the subject. When the subject cannot be completely informed, the consent must be based on trust in the scientist and in the institution sponsoring him. In any case the scientist and his sponsoring institution must insure privacy by the maintenance of confidentiality.

In the end, the fact must be accepted that human behavioral research will at times produce discomfort to some subjects, and will entail a partial invasion of their privacy. Neither the principle of privacy nor the need to discover new knowledge can supervene universally. As with other conflicting values in our society, there must be constant adjustment and compromise, with the decision as to which value is to govern in a given instance to be determined by a weighing of the costs and the gains—the cost in privacy, the gain in knowledge. The decision cannot be made by the investigator alone, because he has a vested interest in his own research program, but must be a positive concern of his scientific peers and the institution which sponsors his work. Our society has grown strong on the principle of minimizing costs and maximizing gains, and, when warmly held values are in conflict, there must be a thoughtful evaluation of the specific case. In particular we do not believe that detailed Governmental controls of research methods or instruments can substitute for the more effective procedures which are available and carry less risk of damage to the scientific enterprise.

Ethical Aspects of Human Research

Greater attention must be given to the ethical aspects of human research. The increase in scientists and in volume of research provides more chance for carelessness or recklessness and, in the hurried search for useful findings, can lead to abuses. Furthermore, if standards are not carefully maintained, there could develop an atmosphere of disregard for privacy that would be altogether alien to the spirit of American society. The increased potentials for damage and for fruitful outcomes from new knowledge are in no small part results of increased Federal support of behavioral science. While no one would suggest that ethical standards should be different for scientists supported by public funds and for those supported by private funds, the Government has an especially strong obligation to support research only under conditions that give fullest protection to individual human dignity. Government must avow and maintain the highest standards for the guidance of all.

To summarize, three parties—the investigator, his institution, and the sponsoring agency—have the responsibility for maintaining proper ethical standards with respect to Government-sponsored research. The investigator designs the research and is in the best position to evaluate the propriety of his procedures. He has, therefore, the ultimate responsibility for insuring that his research is both effective and ethical. The formalization of our ethics concerning privacy in connection with research is too recent, and perhaps too incomplete, to permit the assumption that all investigators have a full understanding of the proper methods for protecting the rights of subjects. Furthermore, the investigator is first and foremost a scientist in search of new knowledge, and it would not be in accord with our understanding of human motivation to expect him always to be as vigilant for his subject's welfare as he is for the productiveness of his own research.

We conclude, therefore, that responsibility must also be borne by the institution which employs the investigator. The employing instituion is often a university or a Government laboratory in which there are other scientists capable of reviewing the research plan. Such persons, drawn in part from disciplines other than the behavioral sciences, can present views that are colored neither by self-interest nor by the blind spots that may characterize the specific discipline of the investigator.

Finally, the sponsoring agency is obligated to make certain that both the investigator and his institution are fully aware of the importance of the ethical aspects of the research and that they have taken the necessary steps to discharge their responsibility to the human subjects involved. We believe that, in the majority of instances, it is neither necessary nor desirable for an agency to exceed this level of responsibility.

Conclusions

From our examination of the relation of behavioral science research to the right to privacy, we have been led to the following conclusions.

1 While most current practices in the field pose no significant threat to the privacy of research subjects, a sufficient number of exceptions have been noted to warrant a sharp increase in attention to procedures that will assure protection of this right. The increasing scale of behavioral research is itself an additional reason for focusing attention in this area.

2 Participation by subjects must be voluntary and based on informed consent to the extent that this is consistent with the objectives of the research. It is fully consistent with the protection of privacy that, in the absence of full information, consent be based on trust in the qualified investigator and the integrity of his institution.

3 The scientist has an obligation to insure that no permanent physical or psychological harm will ensue from the research procedures, and that temporary discomfort or loss of privacy will be remedied in an appropriate way during the course of the research or at its completion. To merit trust, the scientist must design his research with a view to protecting, to the fullest extent possible, the privacy of the subjects. If intrusion on privacy proves essential to the research, he should not proceed with his proposed experiment until he and his colleagues have considered all of the relevant facts and he has determined, with support from them, that the benefits outweigh the costs.

4 The scientist has the same responsibility to protect the privacy of the individual in published reports and in research records that he has in the conduct of the research itself.

5 The primary responsibility for the use of ethical procedures must rest with the individual investigator, but Government agencies that support behavioral research should satisfy themselves that the institution which employs the investigator has effectively accepted its responsibility to require that he meet proper ethical standards.

6 Legislation to assure appropriate recognition of the rights of human subjects is neither necessary nor desirable if the scientists and sponsoring institutions fully discharge their responsibilities in accommodating to the claim of privacy. Because of its relative inflexibility, legislation cannot meet the challenge of the subtle and sensitive conflict of values under consideration, nor can it aid in the wise decision making by individuals which is required to assure optimum protection of subjects, together with the fullest effectiveness of research.

Recommendations

These conclusions lead us to make the following recommendations.

1 That Government agencies supporting research in their own laboratories or in outside institutions require those institutions to agree to accept responsibility for the ethical propriety of human research performed with the aid of Government funds.

2 That the methods used for institutional review be determined by the institutions themselves. The greatest possible flexibility of methods should be encouraged in order to build effective support for the principle of institutional responsibility within universities or other organizations. Institutions differ in their internal structures and operating procedures, and no single, rigid formula will work for all.

3 That investigators and institutions be notified of the importance of consent and confidentiality as ethical requirements in research design, and that when either condition cannot be met, an explanation of the reasons be made in the application for funds.

4 That when research is undertaken directly by, or purchased on specification by, a Government agency, responsibility for protection of privacy lies with the agency. When independent research is funded by the Government, however, responsibility lies primarily with the scientist and his institution, and research instruments or design should not be subject to detailed review by Government agencies with respect to protection of privacy.

5 That universities and professional associations be encouraged to emphasize the ethical aspects of behavioral research. When a training grant is made, a university should be requested to indicate its understanding that support of education on the ethics of research is one of the purposes of the grant.

Another topic that psychologists worry about in assessing their social responsibility is the matter of deception. To the extent that the investigator tries to keep the subject in the dark about the precise purpose of his research, deception enters into almost every experiment. It has always been assumed that if the subject were aware of exactly what the experimenter wants to know, he might not be able to respond in a natural way. The situation is somewhat analogous to that of the sandlot baseball player who, at the moment of truth, concentrates on how to swing the bat rather than on the ball. On the other hand, some scientists are beginning to question the advisability of an impersonal, artificial approach to the subject (e.g., Jourard, 1968; Kelman, 1969, pp. 223-225). Different results, which in many cases seem more valid, are obtained when the subject is treated as a full-fledged participant in the research.

Then there is the matter of unconscious motivation. The typical subject invests something of himself in the research and, presumably, would like to see it succeed. Without being aware of this bias he may respond differently than he would on other occasions. In Part Four we will see that the experimenter as well as the subject is susceptible to unconscious influences. In some cases it has been shown that a supposedly objective hypothesis may be subconsciously transformed into a self-fulfilling prophecy.

In certain types of studies the investigator may wish to induce a particular mental set in his subjects. A simple way to do this is through deception. The subject may be asked to complete a series of tasks and given the impression that he has failed on all of them. Or he may be led to believe that he possesses some very desirable or undesirable trait to see how this perception influences his self-image. Julius Seeman addresses himself to some of these issues.

Deception in Psychological Research

Since the development of psychology as a behavioral science, the issue of experimental controls has been a central one. In the early history of psychology, when attention was centered on studies of sensation, perception, and learning, the problem of controls was readily managed. In recent years, however, psychologists have turned to the study of more complex phenomena, including attitudes, motivational states, expectancies, anxiety, dissonance, and stress. The study of these variables imposes more difficult demands on the control of the experimental setting.

One of the ways that psychologists have sought to construct relevant experimental controls is to devise what I shall call fictional environments—that is to say, environments that appear to have certain properties but that in fact do not have these properties. These fictional environments are designed to induce specified sets or expectancies in the subject. Illustrations of such fictional environments are, for example, the creation of fictional social norms through the use of confederates, the use of false verbal instructions, or the use of nonfunctional visual props such as electronic gear and wires.

One of the distinguishing characteristics of these fictional environments is that they typically involve the use of deception. This article will focus on the issue of deception in research and consider four aspects of the problem: the frequency with which deception is employed in research, the pragmatic complications that result from the use of deception, the public policy issues inherent in the problem, and the ethical issues involved.

With respect of the incidence of deception, it may be useful to note the frequency with which deception appears in the published literature and to determine whether any long-term trends are evident. For this purpose, the total published literature in several journals was analyzed for the years 1948 and 1963. Journals were chosen to reflect different fields within psychology.

Table 1 portrays the incidence of studies using deception for these two time periods. It will be seen from the table that journals emphasizing "experimental" and "clinical" areas had a relatively low incidence of deception studies in comparison with "personality and social" areas. The latter areas also showed a distinct rise in the use of deception. When the figures for the *Journal of Personality* and the *Journal of Abnormal and Social Psychology* are combined, the mean for 1948 is 18.47% and the mean for 1963 is 38.17%. It seems safe to conclude that to some degree deception has come to be the method of choice in this area of research.

The use of deception poses formidable pragmatic problems in psychological research. Many studies assume the existence either of a neutral and naïve set or some particular set specified by the experimenter. The validity of the study rests on the ability of the experimenter to explain the variance in subject behavior on the basis of particular experimental variables. But the use of deception introduces a whole series of new variables that may influence the set of the subjects in unspecified ways and introduce behavioral variations entirely unknown to the experimenter.

The recent literature on the social psychology of experiments emphasizes these problems. In particular, Orne (1962) and Rosenthal (1963) have pointed out the influence of subject set on experimental results. Orne has described what he calls the demand characteristic of an experiment. By this he means the cues that implicitly communicate to the subject what is expected of him and that mediate his role in the experiment. Orne has shown that subject set alone can produce effects comparable to those produced by the experiment itself. Rosenthal similarly found that expectations by either subject or experimenter influenced significantly the outcomes of studies.

Thus we cannot ignore the problems brought about by subject set. When a subject has once participated in a study using deception he is no longer a naive subject but a sophisticated subject who brings to subsequent studies a variety of personal theories and hypotheses that guide the behavior of the subject quite as decisively as theories and hypotheses guide the behavior of an experimenter. In view of the frequency with which deception is used in research we may soon be reaching a point where we no longer have naive subjects, but only naive experimenters. It is an ironic fact that the use of deception, which is intended to control the experimental environment, may serve only to contaminate it.

Let us now move from the realm of pragmatics to the realm of public policy. In order to clarify the issue here, it may be useful to highlight the

Table 1   Incidence of Studies Using Deception in 1948 and 1963

Journal	1948			1963		
	Total no. human-subject studies	No. using deception	%	Total no. human-subject studies	No. using deception	%
Journal of Abnormal and Social Psychology	28	4	14.3	190	70	36.8
Journal of Personality	21	5	23.8	41	18	43.9
Journal of Consulting Psychology	34	1	2.9	118	11	9.3
Journal of Experimental Psychology	48	7	14.6	167	18	10.8

central dilemma posed by the use of deception. The crux of the issue is the conflict between the rights of the individual and the needs of society. Those who justify the use of deception argue that the accumulation of scientifically derived knowledge sometimes exacts a price from individuals, and that this knowledge is worth the price. What does our society have to say on this point? The democratic ethic reflects continuing tensions generated by conflicts between individual and collective good. These conflicts rarely fail to take account of the central position that the rights of the individual hold in our social system. Even where there is collective danger, individual rights have a pivotal position. For example, our laws provide that even in time of war a person conscientiously opposed to military service may undertake civilian service.

Another illustration may be found in the recent Supreme Court decision in the Escobedo and the Miranda cases. In these cases the issue turned on the rights of individuals interrogated in connection with alleged crimes. In two separate actions, Danny Escobedo and Jose Miranda each confessed to major criminal offenses. It was later argued that the confessions should be set aside because the rights of the defendants had not been adequately protected through timely representation by attorneys. The Supreme Court set aside the convictions on the grounds of (a) the respect a government must accord to the dignity and integrity of its citizens and (b) the right to remain silent unless the person chooses to speak in the unfettered exercise of his own will. The principle here is one of informed consent to an action affecting the welfare of the individual.

It is this principle of informed consent that has characterized the evolving public policy with regard to the rights of a research subject. Recent government regulations speak clearly to this point, and insist that those who use human subjects for research do so only with the informed consent of the subject or, in the case of children, the parent or guardian. These regulations seem entirely congruent with the values of a society that accords the individual a place of primary importance in the social structure.

I want to move now to the ethics of deception. It is possible that the most correct position with regard to the use of deception may turn out to be an absolutist position. Such a position would advance the ends-means argument; namely, that the outcome of any process is inexorably embedded in the means used. Thus, a process that used deceptive means could not lead to a "good" end.

There is much to be said for such a view, both ethically and pragmatically. In learning experiments, for instance, it is clear that the end point of a learning curve is lawfully related to its antecedent properties. In psychotherapy, the outcome is simply the end point of a process continuum. In an analogous way, the end point of an experience in which deception is embedded is functionally related to the deception process.

The ends-means view happens to be the view I hold. But one does not need to take an absolutist position in order to have reservations about the ethics of deception. One could argue that there are instances of innocuous deception that have no adverse consequences. This still leaves the question open with regard to other studies. The ethical issue is drawn most sharply in those studies that use noxious deception. Consider, for instance, the three studies that follow.

The first study was intended to measure the effects of cognitive dissonance. Measures were taken of psychiatric patients' reported self-esteem and of the esteem in which they held their nurses. Subjects used were those who reported high positive esteem both for themselves and their nurses. The subjects were then given rating sheets that had purportedly been made by the nurses with respect to the patients. These fictitious ratings in all cases showed that the nurses held these patients in low exteem. Actually the nurses had not made any ratings at all.

The second study concerned the effect of persuasive messages on attitudes. In this study, self-ratings were obtained from psychiatric patients on a hostility continuum. Subjects selected were patients who rated themselves as less hostile than the average person. These subjects were later given fictitious "profiles" of themselves indicating that they were more hostile than the average person. The subjects were not informed of the deception, nor deconditioned by the experimenter after the experiment was over.

In the third study, the experimenter told a group of randomly selected college males that they had latent homosexual drives, when in fact no data were collected to support such a statement. The experimenter never bothered to explain his deception afterward, on the ground that he might want to do another study with the same subjects later on.

One notes in these studies some disturbing human relations side effects. In the first study, the experimenter intruded upon the nurse-patient relationship in a profoundly disruptive way without communication to the nurses themselves. In the second and third studies, the experimenters left the subjects to live with the fictions about their personal characteristics. None of the procedures was necessary to the conduct of the studies themselves. The occurrence of these unethical side effects is congruent with the ends-means hypothesis.

There is a further problem in the deception studies cited above. It is usually thought that telling subjects about the deception corrects the situation and extinguishes the attitude. But this assumption needs further examination. When a person is told that he has been deceived, he may quite conceivably be confused as to when the deception had really taken place. Since he will quite appropriately have lost confidence in the person's veracity, the subject may never be able to disentangle the times of truth and the times of falsity in his relationship to the experimenter. Ray Norris has suggested, on these grounds, that some deceptions may have irreversible consequences.

With regard to the deception procedures used in the studies themselves, I would like to suggest that they may be classified accurately as *antitherapy.* An analysis of the deception situation will reveal systematic reversal of the major properties of the therapy environment. I want to elaborate this point in some detail because it is a central point in the understanding of deception.

In the therapeutic situation the therapist tries to establish conditions of *trust, congruence,* and *reality.* He acts consistently in ways that will develop trust in him by the client. This trust is an essential precondition of self-disclosure by the client. This condition of trust is not a contrived condition, but a genuine condition. It develops as the therapist becomes more and more a genuine person to the client, a person who is just what he seems to be. This genuine condition is an aspect of the therapist's self-congruence. This is to say that the therapist's underlying attitudes and intentions are congruent with his outward behavior to the client.

The third property of the therapeutic situation is the reality condition. The therapist knows that a disturbed person often behaves in terms of reality distortion. Prior experience has led the client to modify the reality situation and, out of his own needs, to create fictional environments of his own. The task of the therapist here is to help the client discard the reality distortion and to learn how to respond in terms of accurate reality perceptions.

If we turn now to the deception studies, we shall see that they reverse each of the three conditions I have enumerated and involve conditions of *distrust, incongruence,* and *unreality.*[1] It is self-evident that the subject learns to distrust the experimenter, and perhaps by generalization to distrust any

---

[1] The author [Seeman] wishes to thank Theodore Newcomb for pointing out the trust-distrust aspect of the comparison between therapy and deception.

experimenter. The deception situation also involves incongruence on the part of the experimenter. He is not, after all, what he appears to be. And finally, the deception experiment reverses the reality situation. The experimenter presents reality distortion in the guise of reality and asks the subjects to act upon this distortion as though it were reality. This, I think, is the crux of the antitherapy situation. Where the therapist helps the client to give up reality distortion as a basis for action, the experimenter in a deception study leads the subject to adopt reality distortion as a basis for action. No more exact reversal seems possible.

There is one final consideration with respect to the use of deception. It is a difficult point to make because it requires a reexamination of the psychologist's most basic assumptions about his discipline. An empirical discipline takes for granted that the primary goal of its efforts is the accumulation of knowledge. Psychologists have been trained to a finely honed position with regard to empirical processes and they have learned to value knowledge above all else. Thus it is scarcely possible to argue for the importance of a nonempirical process. Yet that is what I propose. I suggest that the ultimate goal of the scientific enterprise ought to be not knowledge but wisdom. Knowledge alone has a neutrality that can be deadly in our time. It can destroy as well as create. The existence of a Hiroshima in man's history demonstrates that knowledge alone is not enough, and that the old question of "knowledge for what?" must still be asked. If knowledge in psychology is won at the cost of some essential humanness in one person's relationship to another, perhaps the price is too high.

From what has been said so far in this chapter the student may gain the impression that psychological research is a game in which the experimenter tries to outwit the subject. Nothing could be further from the truth. What we have been discussing are questionable practices and some abuses which psychologists wish to bring out into the open in order to guard against them. The American Psychological Association is keenly aware of the ethical issues involved in the use of human subjects. A thorough revision of the standards for psychological research is under way at the present time. A proposed set of principles covering all the problems raised in this chapter and many others has been published by the Ad Hoc Committee on Ethical Standards (Cook et al., 1971) and comments solicited from the entire membership before they are submitted for approval.

SUMMARY

Psychologists are becoming increasingly concerned about the potential dangers of certain types of research to experimental subjects. Stringent regulations have been promulgated for the laboratory care and use of animals. Various committees are engaged in continuing studies of the investigator's ethical obligations to human subjects. A report of the Panel on Privacy and Behavioral Research was cited as an example. The harmful aftereffects of some uses of deception were discussed at length. Such questionable practices are not typical of psychological investigation in general, and measures are being taken to insure the safety, integrity, and human dignity of all who participate as subjects.

DISCUSSION TOPICS

1 How successful is the investigator in deceiving the typical subject from a psychology class about the precise purpose of his experiment?

2 Is the experience of having been deceived by an investigator likely to influence the performance of a subject in a future experiment in any significant way?

3 What is your attitude toward experiments in which the other "subjects" are accomplices who have been instructed by the experimenter to deceive the real subject by making erroneous observations?

4 In some studies subjects were led to believe that they possessed homosexual tendencies or that their lives were in actual danger while flying in an airplane. The deception was explained in the debriefing at the end of the experiment. Would you use such techniques? Give the reasons for your answer.

5 What are the ethical implications of power groups on the campus manipulating students so that they unwittingly support causes to which they do not subscribe?

6 State the conditions under which you as an experimenter would consider the use of deception permissible.

7 How can the negative effects of deception on the subjects and on the experiment be minimized?

8 Discuss the method of role playing as a possible alternative to the use of deception.

9 Comment on the conclusions of the Panel on Privacy and Behavioral Research.

ADDITIONAL READINGS

Baumrind, D. Some thoughts on ethics of research: After reading Milgram's "Behavioral study of obedience." **American Psychologist,** 1964, **19,** 421-423. Human subjects must be treated with dignity and respect and safeguarded against unwholesome aftereffects.

Conrad, H. S. Clearance of questionnaires with respect to "invasion of privacy," public sensitivities, ethical standards, etc. **American Psychologist,** 1967, **22,** 356-359. Address given at a symposium sponsored by the National Council on Measurement in Education.

Fischer, C. T. Ethical issues in the use of human subjects. **American Psychologist,** 1968, **32,** 532. Questions are raised about the aftereffects on character of certain types of research and about the requirement for students to participate in research as subjects.

Gibbons, C. G. Can sensitivity training be destructive? **American Psychologist,** 1968, **23,** 288. Analogous to drug therapy, the contraindications for sensitivity training should be determined and published in the publicity brochures.

Kelman, H. C. **A time to speak: On human values and social research.** San Francisco; Jossey-Bass, 1968. Ch. 8 is entitled "The human use of human subjects."

Reubhausen, O. M., and Brim, O. G., Jr. Privacy and behavioral research. **American Psychologist,** 1966, **21,** 423-437. The moral right to privacy sometimes conflicts with the community's need for research on social problems. Guidelines for a code of ethics are suggested.

Rubin, Z. Jokers wild in the lab. **Psychology Today,** 1970, **4**(7), 18-24. Several striking examples are given of deception in psychological experiments which offend the ethical sensitivities of most people.

Smith, M. B. Conflicting values affecting behavioral research with children. **Children,** 1967, **14,** 53-58. Smith discusses the special ethical issues that arise in research with children.

Chapter 11

Professional Responsibility

No part of science is categorically free of social values. The scientist shares responsibility for the uses that are made of his discoveries.

Edward L. Walker

When anyone acts in a private capacity, he is likely to feel personally responsible for whatever he does. His actions are his own and he alone is accountable for them. When he joins a group, the situation changes. A group is amorphous and rather impersonal. While each member may have a voice in decision making, and perhaps even a vote, responsibility can easily be shifted from one's own shoulders to those of the vague corporate entity. It is even possible to assume the attitude of a passive onlooker characterized by the expression, "Let George do it." Sometimes through inertia, sometimes through a spirit of defeatism, a person may say to himself, "How can I, a single voter, change the whole U.S. foreign policy?" Or, "What can I do as a lone voice crying in the wilderness to transform public attitudes toward race, education, or anything else?" The excuses are many and persuasive. "I already have more work than I can do. Do you expect me to become a secular missionary? Besides, how would I start and where could I get a hearing?" If, in addition, the individual is a scientist concentrating all his energies on some research problem in hope of a breakthrough, such a distraction might possibly appear as the thin edge between failure and success.

Usually some dramatic event is needed to shake people out of their lethargy. In the case of physicists it was the atomic bomb. For a century or more the Western world had lulled itself into the comfortable belief that science has all the answers. No one could deny the control it was gaining over the forces of nature to make them serve mankind. Looking into the future most people could envision a happy world in which the needs of everyone were plentifully supplied.

Then came Hiroshima and the sudden realization that society's moral and social development had not kept pace with technical progress. The awesome natural forces that physicists had unleashed could be used for evil purposes as readily as for good. Many scientists were guilt stricken. Was it right for them to make discoveries that society might be counted on to misuse? What responsibility did each of them bear for 78,000 deaths, hundreds of thousands of casualties, and a city leveled to the ground?

Fortunately for psychology, our knowledge of behavior has not advanced to the stage where it constitutes an imminent danger in the hands of those minded to abuse it. There is still time to ponder the most urgent ethical questions with the expectation of finding at least tentative answers. Fortunately, also, many psychologists are beginning to respond to the challenge. We cannot hope to achieve instant agreement on what is to be done or left undone, but we can and should become involved in the discussion. Rollo May raises some issues that deserve consideration.

Social Responsibilities of Psychologists

The moral man is not the one who merely wants to do
what is right and does it, nor the man without guilt, but
he who is conscious of what he is doing.

Hegel (1770-1831)

This topic challenges us not only because of its importance to us as social scientists, but also as human beings living in a precarious period of our world. During the days when I was first working on the essay on which this . . .

is based, the President had just announced that there was one slim chance still open of getting a test ban, failing which the genie of thermonuclear war power and its companion devil, overkill, would be out of the bottle for good. Those same days the news was full of reports of the hundreds imprisoned in Birmingham. And the very evening I was writing down some of these ideas, a riot occurred in Harlem and a march down Amsterdam Avenue in New York City, past Columbia University and half a block from our home. A couplet from Shakespeare's last four lines in King Lear kept running through my mind,

> The weight of this sad time we must obey,
> Speak what we feel, not what we ought to say.

If we then had the illusion that as soon as those two problems quieted down, we should be relieved of our precarious state, we were disillusioned soon enough. For we soon saw our marines land in the Dominican Republic, with the result that a "permanently precarious" state is insured, and since then the war has escalated in Vietnam—for which, no matter what one's political views, there seems no ultimate outcome which is not negative. I mention these things to indicate that there seems little doubt but that we shall be in a precarious world situation for some decades to come: unless we blind ourselves to the realities, we shall live "in crisis" for a good while. It therefore behooves us the more as psychologists to be concerned with the question of social responsibility.

The first thing that strikes us as we consider this topic is that we as psychologists, until four or five years ago, did not take our social responsibility in any adequate way or to the degree our society has a right to expect from us. In 1954 Arthur Compton called a conference on Science and Human Responsibility. It was, I fear, indicative of our detachment that there was only one psychologist present. The conference was made up of physicists, like Compton and Heisenberg, biologists, philosophers, and humanists. Nuclear physicists in particular have been way ahead of us in taking responsibility on the overriding issue in our world, namely, thermonuclear war. Fortunately the situation has changed in the last several years: psychologists have taken their place in the front ranks on these issues. I think there is this difference from the physicists: the psychologists have taken their part as responsible citizens, and so far as I can see, what is still lacking is a responsible concern with the fact that the development of the science of psychology itself contains dangers to the society, just as did the development of physics.

Why was it that the nuclear physicists committed themselves a number of years before psychologists? Not because they alone know the tremendous destructive power of nuclear weapons: we all knew that after Hiroshima. Their own hands had had a part in making the bomb, and their social detachment was irrevocably shaken. Can their commitment and responsible concern not be rightly interpreted as a constructive reaction to their own guilt? One of the physicists remarked at the time of the first fission, "Not one of us walked away from that look-out point at Los Alamos without saying to himself, 'God! What have we done?' " Not that any serious number of them believed that they should not have developed the atomic fission that made the bomb possible—that would have meant a scientific turning back which, even if it were possible, is unthinkable from their point of view or ours. But the shaking of their self-world relationship which they directly experienced fortunately did result among many of them in the emergence of a new level of consciousness, a level which now perforce was to include social responsibility.

I propose, similarly, that a constructive facing of our own guilt as psychologists is our healthiest place to start. This may well sound strange in most psychology departments, where at the most it would be admitted that this guilt is only potential, not actual. But it would be a pity indeed if we had to wait, as a profession, until some such cataclysmic change in the mind and spirit of modern man forced us to wake up to the power we are playing with. Robert Oppenheimer (1956a) has already reminded us, in his speech before the American Psychological Association convention in 1955, that the psychologist's responsibility is even greater than the physicist's. "The psychologist can hardly do anything," said Oppenheimer, "without realizing that for him the acquisition of knowledge opens up the most terrifying prospects of controlling what people do and how they think and how they behave and how they feel."

If Oppenheimer's words are correct—and to me it seems obvious that they are—the logic of our situation requires that we strip away professional trappings and make a more profound and searching self-examination than we or any profession is used to. Perhaps it is fitting that a psychoanalyst take the role of Socrates' gadfly in submitting some queries for such a self-examination.

The first query is our tendency to rationalize lack of commitment by the rubric "wait-till-all-the-evidence-is-in." But are not the critical situation of our contemporaneous world and the nature of the issues precisely such that they cannot wait for critical tests? We cannot wait for a test of thermonuclear war; we cannot wait for a full test of radiation. The irony of our situation is that if we wait for all the evidence, we shall not be here to use the evidence when it comes. My argument, of course, is not at all against the disciplined endeavor to gain all the evidence we can. It is, rather, against the use of this respectable ideal as a substitute for commitment. As though if we waited around long enough, the evidence would make our decisions for us! Robert Lifton (1961) well remarks in his study of thought control, any complete "personal or moral detachment in psychological (or any other) work is at best self-deception, and at worst a source of harmful distortion."

But an even more important point for us as psychologists in this connection seems to me to be this: that the nature of the issues we face is such that *we cannot know the truth except as we commit ourselves.* [Elsewhere] we mentioned the statement of a participant in a debate on the issues of nuclear war, addressed to the people listening, "you cannot have any influence whatever on the question of whether there will be war or not. This is decided by the councils of the few high political men who gather in Berlin or Moscow." My answer was, "I admit what you say *seems* to be true, and you have plenty of evidence for it. But even if you had all the evidence in the world, I still would not believe it."

As the audience well realized, I was not making an anti-intellectual statement. I was saying, rather, that if we accepted my opponent's statement, we would remain passive; and the statement would become true by virtue of our accepting it. If, on the other hand, we refused to accept it, but did what little we could to influence Congress, the President, and other leaders, then even a group as small as several hundred would have some significance.

This is the point where political freedom begins, infinitesimally small as it may be to begin with. And it is the faith of democracy that such influence can increase geometrically like a benevolent chain reaction. We all know that democracy can deteriorate into a blind faith in quantities and numbers and gross statistics. But is not democracy in its origins, and in its highest representatives, something quite else, namely, a faith in a *quality of personal commitment?* By the same token, is not freedom not at all a matter of "doing as you please," but rather the power of one's actions as a person to have significance, to *matter,* to his group?

My point is that the critical experiences of life, such as love, war, and peace, cannot come into being until we commit ourselves to them. And statements about these experiences cannot be true except as we, or somebody, commit ourselves responsibly to the beliefs. We shall return to this question in our discussion of values below.

A second question that arises in such a self-examination is our *naiveté about the problem of power.* As I observe psychologists, I find us sharing in abundant measure that aspect of the vocational disease of the Western intellectuals—the failure to see, indeed playing ostrich with, the tragic, demonic aspects of power. In the earlier studies of race relations, I failed to see in the work of psychologists an awareness of the explosions in desegregation and in race relations that were to occur.[1] Did we not underestimate the

---

[1] Kenneth Clark has pointed out this problem of power in race relations, and the challenge it poses for psychological and psychoanalytic theory. Cf. *Dark Ghetto, A Study in Powerlessness,* New York, 1965.

degree of explosive power of the accumulated repressed passion (in a Freudian sense) and the pressure of economic determinants in the suppressed group (in a Marxian sense)? The artists, in the persons of novelists like Lillian Smith and James Baldwin, turned out to be better predictors of the turmoil and rioting in desegregation than we were.

The basic problem here is that our frame of mind as psychologists seems to be one which denies and represses power. As I see it, we tend—again sharing in that symptom of the vocational illness of Western intellectuals, overemphasizing rationality—to take literally Aristotle's dictum that man is a rational animal because it makes our hypotheses simpler, permits us the comfort of continuing as mild-mannered men who assume that other men act as rationally as we *think we* do. And since our tests are set up on our own presuppositions which overlook or deny power, they naturally come up with results which fail to reveal the power needs which drive people or groups.

I have often thought, as I have interviewed psychologists for analytic schools, that there is a selective factor at work in that our profession tends to attract the type of individual who denies and represses his own power needs. These repressed power needs then have room to come out in his proclivities for controlling other people in therapy or in his identification with the power of his laboratory techniques and machines. In candidates wanting to be trained as therapists, I see not infrequently the pattern of the isolated person who wants relationship and gets attracted into doing therapy because it gives a simulated relationship which makes him feel less isolated—a "captive" love affair or friendship, which of course is no love or friendship at all, and a failure of therapy, to the extent that it is captive. Similarly, the unexpressed and unfaced power needs of psychologists going into research find a made-to-order form in which to find expression, namely, preoccupation with the power of techniques to control others.

One aspect of self-deception in connection with the above is that our belief that the pen is mightier than the sword tends to slip over into an unexamined assumption that therefore the sword, or power, is irrelevant. And *mirabile dictu,* we then fail to see that the spoken or written word can be as irresponsible and as vicious as the sword. When someone attacks you with the sword or attacks you economically as in Madison Avenue business competition, you at least can see what you're up against; whereas words which are used for power purposes, as in thought control, can be more vicious and harder to withstand in the respect that they attack the center of identity and self-consciousness.[2]

The less we play ostrich with the problem of destructive power, the more we can effectively help ourselves and our society shift our power needs toward positive goals. Take, for example, the problem of peace. In my college

[2] Cf. Lifton's study (cited above), to which I shall return later. [See Additional Readings—Ed.]

days, we believed in peace, marched for it, campaigned for it, and were so conditioned to "think peace" that we never let a thought enter our minds that there might be another war. But this made us totally unprepared to see or deal with Hitler; we did not even *perceive* this emergence of evil power (for a length of time I am ashamed to remember) because such irrational, primitive power just did not fit our categories and concepts. It simply could not exist. But it *did* exist, whether we could let ourselves see it or not. The liberal intellectuals of Germany and Europe fell into the same trap; they played into the hands of the dictators because of their failure to take the tragic realities of power into account, and they thus consequently failed to commit themselves in time.

What I am advocating—as a hoped-for consequence of this self-examination—is a widening and deepening of our consciousness to take in the problem of power in its tragic, dynamic, and demonic aspects. If I were teaching a course in beginning psychology, I would assign some reading of Karl Marx, not for the sake of his economic philosophy, but because he understood the basic significance of irrational economic and social power, and he saw how the way you get your power conditions the particular set of "rational" beliefs ("ideology") you choose. It is possible thus to reconstitute our consciousness in wider dimensions to include perceiving and understanding the socially destructive aspects of power, and also to enlist our own aggression and power needs on the constructive side of social issues. Is this not what William James sought as the "moral equivalent of war"? Peace will then not be a vacuum—a passive, zestless, unheroic and boring state—but will challenge and require our full potentialities.

A third question for self-examination is the antihistorical tendency in psychology. We are prone to see ourselves as "above" history and to fail to see that our psychology, and indeed modern science itself, are historical products like any other aspect of culture. Science has taken several quite different forms in Western culture; and it is surely arrogance to assume that our own is the absolute and final form of science. The Greek view, that science is the uncovering of *logos,* a meaningful structure of the universe, was based upon the Greek's special respect for nature. The medieval view, formulated by the scholastics and Aquinas, that all nature fits together into a rational order, became the basis for modern experimental science; it gave scientists the faith that all the segments of their diverse research could fit together and make sense. In modern times *power over* nature rather than uncovering and understanding became the goal (vide Bacon's dictum, "Knowledge is power"). And methods of attaining power were to be based on the model of the machine. Thus began the preoccupation of Western man with the calculation and control of physical nature.

Two developments, then, have been fateful for our dilemma as psychologists in our contemporary world. One was the shifting, in the seventeenth century and subsequently, of the moral absolutism and authority of the church to science. The second was the endeavor, beginning in the nineteenth century, to make *man also* an object of calculation and control, and to apply the methods which were still so impressively productive in gaining power over physical nature to gaining power over human beings.

Precisely here, it seems to me, lies the dilemma of modern pyschology. We are the representatives of modern science who are ordained to function in the realm of man's mind and spirit. (And the dilemma surely cannot be escaped by our substituting other terms like "behavior" and "awareness.") We are heirs, whether we are conscious of it or not, to the mantle of moral absolutism of science, and the mantle weighs upon us (like Hercules' shirt) more precariously than upon the physicists, who deal with inanimate nature, or the physicians, who can at least tell themselves they deal with the body. We are handed by society, whether we wish it or not, the requirement of producing answers to the ultimate questions of ethics and the spirit; and it is expected in many quarters, both outside scientific fields and inside, that we shall produce these answers by our techniques and our machines. Our dilemma, then, is whether we can have a science of man and at the same time avoid the tendency to make man over into the image of the machines and techniques by which we study him. That is, whether we can have a science of psychology and still preserve the values and distinguishing characteristics which make man a person, the values that constitute his humanity.

There are no easy answers to these questions; but I believe there *are* answers; and many of us would not be in the field of psychology at all if we believed there were not. The question above, then, is not *whether* but *in what way* can we have a science of man and preserve these values?

Rollo May is rightly concerned about the impersonal image of man that our objective methodology creates. Some of the human psychological models we construct seem about as true to real life as modern paintings of people with split faces and misplaced body members. The danger of telling people this is how they really are, is that self-concepts have a way of becoming self-fulfilling prophecies. When anyone accepts a certain image of himself he tries to be that kind of person. Rosenthal and Jacobson (1966) and Evans and Rosenthal (1969) have shown that randomly selected pupils who were given the false impression that they possessed unusual latent talent actually made significant gains over other children in measured IQ within a few months. One of the greatest obstacles to self-actualization in most children reared in the slums is that they usually have a very low estimate of their own abilities. Being convinced that they will "never amount to anything," they lack the motivation to try.

The typical assumptions that psychologists make about the nature of man (see Part Two) in order to study behavior scientifically may serve some limited purpose in the laboratory. They are not meant to describe real people any more than abstract paintings are intended to be photographic. None of us experiences his friends as passively determined organisms in everything they do, but rather as spontaneous, self-activated persons who make frequent choices based on reason. Nor do they seem to react in a machinelike manner to stimuli over which they have no control. A negative self-concept such as the one just disclaimed openly invites external controls. If enough people were to think of themselves in this way, despotic forms of society might appear to be both scientific and humanitarian.

Carl Rogers, in the following article, presents an awesome picture of what could happen in the near future as impersonal psychological techniques are perfected for overriding voluntary control. Disturbing as these prospects may be, there is reassurance in a suggestion he makes elsewhere that a cold, impersonal "Science" can never make such decisions: only people can.

The Place of the Person in the New World of the Behavioral Sciences

The science of psychology, in spite of its immaturities and its brashness, has advanced mightily in recent decades. From a concern with observation and measurement it has increasingly moved toward becoming an "if-then" science. By this I mean it has become more concerned with the discernment and discovery of lawful relationships such that *if* certain conditions exist, *then* certain behaviors will predictably follow. It is rapidly increasing the number of areas or situations in which it may be said that if certain describable, measurable conditions are present or are established, then predictable, definable behaviors are learned or produced.

Now in one sense every educated person is aware of this. But it seems to me that few are aware of the breadth, depth, and extent of these advances in psychology and the behavioral sciences. And still fewer seem to be aware of the profound social, political, ethical, and philosophical problems posed by these advances. I would like to focus on some of the implications of these advances.

Let me venture first to review a few selected examples of what I mean by the increased ability of psychology to understand and predict or control behavior. I have chosen them to illustrate the wide range of behaviors involved. I shall summarize and greatly simplify each of the illustrations, with only a suggestion of the evidence which exists. As a general statement I may say that each illustration I will give is supported by reasonably rigorous and adequate research, though like all scientific findings, each is open to modification or correction through more exact or imaginative future studies.

What then, are some of the behaviors or learnings for which we now know how to supply the antecedent conditions? I would stress that we know how to produce these effects in the same way, though not with the same exactitude, that the physicist know how to set up the conditions under which given substances will go through a process of atomic fission or fusion. They are instances of what we know how to achieve or accomplish.

We know how to set up the conditions under which many individuals will report as true, judgments which are contrary to the evidence of their senses. They will, for example, report that Figure A covers a larger area than Figure B, when the evidence of their senses *plainly* indicates that the reverse is true. Experiments by Asch (1952) later refined and improved by Crutchfield (1955) show that when a person is led to believe that everyone else in the group sees A as larger than B, then he has a strong tendency to go along with this judgment and in many instances does so with a real belief in his false report.

Not only can we predict that a certain percentage of individuals will thus yield and disbelieve their own senses, but Crutchfield has determined the personality attributes of these who will do so and by selection procedures would be able to choose a group who would almost uniformly give in to these pressures for conformity.

We know how to change the opinions of an individual in a selected direction, without his ever becoming aware of the stimuli which changed his opinion. A static, expressionless portrait of a man was flashed on a screen by Smith, Spence and Klein (1959). They requested their subjects to note how the expression of the picture changed. Then they intermittently flashed the word "angry" on the screen, at exposures so brief that the subjects were consciously completely unaware of having seen the word. They tended, however, to see the face as becoming more angry. When the word "happy" was flashed on the screen in similar fashion, the viewers tended to see the face as becoming more happy. Thus they were clearly influenced by stimuli which registered at a subliminal level, stimuli of which the individual was not, and could not be, aware.

We can predict, from the way individuals perceive the movement of a spot of light in a dark room, whether they tend to be prejudiced or unprejudiced. There has been much study of ethnocentrism, the tendency toward a pervasive and rigid distinction between ingroups and outgroups, with hostility toward outgroups, and a submissive attitude toward, and belief in the rightness of, ingroups. One of the theories which has developed is that the more ethnocentric person is unable to tolerate ambiguity or uncertainty in a situation. Operating on this theory Block and Block (1951) had subjects report on the degree of movement they perceived in a dim spot of light in a completely dark room. (Actually no movement occurs, but almost all individuals perceive movement in this situation.) They also gave these same subjects a test of ethnocentrism. It was found, as predicted, that those who, in successive trials, quickly established a norm for the amount of movement they perceived, tended to be more ethnocentric than those whose estimates of movement continued to show variety.

This study was repeated, with slight variation, in Australia (Taft, 1956), and the findings were confirmed and enlarged. It was found that the more ethnocentric individuals were less able to tolerate ambiguity, and saw less movement than the unprejudiced. They also were more dependent on others and when making their estimates in the company of another person, tended to conform to the judgment of that person.

Hence it is not too much to say that by studying the way the individual perceives the movement of a dim light in a dark room, we can tell a good deal about the degree to which he is a rigid, prejudiced, ethnocentric person.

We know the attitudes which, if provided by a counselor or a therapist, will be predictably followed by certain constructive personality and behavior changes in the client. Studies we have completed in recent years in the field of psychotherapy (Rogers, 1951; Rogers & Dymond, 1954; Seeman & Raskin, 1953; Thetford, 1952) justify this statement. The findings from these studies may be very briefly summarized in the following way.

If the therapist provides a relationship in which he is (a) genuine, internally consistent; (b) acceptant, prizing the client as a person of worth; (c) empathically understanding of the client's private world of feelings and attitudes; then certain changes occur in the client. Some of these changes are: the client becomes (a) more realistic in his self-perceptions; (b) more confident and self-directing; (c) more positively valued by himself; (d) less likely to repress elements of his experience; (e) more mature, socialized and adaptive in his behavior; (f) less upset by stress and quicker to recover from it; (g) more like the healthy, integrated, well-functioning person in his personality structure. These changes do not occur in a control group and appear to be definitely associated with the client's being in a relationship with these qualities.

We know how to provide animals with a most satisfying experience consisting entirely of electrical stimulation. Olds (1955) has found that he can implant tiny electrodes in the septal area of the brain of laboratory rats.

When one of these animals presses a bar in his cage, it causes a minute current to pass through these electrodes. This appears to be such a rewarding experience that the animal goes into an orgy of bar pressing, often until he is exhausted. Whatever the subjective nature of the experience it seems to be so satisfying that the animal prefers it to any other activity. I will not speculate as to whether this procedure might be applied to human beings, nor what, in this case, its consequence would be.

We know how to provide psychological conditions which will produce vivid hallucinations and other abnormal reactions in the thoroughly normal individual in the waking state. This knowledge came about as the unexpected by-product of research at McGill University (Beston, Heron, & Scott, 1954). It was discovered that if all channels of sensory stimulation are cut off or muffled, abnormal reactions follow. If healthy subjects lie motionless to reduce kinaesthetic stimuli, with eyes shielded by translucent goggles which do not permit perception, with hearing largely stifled by foam rubber pillows as well as by being in a quiet cubicle, and with tactile sensations reduced by cuffs over the hands, then hallucinations and bizarre ideation bearing some resemblance to that of the psychotic occur within a relatively short time in most subjects. What the results would be if the sensory stifling were continued longer is not known because the experience seemed so potentially dangerous that the investigators were reluctant to continue it.

I hope that these few illustrations will have given some concrete meaning to the statement that the behavioral sciences are making strides in the understanding, prediction, and control of behavior. In important ways we know how to select individuals who will exhibit certain behaviors: to establish conditions in groups which will lead to various predictable group behaviors; to establish conditions which, in an individual, will lead to specified behavioral results; and in animals our ability to understand, predict, and control goes even further, possibly foreshadowing future steps in relation to man.

If your reaction is the same as mine then you will have found that this picture I have given has its frightening as well as its strongly positive aspects. With all the immaturity of this young science, and its vast ignorance, even its present state of knowledge contains awesome possibilities. Perhaps it makes clear the reason why Robert Oppenheimer, one of the most gifted of our natural scientists, looks out from his own domain of physics, and out of the experiences in that field voices a warning. He says that there are some similarities between physics and psychology, and one of these similarities "is the extent to which our progress will create profound problems of decision in the public domain. The physicists have been quite noisy about their contributions in the last decade. The time may well come—as psychology acquires a sound objective corpus of knowledge about human behavior and feeling—when the powers of control thus available will pose far graver problems than any the physicists have posed" (Oppenheimer, 1956a).

Among behavioral scientists it seems to be largely taken for granted that the findings of such science will be used in the prediction and control of human behavior. Yet most psychologists and other such scientists have given little thought to what this would mean.

I should like to try to present, as well as I can, a simplified picture of the cultural pattern which emerges if we endeavor to shape human life in terms of the behavioral sciences. This is one of two possible directions I wish to consider.

There is first of all the recognition, almost the assumption, that scientific knowledge is the power to manipulate. Dr. B. F. Skinner (1955-1956) of Harvard says: "We must accept that fact that some kind of control of human affairs is inevitable. We cannot use good sense in human affairs unless someone engages in the design and construction of environmental conditions which affect the behavior of men."

Let us look at some of the elements which are involved in the concept of the control of human behavior as mediated by the behavioral sciences. What would be the steps in the process by which a society might organize itself so as to formulate human life in terms of the science of man?

First would come the selection of goals. In a recent paper [Freedom and the control of men] Dr. Skinner (1955-1956) suggests that one possible goal to be assigned to the behavior technology is this: "Let man be happy, informed, skillful, well-behaved, and productive." In his book, *Walden Two* (1948), where he can use the guise of fiction to express his views, he becomes more expansive. His hero says, "Well, what do you say to the design of personalities? Would that interest you? The control of temperament? Give me the specifications, and I'll give you the man. What do you say to the control of motivation, building the interests which will make men most productive and most successful? Does that seem to you fantastic? Yet some of the techniques are available, and more can be worked out experimentally. Think of the possibilities   Let us control the lives of our children and see what we can make of them."

What Skinner is essentially saying here is that the current knowledge in the behavioral sciences, plus that which the future will bring, will enable us to specify, to a degree which today would seem incredible, the kind of behavioral and personality results which we wish to achieve. [Also see Skinner, 1971—Editor.]

The second element in this process would be one which is familiar to every scientist who has worked in the field of applied science. Given the purpose, the goal, we proceed by the method of science—by controlled experimentation—to discover the means to these ends. The method of science is self-correcting in thus arriving at increasingly effective ways of achieving the purpose we have selected.

The third element in the control of human behavior through the behavioral sciences involves the question of power. As the conditions or methods are discovered by which to achieve our goal, some person or group obtains the power to establish those conditions or use those methods. There has been too little recognition of the problem involved in this. To hope that the power which is being made available by the behavioral sciences will be exercised by the scientists, or by a benevolent group, seems to me a hope little supported by either recent or distant history.

It seems far more likely that behavioral scientists, holding their present attitudes, will be in the position of the German rocket scientists specializing in guided missiles. First they worked devotedly for Hitler to destroy Russia and the United States. Now, depending on who captured them, they work devotedly for Russia in the interest of destroying the United States, or devotedly for the United States in the interest of destroying Russia. If behavioral scientists are concerned solely with advancing their science, it seems most probable that they will serve the purposes of whatever individual or group has the power.

But this is, in a sense, a digression. The main point of this view is that some person or group will have and use the power to put into effect the methods which have been discovered for achieving the desired goal.

The fourth step in this process whereby a society might formulate its life in terms of the behavioral sciences is the exposure of individuals to the methods and conditions mentioned. As individuals are exposed to the prescribed conditions this leads, with a high degree of probability, to the behavior which has been desired. Men then become productive, if that has been the goal, or submissive, or whatever it has been decided to make them.

To give something of the flavor of this aspect of the process as seen by one of its advocates, let me again quote the hero of *Walden Two*. "Now that we *know* how positive reinforcement works, and why negative doesn't," he says, commenting on the method he is advocating, "we can be more deliberate and hence more successful, in our cultural design. We can achieve a sort of control under which the controlled, though they are following a code much more scrupulously than was ever the case under the old system, nevertheless *feel free.* They are doing what they want to do, not what they are forced to do. That's the source of the tremendous power of positive reinforcement— there's no restraint and no revolt. By a careful cultural design, we control not the final behavior, but the *inclination* to behave—the motives, the desires, the wishes. The curious thing is that in that case *the question of freedom never arises*" (Skinner, 1948, p. 218).

The Picture and Its Implications

Let me see if I can sum up very briefly the picture of the impact of the behavioral sciences upon the individual and upon society, as this impact is explicitly seen by Dr. Skinner and implied in the attitudes and work of many, perhaps most, behavioral scientists. Behavioral science is clearly moving forward; the increasing power for control which it gives will be held by some one or some group; such an individual or group will surely choose the purposes or goals to be achieved; and most of us will then be increasingly controlled by means so subtle we will not even be aware of them as controls. Thus whether a council of wise psychologists (if this is not a contradiction in terms) or a Stalin or a Big Brother has the power, and whether the goal is happiness, or productivity, or resolution of the Oedipus complex, or submission, or love of Big Brother, we will inevitably find ourselves moving toward the chosen goal, and probably thinking that we ourselves desire it. Thus if this line of reasoning is correct, it appears that some form of completely controlled society—a Walden Two or a 1984— is coming. The fact that it would surely arrive piecemeal rather than all at once, does not greatly change the fundamental issues. Man and his behavior would become a planned product of a scientific society.

You may well ask, "But what about individual freedom? What about the democratic concepts of the rights of the individual?" Here too Dr. Skinner (1948, p. 447) is quite specific. He says quite bluntly, "The hypothesis that man is not free is essential to the application of scientific method to the study of human behavior. The free inner man who is held responsible for his behavior . . . is only a prescientific substitute for the kinds of causes which are discovered in the course of scientific analysis. All these alternative causes lie outside the individual."

I have endeavored, up to this point, to give an objective picture of some of society which might emerge out of those developments. I do however have strong personal reactions to the kind of world I have been describing, a world which Skinner explicitly (and many another scientist implicitly) expects and hopes for in the future. To me this kind of world would destroy the human person as I have come to know him in the deepest moments of psychotherapy. In such moments I am in relationship with a person who is spontaneous, who is responsibly free, that is, aware of his freedom to choose who he will be and aware also of the consequences of his choice. To believe, as Skinner holds, that all this is an illusion and that spontaneity, freedom, responsibility, and choice have no real existence would be impossible for me.

I feel that to the limit of my ability I have played my part in advancing the behavioral sciences, but if the result of my efforts and those of others is that man becomes a robot, created and controlled by a science of his own making, than I am very unhappy indeed. If the good life of the future consists in so conditioning individuals through the control of their environment and through the control of the rewards they receive, that they will be inexorably productive, well behaved, happy or whatever, then I want none of it. To me this is a pseudo-form of the good life which includes everything save that which makes it good.

And so I ask myself, is there any flaw in the logic of this development?

Is there any alternative view as to what the behavioral sciences might mean to the individual and to society? It seems to me that I perceive such a flaw and that I can conceive of an alternative view. These I would like to set before you.

Ends and Values in Relation to Science

It seems to me that the view I have presented rests upon a faulty perception of goals and values in their relationship to science. The significance of the purpose of a scientific undertaking is, I believe, grossly underestimated. I would like to state a two-pronged thesis which in my estimation deserves consideration. Then I will elaborate the meaning of these two points.

    1 In any scientific endeavor—whether "pure" or applied science—there is a prior personal subjective choice of the purpose or value which that scientific work is perceived as serving.

    2 This subjective value choice which brings the scientific endeavor into being must always lie outside of that endeavor and can never become a part of the science involved in that endeavor.

Let me illustrate the first point from Dr. Skinner's writings. When he suggests that the task for the behavioral sciences is to make man "productive," "well-behaved," etc., it is obvious that he is making a choice. He might have chosen to make men submissive, dependent, and gregarious, for example. Yet by his own statement in another context man's "capacity to choose," his freedom to select his course and to initiate action—these powers do not exist in the scientific picture of man. Here is, I believe, the deep-seated contradiction or paradox. Let me spell it out as clearly as I can.

Science, to be sure, rests on the assumption that behavior is caused—that a specified event is followed by a consequent event. Hence all is determined, nothing is free, choice is impossible. But we must recall that science itself and each specific scientific endeavor, each change of course in a scientific research, each interpretation of the meaning of a scientific finding, and each decision as to how the finding shall be applied rests upon a personal, subjective choice. Thus science in general exists in the same paradoxical situation as does Dr. Skinner. A personal, subjective choice made by man sets in motion the operations of science, which in time proclaims that there can be no such thing as a personal, subjective choice. I shall make some comments about this continuing paradox at a later point.

I stressed the fact that each of these choices, initiating or furthering the scientific venture, is a value choice. The scientist investigates this rather than that, because he feels the first investigation has more value for him. He chooses one method for his study rather than another because he believes the first way is closer to the truth, or more valid—in other words that it is closer to a criterion which he values. Now these value choices are never a part of the scientific venture itself. The value choices connected with a particular scientific enterprise always and necessarily lie outside of that enterprise.

I wish to make it clear that I am not saying that values cannot be included as a subject of science. It is not true that science deals only with certain classes of "facts" and that these classes do not include values. It is a bit more complex than that, as a simple illustration or two may make clear.

If I value knowledge of the "three R's" as a goal of education, the methods of science can give me increasingly accurate information as to how this goal may be achieved. If I value problem-solving ability as a goal of education, the scientific method can give me the same kind of help.

Now if I wish to determine whether problem-solving ability is "better" than knowledge of the three R's, then scientific method can also study those two values, but only—and this is very important—only in terms of some other value which I have subjectively chosen. I may value college success. Then I can determine whether problem-solving ability or knowledge of the three R's is more closely associated with that criterion. I may value personal integration or vocational success or responsible citizenship. I can determine whether problem-solving ability or knowledge of the three R's is "better" for achieving any one of these values. But the value or purpose which gives meaning to a particular scientific endeavor must always lie outside of the endeavor.

Though our concern here is largely with applied science what I have been saying seems equally true of so-called pure science. In pure science the usual prior subjective value choice is the discovery of truth. But this is a subjective choice, and science can never say whether it is the best choice, save in the light of some other value. Geneticists in Russia, for example, had to make a subjective choice of whether it was better to pursue truth, or to discover facts which upheld a governmental dogma. Which choice is "better"? We could make a scientific investigation of those alternatives, but only in the light of some other subjectively chosen value. If, for example, we value the survival of a culture then we could begin to investigate with the methods of science the question as to whether pursuit of truth or support of governmental dogma is most closely associated with cultural survival.

My point then is that any scientific endeavor, pure or applied, is carried on in the pursuit of a purpose or value which is subjectively chosen by persons. It is important that this choice be made explicit, since the particular value which is being sought can never be tested or evaluated, confirmed or denied, by the scientific endeavor to which it gives birth and meaning. The initial purpose or value always and necessarily lies outside the scope of the scientific effort which it sets in motion.

Perhaps, however, the thought is that a continuing scientific endeavor will evolve its own goals; the initial findings will alter the directions, and subsequent findings will alter them still further and that the science somehow develops its own purpose. This seems to be a view implicitly held by many scientists. It is surely a reasonable description, but it overlooks one element in this continuing development, which is that subjective, personal choice enters in at every point at which the direction changes. The findings of science, the results of an experiment, do not and never can tell us what next scientific purpose to pursue. Even in the purest of science, the scientist must decide what the findings mean and must subjectively choose what next step will be most profitable in the pursuit of his purpose. And if we are speaking of the application of scientific knowledge, then it is distressingly clear that the increasing scientific knowledge of the structure of the atom carries with it no necessary choice as to the purpose to which this knowledge will be put. This is a subjective personal choice which must be made by many individuals.

Thus I return to the proposition with which I began this section of my remarks—and which I now repeat in different words. Science has its meaning as the objective pursuit of a purpose which has been subjectively chosen by a person or persons. This purpose or value can never be investigated by the particular scientific experiment or investigation to which it has given birth and meaning. Consequently, any discussion of the control of human beings by the behavioral sciences must first and most deeply concern itself with the subjectively chosen purposes which such an application of science is intended to implement.

An Alternative Set of Values

If the line of reasoning I have been presenting is valid, then it opens new doors to us. If we frankly face the fact that science takes off from a subjectively chosen set of values, then we are free to select the values we wish to pursue. We are not limited to such stultifying goals as producing a controlled state of happiness, productivity, and the like. I would like to suggest a radically different alternative.

Suppose we start with a set of ends, values, purposes, quite different from the type of goals we have been considering. Suppose we do this quite openly, setting them forth as a possible value choice to be accepted or rejected. Suppose we select a set of values which focuses on fluid elements of process, rather than static attributes. We might then value:

Man as a process of becoming; as a process of achieving worth and dignity through the development of his potentialities;

The individual human being as a self-actualizing process, moving on to more challenging and enriching experiences;

The process by which the individual creatively adapts to an ever new and changing world;

The process by which knowledge transcends itself, as for example the theory of relativity transcended Newtonian physics, itself to be transcended in some future day by a new perception.

If we select values such as these, we turn to our science and technology of behavior with a very different set of questions. We will want to know such things as these.

Can science aid us in the discovery of new modes of richly rewarding living? More meaningful and satisfying modes of interpersonal relationships?

Can science inform us as to how the human race can become a more intelligent participant in its own evolution—its physical, psychological, and social evolution?

Can science inform us as to ways of releasing the creative capacity of individuals, which seem so necessary if we are to survive in this fantastically expanding atomic age? Dr. Oppenheimer (1956b) has pointed out that knowledge, which used to double in millennia or centuries, now doubles in a generation or a decade. It appears that we will need to discover the utmost in release of creativity if we are to be able to adapt effectively.

In short, can science discover the methods by which man can most readily become a continually developing and self-transcending process, in his behavior, his thinking, his knowledge? Can science predict and release an essentially "unpredictable" freedom?

It is one of the virtues of science as a method that it is as able to advance and implement goals and purpose of this sort as it is to serve static values such as states of being well-informed, happy, obedient. Indeed we have some evidence of this.

A Small Example

I will perhaps be forgiven if I document some of the possibilities along this line by turning to psychotherapy, the field I know best.

Psychotherapy as Meerloo (1955) and others have pointed out can be one of the most subtle tools for the control of one person by another. The therapist can subtly mold individuals in imitation of himself. He can cause an individual to become a submissive and conforming being. When certain therapeutic principles are used in extreme fashion, we call it brainwashing, an instance of the distintegration of the personality and a reformulation of the person along lines desired by the controlling individual. So the principles of therapy can be used as a most effective means of external control of human personality and behavior. Can psychotherapy be anything else?

Here I find the developments going on in client-centered psychotherapy (Rogers, 1951) an exciting hint of what a behavioral science can do in achieving the kinds of values I have stated. Quite aside from being a somewhat new orientation in psychotherapy, this development has important implications regarding the relation of a behavioral science to the control of human behavior. Let me describe our experience as it relates to the issues of today's discussion.

In client-centered therapy, we are deeply engaged in the prediction and influencing of behavior. As therapists we institute certain attitudinal conditions, and the client has relatively little voice in the establishment of these conditions. Very briefly, as I indicated earlier, we have found that the therapist is most effective if he is: (a) genuine, integrated, transparently real in the relationship; (b) acceptant of the client as a separate, different, person and acceptant of each fluctuating aspect of the client as it comes to expression; and (c) sensitively empathic in his understanding, seeing the world through the client's eyes. Our research permits us to predict that if these attitudinal conditions are instituted or established, certain behavioral consequences will ensue. Putting it this way sounds as if we are again back in the familiar groove of being able to predict behavior, and hence able to control it. But precisely here exists a sharp difference.

The conditions we have chosen to establish predict such behavioral consequences as these: that the client will become more self-directing, less rigid, more open to the evidence of his senses, better organized and integrated, more similar to the ideal which he has chosen for himself. In other words we have established, by external control, conditions which, we predict, will be followed by internal control by the individual, in pursuit of internally chosen goals. We have set the conditions which predict various classes of behaviors—self-directing behaviors, sensitivity to realities within and without, flexible adaptiveness—which are by their very nature *unpredictable* in their specifics. The conditions we have established predict behavior which is essentially "free." Our recent research (Rogers & Dymond, 1954) indicates that our predictions are to a significant degree corroborated, and our commitment to the scientific method causes us to believe that more effective means of achieving these goals may be realized.

Research exists in other fields—industry, education, group dynamics—which seems to support our own findings. I believe it may be conservatively stated that scientific progress has been made in identifying those conditions in an interpersonal relationship which, if they exist in B, are followed in A by greater maturity in behavior, less dependence upon others, an increase in expressiveness as a person, an increase in variability, flexibility, and effectiveness of adaptation, an increase in self-responsibility and self-direction.

Thus we find ourselves in fundamental agreement with John Dewey's statement: "Science has made its way by releasing, not by suppressing, the elements of variation, of invention and innovation, of novel creation in individuals" (Ratner, 1939). We have come to believe that progress in personal life and in group living is made in the same way, by releasing variation, freedom, creativity.

A Possible Concept of the Control of Human Behavior

It is quite clear that the point of view I am expressing is in sharp contrast to the usual conception of the relationship of the behavioral sciences to the control of human behavior, previously mentioned. In order to make this contrast even more blunt, I will state this possibility in a form parallel to the steps which I described before.

1 It is possible for us to choose to value man as a self-actualizing process of becoming; to value creativity, and the process by which knowledge becomes self-transcending.

2 We can proceed, by the methods of science, to discover the conditions which necessarily precede these processes, and through continuing experimentation, to discover better means of achieving these purposes.

3 It is possible for individuals or groups to set these conditions, with a minimum of power or control. According to present knowledge, the only authority necessary is the authority to establish certain qualities of interpersonal relationship.

4 Exposed to these conditions, present knowledge suggests that individuals become more self-responsible, make progress in self-actualization, become more flexible, more unique and varied, more creatively adaptive.

5 Thus such an initial choice would inaugurate the beginnings of a social system or subsystem in which values, knowledge, adaptive skills, and even the concept of science would be continually changing and self-transcending. The emphasis would be upon man as a process of becoming.

I believe it is clear that such a view as I have been describing does not lead to any definable Utopia. It would be impossible to predict its final outcome. It involves a step by step development, based upon a continuing subjective choice of purposes, which are implemented by the behavioral sciences. It is in the direction of the "open society," as that term has been defined by Popper, where individuals carry responsibility for personal decisions. It is at the opposite pole from his concept of the closed society, of which *Walden Two* would be an example.

I trust it is also evident that the whole emphasis is upon process, not upon end states of being. I am suggesting that it is by choosing to value certain qualitative elements of the process of becoming, that we can find a pathway toward the open society.

The Choice

It is my hope that I have helped to clarify the range of choice which will lie before us and our children in regard to the behavioral sciences. We can choose to use our growing knowledge to enslave people in ways never dreamed of before, depersonalizing them, controlling them by means so carefully selected that they will perhaps never be aware of their loss of personhood. We can choose to utilize our scientific knowledge to make men necessarily happy, well-behaved, and productive, as Dr. Skinner suggests. We can, if we wish, choose to make men submissive, conforming, docile. Or at the other end of the spectrum of choice we can choose to use the behavioral sciences in ways which will free, not control; which will bring about constructive variability, not conformity; which will develop creativity, not contentment; which will facilitate each person in his self-directed process of becoming; which will aid individuals, groups, and even the concept of science to become self-transcending in freshly adaptive ways of meeting life and its problems.

If we choose to utilize our scientific knowledge to free men, then it will demand that we live openly and frankly with the great paradox of the behavioral sciences. We will recognize that behavior, when examined scientifically, is surely best understood as determined by prior causation. This is the great fact of science. But responsible personal choice, which is the most essential element in being a person, which is the core experience in psychotherapy, which exists prior to any scientific endeavor, is an equally prominent fact in our lives. That these two important elements of our experience appear to be in contradiction has perhaps the same significance as the contradiction between the wave theory and the corpuscular theory of light, both of which can be shown to be true, even though incompatible. We cannot profitably deny the freedom which exists in our subjective life, any more than we can deny the determinism which is evident in the objective description of that life. We will have to live with that paradox.

The fanciful power of fairy godmothers and evil witches, harmless enough in children's story books, now threatens to become a reality in the hands of psychologists. Experiments with social suggestion, drugs, brain stimulation, and similar techniques raise the prospect of almost unlimited control over the thoughts and actions of other people. Assuming that this possibility is not exaggerated, how will this knowledge be used once nature's secrets are unlocked? Should we adopt a plan that manipulates the individual from birth to death to make him happy according to a plan someone else predetermines? Or one designed to lift the individual to new heights of freedom and dignity? Rogers espouses the second alternative but may overstate his case in vindicating the right of every individual to arrange his life the way he chooses. Herbert C. Kelman believes that Rogers's position should be slightly modified in order to take into account all the realities of the situation.

From A Time to Speak

With Rogers (Rogers & Skinner, 1956) on the other hand, I feel a complete affinity at the value level. He values "man as a self-actualizing process of becoming" and in general proposes that "we select a set of values that focuses on fluid elements of process rather than static attributes" (p. 1063). He favors a society "where individuals carry responsibility for personal decisions" (p. 1064). He regards "responsible personal choice" as "the most essential element in being a person" (p. 1064). But, as I have pointed out, Rogers tends to minimize the second horn of the dilemma presented here: the inevitability of some degree of manipulation in any influence attempt. He makes what appears to me the unrealistic assumption that by choosing the proper goals and the proper techniques in an influence situation one can completely sidestep the problem of manipulation and control. He seems to argue that, when an influencing agent is dedicated to the value of man as a self-actualizing process and selects techniques that are designed to promote this value, he can abrogate his power over the influencee and maintain a relationship untainted by behavior control. This ignores, in my opinion, the dynamics of the influence situation itself. I fully agree that influence attempts designed to enhance the client's freedom of choice and techniques that are consistent with this goal are ethically superior, and that we should continue to push and explore in this direction. But we must remain aware that the nature of the relationship between influencing agent and influencee is such that inevitably, even in these influence situations, a certain degree of control will be exercised. The assumption that we can set up an influence situation in which the problem of manipulation of behavior is removed, because of the stated purpose and formal structure of the situation, is a dangerous one. It makes us blind to the continuities between all types of influence situations and to the subtle ways in which others can be manipulated. It lulls us into the reassuring certainty that what we are doing is, by definition, good. I would regard it as more in keeping with both the realities of behavior change, and the ethical requirements of minimizing manipulation, to accept the inevitability of a certain amount of control as part of our dilemma and to find a *modus vivendi* in the face of the ethical ambiguities thus created.

We should not expect to find complete agreement in any group about its obligation to society. Corporate responsibility is easier to identify in some professions than in others. The duty of a doctor to make every effort to preserve human life and health has been recognized from the beginning. The Hippocratic oath of physicians dates back to at least 400 B.C.

Not every professional obligation is so obvious. Psychologists scarcely ever discuss their personal responsibility for the social consequences of their theories, even though millions of people may be affected by them. When a psychologist, either with or without sufficient evidence, undertakes to tell parents how to raise their children, he is accountable to the whole of society. Judging from current child-rearing practices, Watson's advice in this respect was certainly premature. Theories of education, psychotherapy, and counseling also influence the lives of countless persons. It would be difficult for any psychologist to absolve himself from all social responsibility on the plea that he is just a private individual speaking his mind.

Following the pattern established by Freud in such studies as **Totem and taboo, The future of an illusion,** and **Moses and monotheism,** some theorists seem to be intent on taking over the functions of religion. While dismissing all religions as myth, they pronounce on questions of right and wrong in human conduct and man's purpose in existence. How as scientists they find rigorous evidence to speak authoritatively on such subjects is something of a mystery. That they have the right to private speculation which is plainly indicated as such, no one will deny, nor is there any objection to an attempt to integrate philosophy, theology, and science as long as this is clear to the reader. What seems inadmissible is the attempt to blend them all together in one pot and label the whole broth science. Science is a magic word that disposes the reader to accept as fact whatever is said. Professional responsibility requires complete honesty in this regard. There is no need or excuse for wrapping one's self in the robe of science to speculate about religion.

SUMMARY

The blinding flash of the atomic bomb that ignited the skies over Hiroshima deeply seared the consciences of most of the scientists who built it. "What responsibility," they asked themselves, "does each of us bear for the inconceivable slaughter and destruction that we made possible?" Some years later Robert Oppenheimer, one of their number, reminded psychologists that our social responsibility is even greater than the physicists'. "The psychologist," he said, "can hardly do anything without realizing that for him the acquisition of knowledge opens up the most terrifying prospects of controlling what people do and how they think and how they behave and how they feel."

Rollo May suggests that the most constructive way to deal with this potential guilt is to begin with a searching self-examination. Some particulars we should inquire about are (1) the tendency to rationalize our lack of moral commitment on the grounds that not all the evidence is in, (2) repression and denial of our own power needs, and (3) how, in the light of psychology's historical development, we can preserve the values and characteristics that make a man a person. We might add that the danger of confronting people with an inadequate self-image is that they may take it seriously. Anyone who thinks of himself as a passively determined organism invites external controls.

Rogers discusses the possibility of a society in which the citizens could be manipulated as puppets without being aware of the strings. He then goes on to show how instead of enslaving people, psychological techniques can free them to become fully functioning persons. Kelman reminds us that in championing the rights of individuals we must not forget that some external controls are essential to the existence of any society.

Some facets of professional ethics have received little attention. One is the social accountability of the psychologist for the theories he proposes, especially in areas that affect human living. Another is the attempt of a few psychologists to create the myth that psychology has now supplanted religion.

DISCUSSION TOPICS

1 List other facets of the social responsibility of the psychologist in addition to those mentioned in the above chapter.

2 What can psychologists do to ensure that the knowledge of behavior they gain is not used to manipulate people?

3 Is it ethically responsible to use the insights of depth psychology in advertising to persuade people to buy a given product without their awareness of this hidden influence?

4 Suppose that a humane technique is discovered for changing the antisocial attitudes of hardened criminals without their consent. Would society be justified in using it?

5 In some experiments on honesty, small children were placed in situations that provided the opportunity to cheat or steal. Discuss the ethical implications of such research.

6 Some experiments have been designed to evoke fear, humiliation, or indignation in the subject, but before leaving the laboratory he is taken into confidence and the entire procedure is explained. How do you evaluate the investigator's responsibility in this situation?

7 It has been suggested that if the legal body to which a person belongs already possesses and grants the right needed by the experimenter, the consent of the subject is not required. How would this guideline apply in the following cases?

    a. Children in a family.

    b. Schizophrenic patients in a psychiatric ward.

    c. Members of the Armed Forces.

    d. Employees in an industrial plant.

    e. An assessment in depth of the personality and private life of an employee being considered for promotion to vice president of his firm.

    f. Experiments in which the subjects are deceived about some of their own personal traits.

8 Would you respond differently to the above items in research studies involving:

    a. No foreseeable risk.

    b. A low but definite risk such as disturbed behavior resulting from sensory deprivation or sensitivity training.

    c. Temporary surrender of autonomy as in hypnosis.

    d. Considerable physical or mental discomfort.

9 In the following situations where does one draw the line between the right of individuals to privacy and the need of the community to know?

    a. Witetapping to monitor the illegal activities of organized crime.

    b. The use of false credentials to gain access to a meeting of radical leaders in order to study the dynamics of such social movements. It is presumed that all specific information obtained would be kept confidential.

10 To what extent is free scientific inquiry threatened by a public opinion backlash in the matter of professional ethics.

ADDITIONAL READINGS

Chennault, J. Help-giving and morality. **The Personnel and Guidance Journal,** 1969, **48,** 89-96. "A responsible profession giving help must examine the morality of its use of power over the individuals it serves."

Grossman, B. D. Knowledge and responsibility. **American Psychologist,** 1966, **21,** 164. Psychologists should take responsibility for regulating the area of testing and evaluation.

Lifton, R. J. **Thought control and the psychology of totalism: A study of "brainwashing" in China.** New York: Norton, 1961. This is a study of how the systematic knowledge of behavior can be used to enslave the minds of people.

McConnell, J. V. Criminals can be brainwashed now. **Psychology Today,** 1970,

3, pp. 14, 16, 18, 74. The author denies that anyone owns his own personality which he conceives as being forced on the individual by heredity and society. He feels that the Constitution does not give us the right to maintain this personality inviolable.

Milner, E. Social responsibility. **American Psychologist,** 1968, **23,** 763. This brief letter to the editor indicates three instances of irresponsibility in social science research.

Schwitzgebel, R. Electronic innovation in the behavioral sciences: A call to responsibility. **American Psychologist,** 1967, **22,** 364-370. Scientists are urged to guard against possible misuses of electronic devices which may infringe upon the rights and civil liberties of others.

Simon, G. B. Obligation of psychologists. **American Psychologist,** 1968, **23,** 72. Psychologists have an obligation to contribute to the solution of major social problems on a national and international level.

Smith, M. B. Toward scientific and professional responsibility. **American Psychologist,** 1954, **9,** 513-516. To act responsibly, psychologists must be explicit about their values and about the relation of these values to their behavior. Examples are given.

Sykes, G. M. Feeling our way: A report on a conference on ethical issues in the social sciences. **The American Behavioral Scientist,** 1967, **11,** 8-11. This report gives an overview of the issues at stake.

Walker, E. L. Experimental psychology and social responsibility. **American Psychologist,** 1969, **24,** 862-868. The psychologist cannot proceed as if his role as a scientist and as a human being were completely separate. Four obligations of experimental psychology are discussed.

Wolfensberger, W. Ethical issues in research with human subjects. **Science,** 1967, **155,** 47-51. "I write not in order to propose a definitive set of rules but to demonstrate how situations posing ethical problems can be reduced and more readily resolved by rational analysis of underlying issues and principles. . . ."

Chapter 12

The Enigma of Values in Counseling Relationships

If we agree that value judgments are implicit in every action we take, we should also agree that counselors cannot fully escape introducing their own value systems into the counseling interview.

Edmund G. Williamson

The basic liberty in any democracy is freedom of self-determination. Each individual has, at least in theory, an inalienable right to develop his potentialities as he wishes so long as he does not interfere with the same right of other people. In a pluralistic society, there is little agreement about ultimate goals toward which either the individual or the group as a whole should strive. Instead, each person is confronted with a broad range of value systems from which he must select the one that appears valid to him.

Respect for the right of every individual to control his own destiny creates something of a paradox for the guidance worker. How can he be true to himself and remain authentic if he dissembles his own value system in the counseling interview? If he does not, how can he guard against imposing his own philosophy of life on the client? One solution that appealed to many counselors in the past because of its simplicity and its association with earlier notions of scientific methodology was to deny that values enter into the counseling relationship in any way. They thought of themselves as scientists applying objective techniques to the solution of personal problems without influencing the client's motives and goals.

For many years this widely held opinion was scarcely challenged, but more recently it has become obvious that no one can avoid communicating his primary commitments at least at the nonverbal level. Value judgments are implied even in the structuring of the counseling situation and the selection of techniques to be used (Williamson, 1958). The counselor's choice in these matters will be guided by what he believes the outcome of counseling should be. More central to the problem is Gardner Murphy's (1955) reflection that "if he who offers guidance is a whole person, with real roots in human culture, he cannot help conveying directly or indirectly to every client what he himself sees and feels, and the perspective in which his own life is lived." He might have added that this will happen whether or not the counselor is a whole person and whether or not he is fully aware of what his beliefs are. A thorough understanding of one's own hierarchy of motives and values is an essential qualification for any guidance worker. Without such a clearcut private philosophy he can neither order his own life consistently nor guard against unwittingly imposing his values on others. John Hipple discusses some of the elements that underlie such personal convictions.

Development of a Personal Philosophy and Theory of Counseling

To many people, *philosophy* is a threatening term. They do not understand it, so they shy away from considering it. This is a very dangerous practice for a counselor because philosophy is the rock upon which his effectiveness rests. If there is any weakness or confusion in the counselor's philosophy, he will probably not be really effective.

Each counselor must formulate a personal philosophy and theory of counseling if he is to really know himself. It is easy to function without formulating a specific philosophy, but it can be very ineffective. Many errors can be made if the counselor does not really know why he is doing what he is doing and does not know exactly where he is going with his method.

One might wonder why it is so important for a counselor to have a concrete expression of his philosophy. It is essential because it is impossible for the counselor to divorce his true self from his practice of counseling. For this reason, the counselor must be consciously aware of his own life values, beliefs, and feelings. It is impossible for a counselor to be completely removed from his personal values during the counseling relationship. All of the many factors that set him apart as an individual will be expressed at either a verbal or nonverbal level to all his clients. There are many ways in which the counselor's personal values are brought out in the counseling relationship. These would include subtle reinforcement of "desirable" responses, nonverbal cues, and counseling style. If the counselor does not fully understand and recognize his own feelings and their effect on his counseling philosophy, all of these factors can affect the counseling relationship in strange ways.

In order to develop a philosophy, the counselor must begin with a definition of terms. According to Webster, a philosophy is a search for the underlying causes and principles of reality. A theory, on the other hand, is a belief, policy, or procedure proposed or followed as the basis of action. Thus, the counselor might use his theories in an effort to establish his philosophy. Theory allows the counselor to bring together various information and to classify and give it order. It must always be remembered that a theory is flexible; it is never unchangeable. For it to be unchangeable would be to say that the theory has "become," and that is impossible. Counseling is the process of one individual assisting another to increase in self-knowledge, with self-clarification and self-determination the ultimate goals.

The search for and development of counseling theories and statements of philosophy has gone on for some time. Many writers from many fields of personality theory and counseling technique have expressed themselves on it, yet a review of these writings reveals many similarities among the various theories.

Carkhuff (Truax & Carkhuff, 1964) wrote that all 15 authors he reviewed wanted the therapist to know the client, to respond and communicate understanding, and to be warm and accepting. The process of counseling would include *client* exploration of personal feelings, values, perceptions of others, personal relationships, fears, turmoils, and life choices. All of this would seem to indicate that there are probably more significant similarities than differences among the various schools of thought. So in the development of a personal philosophy and theory, the counselor would be mainly concerned with a formal conceptualization of his own views. The counselor would probably not be developing anything too new or unique.

The formation of a personal philosophy of counseling is often put off until the counselor has had an opportunity to stabilize his technical and practical approaches to the counseling relationship. The counselor often experiences much trial and error in his day-to-day counseling before his views and attitudes become crystalized and he feels capable of setting his personal position down on paper.

The counselor's working philosophy must, in all ways, be consistent with what he is as a person. This systematic set of beliefs and attitudes is often based on a compromise position gained through the interaction of the counselor's formal academic training and his practical experience.

Counseling has many factors and each factor can be interpreted several ways. For example, the counselor's concept of the client's intrinsic worth (McGowan & Schmidt, 1962) can be applied in the following diverse ways: (a) The client must be directed since he does not have the capacity for growth; (b) The client needs little or no direction since he is capable of self-determination; (c) The client must be told what is good and what is bad for him since he is incapable of determining right from wrong. To treat each individual client in a consistent manner, the counselor must have decided for himself just how the client can function independently. For example, the counselor can choose between the following philosophies:

1 Respect for the integrity of the individual implies respect for the right of the individual to make his own decisions as to what might be good or bad for him.

2 The client cannot be trusted to take positive action.

3 The client can be trusted to take action that is generally socially acceptable.

The counselor must come to terms with these and many other factors in his formulation of a mode of operation.

The following structural factors must be considered in constructing a personal philosophy. If the counselor systematically considers them he will be able to construct a framework for a personal philosophy.

1 *Nature of Man.* Unless the counselor knows exactly what his concept of man is, he will not be able to function with any consistency or efficiency. The counselor must decide whether man is basically good or evil and whether or not man is capable of total self-direction.

2 *Learning Theory.* If a counselor is to help his client, he must be cognizant of the processes that affect the client as his knowledge of self increases. Because it affects the end result of any counseling contact the counselor must be aware of how and why learning takes place.

3 *Behavior Change.* The counselor must know what clues to look for as his client develops through the process of therapy. Behavior is constantly changing and developing, and the counselor must be able to recognize this process.

4 *Goals of Counseling.* Deciding what is to be expected during the counseling relationship is especially important. It takes a great deal of consideration because the counselor must decide between the goals of the client, the goals of society, and the counselor's personal goals. At times there can be a great deal of conflict between these various goals, and the counselor must know which direction to go according to his stated philosophy. The counseling process attempts to assist the individual in self-examination, analysis, and clarification of reality and self. The goals of counseling will set the limits for manipulation of the client.

5 *Role of the Counselor.* In order to facilitate fully the counseling process, the counselor must have a definite concept of his own role. He must know himself before he can attempt to know his client. The counseling relationship is a very special one. In most situations there is no one quite like the counselor. Counseling is creative; some people call it an art. There is no set of techniques that will apply to all situations. It is the task of the counselor to apply the appropriate feeling to each situation. Therefore, it is essential that the counselor have a complete understanding of his role.

6 *Responsibilities to Society.* To whom does the counselor owe his allegiance? This is the question that must be answered by every professional counselor. Is the counselor responsible to the client, the school, the society, himself, or to any combination of these? There can be many perplexing problems in this area; for example, if a client told his counselor of a forthcoming gang fight between two rival school factions what should the counselor do? What would you do?

In answer to this last question, every counselor must have established a clear philosophy and theory of counseling. Counseling is a very difficult task; all road blocks must be quickly removed. It must also be remembered that a philosophy is never completely developed. As the counselor gains experience, weak points will become strong, cloudy points clear.

The counselor who is already perplexed by the plurality of value systems may feel completely at a loss when the subject of religion is introduced. A more basic philosophy of life can scarcely be imagined than one giving meaning and significance to all reality. More baffling still, religion deals with ultimate purposes that lie beyond the scope of empirical research. Scientific methods rely largely for their data on sense perception. They are unable to investigate problems that do not permit some type of observation or measurement as we shall see in Part Four. No laboratory on earth can give a final reply to the question, "What is man for?" without presupposing the answer from the beginning. The same is true of the more basic ethical problems. While social psychology can study the **prevalence** or **utility** of monogamy or euthanasia, it cannot establish on **scientific grounds** whether either is morally right or wrong. We must look to philosophy or religion for this answer. Moral rectitude does not depend on either expediency or what people do in actual practice. If it did, Hitler could have justified his policy of exterminating a segment of the population which he considered undesirable. And if a person reasons from the nature of man to how he should act as Maslow (1963) does, he is speaking for the moment as a philosopher rather than a scientist.

As in the case of a parent's commitment to his children, religion can be a dynamic force that shapes one's whole style of living or merely an empty verbal formula. Similarly it is capable of inspiring intense loyalties and emotional involvement. Whether or not the counselor is a religious person and whether or not he shares his client's beliefs, religion remains an important factor in the lives of many people which must be taken into account in any helping relationship. C. Gilbert Wrenn explains how this can be done in a professional manner.

Psychology, Religion, and Values for the Counselor

The postulate . . . is that religion and psychology complement each other. Psychology contributes to an understanding of the *nature* of self and of one's relationships with others, religion to an understanding of meaning and purpose in life, and the *significance* of these same relationships. Both may contribute to more effective living. Their purposes are parallel and supporting, not antagonistic. The psychologist conceives of emotional maturity as including an awareness of others, as a development beyond infantile Narcissism toward social perceptivity. The religious counselor speaks of one's concern for others as an extension of the love of God for us. One is concerned in a pragmatic sense with social development which contributes to personality integration, the other with purposeful concern for those who are brothers in the family of man. The personality goal for the client of each has much in common with the other.

Psychology (in its therapeutic sense) can be more effective if it considers the place of religious values and relationships in a client since these attitudes and values are as real as are aptitudes and skills. They cannot be disregarded. Beyond this, to be sure, psychology can meet some human needs that cannot be met by religion. An understanding of *self* involves, perhaps, a

C. Gilbert Wrenn. Psychology, religion and values for the counselor. **The Personnel and Guidance Journal**, 1958, **36**, 331-334. Copyright © 1958, by the American Personnel and Guidance Association. Reprinted by permission.

different discipline than an understanding of *life*. A counselor[1] uses his particular psychological knowledges and skills to help a person understand himself better, his life realities, his daily behavior, his personality potentials. Upon occasion, and if he deems himself competent, he deals with repressed feelings and experiences and attempts to secure better self-acceptance on the part of the client, some resolution of inner conflicts and anxieties. This *is* psychology's domain, the application of what is known about behavior to client needs, the use of relationship and communication procedures in a manner that is a normal outgrowth of the counselor's unique personality style. He may or may not (and this decision is important) go beyond this and assist the client in an understanding of life's purposes and meanings, and the alternate ways in which one may relate oneself to the Infinite.

The Counselor and Religion

Most counselors would accept what I have just written about the psychological functions of the counselor. But does he have any religious functions? This question brings out the goose pimples on any counselor—including the writer! I do not know just what these functions are but I am sure that counselors can no longer act as though religion—the client's and the counselor's—does not exist. We are fearful of admitting religion into our professional thinking for a variety of reasons—the emotional imbalance involved in some religions, the seeming artificiality in others, the exclusive attention that has been given in the professional education of the counselor to the empirical and the intellectual with a consequent neglect of the spiritual and the aesthetic, the counselor's own religious insecurity or his failure to convert creed (belief) and cult (ritual) into conduct. These threats to the counselor's peace of mind still do not deny the reality of religious problems among clients, or keep him from a further fear that he is neglecting a resource that might be tapped in the interests of his client.

Mowrer (1957) clearly points up the danger in neglecting religion as a resource because we have been so much under the influence (and properly so) of objective and analytic psychology in the development of psychology as a field of study. Both objective psychologists and analysts, writes Mowrer, have erred in making the mind a product of or a servant of the body in assuming

---

[1] A counseling psychologist is a psychologist who has had special emphasis on counseling in his professional education and in his practice. The counseling psychologist, as distinct from other psychologists, is concerned primarily with developmental counseling, with appraisal of potentials and assets, with the client's understanding of and integration with social reality, with the various roles played by the client in different areas of life, with client awareness of his own dynamics and of the nature of his psychological defenses. And the counselor, in the sense used in this paper, is a person with at least modest psychological knowledge and sophistication. Some recent statements on counselor and counseling psychologists are found in Wrenn (1954), Perry (1955), and Committee on Definition (1956).

that mind (or spirit) has no independent and autonomous function and existence. All is not well with behaviorists and psychoanalysts who cling to this barren rock. Rather than to be objective and to study *about* religion or to reduce it to a form of psychopathology, religion might well be considered as something having *psychological survival value.* It is now being studied as a resource and as having survived because it has developed in response to man's unique personality needs.

It is hard for the counselor to brush aside the significance of this resource when he hears deeply serious and influential psychiatrists of the National Academy of Religion and Mental Health (1956) making such statements as these: "What a man believes is a factor in his emotional health. The problems of mental illness include the disorganization of an individual's philosophy of life. It concerns the sufferer's attitude toward the world and other people. . . .Religion has always, in many times and many places, played its part in healing. The ultimate values of mankind are spiritual."

Or these: "The Academy does not advocate psychiatric treatment by the ministry, or religious instruction by psychiatrists. It seeks to discover and make known, for the benefit of the people and the professions, the psychiatric and religious resources now available and usable in developing healthy emotional attitudes, in preventing mental illness, and in healing."[2]

The counselor does not need to know the concern of the psychiatrist about religion or to have authority invoked, however, to be convinced. All that he needs is a little reflection on the place of religion in the thoughts and feelings of people, its incalculable potential for societal welfare, the need among young people for an enduring and integrated value structure, a memory recall of clients and students who have been troubled about their place in life, their significance as human beings. All he needs to do is to reflect upon his own uneasiness when confronted by his client with problems of religion. This is an uneasiness that may spring from his own religious immaturity or from his uncertainty about the appropriateness of communicating what are to him personal certainties.

Many of us do not know how to manage *ourselves* in counseling when the client appears to have a religious need. Can we continue to be accepting or should we propound our faith? Can we be empathic and nonjudgmental and still keep faith *with* our faith? Arbuckle (1953) deals sympathetically with this problem in his discussion of those who consider "client-centered"

[2] The officers and advisory council of The National Academy of Religion and Mental Health includes such psychiatrists and psychologists as Kenneth E. Appel, Edward J. Humphreys, Otto Klineberg, Charles A. Curran, Francis Braceland (President, American Psychiatric Association), Arthur Noyes (Past-President, APA), William C. Menninger (Past-President, APA), and such theologians as Paul J. Tillich and Albert C. Outler. In July, 1957, the Academy dropped the word "National" from its title to permit it to develop its influence beyond our national borders. It is now simply The Academy of Religion and Mental Health.

counseling as antagonistic to religious counseling which should be "God-centered." He writes that "client-centered" is not "self-centered" and that whether one is troubled about religious counseling in this sense depends upon both one's concept of God and one's concept of the process of counseling.

What may a counselor do about religion—his own and others? These things at least:

1 Study the significance of religion, positive and negative, in personality development.

2 Be prepared, by thought in advance, to deal with religious problems as permissively and thoughtfully as he would any other emotion-laden experience of the client—marriage relations, parental relations, sexual experiences and fears, repressed guilt, shyly expressed hopes and dreams.

3 Clarify his own religious experience so that immaturity and confusion here will not act as an interference in the counseling relationship.

Values, Ethics, and Religion

As "life in these United States" becomes more complex and our relation to the other parts of the world more intimate, the need for meanings and purposes becomes more urgent, the possession of a carefully considered value system becomes a requirement. A clinical psychologist's discussion of the relation of values to mental health, involving the phenomenon of "value lag," is found in a recent article by Korner (1956). He is concerned with the reluctance with which the social scientist in the past has dealt with values, speaks of the matrix of values within which the adjustment mechanisms function to protect the ego from value conflict and value lag, touches on the difference between short-term values and stable values. The discussion is well worth reading (his "arteriosclerotic" and "super ego deadwood" values must be read to be appreciated) but I am here concerned with Korner's stable, "relatively immutable," values and their relation to religion.

Several years ago I attempted to point up the central ethical conflict with which counselors are often confronted, loyalty to the integrity of the counselor-counselee relationship versus loyalty to society and to the institution of society for which one may work—the integrity of the individual or the integrity of the state? Do I keep faith with the confidence of my client, or tell my boss what he is demanding to know? The adopted code of ethics of the American Psychological Association from which I made my adaptation to the ethics of the counselor is based upon the value system of our American culture.

But such a code of ethics merely defines the problem, it does not solve it. When a person is faced with a conflict of loyalties he is thrown back upon his own personal values, those convictions and beliefs of what is "most right," which are in part, at least, the product of his religious experience. "Each man has his own pattern of values—(but) back of these personal values, which are sometimes pitted against those of his society, is another set of values. These are part of our great human heritage, great principles of truth and mercy and justice that are as yet, and perhaps always will be, only dimly understood" (Wrenn, 1952). Systematic and dedicated religious thinking is the source of much of our mature values system and a thoughtful religious faith appears to the writer to be the best of backlog resources for a counselor when problems of ethics arise.

In conclusion, allow me to comment upon what appears to me to be the psychological pertinence of many value statements. Values are the tested outcome of experience and have proved their pragmatic worth. They would necessarily be reflections of behavior. But so frequently do psychologists eschew value considerations, that it seems desirable to point out that *values do not necessarily exist in a non-psychological world.* Some years ago I heard Dr. Kenneth Brown, Director of the Danforth Foundation, speak on a hierarchy of values that made much psychological sense. There are no notes of this address available to me but three points are recalled as at the apex of a hierarchy of values in our culture: (1) Man is distinguished from all other creatures by his endless quest for the ultimate, his never-ceasing search for the absolute in truth and beauty; (2) Each human being is to be respected for own personal worth; (3) Living is giving, life is a service, growth is through giving of self not through withholding. These are value statements to be sure, but they have a pragmatic psychological integrity as well.

More recently I have tried to state concisely some principles of human relations that I have used in both educational and industrial consulting work, principles that can be justified psychologically. As one reads these, they also appear to be value statements. In either sense they may be useful to the counselor as he deals with colleagues and family as well as with clients. Behavior objectives such as these are a stiff test of one's psychological sophistication as well as of one's religious maturity. (1) I shall strive to see the positive in the other person and praise it at least as often as I notice that which is to be corrected; (2) If I am to correct or criticize someone's action I must be sure that this is seen by the other as a criticism of a specific behavior and not as a criticism of himself as a person; (3) I will assume that each person can see some reasonableness in his behavior, that there is meaning in it for him if not for me; (4) When I contribute to another person's self-respect I increase his positive feelings toward me and his respect for me; (5) To at least one person, perhaps many, I am a person of significance, and he is affected vitally by my recognition of him and my good will toward him.

SUMMARY

If no one can function in a helping relationship without implicitly betraying some of his personal commitments, how can a counselor avoid imposing his value system upon defenseless clients? Above all else he must clearly understand what his own values are and how they are integrated into an overall philosophy of life. Hipple describes what goes into the making of such a philosophy as it applies to the practitioner's theory of counseling.

Not every mention of value judgments, even the counselor's own, necessarily encroaches upon the individual's inviolable right to make his own decisions. Nor is a frank discussion of the possible range of values from which an adolescent may choose always to be avoided. What is important is that the counselor remember that even when he speaks of values as relatively established as those of Western Culture, he views them in a framework of his own personal commitments

The problem of values is further complicated when the topic of religion arises. Wrenn explains that psychology and religion are not inimical. They play supporting roles in the development of a mature person. The counselor should no more ignore religion than any other personality potential that can be used constructively. His task is to help the client integrate into his pattern of living whatever positive convictions he possesses.

DISCUSSION TOPICS

1 How is the task of a school counselor related to the general aims of education?

2 In what way does the counselor's task resemble that of a teacher and in what way does it not? (Williamson, 1958)

3 If you were counseling a young man who seemed intent on some antisocial act that might cause serious injury to another person, how would you proceed?

4 Suggest ways in which the counselor might impose his values on a client without being aware that he is doing so.

5 Is it ever legitimate for the school counselor to teach values? If your answer is affirmative, what kind of values and under what conditions?

6 Discuss the chief value judgments underlying one's personal philosophy of counseling.

ADDITIONAL READINGS

Dreyfus, E. A. Humanness: A therapeutic variable. **The Personnel and Guid-ance Journal,** 1966, **45,** 573-578. More important than the counselor's theoretical orientation is his ability to be human in his professional relationships.

Feifel, H., et al. Symposium on relationships between religion and mental health. **American Psychologist,** 1958, **13,** 565-579. Seven distinguished psychologists contributed to this symposium.

Holden, G. S. On openness and authenticity. **The School Counselor,** 1969, **17,** 3-9. A distinction is made between openness to see and experience oneself and openness that encourages blunt, unsolicited opinions that bring nothing but pain to the recipient.

Lowe, C. M. Value orientations—an ethical dilemma. **American Psychologist,** 1959, **14,** 687-693. Both counselor and client should be aware of each other's value orientation.

Patterson, C. H. The place of values in counseling. **Journal of Counseling Psychology,** 1958, **5,** 216-223. The counselor who realizes that he is not neutral about values can deal more effectively with his clients.

Rogers, C. R. **On becoming a person.** Boston: Houghton Mifflin, 1961, Ch. 3. The characteristics of a helping relationship are described.

Tomilson, T. M. The psychotherapist as a codeterminant in client goal setting. In C. Bühler and F. Massarik, **The course of human life,** New York: Springer, 1968, Ch. 13. " . . . the therapy which grows out of human-istic considerations moves beyond conventional treatment interests in the direction of not only helping the disturbed person but also of providing him with an experience which will contribute to his long-range growth and self-realization."

Williamson, E. G. Value orientation in counseling. **The Personnel and Guid-ance Journal,** 1958, **36,** 520-529. An in-depth study of the role of values in counseling.

Part Four

In Search of a Human Science

This new scientific age will bring with it more than a mere increase in physical well-being. It will entail new ways of thinking and a modification of our system of sentiments. We will find ourselves with some new beliefs and, above all, some changes in the ways we hold those beliefs, whatever they may be.

A. NORTH WHITEHEAD

Chapter 13

Traditional Science

There seems to be the following "law" at work: the more absolutely and completely we formulate the forces or drives, the more we are talking about abstractions and not the living human being.

Rollo May

Great movements in history do not appear at random. Each is the product of a distinctive intellectual climate that shapes its development. Modern science is no exception. What destined the Western world to be its birthplace rather than the far East was not fate but the type of problems that interested thinkers on opposite sides of the globe. Oriental philosophers have traditionally concerned themselves with the conduct of life and moral behavior, whereas the West has been more typically preoccupied with the problem of knowledge. What precisely do we know about the world outside the mind and how do we know it? In raising such questions early Greek philosophers set our civilization on a path that led to the development of scientific methodology.

THE PARTICULAR AND THE UNIVERSAL

Not all the issues raised by Plato, Aristotle, and their contemporaries have been satisfactorily resolved. One item of unfinished business that has enlivened philosophical debates ever since is the problem of universals. How can a universal concept, such as **girl**, do justice to each individual in all her particularity while at the same time referring to every female child? Since this notion is, in effect, a general classification does it point to anything that actually exists or is it just an idea?

The question arises every time we use a noun or common name. Take the case of a boy who buys his first car and thinks of it as an extension of his own personality. He is immensely proud of all the special features which he enthusiastically describes to anyone willing to listen. It is a red Mustang, with power disk brakes, leather interior, vinyl roof, and air conditioning. What happens to all these exciting characteristics of his prized possession when mother casually writes grandfather, ''Joe bought a **car** yesterday?'' The sleight of hand that allows her to place Joe's Mustang in a general category along with every other automobile effectively robs it of all that is most meaningful to him. Precisely the same thing happens to the living person when we think of him in terms of scientific generalizations or findings based on group data. The only way that many objects, persons, or observations can be forced into a single mental category is first to divest them of all their individual and unique characteristics. Every universal concept is a pigeonhole for representations of things that have been stripped down to their least common denominator, that is, to their essence consisting of whatever meaning they mutually share. In the same category with Joe's Mustang are jalopies, jeeps, Buicks, and every other conveyance which by any stretch of the imagination can be called a car. If there were no more than this to automobiles, few people would buy Cadillacs.

Joe may be satisfied to call his Mustang a car because he has enough firsthand experience (phenomenal knowledge) of this particular vehicle to flesh out the skeleton idea. Grandfather is not in a position to do so. He cannot picture the car with any accuracy and can only guess at the color, the ''extras,'' and whether or not it was previously owned by someone else. At the same time the common noun **car** does give him some useful information even though it is not comprehensive. Joe did not purchase a Honda or a pony; it was an automobile.

UNIVERSAL CONCEPTS IN SCIENCE

What is said here of universal ideas holds true in its own way for all scientific terminology and every generic conclusion, principle, law, or theory arrived at by traditional science. It would be difficult to communicate with other people without using universal concepts and general statements, although the convenience exacts a heavy toll, in statistics, where individual measurements as well as people are lost sight of when crowded together into intervals. Frequently enough the advantages of mass treatment of data outweigh the loss of individuality, but the consumer of psychological research must realize that he is dealing with only partial information about human beings, not with existing persons. High correlations between test scores and job success may enable a vocational counselor to suggest to his client alternate choices with favorable odds, but at the same time he must never lose sight of the fact that predictions based on group trends may or may not be valid for this particular individual. A school psychologist whose only information about a new student is that he ranks high on the obsessive-compulsive scale of a personality test must first study him in action to be able to judge how this trait pattern will affect his behavior. On the one hand the compelling need to repeat certain senseless rituals again and again may all but incapacitate him in the classroom. On the other hand it might drive him to the heights of scholarship if his passion for completing anything he starts allows him no rest as long as important questions remain unanswered. A former colleague of the author expressed this insight in the jest, "A student doesn't have to be compulsive to earn a doctorate, but it helps." A writer of his acquaintance puts it this way: "Few things contribute more to erudition than a well-administered inferiority complex."

PSYCHOLOGY NEEDS BOTH KINDS OF KNOWLEDGE

By this time it should be clear that the ancient paradox of the particular and the universal is not confined to elementary ideas and class names. When psychologists debate whether the objective or the phenomenological method should be used to study human beings, they are confronting the same issue at a different level. Both methods are needed. No one can function effectively in everyday life without concrete knowledge about actually existing objects such as Joe's Mustang. At the same time, unless he has at his disposal generic classifications, such as **car**, everything knowable would have to be treated as a unique event isolated from all others. Since this would preclude any effort to deal with the world in an orderly way, not only science but even a mode of life beyond mere survival would be impossible. Whatever methodological difficulties may be involved, psychologists can ill afford to ignore either approach.

Some types of problems allow little choice. Suppose you were given the assignment of standardizing an intelligence test for the armed services with a base of half a million cases. You might stack the answer sheets in a warehouse and carefully inspect them one by one, but when finished you would probably be more confused than before. Statistical methods and a computer would greatly facilitate the task of developing objective norms for interpreting the score of any serviceman. Yet however accurate a standard score of 67 might appear to be on the personnel record of a recruit, it may prove to be a faulty measure of what he can or will do in given circumstances. Leaving aside for a moment the technical limitations imposed by all objective research, many personal equations must be taken into consideration. Was the testing arrangement as a whole too threatening for him? How many errors were due to unfamiliarity with the use of an answer sheet? Is the person too indolent to make full use of his ability in real-life situations? Does his inability to work with others rule out certain types of employment? Will he refuse to participate in military projects which conflict with his value system?

One demand of the human condition that not even the scientist can change is the necessity of learning to live with a certain amount of ambiguity.

BEHAVIORISM AND NINETEENTH-CENTURY SCIENCE

One of the turning points in the history of psychology was marked by John Watson's decision to canonize the objective approach as the **only** legitimate method of research in psychology. What this amounted to was a declaration of intention to deal with only abstract constructs of universal applicability in order to avoid contaminating the data of psychology with direct human experience which he considered untrustworthy. In such a paradigm the subject is of interest to the investigator, not as an individual, but only insofar as he contributes to the elaboration or testing of general laws. Nothing else about him matters. His rich inner life, and for all practical purposes his humanness is considered beyond the scope of psychology. What the subject thinks, feels, or intends may be of interest to the philosopher, theologian, or poet, but not to the scientist who wishes to observe him from the outside as if he were just another object in nature. With one sweeping gesture Watson resolved the problem of universals by ruling flesh-and-blood individuals out of bounds for psychology.

The avowed purpose of behaviorism was to establish a purely natural science of man based on laws of behavior. Unfortunately the concept of science then current and still held by some psychologists was based on the nineteenth-century model of physics. Not until recently did we pause to reflect that physicists themselves had long before abandoned this classical prototype. To overgeneralize somewhat but still give a substantially true picture of it, the experimenter was conceived as standing outside the framework of his experiment and exercising no influence upon its outcome. The decisions he has to make in setting up a study, his manipulation of the independent variable, as well as his interpretation of the results once they are obtained, were considered unbiased by human subjectivity. It is difficult to see how these conditions could ever be achieved short of the experimenter becoming a detached spectator situated somewhere in outer space. Giorgi points out some of the ways in which the investigator is inevitably present in all his research.

Concern for the Inevitable Presence of the Scientist in Science

Under the concept of approach, all of the problems dealing with the inevitable presence of the human researcher in his own research are considered. It is not that others have been blind to this fact (e.g., Rosenthal, 1966; Heisenberg, 1966); it is just that very few have seen the need to account for this presence in a consistent and thorough way. Certain writers (e.g., Brody and Oppenheim, 1967) admit that the researcher has to be an experiencing person, but then this fact remains a mere presupposition and in no way influences how the research is practiced and interpreted. Others may admit that it is a problem, but then use this fact as an argument for using "objective" methods.

However, as we saw above, "objective" methods do not remove the presence of the researcher, they simply make him present in another way. The presupposition is that the objective approach is better than any other approach—but, we would add, for what intention? It is conceivable that a "neutral" presence may be the best attitude for the experimenter to assume in certain situations. But the problem is that most traditional psychologists (1) absolutize this presence, and (2) speak of it as a nonpresence. That is, they believe that it is an attitude that is universally valid and that, in a literal sense, the researcher is independent of his experimental situation. Thus, to state that the researcher is present not only initially but throughout the entire course of research, including interpretation and writing, is to introduce many problems. However we feel that the introduction of these problems constitutes an advance because previously they were not absent, but present in a hidden way. Perhaps now we can work towards the solution of some of them.

First of all, let us try to demonstrate the way in which the researcher or theorist is constantly present. Let us first take a research situation. Everyone agreees that a laboratory situation is an artifical situation. But what does that mean? It means that the laboratory situation exists in a way that is not found naturally in the world. But how did the laboratory situation get that way? Precisely through the activities of the experimenter. He is the one who structured it. He constituted the experimental situation by his selection of equipment, his definition of variables, his selection of stimuli, etc. In other words, the laboratory situation is artifical because it is a *human artifact*; it, more than an everyday situation, is the result of a single human person's intervention. Surely, the experimenter draws upon general principles and accumulated knowledge, but the specific variables that are chosen are still selected by him, the number of subjects are determined by him, the procedures used to analyze the data are determined by him, and so on. In other words, rather than being independent of the researcher, the artificiality of the laboratory situation means that more so than many other situations, it represents the viewpoint of *one* other person using the media and knowledge of a community of persons. Human presence cannot be defined by sheer physical presence; it is a far more contextual matter than that. Let us pursue the matter to the stages of data collection, interpretation and writeup. If experiments simply generated objective, independent facts, there would be no need for the organization of the facts, nor for a discussion of them. The simple truth would be there for all to see. However, no published reports ever present merely raw data. The data are always summarized or organized in some fashion and there is always a discussion of them. The discussion tries to indicate the significance of the facts, and it relates them to relevant theories and points out the hypotheses and interpretations that the data support and oppose whenever this is possible. If there were "objective" facts with univocal implications, none of the above would be necessary. In other words, organization and discussion of data are not just pleasant activities a scientist indulges in, but they are necessary to complete the research. That is, human intervention is once again necessary; there is no "reality-in-itself" that man merely registers; he actively participates in the constitution of what he calls "the real" (Boulding, 1967).

Lastly, we can point out that in the case of human subjects, the experimental situation ultimately must *exist for them*, and there is never any guarantee that the way it exists for them is the way the experimenter intended it (Giorgi, 1967a). More important, however, is the simple fact that the experimental situation exists *for* the subject. This means that the situation is once again charged with human significance, and that the primary frame of reference for understanding the data should be the relation between the subject and the situation. One implication of this fact is that it will not be possible to account for results with expressions like "behavior as a function of stimuli" or "differences in behavior as a function of conditions" because they are not accurate (they may be acceptable as shorthand expressions, but it would be better to avoid them so that misinterpretations are not communicated). They are not accurate because the "conditions" or the "stimuli" are constituted in part by the subjects (not necessarily reflectively); it is not in terms of world versus subject or subject versus world that the results must be understood, but rather what kind of change in the subject-world relation is necessary to change any given subject-world relation. This latter terminology already implies human presence.

Note, we have not stated that because laboratory situations are artificial, they are not valuable; indeed we would hold the opposite. What we are simply trying to point out is that the reason that laboratory studies are valuable can be understood in a more adequate way. It is not because they uncover a "truth-in-itself" or because an "objective" attitude eliminates the presence of man from the research. These are not adequate explanations, because laboratory studies are inventions of men and because they are constantly being supported by human activities and awareness. Obviously something right is being done in laboratory situations, but we can still clarify these situations further. The implication we would like to stress, however, is that it is not simply an obvious platitude that science is constructed by man, but rather a highly relevant fact for both scientific understanding and praxis.

For example, if by means of an analysis such as we have just completed, one discovers that an "objective" attitude, in the traditional sense, does not really remove the presence of the observer, and that it is not a universal desideratum but merely describes one way of being present, one way of conducting research, the possibility of other ways of being present immediately presents itself. In other words, might there not be situations in which other ways of being present might be more fruitful? We believe there are, and especially when it comes to dealing with specifically human modes of behavior. The obvious question here is the one of circumventing the bias of the researcher or investigator. How is this to be done? Our answer, just as in the case of presuppositions, is that if biases cannot be eliminated, then they should be included. The reason is simply that they are part of the data that belong to a situation. Moreover, the mode of presence of the researcher is not limited to his own interpretation of it; wherever possible the subjects should also report on *how* the researcher was present. The presence of the bias limits the generality of the data, but this is precisely why a scientific perspective would want this information. An objective attitude is also a biased presence. By means of relating the results of a study with the biases (or perspectives) of a researcher, one would be able to circumscribe the context within which certain results would be valid. This *is* the way science progresses, and levels of high generality are achieved only after a long time.

SCIENTIFIC CONSTRUCTS

Another false premise of classical science is related to the problem of the individual and the universal that was discussed earlier. Nineteenth-century physicists were convinced that Sir Isaac Newton's principles of mechanics dealt with the very foundations of things as they actually exist. His **Principia** explained the whole physical universe in terms of matter, space, time, motion, and causality. What could be more real or self-evident, they thought, than the idea of matter? Everything one sees is matter and the senses experience firsthand its qualities of color, shape, temperature, and so on.

What they forgot is that matter is an idea, not a thing. The tree outside my window is a pin oak 30 feet high. The cloud drifting lazily in the sky above is made up of individualized particles of water vapor, not matter. By a mental operation it is possible to strip away all the unique characteristics of these actually existing objects so that nothing remains except extension, shape, weight, and inertia. When reduced to such notions they can be heaped together with everything else in the universe in the same thought category of **matter**. Obviously we are dealing with words and ideas rather than the concrete building blocks of the universe. Space, time, motion, and causality can be shown to be equally abstract as matter.

Scientist of the last century, however, felt certain that Newton had discovered the fundamental blueprint for all that exists. It was a neat, closed system. Nothing could be added and nothing taken away without destroying the whole design. What is more important, it worked. Applying the principles of mechanics to nature, scientists were able to give an orderly account of the movements of planets, the behavior of fluids and gases, the elasticity of metals, the acceleration of falling bodies, the path of projectiles, and so on and on. As one mystery after another yielded its secrets with almost monotonous regularity, scholars became convinced that at last they possessed the one genuine key for understanding things **as they really are**. Northrup (1962) points out that had this been true, Newton's theory would never have required modification and no trustworthy experimental results would ever have contradicted it. "Being implied by the facts, it would be as indubitable and final as they are."

As it happened, two investigators succeeded in disconfirming the presence of the subtle ether that Newton had visualized as permeating every object and filling outer space. To add to the confusion physicists discovered that classical mechanics not only failed to account for the absorption of heat by black bodies but were at variance with certain celestial observations as well. Not until two new theories, relativity and quantum mechanics, based on quite different assumptions had been developed, could these phenomena be explained. Obviously Newton's principles are valid only within certain limits.

What is said here does not imply that classical mechanics have been completely replaced by something else. Newton's laws still accurately describe much of what goes on in our natural and technological worlds. The reason why rocket engines produce a forward thrust in the near vacuum of outer space is explained by his third law of motion, "To every action force there is an equal and opposite reaction force." Some of his other principles are involved in calculating the precise angle of reentry of a space capsule so that it does not either ricochet off the earth's atmosphere or burn up as it descends through it.

The failure of classical mechanics as a definitive explanation of all that is real was a shattering blow to a world of scientists wholly committed to Newtonian physics. What could account for the collapse of principles so obviously based on things as they are? How could they be at one and the same time so right and yet so wrong? Gradually physicists came to realize that traditional science does not deal with integral objects but only with constructs, that is, with abstractions based on selective aspects of the object under study (Northrup, 1962). The investigator arbitrarily selects what he wishes to observe and rigidly controls or ignores everything else. Constructs such as the cost-of-living index or the IQ reveal something important about reality but not the whole story. Neither do they exist as such outside the mind. The cost-of-living index is not a thing but an idea which is derived by pooling many bits of information and calculating a rough average. In the same way when we take a bite out of an apple or test the resiliency of a foam rubber cushion we are not experiencing **matter** but this specific apple and this sample of foam rubber as they are in themselves. What we call **matter** is a kind of mental classification used to lump together everything having sense qualities. The mistake of classical scientists was to believe that the world we experience consists of actually existing matter. On the contrary such constructs are highly abstract concepts several mental operations removed from concrete reality.

THE FALLACY OF MISPLACED CONCRETENESS

Some constructs are used so frequently in everyday life that eventually people come to mistake them for objective reality. We think of time as something measured by clocks and space as a kind of empty container instead of concepts arrived at by logical thinking. Whitehead (1962, p. 75) calls this human tendency "the fallacy of misplaced concreteness." He suggests that in every generation certain abstractions become so much a part of our thinking that only gradually do we recognize them for what they are. Maslow (1966, pp. 74-75) was thinking of something similar when he wrote:

From The Psychology of Science

For most people the far goal of science, its end and therefore its ideal and defining essence, still is its comprehensive "laws," elegant and "simple" mathematical formulas, pure and abstract concepts and models, ultimate and irreducible elements and variables. And so for these people these ultimate abstractions have become the most real reality. Reality lies *behind* the appearances and is inferred rather than perceived. The blueprints are more real than the houses. The maps are more real than the territory.

The student must be on his guard to avoid making similar errors. When psychology is defined as the science of behavior he is likely to think in concrete terms as if the behavior referred to here meant a particular rat pressing a bar in a given Skinner box. Behavior in the scientific sense does not have this connotation: it is an abstract construct. As was mentioned earlier, traditional science is not concerned with the individual subject except insofar as it contributes to a general principle of some kind. The same can be said of other psychological terms, such as conditioned responses or reinforcement. A food-deprived rodent operating a lever to obtain food pellets is said to illustrate a hunger drive. While its activity can be observed this is not a drive. A good inference is that the animal works the bar because of a **subjective feeling** of hunger. The **drive**, as such, is in the psychologist's mind—in other words, it is a construct.

CONSTRUCTS ARE PARTLY TRUE

As a result of being derived from selective observations, constructs do not tell the whole truth about any phenomenon even though they reveal something that is factual. Newton's first law of motion deals with

From Abraham H. Maslow. **The psychology of science**, pp. 74-75. (Harper & Row, 1966). Reprinted by permission of Harper & Row, Publishers, Inc.

the property of inertia in material things and nothing else. As far as this principle is concerned, the object in question might be a football, a cabbage, or a king. A construct shows how a thing appears from one point of view. Maslow compared it to a single frame of a movie film. Even this partial information is expressed symbolically, often as a mathematical formula or a physical model. For this reason we should not expect it to provide an accurate thumbnail description of the phenomenon under investigation, much less a photograph of something as it exists in nature. Because the construct is so sketchy and tenuous, it sometimes serves a useful purpose even when it is wrong. The classic example concerns two competing theories of light which baffled physicists until they began to understand the true nature of constructs. One theory conceived it as a particle and the other as a wave. Each neatly explained certain aspects of light but not others. By using both schemes, even though they were contradictory, physicists could better understand and predict the behavior of light than on the basis of one alone.

The student who keeps in mind the limitations of constructs will not draw unwarranted conclusions from psychological models. When, for example, some psychologists speak of explaining all conscious functioning in terms of conditioned responses or of reducing all human motivation to drive reduction, he will recognize this approach as just another mental strategy to summarize and hopefully simplify a host of facts. As in the case of light, such statements do not describe people as they actually are.

SCIENCE IS NEVER COMPLETELY OBJECTIVE

Another presupposition of traditional science pictured the entire research procedure as being completely objective just as if no personal decisions were needed in designing or carrying out an experiment. Nor was any account taken of the fact that data are not self-interpreting. Meter readings and other measurements, far from being laws of behavior, are the raw material from which these are fashioned by a process of logical thinking. While it is true that experiments can be and often are replicated by other investigators who go through the same process in order to check the original measurements, there is not certainty that they will arrive at the same end product. Due to different conscious and subconscious presuppositions, evidence that appears overwhelming to one investigator may leave another quite unmoved. Two scientists sometimes begin with identical data and end with quite opposite conclusions, as the following selection from Rollo May clearly illustrates.

From Existential Psychology

Our presuppositions always limit and constrict what we see in a problem, experiment, or therapeutic situation; there is no escape from this aspect of our human "finiteness." The naturalist perceives in man what fits his naturalistic spectacles; the positivist sees the aspects of experience that fit the logical forms of his propositions; and it is well known that different therapists of different schools will see in the same dream of a patient the dynamics that fit the theory of their particular school. The old parable of the blind men and the elephant is written large on the activities of men in the enlightened twentieth century as well as those of earlier, more "benighted" ages. Bertrand Russell puts the problem well with respect to physical science: "Physics is mathematical not because we know so much about the physical world but because we know so little; it is only its mathematical properties that we can discover."

No one—physicist, psychologist, or anyone else—can leap out of his historically conditioned skin. The one way we can keep the presuppositions underlying our particular method from unduly biasing our efforts is to know consciously what they are and so not to absolutize or dogmatize them. Thus we have at least a chance of refraining from forcing our subjects or patients upon our "Procrustean couches" and lopping off, or refusing to see, what does not fit.

In Ludwig Binswanger's little book *Sigmund Freud: Reminiscences of a Friendship,* which relates his conversations and correspondence with Freud, there are some interesting interchanges illustrating this point. The friendship between Freud, the psychoanalyst, and Binswanger, a leading existential psychiatrist of Switzerland, was lifelong and tender; and it marks the only instance of Freud's continuing in friendship with someone who differed radically with him.

Shortly before Freud's eightieth birthday, Binswanger wrote an essay describing how Freud's theory had radically deepened clinical psychiatry; but he added that Freud's own existence as a person pointed beyond the deterministic presuppositions of his theory.

> Now [with Freud's psychoanalytic contribution] man is no longer merely an animated organism, but a "living being" who has origins in the finite life process of this earth, and who dies its life and lives its death; illness is no longer an externally or internally caused disturbance of the "normal" course of a life on the way to its death (Binswanger, 1957, p. 90).

But Binswanger went on to point out that he believed that in Freud's theory man is not yet man in the full sense of the word:

> ... for to be a man does not mean merely to be a creature begotten by living-dying life, cast into it and beaten about, and put in high spirits or low spirits by it; it means to be a being that looks its own and mankind's fate in the face, a being that is "steadfast," i.e., one taking its own stance, or one standing on its own feet. ... The fact that our lives are determined by the forces of life, is only one side of the truth; the other is that we determine these forces as our fate. Only the two sides together can take in the full problem of sanity and insanity. Those who, like Freud, have forged their fates with the hammer—the work of art he has created in the medium of language is sufficient evidence of this—can dispute this fact least of all (Ibid, p. 90).

Then, on the occasion of Freud's eightieth birthday, the Viennese Medical Society invited Binswanger, along with Thomas Mann, to deliver papers at the anniversary celebration. Freud himself did not attend, not being in good health and also, as he wrote Binswanger, not being fond of anniversary celebrations ("They seem to be too much on the American model"). Binswanger spent two days with Freud in Vienna at the time of this birthday and remarked that in these conversations he was again impressed by how far Freud's own largeness and depth of humanity as a man surpassed his scientific theories.

In his paper at the celebration, Binswanger gave credit to Freud for having enlarged and deepened our insight into human nature more, perhaps, than anyone since Aristotle. But he went on to point out that these insights wore "a theoretic-scientific garb that as a whole appeared to me too 'one-sided' and narrow." He held that Freud's great contribution was in the area of *homo natura,* man in relation to nature (*Umwelt*)—drives, instincts, and similar aspects of experience. And as a consequence, Binswanger believed that in Freud's theory there was only a shadowy, epiphenomenal understanding of man in relation to his fellowmen (*Mitwelt*) and that the area of man in relation to himself (*Eigenwelt*) was omitted entirely.

Binswanger sent a copy of the paper to Freud and a week later received a letter from him containing the following sentences:

> As I read it I was delighted with your beautiful language, your erudition, the vastness of your horizon, your tactfulness in contradicting me. As is well known, one can put up with vast quantities of praise. ... *Naturally, for all that you have failed to convince me.*[1] I have always confined myself to the ground floor and basement of the edifice. You maintain that by changing one's point of view, one can also see the

[1] Binswanger's italics.

upper story, in which dwell such distinguished guests as religion, art, etc. . . . I have already found a place for religion, by putting it under the category of "the neurosis of mankind." But probably we are speaking at cross purposes, and our differences will be ironed out only after centuries. In cordial friendship, and with greetings to your charming wife, your Freud (Binswanger, 1957, p. 99).

Binswanger then adds in his book—and this is the central reason I quote the interchange—"As can be seen from the last sentence, Freud looked upon our differences as something to be surmounted by empirical investigation, not as something bearing upon the transcendental conceptions that underlie all empirical research."[2]

In my judgment, Binswanger's point is irrefutable. We can gather empirical data, let us say on religion and art, from now until doomsday, and we shall never get any closer to understanding these activities if, to start with, our presuppositions shut out what the religious person is dedicated to and what the artist is trying to do. Deterministic presuppositions make it possible to understand everything about art except the creative act and the art itself; mechanistic naturalistic presuppositions may uncover many facts about religion; but, as in Freud's terms, religion will always turn out to be more or less a neurosis, and what the genuinely religious person is concerned with will never get into the picture at all.

The point I wish to make . . . is the necessity of analyzing the presuppositions one assumes and of making allowance for the sectors of reality—which may be large indeed—that one's particular approach necessarily leaves out.

S-R CONCEPTS ARE RELATIVE

Another telling argument against S-R psychology's exaggerated claim to objectivity strikes at the very foundation of its most cherished concepts, namely, stimulus, response, and reinforcement (Gibson, 1960; Jessor, 1961). In a scholarly article entitled On the Need for Relativism (summarized in this chapter by consent of the author), Jerome Kagan(1967) points out that:

The psychology of the first half of this century was absolutistic, outer directed, and intolerant of ambiguity. When a college student carries this unholy trio of traits he is called authoritarian, and such has been the temperament of the behavioral sciences. But the era of authoritarian psychology may be nearing its dotage,

---

[2] By "transcendental," Binswanger of course does not refer to anything ethereal or magical: he means the underlying presuppositions that point beyond the given fact, the presuppositions that determine the goals of one's activity.

and the decades ahead may nurture a discipline that is relativistic, oriented to internal processes and accepting of the idea that behavior is necessarily ambiguous.

Like her elder sisters, psychology began her dialogue with nature using a vocabulary of absolutes. Stimulus, response, rejection, affection, emotion, reward, and punishment were labels for classes of phenomena that were believed to have a fixed reality. We believed that we could write a definition of these constructs that would fix them permanently and allow us to know them unequivocally at any time in any place.

Kagan goes on to show that biology began the trend toward relativism when it recognized that a slice of ectoderm tissue grafted in the eye field of an embryo develops differently than one placed in the area where the toe will later emerge. Physics, too, moved in this direction by discovering that mass and movement, which were once thought to be absolute values, are in fact relative. Psychologists, in turn, are finding that a stimulus cannot be considered a fixed, physical quantity as it has been in the past. Instead it varies with the inner dispositions of the experimental subject. Among the considerations that lead to this conclusion are the following:

1 If a stimulus is regarded as something to which a subject responds or is likely to respond, it cannot be described without taking into account the inner states of that subject. Expectancy or the preparation of the organism to receive the stimulus would be an example. Contrast, as every advertiser knows, heightens the probability that a person will respond to his message. But contrast will always be relative to what the organism is experiencing at the moment. A weak illumination that appears bright to the dark-adapted eye may not be noticed at all when the eye is light adapted.

2 Certain forms of inhibition are present in the nervous system which frequently prevent an otherwise effective stimulus from reaching the brain. An object near the face that one subject responds to immediately may not exist at all psychologically for another person. Anyone who has become accustomed to wearing bifocal lenses in his glasses must pay close attention to perceive the distorting effects that were originally so annoying to him.

3 The physical qualities of external stimuli are less important to the human individual than his interpretation of them. A noise filtering through a window sounds different depending upon whether a person thinks of it as emanating from a game of touch football, a fight, a group of drunken revelers, or a riot. The exertion required for mountain climbing which might appear intolerable if associated with an unwelcome class assignment seems exhilarating if climbing is a favorite sport. Thus the term **physical stimulus** loses much of its power and certainty. In man, at least, **contrast, cognitively interpreted, becomes an impor-**

tant key to understanding the incentives for behavior. Since contrast depends largely upon context and expectancy, it must be defined relatively rather than in terms of some fixed quantity.

Many psychologist think of positive reinforcement almost exclusively under the external aspects of reward or pleasure without taking into account more important **internal processes** which are dependent upon **attention.** Kagan argues that (1) sources of pleasure, and therefore of reinforcement, are often relative rather than fixed and (2) learning depends more on the **attentional involvement** of the learner than on the particular qualities of external events. He cites the following experiments with small children to verify these statements.

Change of stimulation is a source of pleasure, but only for a time. A previously novel stimulation soon becomes monotonous. Playing peek-a-boo is pleasant for a three-month-old infant for a quarter of an hour, for a ten month old infant for three minutes, and for a thirty-month-old child for a few seconds. If it is change in stimulation that gives pleasure, should we not look for the explanation inside the organism rather than outside? The human individual is a cognitive creature who tries to make sense out of incoming stimuli by fitting them into some meaningful pattern. The process of creating such a schema can be looked upon as a major source of pleasure. As long as the problem is only partially solved, the stimulus in question is likely to remain interesting and reinforcing. When the schema is perfected to the extent that the event can be consistently predicted, interest is likely to wane. It takes a twelve-week-old infant fifteen minutes to be able to predict the event of "peek-a-boo" whereas the three-year-old child makes the "aha" discovery within a few seconds. If the "peek-a-boo" face pops up from random locations, the infant keeps looking for the face for a much longer time. This difference can be attributed not to a higher level of external stimulation but to the added time required by the child to arrive at a satisfactory cognitive schema. Similarly, when an infant is shown slides of a human face, it does not smile immediately but only after three to five seconds. In other words, the stimulus does not produce pleasure until the projected picture is perceptually recognized as a human face.

At eight months, the frequency of smiling at both regular and distorted faces is dramatically **reduced.** These data do not support the theory that an infant smiles because of the reward value conditioned to its mother's face. At eight months the mother's face should have accumulated more reward value than at four months. An alternative explanation is that by this time the cognitive schema for a face is fixed so firmly in the child's mind that recognition occurs at once and with little effort. Since the pleasure that grew out of the creative activity is no longer present, smiling does not occur with the same frequency.

Kagan musters additional evidence for this point of view from the following observations:

1 Decrease in rate of heartbeat is known to accompany close attention to incoming visual stimuli. In the study cited above the greatest cardiac deceleration occurred not when the infants were shown representations of faces that were either quite familiar or so novel that they were unlikely to be recognized, but when the stimuli were somewhat familiar. We can assume that a large decrease in heart rate is likely to be associated with a surprise recognition of a face. Four-month-old infants showed the largest cardiac deceleration when shown regular faces; eight-month old infants when shown scrambled faces.

2 Thirteen-month-old infants smiled more frequently and exhibited greater change in heart rate when shown a human figure with either three heads or an animal head than when shown a scrambled man or a free form of the same area, color, and texture. Apparently **stimuli that are too easily recognized and those too difficult to recognize** do not elicit smiling and change in heart rate. Those which require active attention and effort afford pleasure to the individual.

The fact that pleasure is derived from a moderate amount of mismatch between a stimulus event and the subject's schema for interpreting it deprives the experimenter of certainty that a given stimulus will always be a source of pleasure. In the past we have been obsessed with the notion that pleasure, pain, and reinforcement are something fixed and invariant. If we look at what psychologists call reinforcement, we are amazed to find that the word is infamously inexact. A shock to an animal's paw, a verbal chastisement, an examiner's smile, a food pellet, a sign indicating tension reduction, a scene in which a killer gets caught in a Hitchcock movie—each is labeled reinforcement. All they have in common is the name. As a matter of fact, learning theorists have been unable to supply a good definition at all. Reinforcement is anything that helps learning. What, then, is it that must be added to the mere occurring together in space or time of two events in order to obtain learning? A good candidate for the missing essential element camouflaged by the term **reinforcement** is **attentional involvement**. A shock, a smile, a food pellet all attract attention to someone or something. That is why, in Kagan's opinion, they facilitate learning.

SCIENCE EXISTS IN PERSONS

Scientists may even repudiate the objective data gathered in an experiment for subjective reasons. Hebb (1951) records one instance of this which is not at all unusual. In spite of the criticism leveled against the Duke University experiments, enough evidence has been offered for the existence of ESP to convince psychologists on almost any other issue provided that the physiological mechanisms involved make sense. Personally Hebb, with the majority of psychologists, does not accept ESP. "I can not see what other basis my colleagues have for rejecting it; and if they are using my bias, they and I are allowing psychological evidence to be passed on by physical and physiological censors. . . my own rejection of his (Rhine's) view is—in the literal sense—prejudice."

Carl Rogers skillfully illustrates still another dimension of subjectivity in science.

A Changed View of Science

In the year which has elapsed since the foregoing material was written, I have from time to time discussed the issues with students, colleagues, and friends. To some of them I am particularly indebted for ideas which have taken root in me.[1] Gradually I have come to believe that the most basic error in the original formulation was in the description of science. I should like, in this section, to attempt to correct that error, and in the following section to reconcile the revised points of view.

The major shortcoming was, I believe, in viewing science as something "out there," something spelled with a capital S, a "body of knowledge," existing somewhere in space and time. In common with many psychologists I thought of science as a systematized and organized collection of tentatively verified fact, and saw the methodology of science as the socially approved means of accumulating this body of knowledge, and continuing its verification. It has seemed somewhat like a reservoir into which all and sundry may dip their buckets to obtain water—with a guarantee of 99% purity. When

From Carl R. Rogers. Persons or science? A philosophical question. American Psychologist, 1955, 10, 267-279. Copyright © (1955) by the American Psychological Association and reproduced by permission.

[1] I would like to mention my special debt to discussions with, and published and unpublished papers by Robert M. Lipgar, Ross L. Mooney, David A. Rodgers, and Eugene Streich. My own thinking has fed so deeply on theirs, and become so intertwined with theirs, that I would be at a loss to acknowledge specific obligations. I only know that in what follows there is much which springs from them, through me. I have also profited from correspondence regarding the paper with Anne Roe and Walter Smet.

viewed in this external and impersonal fashion, it seems not unreasonable to see Science not only as discovering knowledge in lofty fashion, but as involving depersonalization, a tendency to manipulate, a denial of the basic freedom of choice which I have met experientially in therapy. I should like now to view the scientific approach from a different, and I hope, a more accurate perspective.

Science in Persons

Science exists only in people. Each scientific project has its creative inception, its process, and its tentative conclusion, in a person or persons. Knowledge—even scientific knowledge—is that which is subjectively acceptable. Scientific knowledge can be communicated only to those who are subjectively ready to receive its communication. The utilization of science also occurs only through people who are in pursuit of values which have meaning for them. These statements summarize very briefly something of the change in emphasis which I would like to make in my description of science. Let me follow through the various phases of science from this point of view.

Science has its inception in a particular person who is pursuing aims, values, purposes, which have personal and subjective meaning for him. As a part of this pursuit, he, in some area, "wants to find out." Consequently, if he is to be a good scientist, he immerses himself in the relevant experience, whether that be the physics laboratory, the world of plant or animal life, the hospital, the psychological laboratory or clinic, or whatever. This immersion is complete and subjective, similar to the immersion of the therapist in therapy, described previously. He senses the field in which he is interested. He lives it. He does more than "think" about it—he lets his organism take over and react to it, both on a knowing and on an unknowing level. He comes to sense more than he could possibly verbalize about his field, and reacts organismically in terms of relationships which are not present in his awareness.

Out of this complete subjective immersion comes a creative forming, a sense of direction, a vague formulation of relationships hitherto unrecognized. Whittled down, sharpened, formulated in clearer terms, this creative forming becomes a hypothesis—a statement of a tentative, personal, subjective faith. The scientist is saying, drawing upon all his known and unknown experience, that "I have a hunch that such and such a relationship exists, and the existence of this phenomenon has relevance to my personal values."

What I am describing is the initial phase of science, probably its most important phase, but one which American scientists, particularly psychologists, have been prone to minimize or ignore. It is not so much that it has been denied as that it has been quickly brushed off. Kenneth Spence has said that this aspect of science is "simply taken for granted."[2] Like many experiences taken for granted, it also tends to be forgotten. It is indeed in the matrix of immediate personal, subjective experience that all science, and each individual scientific research, has its origin.

Checking with Reality

The scientist has then creatively achieved his hypothesis, his tentative faith. But does it check with reality? Experience has shown each one of us that it is very easy to deceive himself, to believe something which later experience shows is not so. How can I tell whether this tentative belief has some real relationship to observed facts? I can use, not one line of evidence only, but several. I can surround my observation of the facts with various precautions to make sure I am not deceiving myself. I can consult with others who have also been concerned with avoiding self-deception, and learn useful ways of catching myself in unwarranted beliefs, based on misinterpretation of observations. I can, in short, begin to use all the elaborate methodology which science has accumulated. I discover that stating my hypothesis in operational terms will avoid many blind alleys and false conclusions. I learn that control groups can help me to avoid drawing false inferences. I learn that correlations, and t tests and critical ratios and a whole array of statistical procedures can likewise aid me in drawing only reasonable inferences.

Thus scientific methodology is seen for what it truly is—a way of preventing me from deceiving myself in regard to my creatively formed subjective hunches which have developed out of the relationship between me and my material. It is in this context, and perhaps only in this context, that the vast structure of operationism, logical positivism, research design, tests of significance, etc., have their place. They exist, not for themselves, but as servants in the attempt to check the subjective feeling or hunch or hypothesis of a person with the objective fact.

And even throughout the use of such rigorous and impersonal methods, the important choices are all made subjectively by the scientist. To which of a number of hypotheses shall I devote time? What kind of control group is most suitable for avoiding self-deception in this particular research? How far shall I carry the statistical analysis? How much credence may I place in the findings? Each of these is necessarily a subjective personal judgment, emphasizing that the splendid structure of science rests basically upon its subjective

[2] It may be pertinent to quote the sentences from which this phrase is taken. ". . . the data of all sciences have the same origin—namely, the immediate experience of an observing person, the scientist himself. That is to say, immediate experience, the initial matrix out of which all sciences develop, is no longer considered a matter of concern for the scientist. He simply takes it for granted and then proceeds to the task of describing the events occurring in it and discovering and formulating the nature of the relationships holding among them." Kenneth W. Spence, in *Psychological Theory*, M. H. Marx (Ed.), Macmillan, 1951, p. 173.

use by persons. It is the best instrument we have yet been able to devise to check upon our organismic sensing of the universe.

The Findings

If, as scientist, I like the way I have gone about my investigation, if I have been open to all the evidence, if I have selected and used intelligently all the precautions against self-deception which I have been able to assimilate from others or to devise myself, then I will give my tentative belief to the findings which have emerged. I will regard them as a springboard for further investigation and further seeking.

It seems to me that in the best of science, the primary purpose is to provide a more satisfactory and dependable hypothesis, belief, faith, for the investigator himself. To the extent that the scientist is endeavoring to prove something to someone else—an error into which I have fallen more than once—then I believe he is using science to bolster a personal insecurity, and is keeping it from its truly creative role in the service of the person.

In regard to the findings of science, the subjective foundation is well shown in the fact that at times the scientist may refuse to believe his own findings. "The experiment showed thus and so but I believe it is wrong," is a theme which every scientist has experienced at some time or other. Some very fruitful scientific discoveries have grown out of the persistent *disbelief*, by a scientist, in his own findings and those of others. In the last analysis he may place more trust in his total organismic reactions than in the methods of science. There is no doubt that this can result in serious error as well as in scientific discoveries, but it indicates again the leading place of the subjective in the use of science.

Communication of Scientific Findings

Wading along a coral reef in the Caribbean this morning, I saw a blue fish—I think. If you, quite independently, saw it too, then I feel more confidence in my own observation. This is what is known as intersubjective verification, and it plays an important part in our understanding of science. If I take you (whether in conversation or in print or behaviorally) through the steps I have taken in an investigation, and it seems to you too that I have not deceived myself, and that I have indeed come across a new relationship which is relevant to my values, and that I am justified in having a tentative faith in this relationship, then we have the beginnings of Science with a capital S. It is at this point that we are likely to think we have created a body of scientific knowledge. Actually there is no such body of knowledge. There are only tentative beliefs, existing subjectively, in a number of different persons. If these beliefs are not tentative, then what exists is dogma, not science. If on the other hand, no one but the investigator believes the finding, then this finding is either a personal and deviant matter, an instance of psychopath-ology, or else it is an unusual truth discovered by a genius, which as yet no one is subjectively ready to believe. This leads me to comment on the group which can put tentative faith in any given scientific finding.

Communication to Whom?

It is clear that scientific findings can be communicated only to those who have agreed to the same ground rules of investigation. The Australian bushman will be quite unimpressed with the findings of science regarding bacterial infection. He knows that illness truly is cause by evil spirits. It is only when he too agrees to scientific method as a good means of preventing self-deception, that he will be likely to accept its findings.

But even among those who have adopted the ground rules of science, tentative belief in the findings of a scientific research can only occur where there is a subjective readiness to believe. One could find many examples. Most psychologists are quite ready to believe evidence showing that the lecture system produces significant increments of learning, and quite unready to believe that the turn of an unseen card may be called through an ability labeled extrasensory perception. Yet the scientific evidence for the latter is considerably more impeccable than for the former. Likewise when the so called "Iowa studies" first came out, indicating that intelligence might be considerably altered by environmental conditions, there was great disbelief among psychologists, and many attacks on the imperfect scientific methods used. The scientific evidence for this finding is not much better today than it was when the Iowa studies first appeared, but the subjective readiness of psychologists to believe such finding has altered greatly. A historian of science has noted that empiricists, had they existed at the time, would have been the first to disbelieve the findings of Copernicus.

It appears then that whether I believe the scientific findings of others, or those of my own studies, depends in part on my readiness to put a tentative belief in such findings.[3] One reason we are not particularly aware of

---

[3] One example from my own experience may suffice. In 1941 a research study done under my supervision showed that the future adjustment of delinquent adolescents was best predicted by a measure of their realistic self-understanding and self-acceptance. The instrument was a crude one, but it was a better predictor than measures of family environment, hereditary capacities, social milieu, and the like. At that time I was simply not ready to believe such a finding, because my own belief, like that of most psychologists, was that such factors as the emotional climate in the family and the influence of the peer group were the real determinants of future delinquency and nondelinquency. Only gradually, as my experience with psychotherapy continued and deepened, was it possible for me to give my tentative belief to the findings of this study and of a later one (1944) which confirmed it. (For a report of these two studies see "The role of self understanding in the prediction of behavior" by C. R. Rogers, B. K. Kell, and H. McNeil, *J. Consult. Psychol.*, 1948, 12, 174-186.)

this subjective fact is that in the physical sciences particularly, we have gradually agreed that in a very large area of experience we are ready to believe any finding which can be shown to rest upon the rules of the scientific game, properly played.

The Use of Science

But not only is the origin, process, and conclusion of science something which exists only in the subjective experience of persons—so also is its utilization. "Science" will never depersonalize, or manipulate, or control individuals. It is only persons who can and will do that. This is surely a most obvious and trite observation, yet a deep realization of it has had much meaning for me. It means that the use which will be made of scientific findings in the field of personality is and will be a matter of subjective personal choice—the same type of choice as a person makes in therapy. To the extent that he has defensively closed off areas of his experience from awareness, the person is more likely to make choices which are socially destructive. To the extent that he is open to all phases of his experience we may be sure that this person will be more likely to use the findings and methods of science (or any other tool or capacity) in a manner which is personally and socially constructive.[4] There is, in actuality then, no threatening entity of "Science" which can in any way affect our destiny. There are only people. While many of them are indeed threatening and dangerous in their defensiveness, and modern scientific knowledge multiplies the social threat and danger, this is not the whole picture. There are two other significant facets. (a) There are many other persons who are relatively open to their experience and hence likely to be socially constructive. (b) Both the subjective experience of psychotherapy and the scientific findings regarding it indicate that individuals are motivated to change, and may be helped to change, in the direction of greater openness to experience, and hence in the direction of behavior which is enhancing of self and society, rather than destructive.

   To put it briefly, Science can never threaten us. Only persons can do that. And while individuals can be vastly destructive with the tools placed in their hands by scientific knowledge, this is only one side of the picture. We already have subjective and objective knowledge of the basic principles by which individuals may achieve the more constructive social behavior which is natural to their organismic process of becoming.

[4]I have spelled out much more fully the rationale for this view in two recent papers: "The concept of the fully functioning person" *Psychotherapy: Research, Theory, and Practice,* 1963, 3, 72-92, and "Toward a theory of creativity," *ETC,* 1954, 11, 249-260.

SUMMARY

This chapter began with a consideration of the philosophical dilemma of the universal versus the particular and how this paradox is encountered in psychology. More specifically it was seen that traditional science confines itself to universals. General laws and conclusions are useful but, in the last analysis, only to the extent that they help us understand the individual.

Up to this point we have been chiefly concerned with the role of traditional science in psychology. Admittedly the discussion has been one-sided. Much has been said about its limitations and little of its virtues. In view of the fact that the natural science approach is so frequently extolled as the only legitimate one in psychology, it seems more appropriate to help restore equilibrium than to tip the balance still further in the direction of unqualified praise. Giorgi calls attention to ways in which an experimenter's presence is reflected in the outcome of his research, while May illustrates how a scientist's presuppositions may determine what conclusions he draws from his data. On closer examination Kagan finds that the concepts of stimulus, response, and reinforcement, which supposedly can be described with precision, are subject to such unobservable factors as shifting attention. Finally, Rogers pictures science as a human attainment with all the subjectivity that this implies.

Earlier in the chapter a distinction was made between abstract scientific constructs based on selective observations and the way things exist in reality. Unlike theoretical mathematics which is as much at home with unreality as reality, psychology ultimately must be able to operate on a person-to-person level to reach most of its objectives. Accordingly, we shall now turn our attention from people as an abstraction to the existing person.

DISCUSSION TOPICS

1 Comment on the characteristics, the limitations, the use and the abuse of scientific constructs. Explain the fallacy of misplaced concreteness. Why is it that two contradictory constructs may both be useful?

2 Describe the way a person goes about formulating a universal idea such as **tree** or **stimulus**. How does this type of concept differ from the knowledge of an actually existing concrete object?

3 In drawing a conclusion does a scientist speak in terms of real objects or mental constructs? (Heisenberg, 1962, pp. 196-200; Northrup, 1962, pp. 5-6) What are the implications of your answer for psychology?

4 Discuss the effect of an experimenter's presence on the outcome of his research.

5 Cite all the evidence you can find favoring and opposing the use of natural science methodology for the study of man.

6 Explain the concept of reductionism and give several examples. Comment on its application to psychology. How successful do you think behaviorism has been in attempting to account for all psychological functioning in terms of stimulus and response?

7 Clarify the notion of objectivity in science. What factors limit the objectivity of research?

8 In carrying out an experiment a scientist generates an hypothesis, decides on an experimental design, makes the necessary observation, interprets his data, and finally draws a generalized conclusion. Analyze each process in terms of what subjective or objective elements are involved.

9 Describe the popular stereotype of science. How would you correct this view?

10 Draw up a list of the presuppositions that are made in a typical psychological experiment such as the standardization of a personality test.

11 Discuss various ways in which a psychologist may unintentionally bias his findings.

12 Explain the difficulties encountered in attempting to define such notions as stimulus, response, and reinforcement in wholly objective terms.

13 Compare the theories of science proposed by the following writers: May (1969), Polanyi (1958), Rogers (1963), and Skinner (1963). Which approach do you personally prefer?

ADDITIONAL READINGS

Argyris, C. Some unintended consequences of rigorous research. **Psychological Bulletin**, 1968, **70**, 185-197. Human subjects in rigorously organized psychological research are likely to react in a way similar to disaffected employees in industry.

Barber, B. Resistance by scientists to scientific discovery. **Scientific Manpower Bulletin**, 1960, pp. 36-47. Familiar theories tend to perpetuate themselves in the face of disconfirming evidence.

Bronowski, J. The logic of the mind. In W. R. Coulson and C. R. Rogers (Eds.), **Man and the Science of Man**. Columbus, Ohio: Merrill, 1968. ". . . the unwritten aim that the physical sciences have set for themselves since Isaac Newton's time cannot be attained. The laws of nature cannot be formulated as an axiomatic, deductive, formal, and unambiguous system which is also complete."

Carlson, R. Where is the person in personality research? **Psychological Bulletin**, 1971, **75**, 203-219. "That the person is not really studied in current personality research is clearly shown in the survey of the literature."

Farson, R. E. (Ed.) **Science and human affairs: Morrison lectures.** Palo Alto, Calif.: Science and Behavior Books, 1965. The papers by Farson and Koch deal with some of the questions raised in this chapter.

Frisch, O. R. The life of Niels Bohr, mostly through the eyes of his friends. **Scientific American,** 1961, **216** (June), 144-148. "Bohr liked to stress that 'reality' is itself a word What we try in science. . .is to evolve a way of speaking unambiguously about our experiences. How far 'reality' is suitable for that purpose is itself a question to be decided in the light of experience."

Giorgi, A. Phenomenology and experimental psychology: I. **Review of Existential Psychology and Psychiatry,** 1965, **5,** 228-238. Shortcomings of the natural science approach to psychology are discussed.

Kessel, F. S. The philosophy of science as proclaimed and science as practiced: "identity" or "duality?" **American Psychologist,** 1969, **24,** 999-1005. Some inconsistencies between the theory and practice of science are analyzed from the psychologist's point of view.

Lerner, D. (Ed.). **Parts and wholes: The Hayden Colloquium on scientific method and concept.** New York: Free Press of Glencoe, 1963. This interdisciplinary symposium examines the paradoxical relationship of parts to wholes in fields as diverse as physics and poerty.

Maslow, A. H. **The psychology of science: A reconnaissance.** Chicago: Henry Regnery, 1966 (Gateway ed.) A delightful book written in lecture style, replete with subtle insights about the theory of science and the nature of man.

Northrup, F. S. C. Introduction. In W. Heisenberg. **Physics and philosophy: The revolution in modern science** (Torchbook ed). New York: Harper & Row, 1962. The objects that science studies are never known directly but only by way of mental constructs. Theories cannot be separated from the philosophical assumptions that underlie them.

Pfungst, O. **Clever Hans** (Ed. by R. Rosenthal). New York: Holt, Rinehart, and Winston, 1965. The strange case of Herr von Osten's educated horse dramatically illustrates another form of experimenter error.

Polanyi, M. **Personal knowledge.** Chicago: University of Chicago Press, 1958. In this classic work a scientist-philosopher shows that the ideal of scientific detachment can never be attained. Personal participation in the establishment of even objectively based knowledge is not an imperfection but a vital component.

Polanyi, M. Logic and psychology. **American Psychologist,** 1968, **23,** 27-43. "Confidence in science is based on nonstrict data. No strict rules can exist for establishing empirical knowledge."

Rosenthal, R. Self-fulfilling prophecy. **Psychology Today,** 1969, **2**(4), 44-51. This interesting article shows how an experimenter often unintentionally biases his results.

Schultz, D. P. The human subject in psychological research. **Psychological Bulletin,** 1969, **72,** 214-228. Current practices in the use of human subjects frequently bias the data of psychology.

Weaver, W. The imperfections of science. **American Scientist,** 1961, **49,** 99-113. A lucid discussion of five limitations of the scientific approach to knowledge.

Weaver, W. Scientific explanation. **Science,** 1964, **143,** 1290-1300. Two types of scientific explanations and their interrelationships are discussed.

Chapter 14

Phenomenology and
Existential Psychology

... within general psychology there is an increasing conviction that strictly "experimental" methods are incapable of dealing with central aspects of human psychology...

Rae Carlson

In an influential article published in 1941, Donald Snygg called attention to two contrasting frames of reference in psychological research—that of the experimenter and that of the behaving organism. Conclusions derived from these opposing points of view are not only dissimilar, they may even be contradictory. The process of learning provides an excellent example. As seen by an outside observer the task remains unchanged but not the learner. His responses become more relevant and efficient as practice continues.

Thus the objective approach inevitably includes among its derived facts random molar behavior and improvement with repetition usually by association or integration. Educational procedures based on objective facts customarily stress frequency, drill, reward, and punishment.

From the phenomenological point of view, that is to say, from the point of view of the learner, the facts are quite different. The learner remains unchanged. It is his experience of the situation or task that changes. From his point of view his behavior is always insightful, that is to say, it is always relevant to the situation as he interprets it at the moment. Improvement is concurrent with changes in the observed nature of the task, usually described as differentiation, individuation, or increase in detail. These data are in direct contradiction to the data derived from the objective approach; the observed facts of one frame of reference completely contradict the observed facts of the other. Educational procedures based upon phenomenological facts also differ from those based upon objective facts since they stress understanding of the individual child, pacing, and clear presentation of the material (Snygg, 1941).

A more striking example may occur in a communications class if three students are chosen at random to give a five-minute extemporaneous talk on a rather unfamiliar subject. The first speaker may be a typical loquacious bore who loves to have a captive audience. His strong need to maintain the self-image of being witty and interesting may cause him to see people hanging on his words when exactly the opposite is true. The second student, a member of the debate team, has accurately assessed his oratorical ability through past performance. Like an accomplished politican he knows that he can appear to say something important about almost any topic without committing himself in any way. The third character, too, is not altogether unfamiliar. He is extremely fearful of speaking in public and has studiously avoided every opportunity to stand before an audience, except the one time he tried and failed so miserably that his classmates never allowed him to forget the incident.

For all practical purposes the physical setting for all three speakers is identical but how different it appears to each of them. One glows with self-adulation as he deceives himself about the reactions of his audience. Another meets the challenge confidently and with a zestful feeling of self-fulfillment in the exercise of a skill that he has carefully cultivated. The other student's name is Charley Brown. He knows that he is going to fail, just as he always does on the baseball diamond or in his pursuit of the little redheaded girl. Instead of being a challenge, the situation becomes so threatening that he panics and goes blank. The inner turmoil he experiences is more unbearable than the sharpest physical pain.

If this drama were to take place in the psychological laboratory, instead of a classroom, a student investigator might well conclude that, except for the order of presentation, he has controlled all the relevant variables. The important question, however, is not how the situation appears to the experimenter but whether it is **perceived** identically by each individual. Leaving aside the technical flaws which an experienced scientist would find in this particular demonstration, substantially the same thing can happen in serious research. Since most experimenters are interested only in one particular kind of performance rather than the subject's private thoughts, feelings, and perceptions they do not ordinarily interrogate him about the experiment after it is completed (Jourard, 1968, Ch. 4). When they do, some surprising discoveries are made. One boy may be temporarily incapable of sustained attention because his fiancée returned his engagement ring the previous evening. Another has not quite returned from a drug "trip" and is still experiencing some hallucination. Another is more concerned with controlling his anxieties than listening to the instructions with the result that he misinterprets the task. Still others may point out limitations of the procedure from the subjects' point of view that were not foreseen by the investigator.

THE ORIGIN OF PHENOMENOLOGY

There is a broad spectrum of phenomenological approaches to psychology. Most of them acknowledge some tenuous connection with the leading European philosophy of that name, but two American varieties seem to be indigenous (Shlien, 1963, p. 300). The personality theory of Snygg and Combs (1959) is based on the concept of a phenomenological field, while Rogers (1951) was not aware of Husserl's work when he published his **Client-centered Therapy**. How much phenomenological psychology is indebted to its philosophical ancestor can be debated. The German philosopher Edmund Husserl is considered the originator of the latter. He was impressed by how often people "see" things that are not present and "hear" remarks that are never made. Preconceived ideas distort their sensory experience. Such aberrations are not confined to perception but affect our thinking as well.

This observation, of course, is not new to psychology. More than one experiment has shown that, under controlled conditions, many people cannot tell their favorite cigarette from any other or distinguish Coca Cola and Pepsi Cola: they just think they can. The situation is quite different with wine tasters who can reliably grade different vintages that most people distinguish only by the labels. Why this disparity in sensory acuity? Is one person's perceptual mechanism that much superior to another's? The answer seems to consist in schooling one's self to pay close attention to what is actually experienced. Instead of thinking that one is drinking good wine because it is poured from a fancy bottle with the right label, he must develop the habit of forgetting everything else except **how it tastes.** After sufficient practice he will be able to identify minute differences that previously escaped detection because his attention was directed elsewhere.

Husserl felt that our minds are so filled with ideas and theories about how things should be that we seldom experience them exactly as they are. If we wish to make certain that our knowledge is valid, we must begin in a special way. Suppose that a traveler in New Guinea discovers a new flower. If he is a phenomenologist, he will banish from mind for the time all names, memories, preconceptions, and theories and not even reflect on whether or not the plant exists. His whole attention will be focused on **the thing as he experiences it** and only this. As he encounters the flower again and again from different frames of reference, including the use of a microscope, and under a wide variety of circumstances, he will come closer and closer to an understanding of its true nature. One of Husserl's cardinal principles is that things are what they appear to be. If someone objects that the sun seems to rise in the east, a phenomenologist might well reply that from where you stand it does. But before being too certain about your conclusion you should also observe it from other points of view, such as from a spaceship oriented toward the sun. A similar answer could be given to the protest that material objects appear solid even though this is not true at the atomic level.

Husserl's all-absorbing interest was the clarification and validation of knowledge. He envisioned a gigantic phenomenological research project which would eventually integrate all science with philosophy. Phenomenological psychology is less pretentious. Its primary concern is not philosophical speculation but the empirical study of man. In other words it is a **methodological** rather than a **doctrinal** phenomenology. Philosophers in the Husserl tradition confront us with a number of challenges which have an important bearing on the way that we practice a human science. Psychologists can make use of these ideas without committing themselves to a whole philosophy. In particular the extreme forms of phenomenology and existentialism would be difficult for a scientist to accept. They so overemphasize one pole of the particular-universal antinomy, that is, the concrete living individual, as to all but deny the usefulness of any generalization whatever. By contrast behaviorism overreacts in the opposite direction—denying to experience any validity.

THE ROLE OF PHENOMENOLOGY IN PSYCHOLOGY

Some proponents of methodological phenomenology prefer to speak of it as an attitude of mind that is no longer content to think of man as a bundle of operational definitions. Its chief merit, according to others, consists in helping the investigator take a fresh look at a problem in the initial stages of research and in providing certain kinds of data not else-where available. Still others predict a leading role for phenomenology in the years ahead as the specifics of this approach are elaborated in greater detail. Shlien (1963, p. 301) comments that "to understand phenomenology it is more illuminating, and more in keeping with the very style of approach, to look at its characteristics than trace its his-tory." Giorgi (1965) outlines some of these traits.

> The method of phenomenology essentially involves the process of intuition, reflection, and description. This means that one should first concentrate to the best degree possible on what is given or being experienced and only secondly ask more specific questions about the phenomenon. In this manner the researcher can deal with a more complete phenomenon because he first lets it emerge as it is rather than selecting those aspects of it that he wishes to see or manipulate, or defining the phenomenon in terms of his manipulations (p. 232).

PHENOMENOLOGICAL PSYCHOLOGY

Phenomenological procedures begin with what a person experiences here and now, after certain precautions have been taken to minimize distortions due to preconceived ideas. Much psychological research, especially in the area of sensation, requires feedback about the subjects' conscious processes, but the fact that these data are subjective is fre-quently overlooked. Actually, the experimenter may be in a bind. According to behavioristic theory he should studiously avoid any attempt to deal with private experiences; yet many problems cannot be explored without this kind of information. In order to escape from the embarassing dilemma, John Watson introduced a questionable com-promise. After doubting the existence of consciousness and declaring all mental processes out of bounds for psychology, he found a way to bring them back under the guise of objective data. A good example is the psychophysical experiment in which a subject is asked, "Which light looks brighter?" or "Which lines appears to you to be longer?" Watson merely wrote down what the subject said and called it a verbal report. Since this report could be put on data sheets and processed statistically, he considered it to be objective. It is doubtful that calling the subject's introspection a verbal report and acting as if it were objective really changes its nature. He might have a point if the psychologist's primary interest, as a grammarian's, centered about the actual words that were used, but what he is trying to get at is the subject's true perceptions. If the verbal report does not mirror these conscious events, then it is useless.

Phenomenologists point out that psychology, as a latecomer to the scientific scene, was not forced to develop methods in keeping with its unique subject matter. Instead it adopted the highly successful procedures already in existence. To men of the nineteenth century there was only one scientific method, the one pioneered by physics. No one seemed to ask whether or not it is altogether appropriate for psychology and there is reason to doubt that it is. The objects studied by physicists are not conscious, and so there is no necessity of taking into consideration this level of functioning. All they need to know can be discovered by studying things from the outside. Giorgi explains how the situation changes when scientists turn their attention to the study of man.

From Phenomenology and Experimental Psychology

Research vs. Experimentation

To the average psychologist, to do research means to perform an experiment, and to perform an experiment means to follow the methods and procedures that have been established by the natural sciences. It is this automatic chain of associations that must be broken. Since it is one of the characteristics of the phenomenological approach to investigate the foundational aspects of phenomena, the phenomenological psychologist begins by asking the following basic questions: Why does one do an experiment? Why does a scientist engage in research? Are doing research and conducting an experiment identical activities?

It seems necessary to distinguish between experimentation and research. Webster's dictionary defines research as a careful search or studious inquiry; usually, a critical and exhaustive investigation *or* experimentation having for its aim the revision of accepted conclusions in the light of newly discovered facts. Thus, to do research means literally to search again, im-

From A. Giorgi. Phenomenology and experimental psychology II. **Review of Existential Psychology and Psychiatry,** 1966, **6**, 37-50. Copyright © 1966 by the Association of Existential Psychology and Psychiatry. Reprinted by permission.

plying a deeper and more thorough probing, and it is important to note that one need not do an experiment in order to do research. Witness, for example, research done in the areas of history, literature, political science, and so on.

Hence, to engage in research is to participate in an activity that may or may not involve experimentation. Now then, why are experiments conducted? At what particular times do researchers choose to employ experimentation as opposed to other types of research activities? Assuming that experiments are feasible, they are conducted at that point in an investigation when it becomes necessary to unveil aspects or features of phenomena that cannot be ascertained or understood by direct observation. In other words an experiment is a way of supplementing direct observation, a way of obtaining information about phenomena that would be difficult, if not impossible, to obtain in other ways. An experiment was never meant to supplant direct observation nor to become the exclusive means of supplementing direct observation.

The above considerations reveal the significant fact that some type of research activity is already in progress by the time it comes to design an experiment, even if it is only the experimenter's literature search on a problem or his thinking about a particular experimental design. This means that one never really starts doing research with an experiment, but rather one approaches a certain point in an investigation where an experiment may become desirable or necessary. By remembering this fact one is better able to situate the place of experimentation within the whole framework of research activity, and thus, the two can never become identified.

The distinction between research and experimentation has been emphasized because in referring to the human sciences it is highly desirable that *research* be conducted, but it is not necessary that this research take the form of experimentation. A perfect example of nonexperimental research in psychology on a human phenomenon is Straus' (1962) paper, "On Memory Traces." Straus begins with an historical introduction to the problem of memory and is able to show how a theory of traces or engrams came to be the primary explanation of memory. In the next section, he describes the phenomenology of a "trace" and is able to delineate certain essential features that must be true of all examples of the phenomenon "trace." Then he relates the findings he has obtained from the phenomenological analysis to certain undisputed facts of memory, and is able to demonstrate convincingly that the phenomenon of memory cannot be properly understood as a "trace." This result has tremendous implications because a good deal of the neurophysiological experimentation in the area of memory is based upon the "trace" concept. Thus, one cannot deny that the results of this research are significant even though they were not obtained by means of experimentation. Indeed, many experiments on memory have yielded much less fruitful information. On the other hand, one cannot deny that Straus' article was the result of true research. He conducted a scholarly and studious inquiry into a phenomenon for the purpose of revising some accepted conclusions concerning it on the basis of certain insights.

Granting that research of some type is possible in the human sciences, the next logical question would seem to be, is experimentation possible in the human sciences? Is it possible to have an experimental psychology of characteristically human phenomena? This question will be considered as soon as some other factors necessary for a proper understanding of psychological research are dealt with. At the moment, this discussion can be concluded by stating that because of the phenomenological concern for foundations of scientific activity, one is able to distinguish between research activity and experimentation, and in addition, be able to place the latter in its proper context of being one of the ways of conducting research. This distinction in and of itself opens up many new possibilities for psychological research on human phenomena.

Quantity vs. Quality

In Section I it was emphasized that one of the limits of the traditional experimental approach has been its one-sided emphasis on the quantitative dimension. It is true that the natural sciences have made tremendous progress because of the degree of control and sophistication that man has achieved over this dimension. However, the reason why quantitative analysis and measurement has been able to do wonders for the natural sciences has not been sufficiently analyzed. Most researchers think that it is because of quantity *per se,* but it is actually because the manipulation of the quantitative dimension does yield significant, relevant information about the physical world. In other words, quantitative analysis is a fruitful way to understand the world of material objects. Thus, the quantitative dimension is emphasized in the natural sciences because it is fruitful, and not merely because it is quantitative.

However, can quantitative analysis be equally fruitful in studying man? Only by objectifying man, and objectified man is not a human person. Rather, it is suggested here that if one is interested in studying characteristically human phenomena, then one must consider the qualitative dimension. Man is not an object in the world but an experiencing creature, and qualitative questions are meaningful only for experiencing creatures. It is absurd, for example, to try to find out from a falling stone that is part of an experiment in measuring the pull of gravity, what it is like to fall in a vacuum. Thus, in addition to the fruitfulness of the quantitative question (e.g., how fast does the stone fall is a very meaningful question), the very impossibility of utilizing a strict qualitative analysis in the natural sciences has given a tremendous lead in methodological development to the quantitative dimension. (One should not confuse man's description of the qualities of objects with the analysis of the modes of experiencing that man is capable of.) However, no matter how unsophisticated the techniques may be at the moment, it is clear that to understand what the difference between feelings of guilt and feelings of anxiety are, for example, one must know how they differ qualitatively, and not just how many times an individual experiences each, nor just how intense those feelings are when they do occur. Similarly, the essential difference between memory and learning can only be given qualitatively, and not quantitatively. Thus, in order to achieve the same degree of success as the natural sciences, it is suggested that the human sciences explore fully the qualitative dimension with appropriate methods. Obviously, the transformation of an essentially qualitative phenomenon into a quantitative expression such as is done in many scaling techniques, does not capture the essence of the qualitative *as such*. The reasons for this are given in the next section.

Measurement vs. Meaning

Many psychologists feel that the point of departure for all research is to ask the question: How do we measure the phenomenon? However, it is precisely because the measurement question has reached such an unassailable position that it must be challenged. A deep probing into the situation once again reveals a more fundamental reason for the effectiveness of measurement. Measurement is exactly the kind of *description* that is most suitable for answering the quantitative question which is characteristic of the natural sciences. Furthermore, measurement was able to achieve a high level of sophistication because of the availability of a highly developed and relevant eidetic science, viz., mathematics (Husserl, 1962; Gurwitsch, 1964). However, if the measurement question is removed from the context of the quantitative, it is no longer necessarily the most fruitful question. In other words, measurement is not an absolutely good method, but a method that is highly fruitful for a certain well delineated region, the limits of which have not been sufficiently circumscribed as yet.

However, it is clear that the qualitative dimension is essentially different from the quantitative one, and moreover, that it is sufficiently different so that measurement is not the most fruitful form of description for understanding qualities. For example, if I wanted to know what qualities a painting should have in order to fit into the decor of my living room, I am not primarily interested in size or weight but rather color schemes, content, mood, and so on. Similarly, if one wanted to know the qualities of an anxious experience the answer would have to be in terms of the *contents* of the experience. Thus, the question becomes: what method of *description* will be as fruitful for the qualitative dimension as measurement is for the quantitative dimension? Secondly, what is the allied and relevant eidetic science that will aid the development of this method as mathematics has helped measurement?

From the present perspective, the answers to the two questions would be: unprejudiced verbal descriptions and phenomenology understood as the eidetic science of essences, which is one of the meanings of phenomenology (Spiegelberg, 1960). A common concern of both of these answers is the effort after meaning. A verbal description that has an essentially qualitative perspective also reveals the meaning of the phenomenon for the subject. Thus, to ask for the qualities of an anxious experience is really to ask someone what the experience is like for him, and in describing what it is like for him, the subject also discloses some aspects of the *meaning* in arriving at the essence of a phenomenon, one also discloses its meaning. If the essence of a chair is "a support for the human body in the posture of sitting," then this also discloses the meaning of a chair for man. Thus, for the human sciences, the essential question is not, how do we measure phenomena?; but rather, what do the phenomena mean?

Analysis vs. Explicitation

In the empirical tradition, the analysis of a phenomenon into its basic elements as a mode of understanding a phenomenon is so prevalent that it has almost become axiomatic that analytical techniques be employed. However, most of the power of analytical techniques has been in dealing with inanimate objects, where the assumptions underlying the use of analysis are more compatible with the predominant quantitative considerations. However, meaning does not lend itself so well to analysis. Rather, if meaning is to be understood, it is done better by a process that for a lack of a better term can be called explicitation, that is, the process of making explicit or thematizing the locus of any given phenomenon within its horizon.

Whenever a phenomenon appears, it always appears within a certain horizon or context, and the horizon that implicitly is given with the phenomenon is not irrelevent for the understanding of the phenomenon. On the contrary the horizon is essential for the understanding of the phenomenon because the role that the phenomenon plays within the context, even if it is only implicitly recognized, is one of the determiners of the meaning of the phenomenon (Gurwitsch, 1964). The implication of this fact for research on human phenomena is that a phenomenon cannot be studied by abstracting it from the context in which it appears, and still have the same phenomenon. Rather, a process of description and explicitation must precede the investigation so that the precise situation of the phenomenon is known, and then one is better able to know the precise way the meaning of the phenomenon will change if it is studied in another context. Thus explicitation is one manner of description that is especially suited for grasping the meaning of a phenomenon since it discloses the phenomenon's multiple references to its horizon.

Moreover, in the course of explicitation, certain experiential variables that should be controlled emerge; if these variables are not discovered their influence cannot be properly ascertained. In other words, a description of the phenomenon is necessary in order to discover relevant variables that would otherwise remain hidden (Grauman, 1962).

A study conducted by Hunter (1954) will be used to indicate the significance of explicitation for research on human phenomena. Hunter wanted to find out how well straightness could be judged by touch. He used blind subjects and subjects with normal vision, but the latter were blindfolded during experimentation. The task was to determine the "straightness" of a target by touch, and there were a number of targets with various degrees of curvature away from the subjects. Hunter's "analysis" of the experiment was that the task was equated for both groups because they both performed identical activities. The results were that blind subjects were more accurate in estimating straightness by touch than the normal subjects.

But, if one were to determine the meaning of the task for both groups by means of a careful explicitation, it becomes evident that the two groups were not equated. A blind man cannot know "straightness" by any other modality but touch. Hence, for him, it is his normal way of experiencing straightness. But the normal way of perceiving straightness for subjects who are not blind is by sight. Subjects with vision frequently judge straightness by sight in the course of their everyday activities, but rarely, if ever, by touch. (Even a carpenter's level has a bubble sight gauge, so that straightness can be "seen.") Thus, a careful explicitation of the phenomenon of "judging straightness by touch" would have revealed that the contexts surrounding the two groups of subjects was essentially different, and hence, the meaning of the phenomenon was different for each group, and thus the results are not directly comparable. For one group (blind subjects), straightness was determined by their normal mode of perceiving straightness, and for the other group (subjects with vision), an unfamiliar and therefore deficient mode of perception was employed. The above example demonstrates rather clearly that explicitation yields significant information about the meaning of a phenomenon, and therefore should be included as a necessary phase in all research with human phenomena.

TOWARD A PHENOMENOLOGICAL METHODOLOGY

Although phenomenological psychology begins with naïve human experience as data, the reader should not conclude that it is a variety of introspection such as the structuralists, notably Titchener, employed. McLeod (1964) explains how the two methodologies differ. Instead of simply observing objects and events exactly as they present themselves to a relatively unbiased mind, introspectionists required the subject to analyze what he experienced into such irreducible elements as sensations, feelings, and images, or to identify certain specific features.

> It is clear that introspection is not far removed from phenomeno-logical observation and description. Both are directed at experi-ence (Erlebnis). But there are two crucial differences. First, the introspectionist makes the initial assumption that experience is reducible to a finite number of conscious elements and attributes; this is a bias which phenomenologists attempt to bracket. Secondly, and perhaps more important, there is no place in in-trospection analysis for meaning, except insofar as meaning can be reduced to elements and their attributes. For the phenomenol-ogist, meaning is central and inescapable. To try to abstract or extract meaning from the phenomenal world is futile; all we achieve is a change in meaning (pp. 54-55).

How would a phenomenological psychologist carry out an empiri-cal investigation? Although a general methodology is only now being developed, R. von Eckartsberg outlines a possible procedure. In the paragraphs preceding this selection he contrasts the typical laboratory technique with the one he is about to describe. It is in this context that he writes.

From On Experiential Methodology

All in all, the laboratory set-up is quite authoritarian and not very cooperative; it is a manipulative operation to study human behavior functioning in "objective" non-existential circumstances.

There is no question that such a procedure works. It is objective, verifiable, repeatable, etc., fulfilling the canons of psychology as an objective

From R. von Eckartsberg. On experiential methodology. In A. Giorgi, W. F. Fischer, and R. von Eckartsberg, **Duquesne studies in phenomenological psychology.** Vol. 1, pp. 70-76, Copyright © by Duquesne University Press, 1971. Reprinted by permission.

science. The psychologist in such a set-up serves as an "objective" and seemingly non-interfering observer who records and measures the objective behavioral performance data that are being generated in the laboratory situation. He acts as an "operator" as Barker (1965) has called this—meaning that he performs operations to obtain data. Barker (1965) raises some serious criticisms regarding such an approach from an ecological perspective, arguing that the artificiality of the laboratory setting as well as the built-in operations to collect the data do in fact change and distort the reality observed and measured as contrasted to real-life settings. He proposes that psychologists act more as "transducers" by recording the spontaneously manifest behavior in the subjects' natural settings, with minimal distortion through translation.

I think that Barker (1963, 1965) does us a great service in proposing an ecologically-oriented behavioral science and in criticising exclusive reliance on laboratory research.

But there is another aspect to this problem which needs to be stressed. Even Barker still relies on the *"observer point of view"* which can approach human reality only from "outside" by watching behavior, from the "observer perspective" or, as we can also call it, the "third person point of view." There is another possibility that must be considered and that involves asking the question: what is the reality of the person or "subject" who is being observed, how is the reality observed by the scientist psychologist experienced by the person being observed. We can speak here of the *"actor perspective"* or *"first person point of view"* which stresses the priority of experience in human living. In other words what is the experienced reality of the person being studied?

It is primarily the tradition of existential phenomenology which has addressed itself to this problem of formulating a psychology of experience from the actor point of view. This is the perspective underlying this paper. If, as we believe, and as outlined in the anthropology section, man is co-creator of his reality in the sense that he acts on his personal understanding of a given situation, if, as Laing (1967) has formulated it, man is both "center of orientation of the objective universe" in terms of his experience and "origin of actions" as far as his behavior is concerned, and furthermore, if—as we believe with Laing (1967)—"behavior is a function of experience," then we can no longer ignore the reality of individual experience in human psychology. We must begin to study individual human experience in a systematic way.

I now want to consider some of the methodological problems inherent in such a shift of attitude from the observer to the actor point of view.

As long as we perceive things and events "out there" we consider them to be *objective.* They can be reliably recorded by technical means and people can come to an agreement about them. What goes on within the "private sphere of the person," regarding experience, however, psychologists have long held is—by contrast—*subjective* and hence not verifiable or objectively recordable.

Self-report as a method of gaining access to the experience of the individual by means of some kind of self-expression has been viewed with suspicion and has not been considered worthy of scientific seriousness. It is, therefore, not surprising that much of what goes under the name of psychology in this country is concerned with animal behavioral research where the problem of experience is not a relevant issue, because it is essentially inaccessible.

With people, however, we have a different situation in that people can talk, they do like to talk, even, and they do have something to say. Anthropologists using informants have always recognized this possibility and so have clinical and social psychologists. It has been mostly the fraternity of experimental psychologists and within that group the behaviorists, primarily, who have been suspicious of "subjective experientialism." I think the time has come for a change.

People do act as self-observers, they do pay attention to themselves in terms of their activities and experience. Why can we not use their verbal self-reports as legitimate data of their activities and experience? There are problems, however, and one is the fact that although individuals experience themselves in their interaction with their situations, they do so with selective attention. It is primarily this fact of personal selectivity which has given rise to psychologists being suspicious of subjective data. If the person is selective in his awareness and if this selectivity is guided even by "unconscious mechanisms" what good are such data and where is objectivity? This argument seems plausible, but there are several important considerations and implicit assumptions operating here which need comment.

First of all, there is the assumption that there is "objectivity" in human affairs, and that it can be ascertained through a rigorous methodology. I think this is a basic fallacy. We can achieve "presumed objectivity" through rigorous control of variables, but only through an artificial manipulation of the situation, i.e., by taking life out of its natural context and directing a selective focus on one or at best a few variables and their recording and measurement in public and hence repeatable units. This "presumed objectivity," however, is a total artefact. It is a reality synthetically created by the scientist which has little of any existential reality for the "person-subject" utilized in the experiment. In terms of the "person-subject's" life-problems the experiment has little or no meaning. However, as far as the experimental activity itself is concerned, it does have a personal meaning for the subject. He interprets his situation and acts on this understanding. But, in any case, it is his—"the person-subject's"—own understanding of the situation and of the instructions given to him by the experimenter which form the context within which he will act in the situation. The experimenter, if he is really "objective" can never presume to know what this experienced reality is for the subject. Hence, as a first suggestion, he must obtain some knowledge of the experience of the subject in the experiment in order to interpret the meaning of his data.

This is a first proposal that has been elaborated by existential phenomenologists (Strasser, 1963; Giorgi, 1967b). However, such an adding of an experiential inquiry to traditional research is not enough. We have to heed Barker's (1963, 1965) arguments for an ecological approach in psychology. We must also study the individual in his real-life context. This argument leads us to the formulation of the object of study as *experiential ecological psychology.*

We must study actions and experiences of an individual and individuals together in the concrete setting of their life. We must study "lebenswelt-phenomena," i.e., how persons live and experience their lives.

What are some of the methodological problems connected with such a focus of study? Apart from the complexity of such an undertaking of trying to study the total repertory of lived situations of an individual (von Eckartsberg, 1969), there are specific challenges connected with the distinction between objective-public events and subjective-private events discussed before.

What we would need ideally is a combination of exhaustive observation plus personal experiential meaning. In such a research set-up, we could use the established method of participant participation, i.e., the researcher works in the real-life field-situation as a participant in the role of a witness or "shadow," and he also considers the person under study as an informant on his own situation in terms of his experience and engages in prolonged dialogue to gather the person's experience as reported. This double focus of study could do better justice to the full psychological reality under investigation. Such arrangement could meet some of the objections regarding the unreliability of merely subjective data because it would achieve both public-objective as well as private-subjective recording of an identifiable event. Such data would constitute a dialectic through which we could effectively cope with the issue of selective attention of a person.

The role of the "participant-observer" and some of the problems connected with this approach needs clarification. In a sense every observer— even that of the scientific observer under the most stringent laboratory conditions—is also a participant although he tries not to interfere directly in the ongoing event under study. However, his very presence, as part of the research design, changes the experience and action of the person being studied to some extent. In this meaning every observer is a participant. In this connection, we should also remember that even a technical recording device such as a tape recorder has an effect on the "subject's" action and experience in a situation.

However, there is a situation in which the observer is no longer not directly involved, in which the "participant-observer" actually engages in reciprocal action with the person studied, for instance, living through a day as companion with the person studied or generally living-with, in the sense of anthropological field work. In this case the *participant* aspect of the "participant-observer role" gains in prominence.

In order to clarify this situation a distinction introduced by Alfred Schutz (1964) may be of help. He characterizes dyadic interpersonal relationship—of which the researcher-subject relation is a special case—as being of two types: "thou-relations" or "we-relations" depending upon whether we have a one- or two-sided reciprocal focus of attention. In the thou-relation we have a one-way focus—I attend to you but you are otherwise engaged whereas in the we-relation we have a reciprocal form of attending to one another. The thou-orientation is typical of an observer orientation whereas the we-relationship is characteristic of a participant stance. We must remember, however, that in either case the researcher is a co-constititive member of the situation. His presence has an effect on the situation and the experience and action of the person studied, and he is also, in turn, affected by the situation and the person studied.

In the participant mode this is quite evident. It also operates in the observer mode although the effects are more subtle. In order to obtain some idea as to what goes on in such a research situation in which both partners co-constitute their reality with reciprocal effects, we must make this process itself the focus of study and inquiry. This can be done fruitfully by asking both partners to give a report about their experience in the situation which can be recorded. This report must then be made the focus of a second inquiry through questioning by an outsider in order that the full personal meaning of the experience may be elucidated. Again, ongoing change in both partners is a necessary concomitant of such a procedure and we must welcome it and make it a focus of study, rather than ignore it and pretend that it is not a factor and that "objectivity" prevails. We can never get out of the process of change due to new experience, and in any case I think that the concept of "objective invariant relationships" is a fallacy. As viewed from the concrete existential point of view, there is no "invariant objectivity" possible in any situation. As people live, they grow and change. There is no repeat possible, even though on the manifest level of individuals there may be much habitual stereotypy.

However, as we change from an external observer point of view to the first person actor perspective we realize that in terms of experienced meaning there is never static invariance but only process and change. This does not mean, however, that we cannot find and articulate general laws about the structure and process of experience (Gurwitsch, 1964) in spite of always existing unique patterns and differences between individuals. This is quite different from a formulation of empirical generalizations and causal interpretation of lawfulness of behavior in S-R terms derived from anonymous group averages which have a practical actuarial aim of predicting behaviors in types of settings as well as a truth-function of "explaining behavior" in a causal way. In contrast, the aim of phenomenological description and delineation of essential constituents and structures of experience is primarily to serve our understanding of man in his living, and ultimately leads to self-understanding and deepened awareness of one's living. Self-understanding comes in as the essential understanding becomes biographically real and hence existential.

As we shift to the existential-phenomenological point of view we also move toward an integrative system approach as contrasted with a segmentalized view in terms of S-R unit mechanisms. The existential phenomenological approach in being ecological is comprehensive, integrative, and field-oriented. In this orientation it resembles the structures of our electronic age as described by McLuhan who contrasts this integrative circuit system and field oriented approach to those predominant in the age of mechanics which used a sequentialized step-by-step linear and causal approach. In the sense that the person in his world and other relationships and involvement can be conceived of as a dynamic self-regulating system, the field-system approach as an ecological basis seems the most adequate approach to the study and description of human reality. Existential-phenomenology certainly provides such an orientation.

In an existential-biographical focus, the role of psychological research is changed radically as contrasted to the laboratory approach. First of all, we must engage in a *cooperative dialogue* with our "person-subject informants." The method is hence dialogical and the researcher enters into a give and take with the person he studies. If the researcher also uses the participant observation method, he can compare and contrast his own observations with those reported by the person studied and he can fruitfully discuss the role and operation of personal-selective-attention. As he engages in this, he is at the same time providing valuable feedback to the person studied. The dialogical research method outlined here thus has an important *feedback function* and is by necessity involved in a change process. It is important to recognize, however, that this is a *two way change process*. Not only does the subject studied receive valuable feedback from the observer, but the observer also obtains valuable clarifying knowledge regarding what he observed from the experiential report of the person studied regarding his own experience. *Both the person researched as well as the research-person are thus being changed through the existential research method—they change each other.*

I think that this is a necessary and valuable result of experiential methodology. To me, it also seems a more honest admission of what is going on in any interpersonal transaction than has hithertofore been recognized and acknowledged. In a disguised fashion, these mutual change processes also operate in the most stringent laboratory set-up. All experience is transformation of self, particularly interpersonal experience, and in this change there is mutual effect, influencing and being influenced.

Experiential methodology does not have to use participant observers although the chances for fruitful dialogue and fidelity are maximal in this strategy. There is the possibility of using the "self-report method" fruitfully. In self-report, the person studied gives an account of his activities and experiences in the situations either verbally or in writing. In either case we obtain a protocol focussed on the experience of a situation. The focus on a situation gives us a meaningful and comprehensive unit to work with.

Many psychologists object to the notion of phenomenological methods on the grounds that inner experience cannot be properly validated (e.g., Brody and Oppenheim, 1966). For them an unbridgable gap exists between private experience and events that are public in the sense that they can be confirmed directly by others. At the same time a growing body of literature, exemplified by Polanyi (1958) **Personal Knowledge,** challenges this rigid distinction. What is referred to by the terms "public" and "private" can also be viewed as opposite poles of a single continuum rather than a confrontation between "facts" and unverifiable inner experience. Harold McCurdy, among others, shows that a person can speak just as factually about a dream as he can about seeing himself in a mirror or observing an airplane in the sky. An individual's headaches, thoughts, feelings, and future plans are no less observable to him than things outside the boundary of his skin. Although knowledge of inner events cannot be communicated with the same ease and precision as objects open to the view of every passerby, they can be made public in a number of ways. By word, gesture, facial expression, painting, music, and in other ways that will be discussed later, we manage to convey the content of our awareness to other people.

From The Personal World

One can point at the sun in the sky or the face in the mirror, and others can follow the pointing finger and discover out there before them something corresponding to what was pointed at. Sometimes there is a little confusion,

From **The personal world** by Harold Grier McCurdy, 1961. Reprinted by permission of Harcourt Brace Jovanovich, Inc.

and one sees a bird instead of the sun or the frame of the mirror rather than the face in it, but with persistence, we iron out these disagreements. Pointing, however, does not usually suffice for the objects of dreams, or for feelings, intentions, and decisions. The communication principle here is a trifle more difficult, but in principle it is the same problem (pp. 180-181).

Rogers and Dymond (1954) have demonstrated how subtle subjective factors such as restructuring of the self concept in psychotherapy can be objectified, and the former has restated several of May's abstract existential principles in a testable form (Rogers, 1969, pp. 88-89). Zaner (1967) explains that even though phenomenology deals with events which are directly accessible only through reflection, this does not necessarily imply that they are essentially private. Every finding must be capable of intersubjective verification using a criterion which is appropriate to the subject matter. If the phenomenon in question cannot be perceived by the senses, it is unrealistic to demand that it be visible or measurable in order to be considered a "fact." Euclid's discovery that the square on the hypotenuse of a right triangle is equal to the sum of the squares on the other two sides was not a private insight inaccessible to everyone else. Many high school students since his time have probably wished that it were, for then they would not be required to verify this theorem. Not only mathematicians but also every theorist presumes that one person's reflections can be validated against another's.

In discussing the behaviorist's refusal to admit as data such directly accessible parts of the perceptual world as states of the self, Koehler (1966, pp. 85-86) comments:

> I must therefore conclude that, in all his observations the Behaviorist relies on facts that appear in his private experience, the only experience in which he can do any observing. Moreover, when other observers are present, and describe what they have seen during his experiment, their descriptions again refer to occurrences within their private perceptual worlds. Hence, when the Behaviorist says that the private, "subjective" content of the phenomenal world cannot interest a true scientist, this statement is plainly contradicted by his own procedure. He actually proves that certain contents of the directly accessible world must, and can, be used as reliable tools in his science. Why, then, should they not also be accepted as materials which may be studied by psychologists?

Koehler goes on to make the logical deduction that if the perceptions of different experimenters agree in the above situations, then the same principle should hold for other types of observations that the psychologist might wish to make. Such perceptions are directly accessible to at least one person, "While the independently existing objects in the sense of physics, including the physical behavior of physical men and animals, are directly accessible to nobody."

Peter Koestenbaum in analyzing the nature of facts spells out the implications of this viewpoint in greater detail.

From Phenomenological Foundations for the Behavioral Science

A. Accessibility. Regarding accessibility, it must be noted that facts can be accessible to one, several, or most men. Since public verifiability—the ability to repeat experiments with parallel results—is a central requirement of the scientific method, the recognition that there are so-called private or semi-private facts would constitute a significant exception to the demands of the method of science. My inner sense of free will, i.e., my experience of the spontaneity of my actions, is not a public fact in the traditional sense and appears not to conform to the exigencies of the method of science. On the other hand, the observed correlation between blood-pressure readings and certain patterns of behavior (termed "exhaustion," "nervousness," and the like) is a public fact, that is, a fact open to public confirmation.

The problem of the public verifiability of private facts is a major dilemma for the scientifically oriented phenomenologist. However, since all facts are, in some sense at least, first-person experiences, the problem of public verification for private facts is far more pervasive than might have been apparent at first, and not half as perplexing. Although here is not the place to work this matter out in detail, a few guidelines at this point in our discussion should prove helpful.

Since all facts, public and private, are first-person experiences, the public confirmability of a scientific fact must be described as follows. I am confronted with the following illustrative first-person experiences: I perform a set of operations, called experiments, in a chemistry laboratory and reach certain observable and recordable results. These results are also first-person

From Peter Koestenbaum. Phenomenological foundations for the behavioral sciences: The nature of facts. Journal of Existentialism, 1966, **6**, 305-341. Copyright © 1966 by the Libra Press. Reprinted by permission.

experiences. These experiments are repeated elsewhere in the world, their results are published (or I get letters, articles or newspaper accounts regarding them), and I feel now confident that my experimental results have been publicly confirmed. In this oversimplified paradigm, the ontological status of public confirmation is thought to be fundamentally distinct from that of first-person confirmation. First-person confirmation is always an immediate experience, a phenomenon that to me is immediately acceptable, assessable, and describable; whereas public confirmation has the putative ontological status of an inference or a construct, with all its notorious and attendant epistemological difficulties. These difficulties orbit about the problem of the existence of an external world, the status of inferences, the existence of other minds, the validity of inductive techniques, the empirical application of mathematical concepts and operations, the logical status of theories, the propriety of constructs, etc. Thus, even in the ordinary uses of the scientific method, public verifiability does present crucial epistemological problems. Public confirmation is, in the last analysis, an inference or a construct derived from private, first-person experiences or data. To this extent, the distinction between private and public facts is inexact and imprecise. We can then argue that if a public datum is a bona fide fact, then a private datum, since it does not seem to differ in kind, is also a bona fide fact. What happens if we focus on the differences rather than on the similarities?

There are, of course, basic differences between first-person public facts and first-person private facts. A first-person public fact may be a certain experimental result, whereas a first-person private fact may be a stomach ache or a surge of anxiety. I can call a colleague into my laboratory and he will witness my experiment and its results. However, that he has the same experiences I do with respect to the experiment and that he is a person like me are inferences or constructs. On the other hand, I cannot invite a colleague to visit my stomach or my solar plexus to share in my stomach ache and sense of anxiety. To this extent, therefore, private and public facts differ fundamentally. However, just as public confirmation of public facts is in the last analysis a construction, so there can be public confirmation of private facts. The precise technicalities of the procedure here are different from those of testing public facts, but its general logical and ontological characteristics are basically the same. It is true that I cannot have the pain or fear of someone else, but I can search within me for experiences that correspond to the evocative words that he utters. In this manner I infer or construct the fact that he also has a stomach ache and a surge of anxiety. I have no access to my colleague's first-person experience of free will; but, likewise, I have no access to his first-person experience of the results of my chemical experiment. My belief that he has confirmed the existence of the observed results of my experiment is an inference. Similarly, my belief that he has confirmed my description of my sense of free will by comparing that description with his own sense of free will is also an inference.

The conclusion of these observations is that the difference between private and public facts is not absolute. Both contain an element of first-person experience and of inference or construction. From this it follows that first-person private facts, properly delineated and used, are facts in a perfectly legitimate scientific sense and are open to the operations characteristic of the scientific method. If we condemn first-person or private facts (a typical characterization of phenomenological descriptions) as "too subjective" to have any scientific significance, we pari passu condemn public facts. Conversely, if we accept public facts as bona fide facts, we are equally committed to acknowledge the existence and usefulness of first-person facts.

Phenomenology resembles getsalt psychology in its attempt to take cognizance of all the factors operating in a given situation. For this reason it tends to focus attention on the whole person, so far as possible, in preference to arbitrarily singling out small bits of behavior to be analyzed in isolation from everything else that is going on in the individual. Although as a method it can be used in piecemeal research whenever feedback from the subject is needed, ordinarily the phenomenological psychologist is not content to rest here but presses on to broader issues, such as the effect of the process in question on the total behavior pattern.

Phenomenology deals with human beings on a one-to-one basis. The subject is not thought of as a static personality structure but as a spontaneous interacting individual who influences others and is, in turn, influenced by them. Take for example the boy who asks to use the family car to go on a date. What the father says and how he says it will be reflected in his son's reactions and feelings. As in a game of chess, his responses will influence the father's next move. Whether or not both go to bed happy will depend on more than the permission being given or withheld. Attitudes of long standing, memories of past encounters, the ability to feel and express love are among the transactional factors that enter into the picture. Part of what they say to each other is expressed by word or gesture; the rest is gained by intuition. Without knowing precisely how they do it, each is also communicating at a nonverbal level and the other clearly gets the message.

EXISTENTIALISM

While the phenomenological psychologists are attempting to develop a methodology for the use of this approach in human research, existential psychologists have incorporated related philosophical concepts into the theory and practice of psychotherapy.

Existential philosophy, as an outgrowth of Husserl's phenomenology, retains many of its features. Not infrequently the designation
existential-phenomenology is used, although the two movements address themselves to somewhat different issues. Husserl was primarily
concerned with problems of knowledge, in particular, how to clarify
and validate our concepts. Some of his philosophical progeny, notably
Jaspers, Heidegger, Sartre, and Camus, became more interested in the
concrete, immediate emotional experience of an existing human person
in his ongoing interaction with the total environment—**his being-in-
the-world.**

The precise relationship between existential philosophy and existential psychology is somewhat indeterminate. Maslow (1969), who did
not think of himself as an existentialist, represented an eclectic approach when he asked, "What's in it for us [psychologists] ?" Bugental
(1965), Gendlin (1966), and May (1968) make liberal use of existential
concepts and terminology, although the latter warns:

> In psychology and psychiatry, the term demarcates an **attitude**
> [May's emphasis] , an approach to human beings, rather than a
> special school or group. It is doubtful whether it makes sense to
> speak of **an** existential psychologist or psychotherapist in con-
> tradistinction to other schools. Existentialism is not a system of
> therapy but an attitude toward therapy.*

Most existentialists would endorse the complaint of Wallach
(1967) that the multitude of psychological journals bulging with objective research on personality is of little use to the clinician. What he
needs above all else is not a wealth of correlational studies based on
group data but exact knowledge of a particular individual. Any therapist who thinks primarily in terms of models and abstract concepts is
likely to miss the most important things going on inside his client. An
incident related by Shlein (1963) dramatically illustrates this point.

While visiting the home of a former classmate, a psychologist was
asked for advice about the mild behavior problem of a five-year-old
boy. After asking the appropriate case history questions, he agreed to
begin assessing the child's personality by watching him at play on the
lawn. As the psychologist peered through an open door, the boy discovered a large earthworm. He then looked around for a sharp chip,
stretched the worm out to full length, and vigorously cut it in half. As
the psychologist began writing in his notebook, "Seems isolated and

*Reprinted from **Existential psychology**, 2d ed. edited by Rollo May, by permission of Random House, Inc., p. 15. Copyright © 1960 by The American Ortho-
psychiatric Association, Inc. Copyright © 1969 by Random House, Inc.

angry, perhaps over-aggressive," he overheard the boy address the worm in an affectionate tone. "There. Now you have a friend."

In order to understand the motivation of another person it is necessary to enter into his own personal world. The way he sees and interprets situations is the only reality he has. Regardless of how others may assess the facts, for him this is the **objective** world.

Psychoanalysts have long realized that to uncover a patient's unconscious mental content it is essential to use **his** free associations, not their own. An elderly psychoanalyst, now deceased, liked to recall an incident that occurred at one of the initial meetings of the local chapter of his professional organization. They were discussing for the first time the application of Freudian technique to literature as a method of psychoanalyzing the author. One member read a paper in which he gave a devastating account of Shelley's personality based on the imagery he used in poetry. When asked to comment on the paper the elderly psychoanalyst repled, "It has just occurred to me that Dr._____in using his own free associations has told us what the word pictures mean to him rather than the author. As a result he has psychoanalyzed himself, not Shelley."

Since many readers may not be acquainted with the terminology used by existential authors, some clarification may be needed to bring these concepts into clear focus. The following selection by Laurence D. Simkins, although brief, gives an exceedingly lucid summary of the existential position. It should serve as a useful springboard for further reading on the subject.

From The Basis of Psychology
as a Behavioral Science

Existentialism is also an offshoot of the phenomenological orientation. As a philosophy, however, existentialism dates back to the time of Kierkegaard, Heidegger, Nietzsche, and of Sartre. Today the philosophies expressed by these individuals have been used as theoretical guidelines for certain forms of psychotherapy; hence the development of "existential psychiatry or psychology." There are many varieties of existential philosophy, and it is beyond the scope of this text to cover all of the subtle variations. In the most general terms, existential philosophy is concerned with the nature of man, with his existence in the modern world, and with the meaning of this existence to the individual. Its focus is on man's most immediate experience. The individual is seen, not as a static substance or mechanism, but as in a constant state of transition seeking to fulfill his inner potentialities. Existentialism also represents a revolt against any attempt to classify man in terms of "abstract intellectual dimensions." To so classify man would be to destroy the unique inner aesthetic meaning of an individual. Also, man can never be separated from the object which he observes. The meaning of an objective fact depends upon the subject's relationship to it. In this regard Rollo May, a contemporary authority on existential therapy, writes (1958, p. 46):

> Here is the radical original statement of relational truth. . . . Here too is the prediction of what was later to appear in twentieth-century physics, namely the principle of Copernicus that one discovered truth most fully by detaching man, the observer. The Copernican view that nature can be separated from man is no longer tenable. . . . That is to say, the subject man can never be separated from the object which he observes. . . . But the implications of this landmark are even more specific and more incisive in psychology. It releases us from bondage to the dogma that truth can be understood only in terms of external objects.

The existentialists see man as free. External influences are limiting but not determining. Man is the being who can be conscious of and therefore responsible for his existence. It is this capacity to become aware of his own being which distinguishes the human being from other forms of animal life. Life sets tasks for each man, who in meeting them then defines the meaning of life. While life sets the conditions (biological, genetic, environmental, and so on), man is free to take a stand toward these conditions. Man thus does not simply exist. He decides and has the responsibility to decide what his existence or the meaning of his life will be. The indeterminacy implied in existential thought is, of course, antithetical to the assumptions of science. Indeed, as was stated earlier, existentialism, in part, represents a protest against both rationalism and science, since these two forms of epistemology produce only a fractional picture of man.

Existential therapy consists of an attempt by the therapist to see the patient as an individual to be understood rather than as an object to be analyzed. It is the goal of the therapist to assume the responsibility to help the patient discover his own existence. Both existential therapy and client-centered therapy seek to change behavior by first attempting to see the world as the patient sees it. In Rogers' position empathy, or the ability of the therapist to communicate to the patient his understanding of the client's phenomenal experiences, is a necessary condition in any therapeutic interaction. Also Rogers' goal of getting the patient to the point of self-actualization bears some resemblance to the existential therapist's goal of getting the patient to define his existence or being. Although both therapeutic approaches do have some commonalities, existentialism represents a rather extreme form of phenomenology. Since Rogers does make an attempt to develop a theory of behavior and to test his theory by experimentation, he is engaging in a form of abstraction which is clearly a violation of existential philosophy. Rogers is attempting to place phenomenology within the boundaries of science—whereas implicit in the existential position is the assumption that science can never fully understand man.

SUMMARY

In generating scientific knowledge, the role of the individual subject must not be minimized. Not infrequently, as Snygg observes, he views the experimental task in a frame of reference different from the experimenter's. Much of the success of the physical sciences in gaining control over inanimate nature can be directly attributed to the techniques of measurement and analysis. Giorgi explains how psychology is more effective when it does not confine itself to assigning numbers or to searching for irreducible elements but goes on to explicate the **meaning** of human phenomena.

Phenomenological psychology utilizes immediate experience as data after taking precautions to guard against bias insofar as this is humanly possible. Von Eckartsberg suggests a strategy for its use in empirical investigation. Koestenbaum addresses himself to the objection that inner experience can not be validated by showing that public facts can only be confirmed through the instrumentality of first-person private experience.

Although existential and phenomenological psychology are related through their philosophical antecedents, the former is more concerned about problems of psychotherapy than empirical research. Existential psychologists revolt against the notion of dealing with an individual client as if he were an abstract system of drives or similar intellectualized components. What is emphasized is the person's own experience of life, its meaning for him, and the opportunities it affords for self-actualization. Phenomenological psychologists' chief concern is the development of a truly human science of man.

DISCUSSION TOPICS

1 Discuss Giorgi's distinction between research and experimentation.
2 What reasons are usually cited for the use of phenomenological methodology?

3   Contrast the methodology of behaviorism and phenomenological psychology.

4   List the chief characteristics of existential psychology.

5   Comment on the role of measurement in psychology.

6   Suppose that both a behaviorist and an existential psychology wished to assess the personality of a certain individual. Describe how each one is likely to proceed.

7   Trace the origin of phenomenological psychology and describe two versions of this approach.

8   Compare Rogers' client-centered therapy with that of existentialists.

9   Sketch Giorgi's concept of an adequate science of man.

10   Discuss the notion of public and private events as data for psychology.

11   What is meant by intersubjective verification and how is it implemented? Give three examples.

ADDITIONAL READINGS

Bugental, J. F. T. **The search for authenticity: An existential-analytic approach to psychotherapy.** New York: Holt, 1965. "Basically the book describes what I do as an existential-analytic psychotherapist and what I think about when I am doing it."

Collins, J. **The existentialists: A critical study.** Chicago: Henry Regnery, 1952. A highly readable summary of existential philosophy is presented in this slender volume.

Combs, A. W., and Snygg, D. **Individual behavior: A perceptual approach** (Rev. ed.) New York: Harper & Row, 1959. When the first edition of this book appeared in 1949, the phenomenological approach to psychology was so novel that it was given the subtitle, **A new frame of reference for psychology.**

Correnti, S. Comparison of behaviorism and psychoanalysis with existentialism. **Journal of Existentialism,** 1965, **20,** 379-388. Correnti's lucid article highlights certain features of existentialism by contrasting them with two other theories.

Frankl, V. E. **Man's search for meaning: An introduction to logotherapy.** New York: Washington Square Press, 1963. The author recounts his experience in a Nazi death camp that led to the discovery of his existential therapy.

Gendlin, E. T. **Experiencing and the creation of meaning: A philosophical and psychological approach to the subjective.** New York: The Free Press, 1962. In addition to logical and operational dimensions of knowledge there is a concrete affective side of experience, **felt meaning,** which is of central importance in human life.

Giorgi, A. **Psychology as a human science: A phenomenologically based approach.** New York: Harper & Row, 1970. This is a search for a new paradigm to replace the natural science model of psychology.

Giorgi, A., Fischer, W. F., and von Eckartsberg, R. (Eds.) **Duquesne studies in phenomenological psychology: Volume 1.** Pittsburgh: Duquesne University Press, 1971. "Through a utilization of the philosophical tenets of existential phenomenology, we are attempting to found psychology conceived as a human science. The collection of articles contained in this volume expresses this attempt."

Kunzeli, A. E. (Ed.) **The phenomenological problem.** New York: Harper & Row, 1959. The need for phenomenological procedures is the subject of this symposium.

Lyons, J. **A primer of experimental psychology.** New York: Harper & Row, 1965. Dr. Lyons writes of two approaches to experimental psychology: one system-centered and the other person-centered.

May, R., Angel, E., and Ellenberger, H. F. (Eds.) **Existence: A new dimension in psychiatry and psychology.** New York: Basic Books, 1958. The senior editor of this classic work is the leading exponent of existential psychology.

May, R. **Psychology and the human dilemma.** Princeton, N.J.: Van Nostrand, 1967. Existential essays dealing with such topics as modern man's loss of significance, personal identity, the phenomenological approach to psychotherapy, anxiety and values, freedom and responsibility, and the science of man.

May, R. (Ed.) **Existential psychology.** (2d ed.) New York: Random House, 1969. The interesting papers in this small volume were originally presented at a symposium at an annual convention of the American Psychological Association.

Shlien, J. M. Phenomenology and personality. In J. M. Wepman and R. W. Hein (Eds.), **Concepts of personality.** Chicago: Aldine, 1963. A lucid, scholarly description of the existential-phenomenological position in psychology. There is a long list of references.

Wann, T. W. (Ed.) **Behaviorism and phenomenology: Contrasting bases for modern psychology.** Chicago: The University of Chicago Press, 1964. A symposium by the leading proponents of various theoretical approaches to psychology.

Zaner, R. M. Criticism of "Tensions in psychology between the methods of behaviorism and phenomenology." **Psychological Review,** 1967, **74,** 318-324. The author clarifies the position of phenomenological psychology in replying to an article critical of it.

Chapter 15

Changing Patterns
of Thought in Psychology

*Even today in the most sophisticated branches of natural
science, advances are not made by the application of a
single method. There are many techniques, many ways of
stating problems, many methods of analysis. Yet, belief in
a mistaken notion about experimental science is widespread. Many elementary texts in the physical and biological sciences perpetuate it.*

James B. Conant

Change is a fundamental characteristic of science. Every scientific construct or conclusion views nature from a single frame of reference and
hence can never fully account for all its intricate ramifications and complex interrelationships. Progress in science comes about through a series
of successive approximations, each refining to some degree what had
previously been known. As in the case of most intellectual and cultural
evolutions, change in basic concepts takes place slowly and is accompanied by heightened tensions between those who wish to abandon

present theory or practices and others who prefer to cling to modified versions of them as long as possible. Few scholars gladly relinquish postulates to which they have committed themselves over a long period of time, particularly if pride of authorship is at stake. This conservative stance of science serves a useful purpose in maintaining a disciplined approach to empirical investigation, but it may also serve as an obstacle to progress by causing both theorists and experimenters to think in terms of concepts which have outlived their usefulness.

OUTMODED CONVENTIONS IN SCIENCE

In an address to members of the American Psychological Association the noted physicist Robert Oppenheimer (1956a) observed that the greatest of all possible mistakes would be for psychology to model itself on a theory of science that became outdated long ago.

> We inherited, say at the beginning of this century, a notion of the physical world as a causal one, in which every event could be accounted for if we were ingenious, a world characterized by number, where everything interesting could be measured and quantified, a determinist world, a world in which there was no room for individuality, in which the object of study was simply there and how you studied it did not affect the object, it did not affect the kind of description you gave of it, a world in which objectifiability went far beyond merely our own agreement on what we meant by words and what we are talking about, in which objectification was meaningful irrespective of any attempt to study the system under consideration. It was just the given real object; there it was, and there was nothing for you to worry about of an epistemological character. This extremely rigid picture left out a great deal of common sense.

Oppenheimer goes on to explain that much of the business of science lies within the scope of normal experiencing. It is often necessary, especially in the early stages of research, to sort through a vast number of perceptions in order to discover the most fruitful approach. After this, an enormous amount of analysis and observation of relationships is required in any empirical study. Measurement is not always useful, especially if what is measured is not very meaningful. Nor should naturalistic observation and the use of descriptive methods be repudiated. At a time when American psychologists tended to discount the exploratory work of Jean Piaget as unscientific, Oppenheimer held it up as a model of how to begin. "It is just a start; and yet I think he has added greatly to our understanding." His prediction proved to be correct when, a decade and a half later the American Psychological Association conferred on Piaget its distinguished contribution award.

Harman suggests that the traditional scientific method unnecessarily limits the scope of research by self-imposed constraints that frequently go unnoticed. In an attempt to break out of the conceptual mold that considers classical objective methodology the only true path to knowledge, he proposes a broader approach which he calls the "scientific spirit of inquiry."

> I think we could agree without difficulty on the essential characteristics. Probably we could order human experience with the aid of hypothetical constructs intuitively arrived at and experimentally tested. It implies a willingness to apply to these hypotheses such tests as are appropriate, and to discard theories which prove by testing to be inadequate. (This includes testing by experiment and observation, drawing upon the experiences of others by checking with other authorities, insisting upon logical consistency, and testing intuitively—as for example, when the aesthetic test is applied that the deepest truths appear to be expressible with elegant simplicity. (Harman, 1962, pp. 76-77).

Similarly Rychlak (1968) shows that in personality research operational definitions can never hope to capture the full import of such concepts as **love** or **ambition.** Should the psychologist, then, be told to stop thinking about these and similar notions in terms that are meaningful to human beings? Rychlak believes that there is another way. It is better to investigate exciting ideas with loose experimental designs than safe, prosaic ideas with "tight" designs. The lack of precision in single investigations can be compensated for by cross validating the results of a number of independent studies.

CHANGING SCIENTIFIC PARADIGMS

Kuhn (1962) argues rather conclusively from a historical point of view that the progress of science implies more than a gradual accumulation of facts, theories, and research techniques. At any given time each scientific community adopts a paradigm or body of beliefs, presuppositions, rules, and guidelines which define how science is to be practiced. The paradigm that wins out over its competitors is the one that solves the most important problems. It is neither completely successful nor ideologically neutral. Certain arbitrary elements are always present in the beliefs of the scientific community which can never step outside the world of its own historically conditioned concepts. To a large extent the success of normal science depends upon its willingness to defend these assumptions even though to a later age they may appear as mythical as the ancient notion of phlogiston, or the principle of fire thought of as a material substance. It should come as no surprise, then, that science tends to suppress novel ideas which would overturn its fundamental beliefs. Only when persistent unresolved problems point to the existence of serious deficiencies in the paradigm are extraordinary investigations undertaken to replace it. This amounts to a revolution in the way that science is practiced. In dramatic instances the whole world view may be altered as happened when the Copernican solar system and the theory of relativity were accepted.

Although textbook descriptions of science outlaw any appeal to **authority,** nonetheless it plays an important role. Polanyi (1963) cites as an example his potential theory of absorption of gases on solids which was rejected out of hand by scientists because it ran counter to prevailing views. Only half a century later when these concepts had changed was his evidence evaluated objectively. The theory was then accepted. He does not complain about this suppression of novel ideas by authority because he considers it necessary for maintaining scientific discipline.

> I repeat here that I am not arguing against the present balance between the powers of orthodoxy and the rights of dissent in science. I merely insist an acknowledgement of the fact that the scientific method is, and must be, disciplined by an orthodoxy which can permit only a limited dissent, and that dissent is fraught with grave risks to the dissenter. I demand a clear recognition of this situation for the sake of our intellectual honesty as scientists, and I charge that this situation is not recognized today but is, on the contrary, obscured by current declarations of science. . . .

In applying these notions to the present state of American psychology, Amedeo Giorgi notes the following.

From Psychology as a Human Science

Traditional psychology already has a successful paradigm working for itself and while it is aware that this paradigm does not solve everything, i.e., it is aware of the existence of anomalies, it still feels that these anomalies will eventually be explicable in terms of the already existing paradigm. Thus, traditional psychology is exercising its conservative prerogative, and it has every right to do so, for we must not forget that this is one of science's strengths. . . .

On the other hand, we would also like to reserve the right to leave the existing paradigm and to try to work on the construction of a new paradigm, that we feel will comprehend more adequately the existing anomalies that have been reported above. In doing this, we too are acting in a way that thousands of other scientists have acted before us. Kuhn does not reserve the term revolution for the great scientific revolutions that we all hear about, such as those of Copernicus or Einstein, but he observes that the same sort of thing happens over and over again on a smaller scale throughout science. A revolution occurs any time that a particular scientific community agrees that the existing paradigm can no longer be accepted, and they turn to a new paradigm, and when they do so, they begin to act within the perspective of normal science once again. Thus, what is important here is to realize that the practice of science incorporates both attitudes, that is a dialectical process between conservation and progress, between closure and openness, between solidification and expansion, and that with different phases, it is proper to be doing any one of these activities. However, it is equally important to stress that this aspect of science is revealed by an historical perspective; a definitional point of view might have revealed a more static picture.

THE DECLINE OF BEHAVIORISM

In summarizing the history of behaviorism Koch (1964) describes three phases through which it has passed: **classical behaviorism** as proposed by Watson, **neobehaviorism** which attempted to construct broad empirical theories based on physics, and **neo-neobehaviorism** which is turning liberal to the point of losing its distinctive character. Commenting on the papers contributed to **Psychology: A study of a science** (Koch, 1959) by behavioristically oriented theorists, he calls attention to a radical reanalysis of S and R which has softened the behavioristic position regarding objectivity. Guthrie is quoted as saying "we find ourselves inevitably describing (stimuli) in perceptual terms;" moreover, "it is. . .necessary that they have **meaning** for the responding organism" (p. 165; Koch's italics). In a recent publication E. M. Segal and R. Lachman discuss the internal and external influences which have caused behaviorism to lose its dominant position in psychology.

From Complex Behavior or Higher Mental Process: Is There a Paradigm Shift?

Influences for Change External to Psychology

Although a paradigm has a great deal of circularity built into its formulation, with the concepts determining the appropriate data and vice versa, it is not isolated from the world. The observed data, internal analyses of the paradigm, developments in other fields, and changing interests of scientists each furthered the decline of neobehaviorism.

Following World War II, striking advances occurred in several loosely related scientific fields including finite mathematics and probability theory, information theory, linguistic theory, and computer science. These fields all dealt with formal operations on symbolic entities. Since the neobehaviorist concepts had been generalized to verbal learning and concept formation, the scope of these achievements quite naturally attracted the attention of the psychological community. These various developments outside of psychology all had an important characteristic: their scientific credentials were impeccable. Many of the alternatives to S-R behaviorism within psychology had been vilified for their unscientific and metaphysical predilections, often justifiably. Charges of "unscientific" against these external influences would have seemed ludicrous; now a considerable selection of genuine scientific alternatives to neobehaviorism was available.

Starting with the publication of a text by Feller (1950) on probability, followed by an elementary elucidation of concepts in a book by Kemeny, Snell, and Thompson (1957) on finite mathematics, a large group of psychologists and their students were introduced to the power and simplicity of set theory and finite mathematics. These books and the many others on the same topic did not directly provide any substantive theories, but they did provide a way of formally characterizing many different kinds of hypotheses dealing with qualitative and discrete differences. Before the advent of new formalisms, a primary advantage of the behaviorist positions was that these were the only positions which had even the semblance of formal support. It is not clear whether other theoretical positions could have been formalized before the advent of finite mathematics, but in any case they were not. Now, however, for the first time one could discuss such concepts as attention, selection, cognitive states, or stimulus features with much rigor (e.g., Atkinson & Estes, 1963; Restle, 1961).

One of the most potent of the extrapsychological alternatives was information theory. Information theoretical concepts were applied to psychology almost immediately upon the publication of "A Mathematical Theory of Communication" by Shannon in 1948. Interestingly, the main thrust of information theory into psychology came not from its mathematical formalisms, the theorems, but rather from its conceptual characteristics. Information theory provided a rich source of hypotheses about psychological processes, mostly dealing with complex human behavior, and psychologists were quick to develop them. The result was the accumulation of a considerable literature of high quality. Information theoretic concepts such as uncertainty and structure provided viable alternatives to the concept of association and to the conditioning model (cf. Garner, 1962); such alternative concepts were perhaps information theory's most serious blow to neobehaviorism.

Computer science had a manifold influence on psychology. Automata theory, programming technology, and computer principles provided a rich source of concepts, a methodology, and an explanatory formalism. These, singly and in concert, have been incorporated into a variety of approaches to psychological theory and research, which as a group is called the information-processing approach. General methodological and design characteristics of the approach have been described by Haber (1969) with special emphasis on perception and thinking. A new formalism for theory construction, computer simulation, is, of course, applicable independent of information-processing concepts and methodology, but the formalism and the concepts generally have been applied together, especially in the study of cognitive processes (cf. Reitman, 1965). The major concepts of the information-processing approach such as the flow charting of information, transformations of information, and stages in perception and thought offered a view of reality that contrasted sharply with the concepts of neobehaviorism.

Psychologists using this approach, rooted as it was in computer theory, could use a variety of mental concepts to describe mindless automata; the old behaviorist charge of mentalism was thus rendered irrelevant. It is interesting to note that Hull (1943) himself argued that the analogy with a "self maintaining robot" was an effective "prophylaxis against anthropomorphic subjectivism [p. 27]." Computer simulation was thus recommended in the abstract by a leader of the neobehavioristic movement. The appeal of this approach, along with some concurrent internal difficulties in S-R behaviorism, may account for the many defections from neobehaviorism (e.g., Bower, 1967; Mandler, 1967).

The most recent and most intensive undermining of neobehavioristic cohesion came from developments in linguistic theory. More than any other external influence, linguistics had an impact that cannot readily be separated from internal undermining. An excellent illustration is Skinner's application of his neobehaviorist methods and concepts to verbal behavior and

Chomsky's analysis of that position. Chomsky (1959) reviewed Skinner's *Verbal Behavior* (1957), and neobehaviorism has not yet recovered. Although some disagree, we think that Chomsky clearly showed that Skinner's program could not be used to operationalize linguistic concepts and that it was neither a description nor a theory of language. Chomsky (1957, 1965) not only criticized the neobehavioristic position but offered positive alternatives. He demonstrated that language behavior could not be described meaningfully in terms defined solely by empirically delimited variables and also suggested that a formalism which generated sentences of natural language could be devised, provided that it contained certain abstract features. Miller (1962) called the attention of psychologists to Chomsky's theoretical formulations and demonstrated how they might be used as the basis of empirical research. This theoretical approach won many converts; talent that otherwise would have done research in the neobehaviorist tradition started intensive work within this new conceptual system. Evidence for this latter statement is the continuous dialogue between neobehaviorists and transformationalists and losses from the ranks of S-R behaviorism.

Our catalog of the external undermining of the S-R, neobehaviorist paradigm would be incomplete without some brief mention of developments in the philosophy of science. While neobehaviorists were accepting the tenets of logical positivism, this philosophy was coming under continuous and sometimes devastating attacks by other analytic philosophers. Psychologists generally were unaware of these attacks and of new approaches until quite recently. Among more recent work in the philosophy of science, the influential positions enunciated by Kuhn (1970) and Polanyi (1958) convinced many research psychologists that the conceptual frameworks within which science is conducted contain many arbitrary features. Such awareness could not but make research psychologists question their assumptions.

Influences for Changes Internal to Psychology

In 1954, the euphoria of many neobehaviorists was shaken by the publication of a conference report, *Modern Learning Theory* (Estes, Koch, MacCorquodale, Meehl, Mueller, Schoenfeld, & Verplanck, 1954). Although by then the four major neobehavioristic positions were considered to be theories of learning, the conclusions of the conference were that none were, in fact, coherent theories. In particular, none of the theories were formally adequate. They were not shown to be wrong, but more seriously, they *could not* be shown to be wrong because either they had essentially no formalism or they permitted contradictory deductions. Neobehaviorism has yet to recover.

The neobehaviorists started with essential agreement on the data base and the conviction that challenges to the data base would be resolved empirically. Little did they know what despair some of them would feel when the results of arduous experimentation yielded only one more tally in a box score, as occurred, for example, in the place versus response learning controversy. The basic issue was a seemingly simple empirical problem: Did organisms learn what response to make or where to go? Many studies were done, but the results were contradictory and neither position was established. Kendler and Gasser (1948) attempted to solve the problem by arguing that one of the "responses" a subject can learn is "approach," so place learning was identified as a subset of response learning. The discussion ended with Restle (1957) who claimed to resolve the issue by declaring it a pseudo-problem. What was called place or response learning depended on the locus of cues: if there were internal cues, it was response learning; if the cues were external, it was place learning. The original issue of what was associated to the cues was ignored. Thus, an issue that was to be resolved empirically floated away in a cloud of obscurity. Many other problems were "solved" in similar fashion such as latent learning, one-trial learning, and stimulus selectivity, among others.

As we have mentioned, most neobehaviorists believed that complex behaviors are mediated by essentially isomorphic mechanisms through much of the phylogenetic scale. This belief received shattering rebuffs, especially during the last decade. Among the first to be disappointed were those neobehaviorists who did not wait until the empirical issues were resolved on animal subjects to apply the concepts and variants of the methodology to human complex behaviors. The empirical problems in the human domain were, if possible, more intractable than in the animal domain. Serial and paired-associate learning, two tried-and-true methods for investigating learning in humans, both presented problems unresolvable in terms of associations between elements. The stimulus in serial learning became an event that had no direct empirical correlate (cf. Young, 1968). The functional stimulus in paired-associate learning depended upon what was meaningful to the subject (Underwood, 1963). Subjects could use or not use associative connections as they chose (Jenkins, 1963; Postman & Stark, 1969). These and similar results supported the growing conviction that the data base gathered from animal studies was in no simple way capable of encompassing complex human behavior. Now, some even believe that there is a discontinuity between animal learning and human mental processes.

The neobehaviorists continue to hold antimentalistic convictions. Cautions against the value and reliability of human communication in the form of a verbal report continue to be offered. The Skinnerian wing of neobehaviorism believes to this day that verbal behavior is subject to the same laws and controlled by the same variables as the pecking response of pigeons. Their position represents one side of a controversy on the operant conditioning of verbal behavior (Holz & Azrin, 1966). The other side of the controversy holds that verbal behavior is "conditioned" only when the human subject is aware that something is expected of him and is willing to do it. Whatever the resolution of the controversy, psychology changes. One of the central figures in this controversy has recently concluded:

> Paradoxically, perhaps the most significant contribution of verbal conditioning research has been the stimulation of interest in verbal report procedures and in concepts such as "awareness" among psychologists who are inclined to insist that thoughts and ideas are beyond the limits of scientific inquiry [Spielberger & DeNike, 1966, p. 324].

Some psychologists became interested in complex symbolic processes themselves. This shift in interest oriented them to a new data base. This data base held obvious limitations for any system that depends upon learning defined as changes in the probability of responses. Miller (1965) pointed out that English-speaking adults can easily understand more than 10^{20} sentences. These obviously could not have been learned on an individual basis. If explanatory systems depending upon the changing probability of responses are not to become meaningless, one has to specify in a nontrivial fashion how to integrate response units into higher-order units. Claims that sentences are constructed by "autoclitic" responses to other responses (Skinner, 1957) do not meet this criterion. Also, understanding sentences is not clarified by discussing a systematic set of language habits such that, for example, "a," "the," and "this" are associated with one another by contiguous implicit responses, and "the" and "car" are associated explicitly such that all occurrences of the responses "the" would tend to elicit the response "car" (Staats & Staats, 1963). In addition to problems involving grammatical constructions, the need for conceptions other than the accumulation of S-R units is immediately apparent when one considers such behaviors as paraphrase and understanding prose (Lachman & Dooling, 1968).

Psychology Circa 1970

The neobehaviorist position has been somewhat shaken since its heyday, but it still has adherents, although some individuals such as Bever, Fodor, and Garrett (1968) claim that an associationistic position, *in principle,* cannot account for certain higher mental processes. Others, such as Crothers and Suppes (1967), make the claim that associationism, *in principle*, can handle *any* complex mental phenomena. As things currently stand, Crothers and Suppes are right. Let us look at current neobehaviorism. Witness this statement by a leading S-R neobehaviorist: "an objective, functionalist, or even S-R viewpoint carries no necessary theoretical commitments and no necessary aversion to postulating intervening processes [Cofer, 1968, p. 526]." A second distinguished S-R theorist states, "The least controversial, and perhaps most useful, interpretation of S-R associationism is to view it as a technical language system analogous to notations used to represent moves in a chess game" [Kendler, 1968, p. 388].

According to these spokesmen, by 1968 there were no precepts or limitations with which one could identify the neobehaviorist position. This situation was reached because the S-R psychologists as individuals successively modified their positions to account for the new conceptualizations, new formalisms, new methods, and new additions to the data base. They also became cognizant of problems in their explanatory systems. As far as we can tell, with the exception of the radical behaviorists who reject everything but their own research and rhetoric, the structure which was S-R behaviorism has no properties left. It, in short, has vanished. These psychologists, however, did not give up their conceptual lenses with which to view the world, but gained individualized new lenses to replace the old. It is just that for many psychologists their metatheoretical vocabulary lags behind their vision.

With the demise of S-R behaviorism, research in the higher mental processes has flourished (cf. Neisser, 1967). We cannot at this time specify what the future of psychology will be; however, we see the near future containing many and varied approaches. As to our original problem, are we in the midst of a scientific revolution? If the controversies in psychology lead to continuing debate by the nonscientific educated elite and the concept of man is at stake, as we think it is, then in several years we will be able to say that a revolution took place. We can say with assurance that deep conceptual changes in psychology have already occurred.

Summary

The basic nature of scientific paradigms during periods of stability and change was analyzed, and the results of this analysis were applied to scientific psychology. No particular aspect of a scientific viewpoint in isolation determines a paradigm and, surprisingly, a change in all may not signify a revolution. Revolutions are identified as such retrospectively, frequently by nonscientific criteria. Scientific psychology was in a stable period and was dominated by neobehaviorism for most of the middle third of the twentieth century. We present evidence that this domination was justified by both analytic and empirical considerations. After World War II, the bases for this domination began to dissipate. Major formal and theoretical advances outside psychology in finite mathematics, linguistics, computer technology, information theory, and philosophy of science are described. These gave rise to procedures and ideas applicable to formulations in competition with the behavioristic approaches. Problems within S-R behaviorism which were generally conceived to be empirically resolvable proved to be intractable. The strong neobehavioristic positions have weakened so considerably in the face of this competition that neobehaviorism can hardly be identified. Thus, the justification for the domination of psychology by neobehaviorism has eroded, as has the domination itself.

Jessor (1961) suggests that a rapprochement between S-R psychology and phenomenological approaches might be possible if stimulus and response were to be defined in psychological or meaningful terms. It is still too early to predict whether Giorgi's (1970) search for a more appropriate paradigm will ultimately move in this general direction. In the following selection Carl Rogers also shows how changes in ideology similar to those we have discussed in this chapter could affect the evolution of psychology in a wholesome way.

Some Possible Changes in the Behavioral Sciences

Let me bring my remarks to a close. It may seem that the statements I have been making about knowing and science, and the behavioral sciences in particular, add very little to our present conceptions. Yet, I should like to indicate some of the effects that such a view of science might have, particularly if imparted to our graduate students and to the younger men in the field.

    1 It would tend to do away with the fear of creative subjective speculation. As I talk with graduate students in psychology, this fear is a very deep one. It cuts them off from any significant discovery. They would be shocked by the writings of a Kepler in his mystical and fanciful searching for likenesses and patterns in nature. They do not recognize that often it is out of such fanciful thinking that true science emerges. As Bronowski says, "To us the analogies by which Kepler listened for the movement of the planets and the music of the spheres are far-fetched. But are they more so than the wild leap by which Rutherford and Bohr found a model for the atom in, of all places, the planetary system?" (1956, pp. 22-23) We are badly in need of a course on "The Care and Nurture of Infant Ideas." In our desire to be rigorous, we so often strangle the newborn idea, rather than nourishing its growth and development.

2 It would place a stress on disciplined commitment, disciplined *personal* commitment; not methodology. It would be a very healthy emphasis in the behavioral sciences if we could recognize that it is the dedicated, personal search of a disciplined, open-minded individual which discovers and creates new knowledge. No refinement of laboratory or statistical method can do this.

3 It would do away with many of the "oughts" in selecting hypotheses. For example, it is deeply imbedded in most behavioral scientists that we "ought" to be concerned only with the observables in behavior. Until recently, this has tended to inhibit work on dreams, on fantasy, on creative thinking. It has made most psychologists small-caliber scientists, involved only with the simplest problems in the science of man.

4 It would permit a free rein to phenomenological thinking in behavioral science, our effort to understand man and, perhaps, even the animals from the inside. It would recognize that no type of hypothesis has any special virtue in science save only in its relationship to a meaningful pattern which exists in the universe. Thus, a phenomenologically based hypothesis would have as much place in the behavioral sciences as a chemically based, genetically based, or behaviorally based hypothesis. We would develop a broader science (Rogers, 1964).

5 It would do away with those hypotheses which are selected simply because there are tools to measure the variables involved.

6 It would put the machinery of confirmation, the machinery of empirical testing of hypotheses, in its proper place. Method would not occupy a central place as the core of behavioral science.

7 It would put the stress on meaning; not simply on statistical significance at the .01 level.

8 More generally, if the picture of science I have tried to suggest gains some general acceptance in our field, it would give a new dignity to the science of man and to the scientist who commits himself to that field. It would keep the scientist as a human being in the picture at all times, and we would recognize that science is but the lengthened shadow of dedicated human beings.

9 Perhaps most important of all, it would keep the subject of the investigation of the behavioral sciences in the picture as a subjective human being; not simply as a machine; not simply as an object or a determined sequence of cause and effect. We would not be fearful of looking at man as an existing human being, to use Kierkegaard's term, with more to his life than can be compressed into a machine model. Unless we can make progress in this direction, the behavioral sciences have, I fear, the capacity for becoming a threat to society more extreme and more devastating than the physical sciences have been.

It is encouraging to note that in practice psychology has advanced well beyond the restrictive theory of science to which it is verbally committed. A remark that Einstein made about physics applies with equal force to psychology. If you wish to know what physics is all about, he said, pay attention to what physicists actually do, not to what they say they do. In spite of the interdict against phenomeno-logical data, psychologists have never ceased to accept it when, by some artifice, it could be made to look objective, such as labeling a subject's conscious experience a "verbal report."

During the past decade or two, determined efforts have been made to break out of the traditional mold through the frequent use of techniques to measure such subjective experiences as connotative meaning, the intensity of feeling, self-perception, and the strength of an individual's motives for achievement. Even mechanical devices have been employed as illustrated by Shlien's (1962) use of two semitrans-parent disks to estimate the closeness of match between the way a per-son thinks and feels about himself and the way he would like to be. The disks were mounted on moveable arms in such a way that the amount of overlap could be varied from 0 to 100 percent. The subject was told to think of one disk as himself and the other as his self-ideal and to indicate the amount of congruence by adjusting the overlap. His re-sponse was recorded as a coefficient of correlation in terms of the cosine of the angle of separation between the disks.

These and similar developments emphasize the point of view that psychology should never rest content with a research paradigm modeled exclusively on the natural sciences. Of all the empirical disciplines psy-chology should be the most imaginative in developing a variety of ap-proaches and research strategies to probe in every direction for facts about mankind which are beyond the competency of any given type of methodology. The continued health and vigor of our science depends upon such a flexible professional attitude.

SUMMARY

Since constructs can never capture the full reality of any phenomenon, progress in science requires a constant revision of its theories or the substitution of newer ones derived from different postulates. Oppen-heimer warns psychologists not to base their concepts on a notion of science that is already outdated. Kuhn's historical analysis reveals that certain arbitrary elements are contained in the model of science adopted at any given time. These presuppositions and beliefs are rightly defended in the day-to-day practice of science. Novel ideas that would disrupt the paradigm are authoritatively suppressed as long as possible. Only when the hope of harmonizing theory with reality is abandoned does an ideological revolution occur. Not only is the time ripe for a small-scale revolution of this type to occur in psychology—a quiet revo-

lution seems actually under way. Koch as well as Segal and Lachman
have noted a gradual decline in the influence of behaviorism to the
point where it is no longer the dominant force in American psychology.
Rogers illustrates how changing patterns of thought in the behavioral
sciences might influence psychology in a wholesome way. The time has
come to broaden our notions of what constitutes a truly scientific approach to the study of man.

DISCUSSION TOPICS

1 What are the implications for psychology of Kuhn's concept of
scientific revolutions?

2 To what extent is authority an ingredient in the practice of science?

3 Expand the suggestions of Rogers and other writers calling for new
directions in psychology.

4 Discuss the influences for change in psychology that are described
by Segal and Lachman.

5 Show how a psychologist might use Harman's suggested approach to
investigate some neglected area in psychology such as human courage.

6 Analyze and evaluate Part Four of this book in the light of your own
understanding of the role of science in psychology.

ADDITIONAL READINGS

Blackburn, T. R. Sensuous-intellectual complementarity in science. **Science,**
1971, **172**(3987), 1003-1007. Intuitive knowledge based on "naive"
openness to nature and to other people (e.g., through direct sensuous
observation) complements the quantitative study of phenomena. Both
are needed for a complete science.

Carlson, R. Where is the person in personality research? **Research Bulletin**
(Educational Testing Service, Princeton, N.J.), 1969. The fully functioning person is not portrayed in our research on personality. Several
broad solutions to the problem are suggested.

Coulson, W. R., and Rogers, C. R. **Man and the science of man.** Columbus, Ohio: Merrill, 1968. This book is a product of an ongoing
interdisciplinary investigation at the Western Behavioral Science
Institute to help develop a more appropriate model for the behavioral
sciences.

Hall, E. A conversation with Jean Piaget and Barbel Inhelder. **Psychology
Today,** 1970, **3,** 25-32, 55-56. These scientists have developed in-
novative methods for investigating significant problems of human
development.

Kelly, G. A. Humanistic methodology in psychological research, **Journal of
Humanistic Psychology,** 1969, **9,** 53-65. Some fundamental character-

istics of an adequate methodology for humanistic psychology are discussed.

Kelman, H. C. **A time to speak: On human values and social research.** San Francisco: Jossey-Bass, 141-163. Most debates about research models focus on false issues. Systematic thinking about man and society is the central task of the social psychologist.

Koch, S. Psychological science versus the science-humanism antinomy: Intimations of a significant science of man. **American Psychologist,** 1961, **16,** 629-639. Psychology is seen as occupying the area where the sciences and the humanities intersect.

Kuhn, T. S. **The structure of scientific revolutions.** (2d ed.) Chicago: The University of Chicago Press, 1970. Normal science takes its foundations for granted and works within a restricted paradigm. When unresolved problems become too persistent a revolution in theory and practice occurs.

Luchins, A. S., and Luchins, E. H. Some approaches to studying the individual. **Journal of Humanistic Psychology,** 1965, **5,** 82-89. The scientific study of personality need not be confined to abstract generalizations. Methods for assessing individuality are in the making.

Lumpkin, Martin. Walden I and II: A plea for renewed balance in the psychological pursuit of science. **American Psychologist,** 1970, **25,** 1087-1090. "Our science of psychology is in danger of imbalance in the current uproar on methodological priority. There is need for the naturalist's eye and for release from the suffocating overdemands of his brother satellite, scientific psychology."

Maslow, A. H. **Toward a psychology of being.** (Rev. ed.) Princeton, N.J., Van Nostrand, 1968. Maslow sketches the outline for a psychology of growth and self-actualization.

May, R. **Psychology and the human dilemma.** New York: Van Nostrand, 1907. Chapter 13 is devoted to the characteristics of a science and can deal adequately with man as a symbol-making and a free agent capable of ethical behavior.

Polanyi, M. **Personal knowledge.** Chicago: University of Chicago Press, 1958. A scientist's values, commitments, and participation as a person are as much a part of research as the more traditional elements.

Silverman, I., and Shulman, A. D. A conceptual model of artifact in attitude change studies. **Sociometry,** 1970, **33,** 97-107. Much evidence is marshalled to show how subjects' attitudes can bias psychological investigation.

Smith, W. A. S., Royce, J. R., and Jones, D. Development of an inventory to measure ways of knowing. **Psychological Report,** 1967, **21,** 529-535. This study illustrates one of many ways of objectifying private, subjective experience.

References

Abraham, K. (1937) Notes on the psychoanalytical investigation and treatment of manic-depressive insanity and allied conditions. Chapter 6 in Selected papers on psychoanalysis. London: Hogarth.

Adler, M. J. (1967) The difference of man and the difference it makes. Stanford, Calif.: Stanford University Press.

Alexander, F. A. (1958) A contribution to a theory of play. Psychoanalytic Quarterly, 27, 175-193.

Alexander, I. E., Colley, R. S., & Alderstein, A. M. (1957) Is death a matter of indifference? Journal of Psychology, 43, 277-283.

Allport, G. W. (1962) Psychological models for guidance. Harvard Educational Review, 32, 373-381.

Appleton, L. E. (1910) A comparative study of the play of adult savages and civilized children. Chicago: University of Chicago Press.

Arbuckle, D. S. (1953) Student personnel services in higher education. New York: McGraw-Hill. Pp. 170-177.

Arbuckle, D. S. (1960) Counseling: Philosophy or science. Personnel and Guidance Journal, 39, 11-14.

Asch, S. E. (1952) Social psychology. New York: Prentice-Hall.

Atkinson, R. C., & Estes, W. K. (1963) Stimulus sampling theory. In R. D. Luce, R. R. Bush, & E. Galanter (Eds.), Handbook of mathematical psychology. Vol. 2. New York: Wiley.

Bakan, D. (1966) The duality of human existence. Chicago: Rand McNally.

Barker, Roger (1965) Explorations in Ecological Psychology, Amer. Psychologist, 20, 1-14.

Barker, Roger (Ed., 1963). The Stream of Behavior, New York: Appleton-Century-Crofts.

Baumgold, J., Temerlin, M. K., & Ragland, R. (1965) Experience of freedom to choose in mental health, neurosis and psychosis. Psychological Reports, 16, 957-962.

Beach, F. A. (1945) Concepts of play in animals. American Naturalist, **79**, 523-541.

Begelman, D. A. (1966) Determinism vs. free will. The Catholic Psychological Record, **4,** 124-128.

Benedict, R. (1934) **Patterns of culture.** Boston: Houghton Mifflin.

Bennis, W. G., Benne, K. D., & Chin, R. (Eds., 1961) **The planning of change.** New York: Holt, Rinehart & Winston.

Bennis, W. G., Schein, E. H., Berlew, D. E., & Steele, F. I. (Eds., 1964) Interpersonal dynamics. Homewood, Ill.: Dorsey.

Bertalanffy von, L. (1965) On the definition of the symbol. In J. R. Royce (Ed.), **Psychology and the symbol.** New York: Random House.

Bertocci, P. A. (1967) The freedom to be free! Faculty Forum, No. 42, p. 2.

Beston, W. H., Heron, W., & Scott, T. H. (1954) Effects of decreased variation in the sensory environment. Canadian Journal of Psychology, 8, 70-76.

Bever, T. G., Fodor, J. A., & Garrett, M. A formal limitation of associationism. In T. R. Dixon & D. L. Horton (Eds., 1968), **Verbal behavior and general behavior theory.** Englewood Cliffs, N.J.: Prentice-Hall.

Binswanger, L. (1957) **Sigmund Freud: Reminiscences of a friendship.** New York: Grune & Stratton.

Bischof, L. J. (1970) **Interpreting personality theories.** New York: Harper & Row.

Block, J., & Block, J. (1951) An investigation of the relationship between intolerance of ambiguity and ethnocentrism. Journal of Personality, **19,** 303-311.

Boisen, A., Jenkins, R. L., & Lorr, M. (1954) Schizophrenic ideation as a striving toward a solution of conflict. Journal of Clinical Psychology, **10,** 389-391.

Bonner, H. (1965) **On being mindful of man.** Boston: Houghton Mifflin.

Boulding, K. E. (1967) Dare we take the social sciences seriously? American Psychologist, **22,** 563-567.

Bower, G. H. A multicomponent theory of the memory trace. In K. W. Spence & J. T. Spence (Eds., 1967), **The psychology of learning and motivation: Advances in research and theory.** Vol. 1. New York: Academic Press.

Bradford, L. Gibb, J. R., & Benne, K. D. (Eds., 1964) **T-group theory and laboratory method.** New York: Wiley.

Branden, N. (1963) The contradiction of determinism. Objectivist Newsletter (May), **2,** 17, 19-20.

Britt, S. H., & Janus, S. Q. (1941) Toward a social psychology of human play. Journal of Social Psychology, **13,** 351-384.

Brody, N., & Oppenheim, P. (1966) Tensions in psychology between the methods of behaviorism and phenomenology, Psychological Review, **73,** 295-305.

Bromberg, W., & Schilder, P. (1936) The attitudes of psychoneurotics toward death. Psychoanalytical Review, **23,** 1-28.

Bronowski, J. (1956) **Science and human values.** New York: Harper I orchbooks.

Bruch, H. (1957) **The importance of overweight.** New York: Norton.

Bruch, H. (1958) Developmental obesity and schizophrenia. Psychiatry, **21,** 65-70.

Brzezinski, Z. (1968) The technetronic society. Society, **30** (1), 19.

Bugental, J. F. T. (1965) **The search for authenticity: An existential-analytic approach to psychotherapy.** New York: Holt, Rinehart, & Winston.

Bugental, J. F. T. (1966) Humanistic psychology and the clinician. In L. E. Abt & B. F. Reiss (Eds.) **Progress in clinical psychology.** Vol. 7. New York: Grune & Stratton. Pp. 223-239.

Bühler, C. (1933) **The human course of life as a psychological problem.** Leipzig: Hirzel.

Bühler, C. (1959) Theoretical observations about life's basic tendencies. American Journal of Psychotherapy, **13,** 561-581.

Bühler, C. (1962) **Values in psychotherapy.** New York: Free Press.

Bühler, C. (1965) Some empirical approaches to the study of life's basic values. In F. T. Severin (Ed.) **Humanistic viewpoints in psychology.** New York: McGraw-Hill.

Bühler, C. (1967) Human life goals in the humanistic perspective, Journal of Humanistic Psychology, **7,** 36-52.

Bühler, C., & Allen, M. (1972) Introduction to humanistic psychology. Monterey, Calif.: Brooks/Cole.

Buytendijk, F. J. J. (1934) Wesen und sinn des spieles. Berlin: K. Wolff.

Caprio, F. S. (1946) Theological attitudes toward death: A psychoanalytical evaluation. Journal of Criminal Psychopathology, **7,** 737-752.

Caprio, F. S. (1950) A study of some psychological reactions during prepubescence to the idea of death. Psychiatric Quarterly, **24,** 495-505.

Carlson, R. (1971) Where is the person in personality research? Psychological Bulletin, **75,** 203-219.

Carr, H. A. (1902) The survival value of play. Investigations of the department of psychology and education. Boulder: University of Colorado Press.

Casriel, D. (1963) So fair a house. Englewood Cliffs, N.J.: Prentice-Hall.

Cassirer, E. (1944) An essay on man. New Haven, Conn.: Yale University Press. P. 27.

Cervantes, S. (1951) The portable Cervantes. (Trans. and ed. by S. Putnam) New York: Viking Press, 1951. Pp. 760-769.

Chomsky, N. (1957) Syntactic structures. The Hague: Mouton & Co.

Chomsky, N. (1959) Review of verbal behavior. Language, **35,** 26-58.

Chomsky, N. (1965) Aspects of the theory of syntax. Cambridge: M.I.T. Press.

Claparéde, E. (1911) Psychology of the child. New York: Longmans.

Claparéde, E. (1934) Sur la nature el le fonction de jeu. Archives de Psychologie, **24,** 350-309.

Cofer, C. N. Problems, issues, and implications. In T. R. Dixon & D. L. Horton (Eds., 1968), Verbal behavior and general behavior theory. Englewood Cliffs, N.J.: Prentice-Hall.

Coleman, J. C. (1969) Psychology and effective behavior. Chicago: Scott, Foresman.

Combs, A. W., & Snygg, D. (1959) Individual behavior: A perceptual approach to behavior (Rev. ed.). New York: Harper & Row.

Committee on Definition, Division of Counseling Psychology (1956) Counseling psychology as a specialty. American Psychologist, **11,** 282-285.

Cook, S. W. et al. (1971) Ethical standards for psychological research. APA Monitor, **2**(7), 9-28.

Crothers, E., & Suppes, P. (1967) Experiments in second language learning. New York: Academic Press.

Crutchfield, R. S. (1955) Conformity and character. American Psychologist, **10,** 191-198.

Curti, M. W. (1930) Child psychology. New York: Longmans Green.

Dukes, W. F. (1955) Psychological studies in values. Psychological Bulletin, **52,** 24-50.

Durkheim, E. (1954) Suicide. New York: Free Press.

Ellis, A. (1948) Questionnaire versus interview methods in the study of human love relationships. II. American Sociological Review, **13,** 61-65.

English, H. B., & English, A. C. (1958) A comprehensive dictionary of psychological and psychoanalytical terms. New York: Longmans Green.

Erikson, E. H. (1937) Configuration in play—clinical notes Psychoanalytic Quarterly, **6,** 138-214.

Erikson, E. H. (1940) Studies in the interpretation of play: I. Clinical observations of play disruption in young children. Genetic Psychology Monographs, **22,** 557-671.

Erikson, E. H. (1950) Childhood and society. New York: Norton.

Erikson, E. H. (1951) Sex differences in the play configurations of preadolescents. American Journal of Orthopsychiatry, **21,** 667-692.

Erikson, E. H. (1959) Growth and crises of the healthy personality. Psychological Issues, **1,** 50-100.

Erikson, E. (1963) Childhood and society (Rev. ed.). New York: Norton, pp. 216-222.

Erikson, E. H. (1964) Insight and responsibility. New York, Norton.

Estes, W. K., Koch, S., MacCorquodale, K., Meehl, P. E., Mueller, C. G., Schoenfeld, W. N., & Verplanck, W. S. (1954) Modern learning theory. New York: Appleton-Century-Crofts.

Evans, J., and Rosenthal, R. (1969) Interpersonal self-fulfilling prophecies: Further extrapolations from the laboratory to the classroom. **Proceedings, 77th annual convention, APA.**

Feifel, H. (1963) Death. In N. L. Farberow (Ed.), **Taboo topics.** New York: Atherton.

Feller, W. (1950) **An introduction to probability theory and its applications.** New York: Wiley.

Fenichel, O. (1945) **The psychoanalytic theory of neuroses.** New York, Norton.

Fields, P. E. (1932) Studies in concept formation: I. The development of the concept of triangularity in the white rat. **Comparative Psychology Monographs, 2**(2), 1-70.

Frankl, V. E. (1959) **From death camp to existentialism: A psychiatrist's path to a new therapy.** Boston: Beacon Press.

Frankl, V. E. (1961) Dynamics, existence and values. **Journal of Existential Psychiatry, 2,** 5.

Freud, A. (1936) **The ego and the mechanisms of defense.** London: Hogarth. Also publ. in New York by International University Press.

Freud, A. (1953) Losing and being lost. **International Journal of Psychoanalysis, 34,** 288. (Also see same journal, 1954, **35,** 283.)

Freud, E. L. (Ed., 1960) **Letters of Sigmund Freud.** New York: Basic Books.

Freud, S. (1948—original, 1908) **Collected papers.** Vol. IV, 184-191. London: Hogarth.

Freud, S. (1955—original, 1920) Beyond the pleasure principle. In J. Strachey (Ed.), **The standard edition of the complete psychological works of Sigmund Freud,** Vol. XVIII. London: Hogarth.

Freud, S. (1922) **Beyond the pleasure principle.** London: International Psychoanalytic Press.

Freud, S. (1936—original, 1926) **The problem of anxiety.** New York: Norton.

Freud, S. (1934) Mourning and melancholia. **Collected papers.** London: Hogarth. Vol. 4. Pp. 152-170, especially p. 160.

Freud, S. (1935) **The ego and the id.** London: Hogarth.

Freud, S. (1939) Civilization and its discontents. London: Hogarth.

Fromm, E. (1941) **Escape from freedom.** New York: Holt, Rinehart & Winston.

Fromm, E. (1956) **The art of loving.** New York: Harper & Row. (Also published as a Bantam paperback.)

Fromm, E. (1968) **The revolution of hope.** New York: Harper & Row.

Gardner, B. T., & Gardner, R. A. (1971) Two-way communication with an infant chimpanzee. In A. Schrier & F. Stollnitz (Eds.) **Behavior of nonhuman primates,** Vol. III. New York: Academic Press.

Gardner, J. W. (1968) **No easy victory.** New York: Harper & Row.

Gardner, J. W. (1970) **The recovery of confidence.** New York: Norton.

Gardner, R. A., & Gardner, B. T. (1969) Teaching sign language to a chimpanzee. **Science, 165,** 664-672.

Garner, W. R. (1962) **Uncertainty and structure as psychological concepts.** New York: Wiley.

Gendlin, E. T. (1962) **Experiencing and the creation of meaning.** New York: Free Press.

Gibb, J. R. (1964) Climate for trust formation. In L. Bradford, J. R. Gibb, & K. D. Benne (Eds.), **T-group theory and laboratory methods.** New York: Wiley.

Gibson, J. J. (1960) The concept of stimulus in psychology. **American Psychologist, 15,** 694-703.

Giorgi, A. (1965) Phenomenology and experimental psychology: I. **Review of Existential Psychology and Psychiatry, 5,** 228-238.

Giorgi, A. (1966) Phenomenology and experimental psychology: II. **Review of Existential Psychology and Psychiatry, 6,** 37-50.

Giorgi, A. (1967a) The experience of the subject as a source of data in a psychological experiment. **Review of Existential Psychology and Psychiatry, 7,** 169-176.

Giorgi, A. (1967b) A phenomenological approach to the problem of meaning and serial learning. **Review of Existential Psychology and Psychiatry, 7,** 95-106.

Giorgi, A. (1970) Psychology as a human science: A phenomenologically based approach. New York: Harper & Row.

Glaser, B. G., & Strauss, A. L. (1965) Awareness of dying. Chicago: Aldine.

Gordon, T. (1955) Group-centered leadership. Boston: Houghton Mifflin.

Gorer, G. (1955) The pornography of death. Encounter, 5, 49-52.

Grauman, C. F. (1962) Lecture notes, Duquesne University.

Groos, K. (1898) The play of animals. New York: Appleton-Century-Crofts.

Groos, K. (1908a) The play of men. New York: Appleton-Century-Crofts.

Groos, K. (1908b) Das spiel als katharsis. Zeitschrift für Pädagogische Psychologie und Experimentelle Pädogik, Dec. 7.

Gurwitsch, A. (1964) The field of consciousness. Pittsburgh, Pa.: Duquesne University Press.

Haber, R. N. (1969) Perceptual processes and general cognitive activity. In J. F. Voss (Ed.), Approaches to thought. Columbus: Merrill.

Hall, G. F. (1965) A participant's experience in a basic encounter group. (Mimeographed) Western Behavioral Sciences Institute.

Hall, G. S. (1906) Youth. New York: Appleton-Century-Crofts.

Hamachek, D. E. (1971) Encounters with the self. New York: Holt, Rinehart & Winston.

Harman, W. W. (1962) The humanities in an age of science. Main Currents in Modern Thought, 18, 75-83.

Hattis, R. P. (1965) Love feelings in courtship couples: An analysis. Journal of Humanistic Psychology, 5, 22-53.

Hebb, D. O. (1951) The role of neurological ideas in psychology. Journal of Personality, 20, 39-55.

Heidegger, M. (1927) Sein und zeit. Halle: Max Niemeyer.

Heisenberg, W. (1962) Physics and philosophy. New York: Harper & Row (Torchbook).

Heisenberg, W. (1966) Philosophic problems of nuclear science. Greenwich, Conn.: Fawcett.

Henle, M., and Baltimore, G. (1967) Portraits in straw. Psychological Review, 74, 325-329.

Holz, W. C., & Aznin, N. H (1966) Conditioning human verbal behavior. In W. K. Honig (Ed.), Operant behavior. New York: Appleton-Century-Crofts.

Huizinga, J. (1950) Homo Ludens—A study of the play element in culture. Boston: Beacon Press.

Hull, C. L. (1943) Principles of behavior. New York: Appleton-Century-Crofts.

Hunter, I. M. (1954) Tactile-kinesthetic perception of straightness in blind and sighted humans. Quarterly Journal of Experimental Psychology, 6, 149-154.

Hurlock, E. B. (1934) Experimental investigations of childhood play. Psychological Bulletin, 31, 47-66.

Husserl, E. (1962) Ideas. New York: Collier Books.

Huxley, J (1965) Introduction by Sir Julian Huxley. In P. Teilhard de Chardin, The phenomenon of man. (2d Torchbook ed.)

Immergluck L. (1964) Determinism-freedom in contemporary psychology: An ancient problem revisited. American Psychologist, 9, 270-281.

James, W. (1894) Principles of psychology. New York: Macmillan.

James, W. (1897) The will to believe and other essays. New York: Longmans Green.

James, W. (1904) Talks to teachers. New York: Holt, Rinehart and Winston.

Jenkins, J. J. (1963) Mediated associations: Paradigms and situations. In C. N. Cofer & B. S. Musgrave (Eds.), Verbal behavior and learning. New York: McGraw-Hill.

Jessor, J. (1961) Issues in the phenomenological approach to psychology. Journal of Individual Psychology, 17, 27-38.

Jourard, S. M. (1968) Disclosing man to himself. Princeton, N.J.: Van Nostrand.

Kagan, J. (1967) On the need for relativism. American Psychologist, 22, 131-142.

Kelman, H. C. (1968) A time to speak: On human values and social research. San Francisco: Jossey-Bass.

Kemeny, J. G., Snell, J. L., & Thompson, G. L. (1957) Introduction to finite mathematics. New York: Prentice-Hall.

Kendler, H. H. (1968) Some specific reactions to general S-R theory. In T. R. Dixon & D. L. Horton (Eds.), Verbal behavior and general behavior theory. Englewood Cliffs, N.J.: Prentice-Hall.

Kendler, H. H., & Gasser, W. P. (1948) Variables in spatial learning. I. Number of reinforcements during training. Journal of Comparative and Physiological Psychology, 41, 178-187.

Keniston, Kenneth (1965) The uncommitted: Alienated youth in American society. New York: Harcourt Brace Jovanovich.

Kephart, W. M. (1967) Some correlates of romantic love. Journal of Marriage & the Family, 29, 470-474.

Kerr, W. (1962) The decline of pleasure. New York: Simon & Schuster.

Kierkegaard, S. (1944) The concept of dread. Trans. by W. Lowrie. Princeton, N.J.: Princeton University Press.

Klein, M. (1948—original, 1929) Personification in play. In Contributions to psychoanalysis. London: Hogarth. Pp. 215-226.

Klein, M. (1948) A contribution to the theory of anxiety and guilt. International Journal of Psychoanalysis, 29, 114-123.

Klinger, E. (1969) Development of imaginative behavior: Implications of play for a theory of fantasy. Psychological Bulletin, 72, 277-298.

Knight, R. P. (1946) Determinism, freedom, and psychotherapy. Psychiatry, 9, 251-262.

Koch, S. (Ed., 1959) Psychology: A study of a science: Study I, Vols. I-III. New York: McGraw-Hill.

Koch, S. (1961) Psychological science versus the science-humanism antinomy: Intimations for a significant science of man. American Psychologist, 16, 629-639.

Koch, S. (1964) Psychology and emerging conceptions of knowledge as unitary. In T. W. Wann (Ed.), Behaviorism and phenomenology: Contrasting bases for modern psychology. Chicago: The University of Chicago Press.

Koch, S. (1970) Psychology cannot be a coherent science. Psychology Today, 3 (4); 4, 14, 64, 66-68.

Koch, S. (1971) The image of man implicit in encounter group theory. Journal of Humanistic Psychology, 11, 109-128.

Koehler, W. (1956) The mentality of apes. Ch. vii, "Chance and Imitation." London: Routledge & Kegan Paul.

Koehler, W. (1966) A task for philosophers. In P. K. Feyerabend and G. Maxwell (Eds.), Mind, matter, and method: Essays in philosophy and science in honor of Herberg Feigl. Minneapolis: University of Minnesota Press.

Korner, I. N. (1956) Of values, value lag, and mental health. American Psychologist, 11, 543-546.

Krebs, D. L. (1970) Altruism: An examination of the concept and a review of the literature. Psychological Bulletin, 73, 258-302.

Kuhn, T. S. (1970) The structure of scientific revolutions (Rev. ed.). Chicago: The University of Chicago Press.

Kurland, M. (1953) Romantic love and economic considerations: A cultural comparison. Journal of Educational Sociology, 27, 72-79.

Lachman, R., & Dooling, D. J. (1968) Connected discourse and random strings: Effects of number of inputs on recognition and recall. Journal of Experimental Psychology, 77, 517-522.

Laing, Ronald D. (1967) The politics of experience. New York: Pantheon Books.

Lakin, M. (1969) Some ethical issues in sensitivity training. American Psychologist, 24, 923-928.

Lange, K. (1901) Erganzungstheorie. Berlin.

Lazarus, M. (1883) Uber die reize des spiels. Berlin: F. Dummler.

Lewin, K. (1933) Environmental forces. In C. Murchison (Ed.), A handbook of child psychology. Worcester, Mass.: Clark University Press. Pp. 590-625.

Lifton, R. (1961) Thought control and the psychology of totalism: A study of "brainwashing" in China. New York: Norton. Pp. viii.

Lindner, R. (1955) The fifty-minute hour: A collection of true psychoanalytic tales. New York: Holt, Rinehart & Winston.

McCurdy, H. G. (1961) The personal world: An introduction to the study of personality. New York: Harcourt, Brace & World.

McGowan, J. F., & Schmidt, L. D. (1962) Counseling: Readings in theory and practice. New York: Holt, Rinehart and Winston.

MacLeod, R. B. (1964) Phenomenology: A challenge to experimental psychology. In T. W. Wann (Ed.), Behaviorism and phenomenology: Contrasting bases for modern psychology. Chicago: The University of Chicago Press.

Mace, C. A. (1964). Homeostasis, need and values. In John Cohen (Ed.), Readings in psychology. London: Allen & Unwin.

Mailloux, N. (1953) Psychic determinism, freedom, and personality development. Canadian Journal of Psychology, 7, 1-11.

Mandler, G. (1967) Verbal learning. In G. Mandler et al., New Directions in Psychology. Vol. 3. New York: Holt, Rinehart & Winston.

Maslow, A. H. (1963) Fusion of facts and values. American Journal of Psychotherapy, 23, 117-131.

Maslow, A. H. (1966) The psychology of science: A reconnaissance. New York: Harper & Row. (Paperback ed. Chicago: Henry Regnery, 1969)

Maslow, A. H. (1968) Toward a psychology of being (Rev. ed.). Princeton, N.J.: Van Nostrand.

Maslow, A. H. (1969) Existential psychology—what's in it for us? In R. May (Ed.), Existential psychology (2d ed.). New York: Random House.

Maslow, A. H. (1970a) Humanistic education vs. professional education: further comments. New Directions in Teaching, 2, (Spring), 3-10.

Maslow, A. H. (1970b) Motivation and personality (2d ed.). New York, Harper & Row.

May, R. (1953) Man's search for himself. New York: Norton.

May, R. (1967) Psychology and the human dilemma. Princeton, N.J.: Van Nostrand.

May, R. (1968) The daemonic: Love and death. Psychology Today, 1 (9), 16-25.

May, R. (1969) Love and will. New York: Norton.

May, R., Angel, E., & Ellenger, H. F. (Eds., 1958) Existence: A new dimension in psychiatry and psychology. New York: Basic Books, Inc., Publishers.

Menninger, K. (1930) The human mind. New York: Knopf.

Menninger, K. (1942) Love against hate. New York: Harcourt, Brace & World.

Merloo, J. A. M. (1955) Medication into submission: The danger of coercion. Journal of Nervous and Mental Diseases, 122, 353-360.

Miller, G. A. (1962) Some psychological studies of grammar. American Psychologist, 17, 748-762.

Miller, G. A. (1965) Some preliminaries to psycholinguistics. American Psychologist, 20, 15-20.

Minkowski, E. (1934) Le temps vecu. Paris: D'Artrey. Pp. 121ff.

Mitchell, E. D., & Mason, B. S. (1934) The theory of play. New York: A. S. Barnes.

Montagu, A. (1950) On being human. New York: Schuman. Also published as a Hawthorne paperback.

Mowrer, O. H. (1957) Some philosophical problems in psychological counseling. Journal of Counseling Psychology, 4, 103-110.

Mowrer, O. H. (1961) The crisis in psychiatry and religion. Princeton, N.J.: Van Nostrand.

Mumford, L. (1966) The myth of the machine. New York: Harcourt Brace Jovanovich.

Murphy, G. (1955) The cultural context of counseling. The Personnel and Guidance Journal, 34, 4-9.

National academy of religion and mental health. (1956) The National Academy, New York Academy Bldg., 2 E. 103rd St., N.Y.

Neisser, U. (1967) Cognitive psychology. New York: Appleton-Century-Crofts.

Northrup, F. S. C. (1962) Introduction. In W. Heisenberg, Physics and philosophy: The revolution in modern science. New York: Harper & Row (Torchbook ed.).

Nuttin, J. (1962) Psychoanalysis and personality. New York: Sheed & Ward.

Ohmann, R. (1969) Grammar and meaning. In W. Morris (Ed.), The American heritage dictionary, New York: The American Heritage Publishing Co. Pp. xxxi-xxxiv.

Olds, J. (1955) A physiological study of reward, In D. C. McClelland (Ed.), Studies in motivation. New York: Appleton-Century-Crofts.

Oppenheimer, R. (1956a) Analogy in science. American Psychologist, 2, 127-135.

Oppenheimer, R. (1956b) Science and our times. Roosevelt University Occasional Papers, 2.

Orne, M. T. (1962) On the social psychology of the psychological experiment: With particular reference to demand characteristics and their implications. American Psychologist, 17, 776-783.

Packard, V. (1968) The sexual wilderness. New York: David McKay.

Patrick, G. T. W. (1916) The psychology of relaxation. Boston: Houghton Mifflin.

Peller, L. E. (1954) Libidinal phases, ego development, and play. In The psychoanalytic study of the child. New York: International University Press, pp. 178-198.

Perry, W. G. (1955) On the relation of psychotherapy and counseling. In Roy Waldo Miner (Ed.), Psychotherapy and counseling. Annals of New York Academy of Sciences, 63(Art. 3), 396-407.

Polanyi, M. (1958) Personal knowledge. Chicago: University of Chicago Press.

Polanyi, M. (1963) The potential theory of adsorption. Science, 141, 1010-1013.

Popper, K. R. (1945) The open society and its enemies. London: Routledge & Kegan Paul.

Postman, L., & Stark, K. (1969) The role of associative mediation in retroactive inhibition and facilitation. Journal of Verbal Learning and Verbal Behavior, 8, 790-798.

Premack, D. (1970a) A functional analysis of language. Journal of the Experimental Analysis of Behavior, 14, 107-125.

Premack, D. (1970b) The education of Sarah: A chimp learns the language. Psychology Today, 4, (4), 54-58.

Premack, D. (1971) Language in chimpanzee? Science, 172, 808-822.

Prescott, D. A. (1957) The child in the educative process. New York: McGraw-Hill.

Ratner, J. (Ed.) (1939) Intelligence in the modern world: John Dewey's philosophy. New York: Modern Library.

Reaney, M. J. (1916) The psychology of the organized group game. London: Cambridge. University Press.

Reitman, W. R. (1965) Cognition and thought. New York: Wiley.

Restle, F. (1957) Discrimination of cues in mazes: A resolution of the "place-vs.-response" question. Psychological Review, 64, 217-228.

Restle, F. (1961) Psychology of judgment and choice. New York: Wiley.

Riesman, D. (1950) The lonely crowd. New Haven: Yale University Press.

Robinson, E. S. (1920) The compensatory function of make-believe play. Psychological Review, 27, 429-439.

Rogers, C. R. (1951) Client-centered therapy: Its current practice, implications, and theory. Boston: Houghton Mifflin.

Rogers, C. R. (1955) Persons or science? A philosophical question. American Psychologist, 10, 267-278.

Rogers, C. R. (1959) A theory of therapy, personality, and interpersonal relationships, as developed in the client-centered framework. In S. Koch (Ed.), Psychology: A study of a science. Vol. 3. New York: McGraw-Hill.

Rogers, C. R. (1961) On becoming a person. Boston: Houghton Mifflin (Paperback ed. 1970.)

Rogers, C. R. (1962) The interpersonal relationship: The core of guidance. Harvard Educational Review, 32, 416-429.

Rogers, C. R. (1968) Some thoughts regarding the current presuppositions of the behavioral sciences. In W. R. Coulson and C. R. Rogers (Eds.), Man and the science of man. Columbus, Ohio: Merrill.

Rogers, C. R. (1969) Two divergent trends. In R. May, Existential psychology (2d ed.). New York: Random House.

Rogers, C. R., & Dymond, R. F. (Eds., 1954) Psychotherapy and personality change. Chicago: University of Chicago Press.

Rogers, C. R., and Skinner, B. F. (1956) Some issues concerning the control of human behavior. Science, 124, 1057-1066.

Rosenthal, R. (1963) On the social psychology of the psychological experiment. American Psychologist, 51, 268-283.

Rosenthal, R. (1966) Experimenter effects in behavioral research. New York: Appleton-Century-Crofts.

Rosenthal, R., and Jacobson, L. (1966) Teachers' expectancies: Determinants of pupil's IQ gains. Psychological Reports, 19, 115-118.

Rychlak, J. F. (1968) A philosophy of science for personality theory. Boston: Houghton Mifflin.

Sadler, W. A. (1966) Play: A basic structure involving love and freedom. Review of Existential Psychology and Psychiatry, 6, 237-245. Reprinted in W. A. Sadler, Jr., Existence and love: A new approach in existential phenomenology. New York: Scribner's Sons, 1970, Ch. 9.

Sahakian, W. S. (1965) Psychology of personality: Readings in theory. Chicago: Rand, McNally.

St. Matthew, 18/3

Sarason, I., & Smith, R. E. (1971) Personality. In R. H. Mussen & M. R. Rosenzweig (Eds.), Annual review of psychology. Palo Alto, Calif.

Schilder, P. (1939) Notes on the psychology of metrazol treatment of schizophrenia. Journal of Nervous Mental Disease, 89, 133-144.

Schiller, F. (1873) Essays, aesthetical and philosophical. London: Bell & Sons.

Schutz, A. (1964) Collected Papers, Vol. II. The Hague: Martinus Nijhoff.

Seeman, J., & Raskin, N. J. (1953) Research perspectives in client-centered therapy. In O. H. Mowrer (Ed.), Psychotherapy: Theory and research, Ch. 9. New York: Ronald Press.

Shannon, C. E. (1948) A mathematical theory of communication. Bell System Technical Journal, 1948, 27, 379-423, 623-656.

Shilien, J. M. (1962) Toward what level of abstraction in criteria? In H. H. Strupp & L. Luborsky (Eds.), Research in psychotherapy. Vol. 2. Pp. 142-154.

Shlien, J. M. (1963) Phenomenology and personality. In J. M. Wepman and R. W. Heine, Concepts of personality. Chicago: Aldine.

Shoben, E. J., Jr. (1962) The counselor's theory as personal trait. Personnel and Guidance Journal, 40, 617-621.

Silberman, I. (1940) The psychical experiences during the shocks in shock therapy. International Journal of Psychoanalysis, 21, 179-200.

Skinner, B. F. (1940) Walden two. New York: Macmillan.

Skinner, B. F. (1953) Science and human behavior. New York: Macmillan.

Skinner, B. F. (1955-1956) Freedom and the control of men. American Scholar, 25, (Winter), 47-65.

Skinner, B. F. (1957) Verbal behavior. New York: Appleton-Century-Crofts.

Smith, G. J. W., Spence, D. F., & Klein, G. S. (1959) Subliminal effects of verbal stimuli. Journal of Abnormal and Social Psychology, 59, 167-176.

Smith, M. B. (1960) Social psychology and human values. Chicago: Aldine.

Snygg, D. (1941) The need for a phenomenological system of psychology. Psychological Review, 48, 404-424.

Sorokin, P. (Ed.) (1950a) Explorations in altruism. Boston: Beacon.

Sorokin, P. (1950b) Altruistic love: A study of American good neighbors and Christian saints. Boston: Beacon.

Spencer, H. (1873) The principles of psychology. New York: Appleton-Century-Crofts.

Spiegelberg, H. (1960) The phenomenological movement. Vol. 2. The Hague: Nijhoff.

Spielberger, C. D., & DeNike, L. D. (1966) Descriptive behaviorism versus cognitive theory in verbal operant conditioning. Psychological Review, 73, 306-326.

Spitz, R., & Wolf, K. M. (1946) Anaclytic depression. In A. Freud et al., Psychoanalytic Study of the Child, Vol. 2. New York: International University Press.

Staats, A. W., & Staats, C. K. (1963) Complex human behavior. New York: Holt, Rinehart & Winston.

Stefflre, R. (Ed., 1965) Theories in counseling. New York: McGraw-Hill.

Steiner, I. D. (1968) Reactions to adverse and favorable evaluations of one's self. Journal of Personality and Social Psychology, 36, 553-562.

Stekel, W. (1949) Conditions of nervous anxiety and their treatment. New York: Liveright.

Strasser, S. (1963) Phenomenology and the human sciences, Pittsburgh: Duquesne University Press.

Strauss, E. (1962) On memory traces. Tijdschaft voor Filosofie, 24, 1-32.

Sullivan, H. S. (1953) The interpersonal theory of psychiatry. New York: Norton.

Suttie, I. D. (1952) The origins of love and hate. New York: Julian Press.

Swensen, C. H. (1961) Love: A self-report analysis with college students. Journal of Individual Psychology, 17, 167-171.

Swensen, C. H., & Gilner, F. (1964) Factor analysis of self-report statements of love relationships. Journal of Individual Psychology, 20, 186-188.

Taft, R. (1956) Intolerance of ambiguity and ethnocentrism. Journal of Consulting Psychology, 20, 153-154.

Teicher, J. D. (1953) Combat fatigue or death anxiety neurosis. Journal of Nervous Mental Disease, 117, 234-243.

Teilhard de Chardin, P. (1965) The phenomenon of man, New York: Harper & Row. (2d Torchbook ed.)

Thetford, W. N. (1952) An objective measure of frustration tolerance in evaluating psychotherapy. In W. Wolff (Ed.), Success in psychotherapy, Ch. 2. New York: Grune and Stratton.

Thorndike, E. L. (1911) Animal intelligence. New York: Macmillan. Pp. 199ff.

Tillich, P. (1952) The courage to be. New Haven, Conn.: Yale University Press.

Tinklepaugh, O. L. (1942) Social behavior in animals. In F. A. Moss (Ed.), Comparative psychology (2d ed.). Englewood Cliffs, N.J.: Prentice-Hall.

Tolman, E. C., Hall, C. S., & Bretnall, E. P. (1932) A dis-proof of the law of effect and a substitution of the laws of emphasis, motivation, and disruption. Journal of Experimental Psychology, 15, 601-614.

Truax, C. B., & Carkhuff, R. B. (1964) Theory and research in counseling and psycho-therapy. Personnel and Guidance Journal, 42, 860-866.

Tweedie, D. F. (1961) Logotherapy and the Christian faith: An evaluation of Frankl's existential approach to psychotherapy. Grand Rapids, Mich.: Baker Book House.

Underwood, B. J. (1963) Stimulus selection in verbal learning. In C. N. Cofer & B. S. Musgrave (Eds.), Verbal behavior and learning. New York: McGraw-Hill.

van der Leeuw, G. (1963) Sacred and profane beauty: The holy in art. New York: Holt, Rinehart & Winston. P. 112.

van Kaam, A. (1962) Counseling from the viewpoint of existential psychology. Harvard Educational Review, 32, 403-415.

von Eckartsberg, R. (1969) Geography of human experience. Journal for the study of Consciousness, July-December.

Waelder, R. (1933) The psychoanalytic theory of play. Psychoanalytic Quarterly, 2, 208-224.

Wahl, C. W., (1965) The fear of death. In R. Fulton (Ed.), Death and identity. New York: Wiley.

Wallach, M. A. (1967) Thinking, feeling, and expressing: Toward understanding the person. In R. Jessor and S. Fishbach (Eds.), Cognition, personality, and clinical psychology. San Francisco: Jossey-Bass.

Watson, J. B. (1914) Behaviorism: An introduction to comparative psychology. Chicago: University of Chicago Press.

Whitehead, A. N. (1962) Science and the modern world. New York: Macmillan

Williamson, E. G. (1958) Value orientation in counseling. The Personnel and Guidance Journal, 36, 520-529.

Wolfle, D. (1970) Dying with dignity. Science, 168, 1403.

Wrenn, C. G. (1952) The ethics of counseling. Educational and Psychological Measurement, 12, 161-177.

Wrenn, C. G. (1954) Editorial comment. Journal of Counseling Psychology, 1, 124.

Wrenn, C. G. (1962) The counselor in a changing world. Washington, D.C.: American Personnel and Guidance Association.

Wundt, W. (1913) Grundriss der psychologia. Leipzig: Kroner.

Yerkes, R. M. (1943) Chimpanzees: A laboratory colony. New Haven, Conn.: Yale University Press.

Yerkes, R. W., & Yerkes, A. W. (1929) The great apes. New Haven, Conn.: Yale University Press. Pp. 368ff, 520ff.

Young, R. K. (1968) Serial learning. In T. R. Dixon & D. L. Horton (Eds.), Verbal behavior and general behavior theory. Englewood Cliffs, N.J.: Prentice-Hall.

Zaner, R. M. (1967) Criticism of "Tensions in psychology between the methods of behaviorism and phenomenology." Psychological Review, 74, 318-324.

Zilboorg, G. (1938) Loneliness. The Atlantic Monthly, January, 161, 45-54.

Zilboorg, G. (1943) Fear of death. Psychoanalytic Quarterly, 12, 465-475.

Name Index

Page numbers in *italics* indicate references of secondary importance.

Subject Index